Banff, Jasper & Glacier

NATIONAL PARKS

Jasper National Park
p134

D0089191

Banff National Park
p46

Around Banff National Park
p116

Waterton Lakes National Park
p216

Glacier National Park
p176

Around Glacier National Park
p207

THIS EDITION WRITTEN AND RESEARCHED BY

Brendan Sainsbury, Michael Grosberg

PLAN YOUR TRIP

Welcome to Banff,
Jasper & Glacier........ 4

Banff, Jasper &
Glacier National
Parks Map 6

Banff, Jasper &
Glacier's Top 20 8

Need to Know 18

What's New 20

If You Like................21

Month by Month....... 24

Itineraries 26

Travel with Children.... 38

Travel with Pets 42

ON THE ROAD

BANFF NATIONAL
PARK............. 46

Day Hikes 50
Overnight Hikes 68
Cycling 72
Driving 76
Other Activities 77
Sights................. 86
Tours................. 97
Sleeping.............. 98
Eating............... 107
Drinking & Nightlife... 110
Entertainment........ 110
Shopping 110

AROUND BANFF
NATIONAL PARK ...116

Canmore 117
Kananaskis Country 121
Yoho National Park 124
Lake O'Hara........... 127
Mt Assiniboine Provincial
Park 127
Kootenay National Park &
Radium Hot Springs 128
Golden 131

JASPER NATIONAL
PARK............. 134

Day Hikes 138
Overnight Hikes 146

RONNIE CHUA/SHUTTERSTOCK ©

PETE SEAWARD/LONELY PLANET ©

WWING/GETTY IMAGES ©

BANFF SUMMER ARTS FESTIVAL (P25)

FLOWERS IN BLOOM NEAR LAKE LOUISE (P60)

Contents

Cycling 149
Driving 152
Other Activities 152
Sights 156
Tours 163
Sleeping 163
Eating 169
Drinking & Nightlife . . . 170
Shopping 171

GLACIER NATIONAL PARK 176

Day Hikes 180
Cycling 189
Other Activities 189

Driving 192
Sights 195
Tours 199
Sleeping 199
Eating 204
Drinking & Nightlife . . . 205
Entertainment 205

AROUND GLACIER NATIONAL PARK . . 207

West Glacier 208
St Mary 209
East Glacier 210
Blackfeet Indian Reservation 212
Whitefish 212

WATERTON LAKES NATIONAL PARK . . 216

Day Hikes 217
Driving 220
Cycling 222
Other Activities 223
Sights 225
Tours 227
Sleeping 227
Eating 230
Drinking & Entertainment 230
Shopping 230

UNDERSTAND

The Parks Today 234
History 236
Geology 243
Wildlife 246
Conservation 254

SURVIVAL GUIDE

Health & Safety 258
Clothing & Equipment 264
Directory A–Z 267
Transportation 275
Index 281
Map Legend 287

ROCKY MOUNTAINEER TRAIN (P113) PASSING THROUGH BANFF NATIONAL PARK

SPECIAL FEATURES

Travel with Children 38
Travel with Pets 42
Full-color Wildlife feature 246
Clothing & Equipment Checklist 266

Welcome to Banff, Jasper & Glacier

Sit atop a mountain, hike through the forest, feel the spray of a waterfall: Banff, Jasper and Glacier offer outdoor experiences at their simplest and best.

Historical Heritage

While other countries protect ancient ruins and medieval castles, the Rocky Mountains offer up Banff, Jasper and Glacier, legendary natural wonders replete with crenelated peaks, majestic meadows and scenery-shaping glaciers that together make up an important part of North America's historical jigsaw. Of the hundreds of national parks scattered around the world today, Banff, created in 1885, is the third oldest. Associated with the development of America's cross-continental railroads, which lured wealthy visitors into previously unexplored wilderness, these protected areas practically invented modern tourism, and their hold on the popular imagination has not diminished.

Wilderness Walks

There are bucket-loads of things to do in Banff, Jasper and Glacier, from heart-in-your-mouth white-water rafting to an easy round of golf. But arguably the most rewarding activity in the parks is the simplest – hiking. Walking along a well-maintained trail amid classic mountain splendor is one of life's great spiritual diversions. You won't be the first convert: hiking, by default, was the primary means of transportation for the indigenous people of the Rockies and the early European explorers who followed.

Protected Environments

Acting as litmus tests for the tricky balance between ecological integrity and a rip-roaring visitor experience, the Rocky Mountain national parks have long played a key role in safeguarding North America's natural environment. Glacier protects an ecosystem unchanged since Columbus' time, Banff exhibits some of the finest wildlife-watching in North America, and Jasper is a dark-sky preserve free of unnecessary light pollution; underneath the myriad adventure opportunities lies savvy park management paving the way to a greener future.

Outdoor Accessibility

One of the advantages of the Rocky Mountain parks is their accessibility. Banff, in particular, embodies the fragile, sometimes controversial, juxtaposition between the tamed and the untamed. While some frown at the commercialization of Banff Ave, the home comforts have their merits. Outfitters and guides add safety to potentially complicated trip-planning, while speedy gondolas allow people who might otherwise not have the opportunity to get up above the timberline to experience flower-carpeted alpine meadows and wild animals roaming through their natural habitats.

Why I Love Banff, Jasper & Glacier

By Brendan Sainsbury, Writer

Ever since climbing my first Welsh mountain at the age of eight, hiking and trail-running have been in my blood. For me, Banff, Jasper and Glacier offer some of the best trails in North America – suitably wild and rugged, but easily accessible without a car. On a fine day in high summer, there's nothing I like more than roaming alone above the treeline in Banff's Sunshine Meadows or Jasper's Bald Hills, drinking in the views and singing my favorite Smiths songs to ward off the bears.

For more about our writers, see page 288.

Above: Moraine Lake (p95), Banff National Park

Banff, Jasper & Glacier National Parks

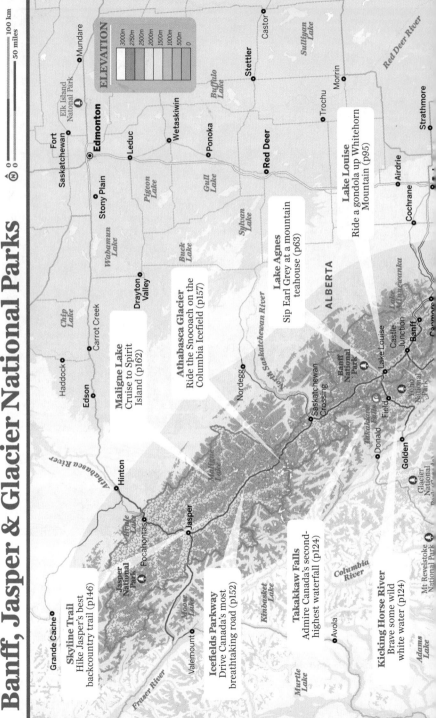

Skyline Trail
Hike Jasper's best backcountry trail (p146)

Icefields Parkway
Drive Canada's most breathtaking road (p152)

Takakkaw Falls
Admire Canada's second-highest waterfall (p124)

Kicking Horse River
Brave some wild white water (p124)

Maligne Lake
Cruise to Spirit Island (p162)

Athabasca Glacier
Ride the Snocoach on the Columbia Icefield (p157)

Lake Agnes
Sip Earl Grey at a mountain teahouse (p63)

Lake Louise
Ride a gondola up Whitehorn Mountain (p95)

ELEVATION

3000m
2750m
2500m
2000m
1500m
1000m
500m
0

100 km
50 miles

Banff Town
Get some mountain culture
at Whyte Museum (p86)

Mt Assiniboine
Hike to the Canadian
Matterhorn (p68)

Carthew-Alderson Trail
Explore high-alpine forests
and meadows (p219)

Moraine Lake
Paddle across an azure
lake (p95)

Radium Hot Springs
Soak in a volcanic
spring (p129)

Going-to-the-Sun Road
Experience Glacier's classic
road trip (p192)

Two Medicine Valley
Spot bears in a mountain
valley (p197)

Banff, Jasper & Glacier's
Top 20

1

Lake Louise

1 No one should leave this mortal coil without first setting eyes upon the robin-egg-blue waters of Lake Louise (p60) nestled below the hulking Victoria Glacier and ringed by an impressive amphitheater of mountains. True, the lakeshore crowds can sometimes resemble a giant emporium of selfie-sticks, but grab your photos from a more unique angle – on Mt Fairview, for instance, or looking back from the Victoria Glacier – and solitude could conceivably be yours.

Icefields Parkway

2 There are amazing road trips, and then there's the Icefields Pkwy (p80). This iconic highway unfurls for 230km (143 miles) between Lake Louise and Jasper, and takes in some of the most mind-blowing mountain panoramas anywhere on the Continental Divide. En route you'll pass cerulean lakes, crashing cascades, gleaming glaciers and the largest area of unbroken ice anywhere in North America, the mighty Columbia Icefield. It's a true trip of a lifetime, so fuel up, sit back, and let one of the world's great scenery shows unfold.

GREG MCLEMORE/500PX ©

ANNA GORIN / GETTY IMAGES ©

Skyline Trail

3 Cross-park views of Jasper are par for the course on the widely celebrated Skyline Trail (p146). It could have had any number of descriptive names conferred upon it – the Homeric path, the celestial walk, the resplendent ramble – but instead its name describes exactly how it is: a 45.8km (28.7-mile) promenade through Jasper's splendidly glaciated high country that offers kilometer after kilometer of seemingly endless skyline. Is there a more spectacular hike anywhere in North America? Possibly not.

Going-to-the-Sun Road

4 The start is inauspicious enough: a signposted turning off US 2, the blink-and-you'll-miss-it village of West Glacier, followed by a serendipitous plunge into dense forest around Apgar. It's only on the shores of Lake McDonald that the views start getting better and better, until you feel as if the Going-to-the-Sun Rd (p192) really is – well – going to the sun. The highpoint is Logan Pass on the Continental Divide. After that it's all downhill to St Mary, amid more jaw-dropping scenery and potent lessons in glacial erosion.

Wildlife Watching

5 Black and grizzly bears may be the holy grail for wildlife spotters, but there are plenty of other animals to seek out. The parks support a hugely diverse range of species, from elk and bighorn sheep to mountain goats, marmots and moose, not to mention an entire aviary of unusual birds. The best time to see wildlife (p246) is always at dawn or dusk; bring along decent binoculars and a telephoto lens to help with the perfect view.

Above: A Rocky Mountain elk

Moraine Lake

6 Canoes have been the preferred method of transport in the Rockies since time immemorial, and they're still an ideal way to explore the region's lakes and rivers. Canoes and kayaks can be hired on many of the region's waterways, but few water journeys can match Moraine Lake (p95) in the scenery stakes. Paddling out across this peacock-blue lake in a traditional canoe, gazing up to the icy summits of Wenkchemna Peak, you'll feel like you've been transported back in time to the days of the early pioneers and voyageurs.

Sunshine Meadows

7 Climb above the treeline in the Rocky Mountains and you're in a different domain, an ethereal world of impressionistic flower meadows, glassy mountain lakes and jagged peaks above the clouds. The easiest access point to this wild terrain is at Banff's Sunshine Meadows (p92), where a summer shuttle replaces a winter ski gondola to take hikers up to the Continental Divide for fabulous short and long hikes, some of them guided. Extra bonus: Sunshine Meadows metamorphoses into Banff's finest ski resort in the winter months.

RYAN CREARY / AGEFOTOSTOCK©

MALIGNE LAKE
BOAT HOUSE

Canmore Nordic Centre

8 The Rockies' rugged landscape of mountains and valleys makes perfect terrain if you're into mountain biking. Many of Banff and Jasper's trails are designated as multi-use, meaning they're open to hikers and horseback riders as well as cyclists, but for the best cycling head for the groomed trails of the Canmore Nordic Centre (p33). There are more than 65km (40 miles) of routes to explore, ranging from easy rolls to epic singletracks, and the regular skills clinics can help you get the most out of your ride.

Maligne Lake

9 Beyond its oft-visited northern shore, Maligne Lake (p162) remains a wilderness lake bequeathed with the kind of grandiose scenery that early explorers such as Mary Schäffer would still recognize. The only way to penetrate this watery kingdom's southern reaches is to hike in through backcountry, venture out solo on a kayak, or – for more relaxed day-trippers – enjoy it communally on a daily boat launch. The object of everyone's longing is the calendar-cover view of tiny Spirit Island backed by an amphitheater of appropriately 'rocky' mountains.

Tonquin Valley

10 In winter, Jasper's visitors drop to a trickle, with the majority never venturing far beyond the comforting skiing hub of Marmot Basin. What they're missing is some of the best icy backcountry in Canada. The Tonquin Valley (p156) – already well known to summer hikers and horseback riders – is a snow-blanketed nirvana equipped with a sprinkling of lodges where you can practice the energetic art of hut-to-hut cross-country skiing. Characterized by manageable elevation and a minimal avalanche risk, it's a 'haute route' without the height, or the danger.

Jasper Skytram

11 It probably wouldn't happen today, but back in the 1960s, in an era when mechanical geeks were experimenting with fancy new gimmicks, the Jasper park authorities built this high-speed cable car (p160) to a lofty knoll on 2466m (8088ft) Whistlers Mountain. Hiking purists may disapprove, but the tramway provides an easy way for people of all ages and abilities to enjoy the beautiful alpine tundra.

DIRK HEDEMANN / ALAMY PHOTO STOCK ©

11

MARTIN CHILD / GETTY IMAGES ©

Takakkaw Falls

12 First Nations people had it right when they named this thundering waterfall (p124): Takakkaw translates as 'it is magnificent' in the Cree language, and you'll probably find yourself thinking the same thing when you first set eyes on it. At a total height of 384m (1259ft), Takakkaw is the second-highest waterfall in Canada, topped only by Della Falls on Vancouver Island. A trail leads through pine forest to the base of the falls, affording grand views across the valley toward Cathedral Mountain and the rest of Yoho National Park.

White-Water Rafting

13 There are few activities that induce a more white-knuckle, heart-in-mouth, seat-of-the-pants adrenaline hit than hurtling downriver in an inflatable raft armed with nothing but a paddle and a prayer. Despite the apparent danger, white-water rafting (p34) is actually well within the capability of most people. Guided trips are run on many rivers, including the Bow, Kananaskis and Kicking Horse, and while you're guaranteed to get soaked to the skin, you're sure to have a huge grin on your face once you're finally back on terra firma.

Mt Assiniboine

14 If it's a taste of the wilds you're yearning for, Assiniboine (p127) is where you'll find it. The mountain's rocket-profile peak marks the start of some of the finest backcountry trails anywhere in the Canadian Rockies. With its secret lakes, soaring mountains and remote backcountry campgrounds, Assiniboine feels like another world compared to the busy trails of Banff. It takes some effort and dedication to get here, though – you'll need legs of steel, sturdy boots, proper supplies and, of course, a sense of adventure.

Radium Hot Springs

15 If it weren't for the geothermal springs that bubble up from beneath the mountains, Banff and its neighboring national parks may never have come into existence. The craze for spa bathing was instrumental in attracting early visitors to the park during the late 19th century. While the original site at the Cave & Basin National Historic Site is now off-limits to bathers, you can still take an outdoor dip at the twin pools of Radium Hot Springs (p129), as well as its sister springs in Banff and Jasper.

Glacier's Historic Hotels

16 As much museums of park history as evocative places to stay, Glacier's historic hotels date from the second decade of the 20th century, when they were built by the Great Northern Railway to accommodate travelers fresh off busy cross-continental steam trains. Paying homage to Swiss-chalet-style architecture and sited in areas of natural beauty, these noble structures survive today with their rustic spirit intact. Old-school rooms in places like the Many Glacier Hotel (p203) lack TVs, air-con and fancy gadgets, but retain bags of gilded-age glamor. Bottom: Many Glacier Hotel

Bears in Two Medicine Valley

17 Bear sightings inspire the whole gamut of feelings in humans, from fascination, intrigue and reverence to shock and blind fear. You can grab a cocktail of all five in the Two Medicine Valley (p197), once one of Glacier National Park's more accessible haunts but, in the days since car traffic diverted to the Going-to-the-Sun Rd, a deliciously quiet corner preferred by hikers, solitary fishers and – er – bears. At last count the park had around 400 grizzlies and substantially more black bears.

Top: American black bear with cubs

Athabasca Glacier

18 Driving on a glacier: sounds more like the kind of stunt pulled on a car-crazy TV show than something you could actually do, right? Wrong. At Jasper's humungous Columbia Icefield, specially adapted Snocoaches crawl and crunch across the Athabasca Glacier (p157), affording amazing views of crevasses, seracs and an endless horizon of ice. You'll even get the chance to disembark briefly and set foot on the 400-year-old snow. The so-called Ice Explorers leave every 15 to 30 minutes from the Columbia Icefield Centre in summer.

Afternoon Tea at Lake Agnes

19 After slogging all day on the mountain trails around Lake Louise, what could be more civilized than a cup of Earl Grey and a slice of homemade cake? The historic teahouse (p63) at Lake Agnes has been serving refreshments to weary walkers since 1901 when it was built by the Canadian Pacific Railway, and it remains an ideal stop-off for parched hikers tackling the trail to the Big Beehive. For an altogether posher experience, you can enjoy the C$43 tea spread in the Chateau Lake Louise. Top: Lake Agnes Teahouse

Waterton's Carthew-Alderson Trail

20 Waterton's diminutive size means that everything's close at hand, from the local cinema and afternoon tea in the Prince of Wales Hotel to the Carthew-Alderson Trail (p219), your highly prized 'day pass' into flower-embellished high-alpine tundra with barely a tree to break the vista. Even better, you don't need a cable car to get there! Just catch the early hiker shuttle to Cameron Lake, climb 4km (2.5 miles) through scented pine forest and you're there – on top of the world, or feeling like it.

Need to Know

For more information, see Survival Guide (p257)

Entrance Fees

Banff & Jasper: adult day pass C$9.80; Glacier: pedestrian/vehicle weekly pass US$12/25; Waterton Lakes: adult day pass C$7.80

Number of Visitors

Banff: 3,606,637 (2014); Jasper: 2,151,791 (2014); Glacier: 2,338,528 (2014); Waterton Lakes: 402,502 (2013)

Years Founded

Banff: 1885; Jasper: 1907; Glacier: 1910; Waterton Lakes: 1895

Money

ATMs in Banff, Jasper and Glacier townsites, scarce elsewhere. Credit and debit cards widely accepted.

Cell Phones

Coverage is patchy outside townsites. Phone must be compatible with Canadian/US network.

Driving

Most major roads are sealed, some minor roads are gravel/dirt. Some roads closed during heavy snowfall. Snow chains required in some areas in winter.

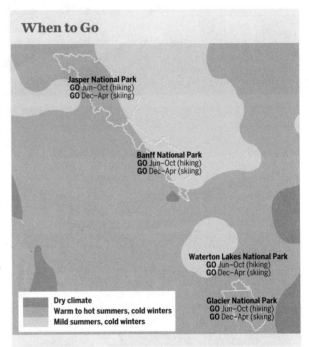

When to Go

Jasper National Park
GO Jun–Oct (hiking)
GO Dec–Apr (skiing)

Banff National Park
GO Jun–Oct (hiking)
GO Dec–Apr (skiing)

Waterton Lakes National Park
GO Jun–Oct (hiking)
GO Dec–Apr (skiing)

Glacier National Park
GO Jun–Oct (hiking)
GO Dec–Apr (skiing)

Dry climate
Warm to hot summers, cold winters
Mild summers, cold winters

High Season (Jul & Aug)

➡ July and August are the busiest months.

➡ Mainly warm weather and sunny skies, but be prepared for sudden thunderstorms.

➡ Trail closures and hiking restrictions during buffalo-berry season (mid-July onwards).

Shoulder (May, Jun, Sep & Oct)

➡ Spring comes late, with snow lingering until May or June.

➡ Many lakes are frozen and some trails remain closed until early summer.

➡ June is the wettest month in Banff and Jasper.

Low Season (Nov–Apr)

➡ Late March to May is the quietest season.

➡ Accommodations can be cheap, but many campgrounds, trails and activities are closed.

➡ Weather permitting, ski areas usually open from early December to early May.

Useful Websites

Lonely Planet (www.lonely planet.com/canada/alberta/banff-and-jasper-national-parks, www.lonelyplanet.com/usa/rocky-mountains/glacier-national-park) Hotel bookings, traveler forum and more.

National Parks Canada (www.pc.gc.ca) Comprehensive info for Canada's national parks.

US National Parks (www.nps.gov) US parks, including Glacier.

Travel Alberta (www.travel alberta.com) Alberta-wide site.

Trail Peak (www.trailpeak.com) User-generated trail guide.

Important Numbers

Banff Information Centre	☏403-762-1550
Jasper Information Centre	☏780-852-6176
Glacier National Park Headquarters	☏406-888-7800
Waterton	☏403-859-2378

Exchange Rates

AUS	A$1	C$0.96	US$0.73
CAN	C$1	C$1	US$0.76
Euro zone	€1	C$1.50	US$1.14
JPN	¥100	C$1.08	US$0.82
NZL	NZ$1	C$0.88	US$0.67
UK	£1	C$2.07	US$1.57
USA	US$1	C$1.32	US$1

For current exchange rates see www.xe.com.

Daily Costs

Budget: Less than C$100

➡ Dorm room in hostel or camping: C$30–C$40

➡ Self-catering from supermarkets: C$20

➡ Hiking on local trails using public transport: free–C$20

Midrange: C$100–C$400

➡ Double room in a hotel: C$150–C$200

➡ Lunch and dinner with drinks in local midrange restaurants: C$50

➡ Compact car hire: C$50

Top End: More than C$400

➡ Suite in a luxury hotel or lodge: C$300

➡ Three-course meal with wine: C$80–C$100

➡ Guided minibus tour: C$100

Opening Dates

Banff

Hwy 1 between Banff and Lake Louise open year-round. Minor roads snowbound in winter. High trails closed until at least mid-June.

Jasper

Icefields Pkwy between Lake Louise and Jasper closes during heavy snowfall. Minor roads snowbound between December and May. Most trails open by late June.

Glacier

The only main road (Going-to-the-Sun Rd) is closed until May or June. Minimal services maintained at Apgar Village in winter.

Waterton

Most facilities open May to September. Red Rock Pkwy closes from September to May;

Akamina Pkwy partially closes November to May.

Park Policies & Regulations

Hunting Not permitted in any of the parks. Firearms are banned in Banff, Jasper and Waterton.

Park passes Anyone intending on stopping in the national parks will require a National Park Pass.

Pets Must be kept on a leash at all times and are not allowed in backcountry shelters. Pets are prohibited from most trails in Glacier National Park.

Trail etiquette and safety Stay on the trails and avoid cutting across switchbacks, which causes unnecessary erosion and damages fragile plants.

Wildlife and cultural artifacts It is illegal to remove any natural or cultural artifacts from the parks, including rocks, stones, minerals and fossils, as well as antlers, nests, bird eggs, plants, cones and wildflowers.

Getting There & Around

All the parks are accessible on good roads. Most visitors arrive in their own vehicle and drive.

Getting around the parks without a car can be challenging, but not impossible, with a small selection of expensive shuttles. Glacier has an excellent free park shuttle linking most of the trailheads (summer only). Public transportation within Waterton is limited.

VIA trains serve Jasper. Amtrak serves Glacier with its transcontinental *Empire Builder* service.

For much more on **getting around**, see p277

PLAN YOUR TRIP NEED TO KNOW

What's New

Via Ferratas

First established by the Italian military during WWI, these fixed-protection climbing routes equipped with ladders, cables and suspension bridges are starting to pop up all over western Canada. New operators at Mt Norquay, in Banff National Park, and at Kicking Horse Mountain Resort (p133), near Golden, BC, run guided hikes across vertiginous mountain crags allowing non-climbers to tackle areas normally only accessible to experienced alpinists. (p82)

Glacier Skywalk

New in 2014, Jasper's glass-floored clifftop walkway juts out over the Sunwapta River valley by the side of the Icefields Pkwy. Visitors are taken over on special buses from the nearby Columbia Icefield Centre. (p159)

Crimson

Jasper has sprouted a plush new downtown hotel. One of six establishments run by Mountain Park Lodges, the Crimson is equipped with a swimming pool, gym and well-regarded casual restaurant. (p166)

Hidden Cove Campground

This small new paddle-in campground beside Jasper's Maligne Lake, just 5km from the busy north shore, has been designed as a handy stepping stone into the brawnier wilderness beyond. (p154)

Jasper Planetarium

Enhancing its role as a Dark Sky Preserve free of artificial light pollution, Jasper upped its stargazing potential in 2015 with the opening of a mini 'inflatable' planetarium. (p157)

'Glamping'

Banff and Jasper have latched onto the trend for 'glamping' (glamorous camping) with the installation of oTENTiks – A-frame tents with electricity, hot water and heating – in several campgrounds.

Paddleboarding

This popular low-impact water sport has taken off in all of the parks, thanks, in part, to the abundance of accessible lakes. You can either bring your own paddleboard or rent one locally.

Refurbished Hotels in Glacier

Some of Glacier National Park's historic hotels are undergoing some much-needed renovations in 2016–17, including the Lake McDonald Lodge, Rising Sun Motor Inn and the Many Glacier Hotel.

New Visitor Center in Apgar Village

Glacier's tiny service 'village' has sprouted an impressive new LEED–certified visitor center that gives out useful information on the national park. It comes equipped with free wi-fi. (p205)

Upgraded 'Jammer' Bus

Glacier has upgraded one of its vintage red 'Jammer' buses (originally dating from the 1930s) to cater for people with disabilities. The bus runs on the park's ever-popular sightseeing routes including the Going-to-the-Sun Rd. (p199)

For more recommendations and reviews, see **lonelyplanet.com/thorntree**

If You Like...

Wildlife Watching

Vermilion Lakes Tranquil lakes within easy reach of Banff Town where you can often spot beavers and grazing elk. (p90)

Bow Valley Parkway Running parallel to the Trans-Canada Hwy, this old forest road is an ideal place to see wildlife from your car. (p78)

Lake Louise Gondola Look out for grizzly bears foraging on surrounding avalanche slopes as you glide upwards. (p96)

Many Glacier One of the best places in Glacier to see bears, mountain goats, bighorn sheep and moose. (p198)

Maligne Lake Road Another good route to cruise with your car, keeping your eyes peeled for elusive woodland caribou. (p151)

Icefields Parkway Lots of traffic doesn't deter the full gamut of Rocky Mountain wildlife from frequenting the roadside. (p152)

Logan Pass A favorite high-altitude hangout for bighorn sheep, mountain goats and hoary marmots. (p196)

Lookouts & Views

Sulphur Mountain Quite possibly the most famous view in Banff National Park. (p88)

Glacier Skywalk This new vertiginous glass-floored lookout juts out from the Icefield Pkwy. (p159)

Fairview Build leg strength climbing to one of the best (and highest) viewpoints of Lake Louise. (p63)

Whistlers Mountain Hike or catch a cable car up to Jasper's best-loved viewpoint amid a backdrop of high-alpine tundra. (p143)

Parker Ridge Gaze across the Saskatchewan Glacier from this windy ridge halfway along the Icefields Pkwy. (p66)

Going-to-the-Sun Road This amazing roller-coaster road boasts 85km (53 miles) of nonstop views. (p192)

Glaciers

Athabasca Glacier This grand glacier is but a fragment of the enormous Columbia Icefield, North America's largest area of ice outside the polar regions. (p157)

Grinnell Glacier See Glacier's most accessible ice river from atop the Continental Divide, or down below from Many Glacier. (p198)

Saskatchewan Glacier Another spur tongue from the Columbia Icefield; this one is best seen from Parker Ridge. (p66)

Stanley Glacier Hike through burned forest to this classic 'hanging valley' glacier in Kootenay National Park. (p129)

Jackson Glacier One of 25 fast-disappearing icefields in Glacier National Park. Don't miss the lookout on Going-to-the-Sun Rd. (p196)

Adventure Activities

Skiing and snowboarding Tackle heart-stopping slaloms and off-piste thrills in Banff's Big Three resorts, or head to Jasper for quieter runs. (p36)

White-water rafting The class IV rapids of the Kicking Horse River are some the wildest in Canada; prepare to get very wet. (p80)

Caving Explore a subterranean world of stalactites and underground pools in the Rat's Nest Cave near Canmore. (p118)

Mountain biking Jasper National Park has, arguably, the best and most varied off-road biking network in Canada. (p149)

Via ferratas Try out these new fixed-protection climbing routes at the top of Banff's Mt Norquay. (p82)

Lakes & Waterfalls

Lake Louise Without doubt one of the most iconic vistas in Canada, despite the omnipresent crowds. (p60)

Johnston Canyon See three waterfalls in a single canyon on cleverly adapted boardwalks crammed with day-trippers. (p58)

Lake McDonald Take a trip or paddle a canoe across the waters of Glacier's stateliest lake. (p189)

Lake Minnewanka Catch a cruise across the largest lake in Banff National Park. (p91)

Maligne Lake Jasper's most famous lake is the ideal place to launch a backcountry kayaking trip. (p162)

Takakkaw Falls This enormous waterfall in Yoho National Park drops 384m (1259ft) to the valley floor. (p124)

Waterton Lake Cross the 49th parallel on a boat cruise with the opportunity to hike back into Canada afterwards. (p227)

Hiking

Healy Pass Multi-terrain hike through forest and meadows to a pass with expansive views across Alberta and British Columbia. (p59)

Highline Trail A sometimes vertiginous, always spectacular trail that traverses Glacier's unique geological formations. (p182)

Cory Pass Loop A knuckle-whitening adventure-hike a stone's throw from the urban comfort of Banff Town. (p57)

Lake Agnes & the Beehives Moderate trek to a wonderful backcountry teahouse perched above the scenic splendor of Lake Louise. (p62)

Top: A white-tailed deer in Vermilion Lakes (p90), Banff National Park
Bottom: A dogsled team racing on the trails of Canmore Nordic Centre (p117)

Skyline Trail Rated by many as one of the best multiday hikes in Canada, with fantastic Jasper views and a pleasant chalet for overnighting. (p146)

Carthew-Alderson Trail One of the finest above-the-treeline hikes in North America through an ethereal world of lakes, passes and peaks. (p219)

Hot Springs

Cave & Basin National Historic Site The first springs to be discovered in the Rockies are now inaccessible to bathers to protect the critically endangered Banff Springs snail. (p89)

Banff Upper Hot Springs The national park's oldest geothermal spa is still its most popular. Come early in the morning or late at night to dodge the crowds. (p88)

Radium Hot Springs Twin pools to indulge in, both with wonderful mountain views on every side – and the water is odorless! (p129)

Miette Hot Springs Jasper's natural springs offer a much quieter alternative to Banff; they are also the region's hottest. (p163)

Quiet Spots

Tonquin Valley No road access means guaranteed tranquillity in this remote Jasper valley. (p148)

Sunshine Meadows The high-altitude trails of these mountain meadows feel empty even on the busiest summer days. (p92)

Consolation Lakes These twin tarns are less than an hour's walk from Moraine Lake, but feel a world away from the tourist bustle. (p60)

Two Medicine Valley No hotels, no restaurants, but plenty of

wildlife and practically zero crowds. (p197)

Kananaskis Country Relatively few people explore the provincial parks that make up K-Country, so you'll probably just be sharing the trails with the locals. (p121)

History & Heritage

Banff Park Museum A wild menagerie of stuffed beasts and animal heads adorns the walls of Banff's oldest museum. (p86)

Whyte Museum of the Canadian Rockies Mountain takes centre stage at this excellent museum in Banff. (p86)

Native American Speaks Regularly held at the St Mary Visitor Center in Glacier. (p205)

Spiral Tunnels Train enthusiasts will find plenty to interest them in Yoho's ingenious railway route across the Rockies. (p125)

Buffalo Nations Luxton Museum This Banff museum has some intriguing examples of First Nations costume, art and craftwork. (p90)

Many Glacier Hotel Classic example of Glacier's woody 'parkitecture' building style dating from 1915. (p203)

Prince of Wales Hotel This gabled Swiss-style architectural beauty, set on a promontory overlooking Upper Waterton Lake, evokes the Empire spirit. (p229)

Off-the-Grid Accommodations

Skoki Lodge Ski lodge dating from 1930s near Lake Louise that offers afternoon tea, great food and comfortable rustic rooms. (p106)

Sperry Chalet A historic Glacier landmark built in 1913 with no

lights, heat, water or road access – but memorable dinners. (p203)

Assiniboine Lodge Cozy backcountry lodge offering helicopter transfers, warm showers and a sauna! (p128)

Granite Park Chalet Historic cook-your-own-meals lodge on Glacier's spectacular Highline Trail, built by Great Northern Railway in 1914. (p203)

Shovel Pass Lodge Jasper's oldest backcountry lodge sits halfway along its finest trail – the Skyline. (p168)

Tonquin Valley Backcountry Lodge Ski in, hike in or ride a horse: this rustic heaven next to Amethyst Lake is 24km from the nearest road. (p168)

Winter Activities

Downhill skiing Three ski areas in Banff and one in Jasper offer nearly 10,000 acres of dry white powder for skiers. (p36)

Ice-climbing The raging torrent of Maligne Canyon transforms into an eerie ice domain when the temperature dips below zero. (p162)

Skating Summer boating lakes become winter skating rinks with a good selection in Jasper, including Pyramid Lake. (p161)

Cross-country skiing Canmore's Nordic Centre hosted the 1988 Winter Olympics and its cross-country ski facilities remain top-notch. (p117)

Snowshoeing Guided snowshoe walks around Apgar Village are one of a few winter options available in low-key Glacier National Park. (p193)

Dogsledding Travel in the manner of Canada's early explorers pulled by a team of huskies in Canmore. (p119)

Month by Month

TOP EVENTS

Banff Summer Arts Festival, August

North American Indian Days, July

Jasper Dark Sky Festival, October

Snow Days, January

Canmore Highland Games, September

January

Chilly temperatures and crisp snow transform the mountains into an eerily quiet white wilderness, except for the slopes around Banff and Jasper, which are crammed with skiers and snowboarders.

👁 Ice Magic

During this annual competition, held at the Fairmont Lake Louise, teams of ice carvers battle it out to create sculptures fashioned from 136kg (300lb) blocks of ice.

Snow Days

Block parties, snow-sliding events, big-name bands and a huge game of street hockey characterize this celebration of all things snowy in downtown Banff.

Jasper in January

Jasper's atmospheric winter festival hosts plenty of family-friendly events, including cross-country skiing, sleigh rides, skating and a chili cook-off.

February

Winter holds the mountains in an icy grip, with frequent snowfalls and sub-zero temperatures still the norm.

Canmore Winter Carnival

This boisterous festival attempts to raise the winter spirits with log-sawing, ice-carving and beard-growing contests, but the Trapper's Ball is the highlight.

March

Little has changed in the mountains by March: snow and ice still cloak the landscape, with the spring thaw still months away.

Jasper Pride Festival

Wrap yourself in a rainbow flag and hit the ski slopes for this four-day LGBT–themed party (www.jasperpride. ca). Save time and energy to hit the town afterwards for special outdoor events, film screenings and – to cap it all off – a drag show.

April

Late April sees the first hints of spring – snowmelt at lower elevations and the odd warm sunny day – but don't put away the balaclava just yet.

👁 Big Mountain Ski Annual Furniture Races

Settees with skis, beds on sleds and even improvised toilets take to the slopes in this zany downhill furniture race at Montana's Whitefish Mountain Resort.

June

The summer season is usually underway by mid-June, with ski areas reopening to host warm-weather activities such as climbing, hiking and cycling. Alpine flower meadows unfurl their first blooms in late June.

🏃 Waterton Wildflower Festival

This nine-day event (www. watertonwildflowers.com) in Alberta's 'hidden secret' park is over a decade old and offers photography workshops and guided walks through the freshly carpeted flower meadows, with accompanying experts identifying the various species.

July

Summer settles in by July, and everyone starts to look forward to long days of hiking, cycling and other outdoor activities. Colorful blooms blanket mountain meadows, and most trails are open.

✈ Canada Day

Food booths, fireworks and outdoor concerts take place beneath the maple-leaf flag in a hot flush of patriotic pride. Look out for ebullient street processions in Banff and Jasper on July 1.

⊙ North American Indian Days

The largest of several celebrations held on the Blackfeet Indian Reservation throughout the year, this event has displays of traditional drumming and dancing, and the crowning of the year's Miss Blackfeet.

August

The warmest month of the year coincides with a host of special events, as well as the Rockies' busiest tourist season. The weather is mostly hot and dry, but watch out for thunderstorms.

☆ Banff Summer Arts Festival

Culture takes center stage for this month-long show-case of artistic activity at the Banff Centre, hosting everything from opera,

theater and street perform-ance to art exhibitions. It kicks off in late July and runs through August.

⊙ Jasper Heritage Rodeo

Since 1926 bull-riders, steer-wrestlers and calf-ropers have been congre-gating in Jasper for this annual hoedown and rodeo (www.jasperheritagerodeo. com), held in mid-August.

September

Fall brings a blaze of color to the mountain parks, making it one of the most spectacular seasons for hiking – especially now the summer crowds have left for home. Days remain warm, but the nights are getting chilly.

☆ Banff International String Quartet Competition

A world-famous contest for the cream of the world's classical string quartets, held at the Banff Centre every three years (next in 2016).

✈ Canmore Highland Games

Canmore celebrates its Scottish roots with a day of caber-tossing, piping, drumming, sheepdog trials and a traditional ceilidh to round things off (www. canmorehighlandgames.ca).

🏃 Lake Louise WonderFall Festival

Lake Louise hosts a series of events to mark the ar-rival of fall when its famous larch trees turn a mellow shade of yellow. Happen-ings include guided walks

and photography exhibi-tions, and many local restaurants present special fall-themed menus.

October

The seasonal interval between the end of summer and the start of the ski season means fewer crowds and lower hotel rates.

☆ Jasper Dark Sky Festival

Introduced in 2011, this annual event (www.jasper darksky.travel) celebrates Jasper's status as a Dark Sky Preserve with classical concerts under the stars and talks at the new planetarium from visiting astronomers and astronauts.

November

Winter is knocking on the door in November, which usually sees the first snowfall of the season and the opening of some of the area's higher elevation ski resorts.

☆ Banff Mountain Film & Book Festival

Since the mid-1970s, this seven-day film and litera-ture festival (www.banff centre.ca/mountainfestival) has celebrated the spirit of mountain adventure through films, videos, read-ings and lectures.

✈ Winterstart

This Banff street party is popular with the snow-boarding and winter-sports crowd, and includes the Ski Big Three Rail Jam and Santa's Parade of Lights.

Itineraries

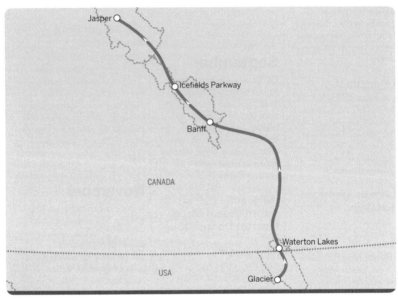

 Rocky Mountain Road Trip

This once-in-a-lifetime trip takes in four parks and covers pretty much everything the Rocky Mountains have to offer.

Start out with three days exploring **Glacier** and the magnificent mountain scenery around Going-to-the-Sun Rd, warming up with some short hikes around Many Glacier. On day four, head north across the Canadian border for **Waterton Lakes** and a hike along the iconic Carthew-Alderson Trail. Spend the next day driving north to **Banff**, your base for the next four days. How you divide the time is up to you, but make sure you factor in the gondola ride up Sulphur Mountain, wildlife spotting around Vermilion Lakes and the Bow Valley Parkway, a boat trip across Lake Minnewanka, and at least one day hike. Day 10 is set aside for more mind-blowing scenery around Lake Louise and Moraine Lake, followed on day 11 by a drive up the **Icefields Parkway** – it won't take long for you to realize why it's often dubbed the world's most spectacular road. Round the trip off with three days in **Jasper**, including a cruise on Maligne Lake, a day hike, a ride on the Jasper Skytram and a dip in Miette Hot Springs.

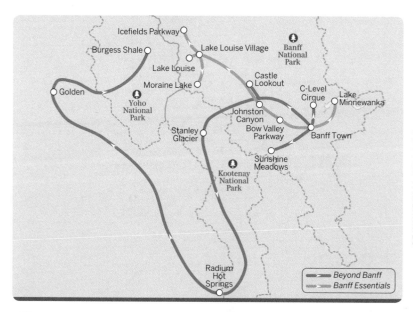

 Beyond Banff

This itinerary combines day hiking around Banff with a side trip into the neighboring (quieter) national parks in British Columbia.

For the first few days, base yourself in **Banff Town** and spend the time breaking in those boots: you could hike up to a hidden icefield at the **C-Level Cirque**, admire the Bow Valley from **Castle Lookout**, or trek through the colorful wildflowers of **Sunshine Meadows**.

From Banff, head west into **Kootenay National Park**. This is one of the most fire-prone areas of the Rockies: you'll still be able to see the damage wrought by the massive 2003 burn. Take the time to hike up to **Stanley Glacier** before chilling in the 'hot' and 'cool' pools of **Radium Hot Springs**, both fed from a volcanic spring hidden deep beneath the mountainside.

From Radium, the route loops north via **Golden**, a lively little town. From here, the road heads east along the Kicking Horse Valley into **Yoho National Park**, where you can spend the remaining few days admiring the sights: don't miss Emerald Lake, Takakkaw Falls and a guided walk to the fossil fields of the **Burgess Shale**.

 Banff Essentials

This five-day itinerary squeezes in Banff's key sights, with the emphasis on sightseeing rather than hiking.

Kick off with a day exploring **Banff Town**, a lively mini-metropolis with a cosmopolitan mix of shops, bistros, pubs and museums. Check in for some chateau luxury at the historic Fairmont Banff Springs hotel, followed by a day exploring **Lake Minnewanka**, canoeing on the Bow River and relaxing in the Upper Hot Springs Pool.

On day three, drive out of Banff and detour off the Trans-Canada Hwy and onto the **Bow Valley Parkway**. Keep your eyes peeled for wildlife, and don't miss the famous waterfalls of **Johnston Canyon**. By mid-afternoon, you'll reach iconic **Lake Louise** and nearby **Moraine Lake**, both renowned for their sapphire-blue waters and stunning mountain settings. Spend day four stretching your legs on the dramatic trail along the Plain of Six Glaciers.

On day five, drive along the breathtaking **Icefields Parkway**, passing jagged peaks, mighty glaciers and sparkling lakes en route to Num-Ti-Jah Lodge, one of the Rockies' most famous mountain retreats.

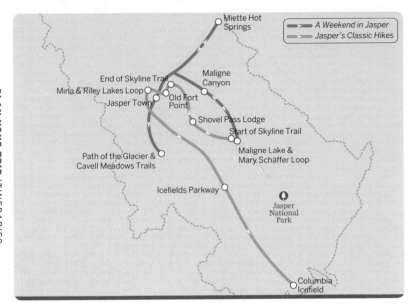

A Weekend in Jasper

Even with only a long weekend at your disposal, it's still possible to get a taste of what makes Jasper special. Base yourself in Jasper Town, and take three little day excursions that combine the main sights with a couple of short trails.

On the first day, tick off **Jasper Town**: get an early morning ticket for the Jasper Skytram, visit the museum, pick up lunch from the Bear's Paw Bakery, then spend an afternoon at Patricia and Pyramid Lakes. Stroll along the Discovery Trail as the sun sets, with a smart dinner at Evil Dave's Grill.

On day two, pack a picnic from Patricia Street Deli and drive along Maligne Lake Rd – a hot spot for wildlife. Explore the crashing cascades of **Maligne Canyon**, and then head for nearby **Maligne Lake** for a guided cruise to tiny Spirit Island and an early evening walk on the **Mary Schäffer Loop**.

On your last day, it's time to hit the trail. Jasper has lots of day hikes, but it's hard to top the spectacular **Path of the Glacier Cavell Meadows Trails**. Reward yourself with an evening soak at **Miette Hot Springs**, followed by farewell drinks and dinner at Jasper Brewing Co.

Jasper's Classic Hikes

You've seen Jasper's must-see sights, so now's the time for something a bit more challenging. This hike-centric itinerary incorporates a couple of short trails with a longer one, after which you can take some time off for glacier viewing.

Warm up with some easy hikes around town. **Old Fort Point** is steep but short. The **Mina & Riley Lakes Loop** is peaceful but never strays too far from civilization.

Now you're ready for the wilder stuff. The two- to three-day **Skyline Trail** is without doubt one of North America's premier overnight hikes, taking in everything from snowy peaks and glacial lakes to lofty passes with mind-boggling views. You don't even have to rough it, thanks to the cozy Shovel Pass Lodge.

After the exertion, it's time to sit back and let the views come to you. Spend a day driving south along the Jasper section of the **Icefields Parkway**, and finish up with a visit to the **Columbia Icefield**, the largest area of ice this side of the North Pole. Most people trundle up in a Snocoach, but a guided walk will give you an even more memorable perspective.

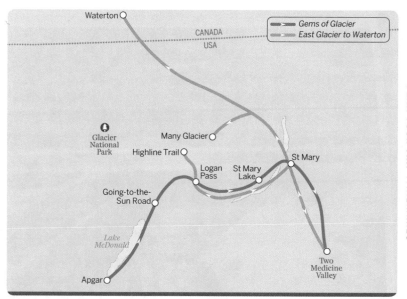

Gems of Glacier
3 DAYS

Three days in Glacier will bag you the highlights if you don't stray too far from the Going-to-the-Sun Rd. Use one of the hotels or motels around Apgar as your launchpad and then employ the park's handy free shuttle to get you from west side to east with various stop-offs en route.

On day one, explore around **Apgar**, West Glacier and nearby Lake McDonald, perhaps taking a walk among ancient rainforest on the Trail of the Cedars, or admiring mountain scenery on the Avalanche Lake Trail.

On day two, travel east along the **Going-to-the-Sun Road**, one of America's most stunning stretches of asphalt. You can take your own vehicle or climb aboard one of the vintage red Jammer buses, which have been trundling along the road since 1936. Stop to see the sights: the tumbling cascades of Bird Woman Falls and the Weeping Wall, the dramatic stretch of highway over **Logan Pass**, and the Jackson Glacier Overlook, which affords a knockout view of one of the park's namesake glaciers.

Stay overnight at the Rising Sun Motor Inn on the shores of **St Mary Lake**, and spend your last day hiking trails and spotting wildlife in **Two Medicine Valley**.

East Glacier to Waterton
1 WEEK

This trip focuses on the eastern side of the Rockies in Glacier National Park, using the small settlement of **St Mary** as a base. Afterwards, you'll be within striking distance of Waterton Lakes just across the border in Canada, a beautifully compact and often-overlooked national park.

Spend the first couple of days exploring north and south around **Going-to-the-Sun Road**. **Two Medicine Valley** is a short drive south of St Mary, while **Logan Pass** lies to the west: both are fantastic areas for walking and wildlife watching. To get underneath Glacier's skin, a hike is essential – the Sun Point to Virginia Falls Trail starts near St Mary Lake, while the Highline Trail starting at Logan Pass is one of the park's most popular – and spectacular.

Then it's north for a couple of days in **Many Glacier**, arguably the national park's most beautiful valley. Reward yourself with a stay in the Many Glacier Hotel, overlooking the sparkling waters of Swiftcurrent Lake.

Finish up with some more hiking and sightseeing in **Waterton**: don't miss the classic Carthew-Alderson Trail and the equally impressive tramp to Crypt Lake.

A climber on Cascade Mountain (p57), Banff National Park

Plan Your Trip
Activities

If you want to sample the full gamut of spine-tingling outdoor activities in a well-equipped but refreshingly pure wilderness, you've come to the right place. Glacier excels in backcountry hiking, Banff and Jasper up the ante with ski resorts, while Canmore and Golden are two of Canada's adrenaline-sports capitals.

Hike Grades

For ease of use and to help you decide which one to take, we've graded our favourite hikes into three difficulty levels.

Easy

Mostly flat, simple walking on clearly defined trails, suitable for families and inexperienced hikers. Some may be paved and suitable for wheelchair users or people with reduced mobility.

Moderate

These hikes will feature significant elevation gain, and include steep sections and possibly some ungroomed areas of trail (such as rubble, stones or moraines). Suitable for any hiker with an average level of fitness.

Difficult

Expect very steep climbs, sections of exposed and unmaintained trail, challenging terrain and occasional route-finding. These hikes are for experienced hikers, and will entail long days and significant distances. Pack appropriate equipment.

Planning Your Trip

Experiencing the great outdoors is undoubtedly one of the top reasons to visit the Rockies. Whether it's plummeting down the slopes on a mountain bike or climbing up them on a classic hike, the mountain parks present a wealth of ways to expend your energy and make the most of the spectacular scenery.

When to Go

When you choose to visit the mountain parks depends on what you want to do. Winter is long in the Rockies, with snow covering the landscape for up to six months of the year (from around November to May). Most summer activities take place between May and September, although the exact periods vary according to seasonal conditions.

Summer Activities

➡ **June–September** This is the peak activity season and usually offers the most reliable weather. Most trails are open by late June or early July. It's worth waiting to do longer overnight hikes for the warmer temperatures of late July and August.

➡ **July–August** By far the busiest times on the trails, so if you prefer to walk in solitude, the shoulder months are a better bet.

➡ **September–October** Both great months to visit, as fall brings autumnal colors and most trails are comparatively quiet.

Winter Activities

➡ The ski season usually runs from late November until April, but can open early or late, depending on seasonal conditions.

➡ Some hiking trails stay open in winter, but you'll need to master the art of snowshoeing!

Outdoor Activities

Hiking & Backpacking

If there's one activity that sums up the spirit of the Rockies, it's hiking. No matter where you travel in the parks, there's a trail nearby that'll whisk you up spectacular mountains, into picturesque forests or down a dramatic gorge.

The Rockies are a destination *par excellence* for experienced hikers, but have plenty to offer novice walkers, too. Some trails have interpretive signs that are ideal for families, while others feature paved sections designed for people with limited mobility.

A good topographical map of the area you're hiking in is essential – the Gem Trek maps are the best for the Canadian parks.

Day Hikes

The term 'day hike' covers everything from an hour-long woodland stroll to an eight-hour haul to a mountain pass. Any route that takes less than eight hours to complete, or covers a round-trip of less than 24km (15 miles), is generally practical for a day hike.

You might not quite reach the edge of the true wilderness in a single day, but you can still experience an astonishing variety of terrain and enjoy plenty of wonderful views.

It's always worth reading up on your chosen route before you set out to make sure it suits your ability level and that you know what to expect from your day on the mountain. Latest trail reports and wildlife warnings are available from park visitor centers or online from the national park websites.

Overnight Hikes

For a true wilderness experience you have to spend a few nights out in the wild. There are hundreds of backcountry routes scattered around the parks. Some string together a few day hikes with a night in a backcountry campground, while others are multiday epics that venture into distant and little-visited corners of the national parks.

➡ Trips can last anywhere from a couple of days to a couple of weeks.

➡ Overnight hikes require a wilderness pass and backcountry campground reservations.

➡ The majority of overnight hikes are within the capabilities of most hikers, as long as you're properly equipped and reasonably fit.

➡ You'll need to pack in food, a tent and sleeping bag, first-aid supplies and all other equipment, and pack out all your rubbish.

Responsible Backcountry Hiking

The general rule in the backcountry is to leave everything as you find it – the Leave No Trace (www.leavenotrace.ca) website has some excellent advice on ways to reduce your impact on the environment.

➡ Pitch on sites previously used by other campers to avoid unnecessary damage to the landscape.

➡ Keep your campsite clean to avoid attracting animals.

➡ Store food, toiletries and cooking equipment in bear-proof lockers if available, or suspend them between two trees at least 4m (13ft) above the ground and 1.3m (4ft) from each trunk.

➡ Use biodegradable soap and wash dishes well away from rivers and streams.

➡ A portable stove is more eco-friendly than a campfire, as it prevents unnecessary scorching of the ground.

➡ If you do have a fire, don't cut anything down to burn as fuel – dead wood is OK, green wood certainly isn't.

➡ Heed any fire restrictions that may be in place.

➡ If you get caught short on the trail, move well away from the path and at least 70m (230ft)

TOP AREAS FOR OVERNIGHT HIKES

➡ Skoki Valley, Banff (p71)

➡ Egypt Lake, Banff (p68)

➡ Mt Assiniboine, Banff (p68)

➡ Kananaskis Country (p121)

➡ Tonquin Valley, Jasper (p148)

➡ Skyline Trail, Jasper (p146)

➡ Gunsight Pass, Glacier (p185)

➡ Lake O'Hara, Yoho (p127)

➡ Northern Highline–Waterton Valley (p190)

---

from any water source, dig a hole, do the deed and cover it with dirt. Pack out toilet paper in a sealed bag.

Rules & Permits

No matter where you're hiking, you'll need a valid park pass and, if you're exploring the backcountry, backcountry campground reservations and a wilderness permit for each night of your stay. All these can be arranged through visitor centers.

It's also a good idea to leave a full trip itinerary with park staff if you're traveling in remote country or doing any hazardous activities (such as mountaineering or rock climbing). Remember to sign in once you're back, otherwise you will be listed as missing and a search party will be sent out to find you.

It's extremely important to stay on the trails – cutting across switchbacks, avoiding muddy patches and tramping trail fringes causes unnecessary 'braiding' of the path and damages the fragile alpine environment.

Trail Guides

A standalone hiking guide can be a useful purchase, as they have extra space to detail precise trail distances, marker points, full elevations and compass bearings for specific routes. There are lots of different guides to choose from.

Standard hiking textbook *The Canadian Rockies Trail Guide* by Brian Patton and Bart Robinson, first published in 1971, is still many people's preferred guide. Simple layout, no-nonsense text, and trail descriptions for 229 hikes are all user-friendly, although the black-and-white format looks dated.

The full-color *Classic Hikes in the Canadian Rockies* by Graeme Pole is more useful if you're after some context on your hike, with glossy photos of views, sights, wildflowers, and flora and fauna. The book is handily divided into color-coded sections for each national park.

The opinionated *Don't Waste Your Time in the Canadian Rockies* by Kathy and Craig Copeland rates hikes in four categories (Premier, Outstanding, Worthwhile and Don't Do). Some of the choices are controversial, but it certainly helps you narrow your selection.

Going Solo

For many people it's the chance for solitude that makes the idea of hiking in the mountains so irresistible, but it's worth thinking carefully if you're heading out solo. If you'd prefer not to go alone, ask around at local hostels and visitor centers to see if you can find some like-minded hikers or an organized walk to tag along with.

Walking alone (especially in the backcountry) is inherently more risky – your chance of encountering wildlife is greater, there's no one to go for help if you get into trouble or sprain an ankle, and no one to blame if you get lost due to bad navigation skills! If you do decide to hike alone, take the following precautions:

➜ Pack a compass and a good trail map, and make sure you're familiar with basic navigation techniques.

➜ Look out for recent wildlife warnings at trailheads, which will also be posted in park visitor centers.

➜ Pay attention to group access restrictions and seasonal trail closures around Lake Louise in summer.

➜ Let someone know where you're planning on hiking and what time you expect to be back.

➜ Sing loudly on the trail, shout and clap your hands to warn animals of your approach.

➜ Be particularly wary about wildlife around noisy streams or dense forest.

➜ Carry bear spray in an easily accessible place, and make sure you know how to use it. Also check expiry dates on the canister.

Cycling

While parks authorities have cracked down on a number of unauthorized bike trails in recent years, there are still plenty of routes

---

EXTREME PURSUITS

Looking for extra adrenaline? No problem! The mountain parks have plenty of ways to get your blood pumping.

➜ Live out your Jack London fantasies on a dogsledding expedition (p119)

➜ Plumb the depths of the Rat's Nest (p118) cave system

➜ Challenge the rapids on the Kicking Horse and Kananaskis Rivers (p80)

➜ Soar through the skies on a heli-hiking expedition (p78)

➜ Scramble around the peaks of Mt Edith Cavell or Canmore (p82)

---

open to mountain bikers in Banff, Lake Louise, Kananaskis and Jasper. Waterton Lakes also has a small selection of routes, but mountain biking is banned on all trails in Glacier.

There are also dedicated bike parks at the **Canmore Nordic Centre** (✏403-678-2400; www.canmorenordic.com; 1988 Olympic Way) and the **Kicking Horse Mountain Resort** (www.kickinghorseresort.com) in Golden, which has its own cyclist-friendly gondola and a huge network of mountain trails.

Road riding is most popular along the Bow Valley Pkwy, Minnewanka Loop and the Icefields Pkwy, but you won't get away without tackling a few hills.

Preparation, Equipment & Safety

➜ Rent bikes and equipment in Banff, Jasper, Waterton, Kananaskis, Canmore and Golden.

➜ Always wear a helmet, take a puncture repair kit and/or spare inner tubes, and a basic trail tool kit including hex keys, screwdrivers and chain tool.

➜ Many rental companies offer shuttle services to trailheads or guided trips along classic routes in the parks.

➜ Trail conditions vary widely, from flat, paved trails to technical singletracks with hazards such as branches, rocks and knotted roots. Do your research before you set out.

➜ Cyclists are particularly prone to surprise bear encounters due to the speed and silence with which they travel. Make plenty of noise,

Backcountry camping, Banff National Park

slow down in dense forests, and take extra care near rivers and on windy days.

Fishing

With hundreds of waterways and lakes open for angling, the mountain parks are, unsurprisingly, a paradise for aspiring anglers. Arctic grayling, rainbow trout, brown trout, brook trout, lake trout, northern pike, mountain whitefish and lake whitefish are all abundant, although some species (such as bull trout, cutthroat trout and kokanee salmon) have suffered a major decline in recent years and are protected by law.

The most popular angling areas include the Bow River and Lake Minnewanka in Banff; Maligne Lake, Pyramid Lake and Princess Lakes in Jasper; and Lake McDonald and St Mary Lake in Glacier.

Rules, Regulations & Seasons

To fish anywhere in Banff and Jasper, you will need to buy a fishing permit, available from park visitor centers. The free *Fishing Regulations Summary* will be included with your permit, detailing angling seasons, catch limits and other useful information. There's also a handy pictorial key for helping to identify your fish: it's important to be sure about your catch, as you'll be fined if you're caught in possession of one of the protected species by park authorities. If in doubt, catch-and-release is the way to go.

No fishing permit is required across the border in Glacier. Casting on the park's boundaries may require a Montana state fishing license, and waters on Blackfeet Indian Reservation land (such as part of Lower Two Medicine Lake) require permits from the reservation.

➡ The season in Canada generally runs from June to September, with a slightly longer season in Glacier.

➡ It's illegal to fish with natural bait, chemical attractants or lead tackle.

➡ You cannot have more than one line at a time in the water and may not fish from two hours after sunset to one hour before sunrise.

➡ Some waters are catch-and-release zones only, while most others have catch limits for particular species.

➡ Consider employing a local guide, who can provide gear and tackle, help you find the choicest waters, and make sure you stay within the rules.

Horseback Riding

People have been taking pack trips around these parts since the days of the earliest settlers, and the horseback tradition remains strong to this day. Many trails in Banff, Jasper and Glacier are open to horseback riders as well as hikers, and horses are also welcome at many backcountry campgrounds and lodges, so there's plenty of opportunity for day trips, as well as more adventurous backcountry expeditions.

Most people choose to saddle up with a local guiding company, but it's possible to bring along your own steed. If you're trotting off into the Canadian backcountry, you'll need a grazing permit in addition to your wilderness pass. Comprehensive listings of pack-trip companies and outfitters are available from **Alberta Outfitters Association** (☑403-722-2692; www.alberta outfitters.com) and **Montana Outfitters & Guides Association** (☑406-449-3578; www. montanaoutfitters.org).

White-Water Rafting & Float Trips

The Rockies have some of the best white water in Canada. Rapids systems are graded into six degrees of difficulty, ranging from I (easy) to VI (near-impossible): most local activity companies tackle rapids rated between I and III. Equipment, safety gear and trained guides are all supplied, and though it can be pretty white-knuckle at times, in general white-water rafting is safe – although you'll obviously need to be able to swim, and be prepared to get very wet.

More sedate float trips on rivers are ideal for families and often provide a good way of spotting waterbirds and wildlife.

The rafting season is May through September, with highest river levels (and therefore the most rapids) in spring.

The best areas for rafting are along the Kicking Horse and Kananaskis Rivers; Canmore and Golden both have plenty of operators that run trips. Jasper also has its own network of white-water rivers, while in Glacier, the Middle and North Forks of the Flathead River offer the best stretches of white water for rafting.

Canoeing & Kayaking

The region's Aboriginal people have been using canoes for thousands of years (an example followed by the early European settlers and voyageurs), and canoeing and kayaking are still the best ways to get out on the water.

Nonmotorized boats (including canoes, dinghies and kayaks) are allowed on nearly all waterways in the Canadian parks, but motorboats are banned, except on Lake Minnewanka. The rules are less strict in Glacier, with most waterways open to boats.

➡ Canoes and kayaks are readily available for hire at many lakes; expect to pay around C$30 to C$55 per hour, including life jackets and paddles.

➡ Banff's best places for canoeing are Lake Louise, Moraine Lake, Bow River and Vermilion Lakes. Cruises are offered on Lake Minnewanka. You can also paddle on Emerald Lake in Yoho.

➡ In Jasper, Maligne Lake offers superb canoeing and commentated cruises to Spirit Island. Pyramid Lake is another good spot.

➡ In Glacier, hire boats and cruises are offered on Lake McDonald, St Mary, Swiftcurrent Lake and Josephine Lake.

➡ In Waterton, Cameron Lake is the best lake for sailing, with rowboats, kayaks and canoes for rent.

Wildlife Watching

With a rich and varied animal population ranging from bighorn sheep to wolverines, elk and grizzly bears, you should have plenty of opportunities to glimpse the parks' wilder residents. As always, the best times for wildlife watching are dawn and dusk. You'll have more luck away from major roads, especially around the more remote areas of Jasper and Glacier, but even in Banff you're bound to cross paths with at least a few wild animals.

In general, wildlife tends to go wherever humans don't, so the quieter areas of Kananaskis and Kootenay are excellent places for wildlife seekers. Kananaskis is also famous for the annual migration of around 6000 golden eagles, which takes place through the valley every fall.

TOP SPOTS FOR WILDLIFE

Vermilion Lakes, Banff Elk

Lake Minnewanka, Banff Bighorn sheep, mountain goats, pika, ground squirrels

Bow Valley Parkway, Banff Elk, moose, occasionally black bears

Smith-Dorrien/Spray Trail Road Mountain goats, bighorn sheep

Lake Louise Gondola, Banff Grizzly bears on the avalanche slopes

Emerald Lake Area, Yoho Moose, black and grizzly bears

Icefields Parkway, Jasper Elk, moose, marmots, bighorn sheep

Maligne Lake Road, Jasper Moose, mountain goats, occasionally wolves

Tonquin Valley, Jasper Moose, bighorn sheep, marmots, some bears

Many Glacier, Glacier Mountain goats, black and grizzly bears

Two Medicine Valley, Glacier Grizzly bears

Horseback riding (p34) on trails near Lake Louise

Wild animals can be highly unpredictable and often perceive humans as a threat, so be careful not to get too close (even seemingly harmless animals such as elk can be dangerous, especially during calving season). A good pair of binoculars or a telephoto lens will help you see the show from a distance.

Rock Climbing & Mountaineering

With so many peaks and rock faces to tackle, Banff and Jasper are both well-known destinations for rock climbers, but the mountainous terrain is generally challenging and technical and mostly more suited to experienced alpinists, rather than novices.

An exception is the new via ferratas (fixed-protection climbing routes) in Banff's Mt Norquay and Kicking Horse Mountain Resort that offer a safe, guided climbing experience on some truly incredible crags.

The **Alpine Club of Canada** (www.alpineclubofcanada.ca) and the **Association of Canadian Mountain Guides** (www.acmg.ca), both based in Canmore, provide general advice on climbing in the Rockies and can put you in touch with local mountain guides.

Skiing & Snowboarding

While perhaps not quite on a par with Whistler, Banff and Jasper have a growing reputation for winter sports – and with more than five months of snow every year, and, of course, no shortage of mountains, it's hardly surprising.

Banff & Jasper

The three main resorts in Banff are Mt Norquay, Lake Louise and Sunshine Village, collectively known as the **Big Three** (www.skibig3.com). Lift passes covering all three resorts are available, or you can buy individual resort passes if you only have a limited time on the mountains.

In Jasper, the main skiing center is **Marmot Basin** (www.skimarmot.com), along the Icefields Pkwy. The slopes and facilities are generally a little quieter than in Banff, so Marmot makes a good destination if this is your first time on the snow.

The facilities at all four resorts are excellent, with ski and snowboarding schools, childcare facilities, terrain parks and half-pipes for snowboarders, as well as public transportation to the slopes and lots of groomed and powder runs.

Other Resorts

Though less well-known than Banff and Jasper, there are a couple of other resorts a short drive away. **Nakiska** (www.skinakiska.com) in Kananaskis Country, about an hour's drive south of Canmore, was originally developed for the 1988 Winter Olympics, and still has a good reputation among skiers and snowboarders. It's usually a lot quieter than Banff, but has fewer runs and simpler facilities. Shuttle buses run throughout the ski season from Banff and Canmore.

The **Kicking Horse Mountain Resort** (p133) is the Rocky Mountains' newest ski resort (and one of the only ones to be granted development permission in the last 20 years). With more than 1120 skiable hectares, over 120 runs and a vertical drop of 1260m (4133ft), it's also fast becoming one of the best.

Whitefish Mountain Resort (p212), 11km (7 miles) south of Whitefish, is another prime ski destination, with the excellent Fishbowl Terrain Parks, a vertical drop of 717m (2353ft) and 93 marked trails spread over a massive 1215 hectares (3000 acres). Look out for the annual furniture race (April) down the slopes of Big Mountain, which has to be seen to be believed.

Cross-Country Skiing

While most skiers choose to bomb down the mountainside, an increasing number of people are taking to cross-country skiing as a way of experiencing the parks in their wintry glory.

Cross-country skiers have the chance to explore the empty backcountry deep into midwinter; many trails around Banff, Lake Louise and Jasper are specifically kept open for use by cross-country skiers from December through March, with a more limited range of trails also open in Glacier, Waterton, Kananaskis and Yoho.

➡ Park authorities supply trail maps of open routes, and you'll find lessons and equipment rental from most outdoor activity operators and some ski schools.

➡ Trails aren't always signposted and can be difficult to make out under heavy snow cover. Check trail conditions before you set out.

HENRY GEORGI / GETTY IMAGES ©

Snowboarder at Lake Louise resort, Banff National Park

➡ Cross-country skiers need to be alert to the dangers of avalanches, especially in remote areas.

➡ Carry emergency supplies, an avalanche beacon, a full repair kit, a compass and a detailed topographical map with you on any cross-country skiing trip.

Snowshoeing

Snowshoeing has been practiced in the Rockies for hundreds of years, and it's one of the easiest and most enjoyable ways to explore the winter wilderness.

Many of the trails kept open for cross-country skiers also have parallel tracks for snowshoers, and there are other routes to explore around the townsites in Jasper, Banff and Glacier. As always, park staff can help with route maps and condition reports for current trails.

Snowshoes can be hired from outdoor equipment stores and activity providers in Banff, Jasper and Glacier.

Travel with Children

The Rocky Mountain parks are the perfect places to entertain and educate children; light on gimmicks, but heavy on inspiration. Listen to fascinating tales from indigenous storytellers, feel the thrill of your first-ever bear sighting, or enjoy the good old-fashioned simplicity of a game of charades around the campfire.

Best Regions for Kids

Banff

The park with the best infrastructure contains a sizeable town that hosts bags of restaurants and hotels, and a good cross section of outdoor adventure companies. Banff also has a gondola ride, hot springs and several museums.

Jasper

A quieter alternative to Banff, Jasper also has a handy townsite, a gondola ride, hot springs and the best off-road bike network in the Rockies.

Waterton Lakes

This pint-sized park has a small townsite equipped with its own large family-friendly campground. Also on offer are boat rides on lakes, and some spectacular trails.

Glacier

The most rugged park has an excellent Junior Ranger program and interesting Native America Speaks.

Banff, Jasper & Glacier for Kids

Sights & Attractions

Compared to the true wilderness parks in Alaska and the Yukon with next-to-zero infrastructure, the Rocky Mountain parks are positively family-friendly, laying on many activities specifically for children.

Inevitably, it's the outdoor pursuits that are going to be the main attraction. Wildlife walks, white-water rafting, canoeing and horseback riding are all popular family pastimes, and most activity providers are well set up for dealing with kids.

Children qualify for discounted entry to nearly all sights (generally around half-price for ages five to 15, while under-fives often go free). Family tickets, which usually include entry for two adults and two children, are also available for many tours and sights.

Hiking

Hiking is one of the best all-round family activities. Many of the trails around the parks are well maintained and easily within the scope of active kids. Older kids should be capable of tackling

TOP HIKES FOR KIDS

Johnston Canyon, Banff (p58)

Sundance Canyon, Banff (p54)

Consolation Lakes, Banff (p60)

Garden Path Trail, Banff (p58)

Mary Schäffer Loop, Jasper (p143)

Moose Lake Loop, Jasper (p143)

Crypt Lake Trail, Wateron Lakes (p219)

Avalanche Lake Trail, Glacier (p181)

Swiftcurrent Lake Nature Trail, Glacier (p187)

some of the shorter overnight hikes, including staying out in the backcountry and cooking dinner over an open campfire with parents or extended family.

Trails that combine the sights are usually more fun for inquiring young minds, and there are many examples of walks that take in a mix of forest, mountain, river and canyon, or those that wind their way through wildlife habitats. Several trails have interpretive panels to help you understand the geographical features, flora and fauna.

If the kids are interested in nature, it might be a good idea to join an organized hike. Many local guides are accredited by the Mountain Parks Heritage Interpretation Association (MPHIA) and can help children really engage with the natural world they're walking through. The main tour operators in Banff run morning and evening wildlife tours, on which you'll have a good chance of spotting elk, moose, bighorn sheep and other animals.

Remember to take along all the necessary supplies, including plenty of water, hats, sun lotion, blister cream and, most importantly, something nice to eat once you reach the end of the trail. Good-quality waterproofs will also come in handy in case of sudden rainstorms.

Cycling

Banff and Jasper have decent on- and off-road cycling networks with plenty of easy grades for kids. Most bike-rental companies offer children's bikes, child helmets and protective pads, as well as child chariots and 'tag-a-longs' for younger children.

One of the best areas for cycling is at the self-contained **Canmore Nordic Centre** (p117), which has a huge system of trails catering for all ages and abilities. The **Kicking Horse Mountain Resort** (p133) is also good for downhill mountain biking in summer.

Canoeing & Rafting

Canoes and kayaks are readily available for hire on Lake Louise, Moraine Lake, Emerald Lake and many others throughout the summer months. For more thrills, white-water rafting on the Kicking Horse and Bow Rivers is a guaranteed knuckle-whitener, although – depending on the class of rapids – there are sometimes minimum age stipulations. More popular with families are relatively sedate 'float trips', such as those offered on the Bow and Athabasca Rivers (in Banff and Jasper, respectively). All canoeing and rafting companies provide suitable boats for kids, or spaces in adult boats, along with child-sized life vests.

If you prefer to let someone else do the steering, there are scenic boat cruises on Lake Minnewanka, Maligne Lake and several of Jasper's lakes.

Horseback Riding

Horse travel is part of Rocky Mountain folklore and requires minimal skills if you're a first-timer. Most horse-trip companies provide small ponies and child-friendly saddles, and cater as much for novices as experienced riders.

Banff Trail Riders (p83) has lots of easy rides in Banff (from one hour in duration) and also offers a great evening trail cookout, complete with BBQ steak and homemade baked beans.

You can usually visit the horses at Spray River Corral and the Warner stables, near the Cave & Basin in Banff; phone ahead to check the stables are open for visitors.

Jasper also has plenty of potential for horseback riding, with popular day trails around Lake Annette and Lake Patricia, and longer trips into Tonquin Valley and Maligne Pass.

Skiing, Snowboarding & Other Winter Activities

In winter, skiing and snowboarding are the main outdoor pastimes. All of the ski resorts in Banff, Jasper and Kananaskis, as well as Whitefish Mountain Resort near Glacier, have runs that are specially tailored for younger users. Child-size skis, snowboards, goggles and gear are all available for hire. Banff's Mt Norquay is deemed particularly family-friendly.

Most resorts offer ski lessons and snowboard schools, as well as day care and babysitting services. For more info, the website for Banff's **Big Three** (www.skibig3.com) ski resorts will give you some idea of what's on offer.

Cross-country skiing and snowshoeing are both fun and unusual ways to explore the winter landscape: The trails around Jasper Townsite and the Lake Louise area are good places to start. Ice-skating is usually possible on some of the park's lakes in winter, depending on seasonal temperatures.

Ranger Programs

Glacier operates the US National Parks Service's excellent **Junior Ranger Program** (www.nps.gov/learn/juniorranger.htm), in which kids pick up a free ranger booklet from park visitor centers. The booklet contains activities, questionnaires, quizzes and games to complete during their stay; they'll earn a Junior Ranger badge and a certificate when the book is completed. Before you even set out for the national park, kids can sign up to become a WebRanger at www.nps.gov/webrangers, where there are plenty of online games, puzzles and activities to pique their interest.

The Canadian Rocky Mountain parks – Banff, Jasper, Yoho, Kootenay and Waterton Lakes – all run an **Xplorers Program** aimed at kids aged six to 11. Kids are given a paperback *Xplorer* booklet full of interesting facts and tasks. They must complete a given number of tasks in order to claim a special souvenir. **Xplorers 2** is a similar program aimed at teens. Booklets are available at any park information center.

Hands-on interpretive activities are often run at day-use areas or on trails in Banff. Activities range from stories about legendary park characters to field studies of bugs. Upcoming activities are displayed on the park website.

Parks Canada also provides regular educational programs at main campgrounds in Banff, Jasper, Waterton Lakes and Kootenay, with slide shows, talks, films and activities exploring many aspects of the parks, including wildlife, natural history and geology. Campgrounds with regular programs include Tunnel Mountain, Johnston Canyon and Lake Louise in Banff, and Whistlers

and Wapiti in Jasper. You don't have to be a campground guest to attend.

In West Glacier in the US, the Glacier National Park Visitor Center holds similarly entertaining ranger talks and slideshows throughout summer, and the Discovery Cabin in Apgar Village holds Junior Ranger programs in July and August.

Children's Highlights
Banff & Around

Banff Gondola Ride the sky-skimming cable car to the top of Sulphur Mountain.

Bow River Float the low-grade rapids below Bow Falls or hire a canoe and paddle up to Vermilion Lakes for some beaver-spotting.

Lake Louise Hike up for afternoon tea at the Lake Agnes Teahouse.

Rat's Nest Cave This cave system near Canmore has over 65km (40 miles) of underground tunnels to explore.

Boo the Grizzly Bear The Rocky Mountains' only captive grizzly bear lives in a refuge on Kicking Horse Mountain Resort, meaning sightings are practically guaranteed.

Cows Ice Cream Banff Ave has an outlet of what is possibly the best icecream maker in Canada.

Jasper

Maligne Lake Jump aboard a cruise boat to Spirit Island.

Jasper Skytram More gravity-defying cable cars.

Columbia Icefield Centre Go for a Snocoach ride on the Athabasca Glacier.

Glacier Skywalk Test your head for heights on this daring glass-floor lookout.

Jasper Town Trails Hike or pedal the scenic trails that fan out directly from Jasper's townsite.

Miette Hot Springs Splash around in geothermally heated waters.

Glacier & Waterton

Going-to-the-Sun Road Ride this spectacular road in a vintage 'Jammer' bus.

Native America Speaks Watch First Nations culture in action at the St Mary Visitor Center.

Many Glacier Valley Top spot for wildlife- and glacier-spotting.

Lake McDonald Dip a canoe oar into the frigid but beautiful water of this picture-perfect lake.

Planning

Accommodations

Most hotels will happily accept kids, and many places allow children under a certain age to stay in their parents' room for no extra charge (the exact age varies according to the hotel, but it's usually under 12, 15 or 16). Extra pull-out beds are often available; otherwise ask for a triple-bed or family room.

➡ Many hotels have extra facilities, such as games rooms, saunas and swimming pools with waterslides, which can help to fend off boredom once the day's activities are done.

➡ For larger families, booking out a whole hostel dorm is usually far cheaper than an equivalent hotel room. The big HI hostel in Banff has private self-catering cabins ideal for families.

➡ Many cabin complexes and some hotels have self-catering suites with fully equipped kitchens.

➡ Larger campgrounds such as Tunnel Mountain, Johnston Canyon and Lake Louise in Banff, or Whistlers and Wapiti in Jasper, host regular interpretive programs and activity sessions for children. Some of them also have playgrounds.

Dining

Most restaurants in the parks are kid-friendly, with the exception of some of the more upmarket establishments. Kids' menus are widespread, especially in hotels and the main town restaurants. This being North America, menus usually arrive with crayons and an activity sheet to pass the time.

Some drinking establishments will serve kids food at sit-down tables in the early evening (usually before 9pm).

Driving

➡ In Alberta and BC, it's a legal requirement that children under six and weighing less than 18kg (40lb) are secured in a properly fitted child-safety seat. In BC kids over 18kg but under 1.45m (4ft 9in) must use a booster seat (this is also recommended in Alberta).

➡ In Montana, US, kids under six years of age or under 27kg (60lb) must use a child-safety seat.

➡ Drivers are responsible for ensuring that other passengers are safely secured and wearing seat belts. Safety seats for toddlers and children are available from all the major rental companies, but you'll incur an extra charge (usually around C$6 to C$10 per day). You'll need to reserve them at the time of booking.

RAINY-DAY ACTIVITIES

Bad weather can put a dent in even the best-laid plans, so here are a few ideas on what to do when the sun won't play ball.

Banff Park Museum Get spooked out by stuffed beasts.

Lux Cinema Centre in Banff Top place for catching the latest flicks.

Jasper Aquatic Centre Get wet in Jasper's municipal pool.

Elevation Place Indoor climbing walls and a fun indoor pool are the highlights at this new Canmore recreation centre.

Banff Skatepark Plenty of bowls, rails and ramps to grind.

Hot springs in Banff, Jasper and Radium Get wet and stay warm.

Museum of the Plains Indian Learn about First Nations culture at this interesting museum on the Blackfeet Indian Reservation.

What to Pack

For Babies & Toddlers

Back sling or child-carrier rucksack Perfect for hiking the trails and keeping your hands free.

Portable changing mat Plus hand-wash gel and other essentials, as trail toilets are very basic.

Child's car seat Avoid the extra expense and hassle of arranging a car seat from your rental company.

Stroller with rain cover The cover is essential in case of bad weather.

For Five to 12 Year Olds

Rain gear A good raincoat and plenty of warm layers will be indispensable.

Proper footwear A pair of boots (or at the very least, decent trail shoes) will help avoid sprained ankles and keep feet dry. Sneakers are not a good idea.

Nature guides Essential for helping to identify wildflowers, birds and animals on the trails.

Binoculars For long-distance wildlife watching.

First-aid kit Including disinfectant, antibiotic cream, Band-Aids, blister cream and moleskin patches for hot spots in boots.

Spare batteries For torches, games etc.

Plan Your Trip
Travel with Pets

The four main national parks in this book have varying rules regarding pets (which primarily means dogs). The Canadian parks have a reasonable cache of pet-friendly facilities, while Glacier is much more limited. For horse owners, decent trail-riding options abound. Pet snakes, iguanas and guinea pigs are probably best left at home.

Best Spots for Dogs

Sundance Trail, Banff
A flat, paved trail near Banff Town, shared with walkers, cyclists and horseback riders.

Marsh Loop, Banff
This pleasant dirt trail is usually peaceful and offers lovely views of the Bow River.

Lake Minnewanka, Banff
The lakeshore makes a perfect place for a family picnic.

Johnson Lake, Banff
A quiet lakeside trail that's often shared with summer sunbathers.

Mary Schäffer Loop, Jasper
Part-wooded walk on the eastern shoreline of Maligne Lake.

Lake Annette, Jasper
You can follow a paved trail around Lake Annette, but be on the lookout for elk and deer.

Moose Lake Loop, Jasper
Offers a quick escape from the Maligne Lake crowds.

Rules & Regulations

➡ In Banff and Jasper, dogs are allowed on most trails and at most campgrounds (both frontcountry and backcountry), but you're required to keep them securely leashed at all times.

➡ In Glacier, dogs are banned from *all* park trails, but are allowed in drive-in campgrounds, along park roads open to vehicles, and in most picnic areas.

➡ You are required by law to clean up after your dog, so remember to bring along plastic bags or a pooper-scooper.

➡ Bring along all necessary supplies, including food and any medications, as they'll be almost impossible to buy outside the townsites.

➡ Guide and service dogs should wear reflective vests to indicate their working status.

Border Crossings

For many people, visiting the national parks is very much a family affair and often that doesn't just mean mom, dad and the kids. Plenty of people also decide to bring their pets along on their park adventure, but you definitely need to be prepared for the added complications that come with having your furry companion in tow.

The same rules and regulations apply to dogs of all sizes, regardless of whether they're a dachshund or a Doberman. If you're crossing the US–Canada border, you may be asked for a pet-health certificate and/or rabies certificate issued by an accredited veterinarian.

For exact rules, consult the relevant government agency.

Canadian Food Inspection Agency (www. inspection.gc.ca/english/anima/imp/petani/petanie.shtml)

US Department of Agriculture (www. aphis.usda.gov/wps/portal/aphis/ourfocus/importexport/sa_animals/sa_pet_travel)

Health & Safety

In addition to the official rules, it's also worth considering how dogs will be perceived by any wild animals you might meet out on the trail. To elk, caribou and moose, dogs will probably be perceived as a threat, while to other beasts (such as cougar and bears) they might resemble prey. Either way, bringing your dog along puts you at increased risk in the event of an animal encounter – previously placid bears have been known to become enraged due to the noise of a barking dog.

➡ Ticks are a common parasite in the Rockies, especially in spring. Check your dog's coat carefully for ticks after any long walk, and remove any you find.

➡ Make sure you keep your dog leashed at all times, and discourage them from eating berries, fungi or other unknown plants.

➡ Urinating near streams and water sources is a major cause of giardia and other water-borne parasites, so discourage your dog from doing so.

Choosing Accommodations

It's important to think about two things before you bring your pet along to the parks: what they'll do while you're out on the trail or exploring the sights, and where they'll stay overnight. Leaving your dog leashed up for hours on end isn't much of a holiday for them – so it's best to decide beforehand what kind of trip you're planning, and how bringing a pet will fit into those plans.

BEST PET-FRIENDLY HOTELS
Tekarra Lodge (p165)

Banff Ptarmigan Inn (p99)

Juniper (p100)

Lake Louise Inn (p105)

Hidden Ridge Resort (p103)

Crimson (p166)

Pocahontas Cabins (p169)

Relatively few hotels in Banff and Jasper accept dogs; those that do will probably charge an extra fee on top of the standard room rate. Most campgrounds accept dogs, but unless they're very obedient, they should always be securely tethered. In Glacier, no hotels accept pets. Campgrounds will accept them (as long as they're kept on a lead).

There's also a useful online directory of animal-friendly accommodations in Canada at **Pet Friendly** (www.petfriendly.ca).

Hotels listed in this book that welcome pets have been given a dog's paw symbol (🐾).

Veterinarians

Veterinary services are nonexistent outside the main town areas.

Alberta Veterinary Medical Association (www.avma.ab.ca) Online listings of veterinary services.

Banff Veterinary Services (☑403-762-3611; petcare@canmorevet.com; 140 Hawk Ave, Banff)

Canmore Veterinary Hospital (☑403-678-4425; 502 Bow Valley Trail, Canmore)

Jasper Veterinary Clinic (☑780-852-5551; jaspervetclinic@telus.net; 6 Stan Wright Dr, Jasper)

Pincher Creek Veterinary Clinic (☑403-627-3900; www.pinchercreekveterinaryclinic.ca; 1124 Waterton Ave, Pincher Creek)

Whitefish Animal Hospital (☑406-862-3178; www.whitefishanimalhospital.com; 713 E 13th St, Whitefish)

Kennels

The Canmore Veterinary Hospital has limited boarding facilities for pets.

Three Dog Ranch (☎406-862-3913; www. threedogranchmontana.com; 5395 Hwy 93, Whitefish) Grooming, day and overnight care, and pet store, 3.3km (2 miles) south of Whitefish, Montana.

Veronica's Dog Grooming (☎403-762-3647; www.762dogs.com; 114 Eagle Cres, Banff) Dog and cat grooming and overnight stays.

Lost & Found

If you have lost or found an animal, contact the relevant authorities as soon as possible.

Banff Animal Control (☎403-762-1218)

Canmore Animal Services (☎403-678-4244)

Jasper Animal Control (☎780-852-5514)

Royal Canadian Mountain Police (RCMP; ☎403-678-5516) For emergencies in Banff and Canmore outside business hours.

Horse Trails & Equestrian Facilities

Horse owners are permitted to bring their own animals to the national parks for recreational use. Many trails in Banff, Jasper and Glacier are open to horses, but seasonal conditions such as mud, swollen rivers, snow cover, plus wildlife activity means this can change at short notice. Some areas are also permanently closed to horse use

and in the backcountry there are strict quotas to prevent overuse and to protect wilderness areas. Contact park authorities for the latest advice on which routes are open or closed to horses, or consult the websites detailed here.

If you just fancy a quick day ride, or you don't want the hassle of transporting your own horse to the park, contact one of the commercial horse – guiding companies, some of which will let you bring your own animal on organized trips and provide stabling facilities.

For more information and advice, pick up the free *Horse User's Guide* from park offices, contact the local **warden's office** (☎Banff 403-762-1470, Jasper 780-852-6167), or consult the following webpages on the official park websites:

Banff (www.pc.gc.ca/eng/pn-np/ab/banff/activ/cheval-horse.aspx)

Jasper (www.pc.gc.ca/eng/pn-np/ab/jasper/activ/ap-bc/gc-hug.aspx)

Glacier (www.nps.gov/glac/planyourvisit/privatestockuse.htm)

Permits & Corrals

➡ If you're trekking into the Canadian backcountry, you'll need a wilderness pass (C$9.80), as well as a grazing permit (C$1.90) for each night.

➡ In Glacier, backcountry permits are free, but advance reservations incur a levy of US$20.

➡ Most backcountry campgrounds in Canada accept horses, but some in Glacier are closed to horse use. Discuss your route and make advance reservations with park staff.

➡ In Banff, public corrals are available at Pipestone River, Mosquito Creek and 2km (1.2 miles) east of Saskatchewan Crossing along Hwy 11.

➡ In Jasper, there are corrals at the trailheads at Portal Creek, Poboktan, Nigel Creek, Athabasca Pass trail, Miette Lake trail and Fiddle Pass trail.

➡ In Glacier, the corrals are not for public use, though there is one small exception. The Many Glacier corral can be used as an overnight stop for riders undertaking the Continental Divide Trail.

➡ Depending on the corral, maximum stays are usually between 48 and 72 hours.

On the Road

Jasper National Park
p134

Banff National Park
p46

Around Banff
National Park
p116

Waterton Lakes
National Park
p216

Glacier National Park
p176

Around Glacier
National Park
p207

Banff National Park

Includes ➡

Day Hikes........... 50
Overnight Hikes 68
Cycling.............72
Driving 76
Other Activities.......77
Sights..............86
Tours...............97
Sleeping............98
Eating.............107
Drinking &
Entertainment.......110
Shopping 110

Best Hikes

➡ Healy Pass (p59)
➡ Plain of Six Glaciers (p60)
➡ Larch Valley (p62)
➡ Cory Pass Loop (p57)

Best Places to Dip an Oar

➡ Lake Louise (p60)
➡ Bow River (p80)
➡ Vermilion Lakes (p90)
➡ Johnson Lake (p54)

Why Go?

In the hit parade of top sights in Canada, Banff justifiably ranks as many people's number one. As much a piece of Canadian history as a natural wonder, the nation's oldest national park, founded in 1885, is what Canada is all about: a feral, but largely accessible, wilderness that attempts to cater for everyone – and by and large succeeds – from bus-tour seniors to hard-core cyclists. Indeed, one of the great beauties of Banff is its juxtaposition of the untamed and the civilized. Grizzly bears roam within growling distance of diners chinking cocktails at the romantic Banff Springs Hotel, while knackered hikers fresh from summit attempts queue up for ice cream with golfers clutching nine-irons. Striking a clever balance between yin and yang, Banff is a park with two distinct personalities. Popcorn in Banff Ave or cold soup at a backcountry campground in the middle of nowhere? Take your pick – or have both.

Road Distance (KM)

	Banff	Canmore	Field (Yoho)	Lake Louise
Canmore	25			
Field (Yoho)	85	110		
Lake Louise	55	80	25	
Saskatchewan Crossing	135	160	100	80

Note: Distances are approximate

Entrances

There are four main road entrances into Banff National Park. All are open year-round, weather permitting. The main East Gate is on Trans-Canada Hwy 1, 7km (4.3 miles) west of Canmore, and has manned tollbooths where you can purchase park passes (they all accept cash, cards and check). If you already have a pass, you can use the right-hand lane to avoid queuing at the tollbooths. The other park entrances are on Trans-Canada Hwy 1 eastbound from Yoho National Park; Hwy 93 eastbound from Kootenay National Park; and Hwy 93 southbound from the Icefields Pkwy. If you're driving, remember to hang your pass from your rearview mirror so that park staff know you've already paid.

DON'T MISS

A major lure of the Lake Louise area is its two hike-in teahouses built in the first half of the 20th century by some of the park's early pioneers. Moderate but well-trodden trails to each establishment help hikers get away from the intense clamor of the lakeside and into a calmer, more serendipitous realm.

The Lake Agnes Teahouse (p63) sits 3.5km up a steep-ish trail in a hanging valley beside a beautiful lake. It was built in 1901 by the Canadian Pacific Railway and has been serving tea and other snacks (including scones) since 1905. The Plain of Six Glaciers Teahouse (p61) is within viewing distance of the Victoria Glacier (behold the thunderous avalanches) at the head of Lake Louise. It was constructed by Swiss guides in 1927 and has been in the tea business since 1959. The 5.5km trail to reach it is slightly gentler than the Lake Agnes trek.

Both teahouses sit at 2100m above sea level. Neither has electricity nor road access; supplies are brought in by foot, horse or helicopter.

When You Arrive

➡ Buy your park pass from the tollbooths at Banff's East Gate or from a park visitor center. Daily passes cost C$9.80/4.90/8.30/19.60 per adult/child/senior/family.

➡ Check the latest trail reports at the Banff Information Centre or online at www.pc.gc.ca/apps/tcond/cond_e.asp?opark=100092.

➡ Most campgrounds operate on a first-come, first-served system: arrive early at your chosen site (ideally by 11am) for the best chance of securing a pitch.

PLANNING TIPS

Accommodations in Banff and Lake Louise are expensive and scarce in summer, so book early. To cut costs, avoid peak months or stay outside the park.

BANFF NATIONAL PARK

Fast Facts

➡ **Area** 6641 sq km (2564 sq miles)

➡ **Highest elevation** 3612m (11,850ft)

➡ **Lowest elevation** 1310m (4297ft)

Reservations

Accommodations bookings are handled by the Banff Tourism Bureau (p112). For advance reservations at Tunnel Mountain, Two Jack, Johnston Canyon and Lake Louise campgrounds, contact the Parks Canada campground reservation service (p99). For backcountry campground reservations and wilderness passes, contact the Banff Visitor Centre (p112).

Resources

➡ **Parks Canada** (www.pc.gc.ca/eng/pn-np/ab/banff/index.aspx)

➡ **Banff & Lake Louise Tourism** (www.banfflakelouise.com)

➡ **Banff Town website** (www.banff.ca)

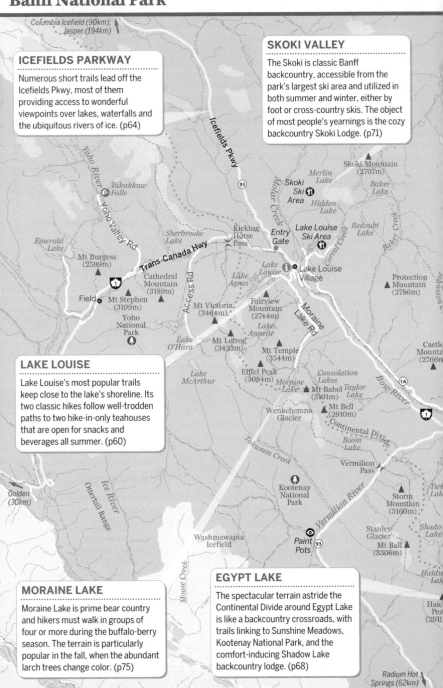

ICEFIELDS PARKWAY

Numerous short trails lead off the Icefields Pkwy, most of them providing access to wonderful viewpoints over lakes, waterfalls and the ubiquitous rivers of ice. (p64)

SKOKI VALLEY

The Skoki is classic Banff backcountry, accessible from the park's largest ski area and utilized in both summer and winter, either by foot or cross-country skis. The object of most people's yearnings is the cozy backcountry Skoki Lodge. (p71)

LAKE LOUISE

Lake Louise's most popular trails keep close to the lake's shoreline. Its two classic hikes follow well-trodden paths to two hike-in-only teahouses that are open for snacks and beverages all summer. (p60)

MORAINE LAKE

Moraine Lake is prime bear country and hikers must walk in groups of four or more during the buffalo-berry season. The terrain is particularly popular in the fall, when the abundant larch trees change color. (p75)

EGYPT LAKE

The spectacular terrain astride the Continental Divide around Egypt Lake is like a backcountry crossroads, with trails linking to Sunshine Meadows, Kootenay National Park, and the comfort-inducing Shadow Lake backcountry lodge. (p68)

Columbia Icefield (90km);
Jasper (194km)

Yoho River

Takakkaw Falls

Yoho Valley Rd

Emerald Lake

Mt Burgess (2599m)

Cathedral Mountain (3189m)

Field

Mt Stephen (3199m)

Yoho National Park

Trans-Canada Hwy

Sherbrooke Lake

Kicking Horse Pass

Access Rd

Lake Agnes

Lake Louise

Mt Victoria (3464m)

Fairview Mountain (2744m)

Lake Annette

Lake O'Hara

Mt Lefroy (3423m)

Mt Temple (3544m)

Lake McArthur

Eiffel Peak (3084m)

Moraine Lake

Wenkchemna Glacier

Consolation Lakes

Mt Babel (3101m)

Mt Bell (2910m)

Taylor Lake

Continental Divide

Boom Lake

Tokumm Creek

Ice River

Ottertail Range

Golden (30km)

Kootenay National Park

Vermilion River

Vermilion Pass

Washmawapta Icefield

Moose Creek

Paint Pots

93

Storm Mountain (3160m)

Stanley Glacier

Mt Ball (3306m)

Radium Hot Springs (62km)

Icefields Pkwy

93

Molar Creek

Skoki Ski Area

Merlin Lake

Skoki Mountain (2707m)

Baker Lake

Hidden Lake

Lake Louise Ski Area

Redoubt Lake

Baker Creek

Corral Creek

Entry Gate

Lake Louise Village

Protection Mountain (2786m)

Johnson C

Moraine Lake Rd

Bow River

1A

Castle Mountain (2766m)

1

Shadow Lake

Twi Lak

Haid Lak

Haic Pea (2919

N 0 ⟩——————————⟩ 10 km
   0 ⟩——————————⟩ 5 miles

BOW VALLEY PARKWAY

Trails – ranging from simple strolls to challenging semi-scrambles – replete with waterfalls, old fire lookouts and steep scree slopes lead off Hwy 1A, the quiet alternative to the Trans-Canada Hwy. (p78)

BANFF TOWN

A good half-dozen trails head out from downtown Banff. All of them emphasize the eerie proximity of the natural world to Banff's urban hub, with some great wildlife-watching opportunities around the local rivers and lakes. (p50)

LAKE MINNEWANKA

You're never far from lake views on the Minnewanka Loop trails located conveniently close to Banff Town. Favorites include a hike to a rocky amphitheater and a stroll to an impressive lakeside canyon. (p76)

SUNSHINE MEADOWS

Banff's best above-the-treeline hikes meander through flower meadows close to the Continental Divide. The meadows are also a launching pad for some excellent backcountry treks. (p92)

Panther River

Panther Mountain (2943m)

Palliser Range

Bonnet River

Goat Lake

Cascade River

Cascade Valley Trail

Vermilion Range

Ghost River Wilderness Area

Banff National Park

Luellen Lake

Sawback Range

Sawback Lake

Forty Mile Creek

Palliser Range

Mt Aylmer (3162m)

Rockbound Lake

Johnston Canyon Trail

Cascade Amphitheatre Trail

Cascade River

C-Level Cirque Trail

Lake Minnewanka

Castle Junction

Bow Valley Pkwy

Trans-Canada Hwy

Red Earth Creek

Red Earth Creek Trail

Massive Range

Mt Edith (2554m)

Mt Norquay (2133m)

Cascade Mountain (2998m)

Mt Inglismaldie (2964m)

Mt Peechee (2935m)

Sawback

Vermilion Lakes

Banff Town

Johnson Lake

Pharaoh Peaks

Mt Bourgeau (2930m)

Sunshine Village Rd

Sunshine Village Parking Lot

Healy Pass Trail

Sunshine Meadows

Sulphur Mountain (2451m)

Spray River

Rundle Riverside Trail

East Gate

Harvie Heights

Egypt Lake

Mt Assiniboine Provincial Park

Canmore

Bow Valley Wildland Provincial Park

Trans-Canada Hwy

Kananaskis Country; Calgary (90km)

🥾 DAY HIKES

Does hiking get any better than this? Banff's astounding 1600km (1000-mile) network of marked trails is a highlight of Canada and a credit to the parks staff who lay out and maintain them. They are regularly checked and meticulously signposted, so you'll rarely get lost in this walkers' paradise. Trails are graded between easy (green), moderate (blue) and difficult (black), and fastidiously logged for weather closures and wildlife warnings. Always check the 'trail report' tab on the Parks Canada website (www.pc.gc.ca) before starting off.

Many trails lead out directly from Banff townsite. Others start within easy driving or cycling distance. Some undulate through thick forest populated by black bears. Others penetrate vast ethereal wilderness above the treeline. You can set out for hours, days, even weeks – anything is possible, from the kid-friendly interpretive Fenland Trail to the adrenaline-loaded Cory Pass Loop.

Successful hiking requires basic common sense. Wear comfortable footwear, take plenty of water and trail snacks, and pack warm, layered clothing and waterproofs for the famously fickle mountain weather.

Banff Town & Around

🥾 Bow Falls & the Hoodoos

Duration Three hours round-trip

Distance 10.2km (6.4 miles)

Difficulty Easy

Start/Finish Buffalo St, Banff Town

Elevation Change 60m (197ft)

Nearest Town Banff

Transportation Bus, bike, foot

Summary A scenic stroll from Banff, tracking the Bow River through woodland all the way to the Hoodoos.

Despite its proximity to downtown Banff, this easy ramble quickly leaves both traffic noise and tourists behind and delves into the forests and rivers east of the main town, ending at the otherwordly landscape of rocky pillars known as the Hoodoos.

Start out on Buffalo St and follow the road east to the start of the gravel trail beside the river, a popular jaunt for Banff cyclists and joggers. The flat trail tracks the Bow River for about 1.2km (0.7 miles), where it reaches a set of two staircases up to the Surprise Corner Viewpoint and parking lot, looking out over the rushing white water of Bow Falls (p86). You could turn around here and retrace your steps, but it's worth carrying on to the Hoodoos.

From the parking lot, the trail descends through larch and pine woodland and again runs parallel to the river, passing several inlets and small beaches en route to a wide, open grass meadow at around the 3km (1.9-mile) mark, from where there are fine southerly views to Mt Rundle on the opposite side of the river.

From here the trail climbs gently up onto the canyon wall above the river, with great views across the Bow Valley – make sure you stick to the main trail, as several faint subtrails veer off along the riverbank and are much tougher going. After 5.1km (3.2 miles) you'll reach the Hoodoos interpretive trail, from where you can look out over the Hoodoos rising above the snaking course of the Bow River. The Hoodoos themselves are predominantly made of limestone, with a hard cap of magnesium-rich rock at the top; eons of wind and rain have carved them into a complex topography of twisted towers and weird spires.

Return along the same route or, if your legs are feeling the strain, catch a bus back to Banff from Tunnel Mountain Dr.

🥾 Fenland Trail & Vermilion Lakes

Duration 30 minutes round-trip

Distance 2.1km (1.3 miles)

Difficulty Easy

Start/Finish Forty Mile picnic area, Banff Town

Elevation Change Negligible

Nearest Town Banff

Transportation Car, bike, foot

Summary Quiet forest walk that follows the green Echo and Forty Mile Creeks through the fenlands.

Popular with Banff cyclists and joggers, this short trail travels through a variety of natural habitats: woodland, marsh, fen, riverbed and wetland. Begin the trail at the Forty Mile Creek Picnic Area (Map p87), just north of the 'Welcome to Banff' sign on Lynx St. If you're coming from downtown, there's a connecting

Banff Town & Around – Day Hikes

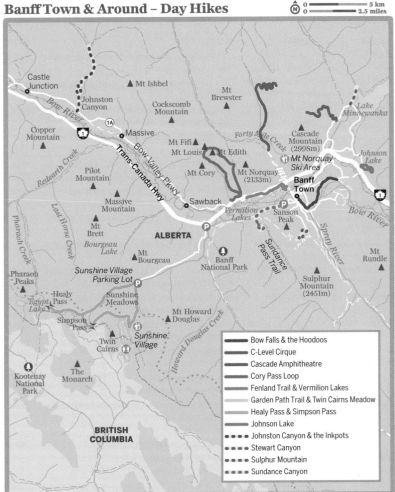

Map labels:

N · 0 — 5 km · 0 — 2.5 miles

Castle Junction
Mt Ishbel
Johnston Canyon
Cockscomb Mountain
Mt Brewster
Lake Minnewanka
Copper Mountain
Massive
1A
Cascade Mountain (2998m)
Johnson Lake
Bow River
Forty Mile Creek
Mt Fifi
Mt Louis
Mt Edith
Mt Norquay Ski Area
Redearth Creek
Trans-Canada Hwy
Bow Valley Pkwy
Mt Cory
Mt Norquay (2133m)
Banff Town
Pilot Mountain
Sawback
Massive Mountain
Vermilion Lakes
Sanson Peak
Bow River
Last Horse Creek
Mt Brett
ALBERTA
Sundance Pass Trail
Mt Rundle
Pharaoh Creek
Bourgeau Lake
Mt Bourgeau
Banff National Park
Spray River
Pharaoh Peaks
Sunshine Village Parking Lot
Sulphur Mountain (2451m)
Healy Pass
Sunshine Meadows
Egypt Lake
Simpson Pass
Mt Howard Douglas
Howard Douglas Creek
Twin Cairns
Sunshine Village
Kootenay National Park
The Monarch
BRITISH COLUMBIA

Legend:

— Bow Falls & the Hoodoos
— C-Level Cirque
— Cascade Amphitheatre
— Cory Pass Loop
— Fenland Trail & Vermilion Lakes
— Garden Path Trail & Twin Cairns Meadow
— Healy Pass & Simpson Pass
— Johnson Lake
•••• Johnston Canyon & the Inkpots
•••• Stewart Canyon
•••• Sulphur Mountain
•••• Sundance Canyon

trail on the left side of Lynx St, just over the rail tracks. Bring along some mosquito repellent as the biting bugs can be rampant along here, and pick up one of the free trail leaflets from the start of the trailhead.

The flat dirt trail travels through the trees and crosses several wooden bridges where you can view the river and the rich fenland; look out for wooden posts that match points of interest on the trail leaflet. It's a rich habitat for wildlife – listen for tapping woodpeckers, whistling chickadees, honking Canada geese and, in autumn, bugling elk. Try also to spot the many flowers and plants that thrive in the

fenland – sedges, grasses, willows, poplars and dogwoods all flourish in the nutrient-rich groundwater. The only drawback is the constant thrum of traffic traveling along the Trans-Canada Hwy nearby, but it does at least give you a sense of how the local wildlife must feel about the racket on the main road.

If you want a longer hike, you can extend the walk by crossing the large bridge about halfway around the loop and heading left down the road to the Vermilion Lakes (p90), a wetland that's popular with wildlife-spotters. The lakes are a 4km (2.5-mile) round-trip. In late May and early June the

HIKING IN BANFF NATIONAL PARK

REGION	NAME	DESCRIPTION	DIFFICULTY
Banff Town	Fenland Trail & Vermilion Lakes	Flat woodland trail leading to network of lakes where you'll often spot grazing elk	easy
Banff Town	Sundance Canyon	Wild canyon walk reached via paved riverside trail from Banff	easy
Banff Town	Bow Falls & the Hoodoos	Riverside walk to Banff's most famous waterfalls and a landscape of weird rock towers	easy
Banff Town	Sulphur Mountain	Steep hike up flank of Sulphur Mountain with wrap-around views	moderate
Banff Town	Cascade Amphitheatre	High-level trail across ski fields to classic glacial cirque hidden among mountains	moderate-difficult
Bow Valley Parkway	Johnston Canyon & the Inkpots	Visits Bow Valley's best-known waterfalls and continues to colorful mountain tarns	moderate
Bow Valley Parkway	Cory Pass Loop	Tough climb to a rugged pass followed by a scree descent	difficult
Icefields Parkway	Mistaya Canyon	Short walk to a spectacular deep-cut river canyon with few crowds	easy
Icefields Parkway	Bow Glacier Falls	Start at Num-Ti-Jah Lodge and walk across boulders and moraines to impressive glacial cascade	easy-moderate
Icefields Parkway	Parker Ridge	Switchbacking climb to stunning knife-edge ridge above Saskatchewan Glacier	moderate
Icefields Parkway	Peyto Lake & Bow Summit Lookout	Busy trail to lookout above Peyto Lake, leading to quieter climb to old fire lookout	moderate
Icefields Parkway	Sunset Lookout	Little-used trail to superb fire lookout with views of rivers, glaciers and peaks	moderate
Icefields Parkway	Helen Lake	Often-overlooked route up to lake-filled mountain meadow with vistas of Icefields Pkwy	moderate
Lake Louise	Plain of Six Glaciers	Superb walk to glacier viewpoint, with option to stop at historic teahouse	moderate
Lake Louise	Lake Agnes & the Beehives	Steep walk to Lake Louise's most famous teahouse and lofty summit high above	moderate-difficult
Lake Louise	Saddleback & Fairview	Double summit trail from shores of Lake Louise to above-the-clouds viewpoint at top of Fairview	moderate-difficult
Lake Louise	Skoki Valley	True classic of the Rockies, exploring one of the most beautiful backcountry valleys near Lake Louise	moderate-difficult
Lake Louise	Paradise Valley & the Giant's Steps	Difficult Lake Louise trail, hiking through wild valley frequented by goats, marmots and grizzly bears	difficult
Lake Minnewanka	Johnson Lake	Short ramble around a small placid lake	easy
Lake Minnewanka	Stewart Canyon	Flat lakeshore trail to hidden forest canyon; canoeing possible	easy
Lake Minnewanka	C-Level Cirque	Hike past old mine workings to ice amphitheater high above Lake Minnewanka	moderate
Moraine Lake	Consolation Lakes Trail	Escape Moraine Lake crowds into wild mountains past glassy lakes	easy

 Drinking Water   *Restrooms*   *Great for Families*   *Fishing*

DURATION	DISTANCE	ELEVATION CHANGE	FEATURES	FACILITIES	PAGE
30min	2.1km (1.3 miles)	negligible			p50
2½-3hr	8km (5 miles)	145m (476ft)			p54
3hr	10.2km (6.4 miles)	60m (197ft)			p50
4hr	11km (6.8 miles)	655m (2149ft)			p55
6hr	15.4km (9.6 miles)	640m (2100ft)			p57
4hr	10.8km (6.7 miles)	215m (705ft)			p58
5-6hr	13km (8.1 miles)	920m (3018ft)			p57
30min	1km (0.6 miles)	negligible			p64
3hr	7.2km (4.4 miles)	155m (509ft)			p65
2hr	4km (2.5 miles)	250m (820ft)			p66
2hr	6.2km (3.8 miles)	245m (803ft)			p66
3hr	9.4km (5.8 miles)	250m (820ft)			p67
4hr	12km (7.5 miles)	455m (1493ft)			p67
4-5hr	13.5km (8.4 miles)	365m (1198ft)			p60
4hr	10.8km (6.6 miles)	495m (1624ft)			p62
5-6hr	10.2km (6.4 miles)	1013m (3323ft)			p63
4 days	50.4km (31.3 miles)	up to 1136m (3727ft)			p71
6-7hr	20.3km (12.6 miles)	385m (1263ft)			p64
45min	3km (1.9 miles)	negligible			p54
1½-2hr	5.6km (3.5 miles)	negligible			p56
4hr	8.8km (5.4 miles)	455m (1493ft)			p56
2hr	6km (3.8 miles)	65m (213ft)			p60

 Swimming   Grocery Store Nearby   Restaurant Nearby   Wildlife Watching

HIKING IN BANFF NATIONAL PARK (CONTINUED)

REGION	NAME	DESCRIPTION	DIFFICULTY
Moraine Lake	Larch Valley & Sentinel Pass	Wildflowers and native larches in mountain meadow overlooking Ten Peaks, with add-on to high-level pass	moderate
Sunshine Meadows	Garden Path Trail & Twin Cairns Meadow	Wonderful walk through high mountain meadows and past lakes	easy
Sunshine Meadows	Healy Pass & Simpson Pass	Rewarding walk that affords fantastic glimpses over Continental Divide	moderate-difficult
Sunshine Meadows	Egypt Lake & Gibbon Pass	Great option for first-timers in backcountry, taking in lakes and moderately demanding mountains	moderate-difficult
Sunshine Meadows	Mt Assiniboine	Unforgettable journey into wild backcountry around shining pinnacle of Mt Assiniboine	difficult

〰️ Waterfalls	🛶 Canoeing	🔺 Backcountry Campsite	⛺ Picnic Sites

trail is often closed due to aggressive female elk, which use the area for calving.

🚶 Sundance Canyon

Duration 2½-3 hours round-trip

Distance 8km (5 miles)

Difficulty Easy

Start/Finish Cave & Basin National Historic Site

Elevation Change 145m (476ft)

Nearest Town Banff

Transportation Bike, foot

Summary A delightful route around a river canyon, with views of a gushing waterfall, rugged mountains and the Bow Valley.

The tarmacked Sundance Trail begins just beyond the Cave & Basin National Historic Site (p89), 1km from downtown Banff. The first part is flat and easy with views of the Bow River on your right and Sulphur Mountain to your left, passing through a few sections of marsh and wetland, where you'll often spy wading birds and dragonflies. Beware summer ticks. Bring repellent!

There's a dirt track on the left side of the trail that is reserved for horses, which is handy as it keeps the main trail free of horse manure. If you fancy taking a break, you'll find riverside benches dotted along the trail.

After around 2km (1.2 miles) you'll reach a junction. Fork left on the tarmacked trail veering away from the river and climb gently uphill.

The canyon hike proper starts at the end of the tarmacked trail, where there is a bike rack, and passes steeply up the left side of a tumbling waterfall. After crossing the wooden bridge and scrambling up a section of rocks and boulders, you'll come out on the mainly flat, sun-dappled trail, which tracks a bubbling stream through the wooded canyon. In summer it's always filled with birdsong and butterflies, and the shady forest makes a rich habitat for lichen, mosses and wildflowers; take along a nature guide to help you spot the species.

After crossing a couple more wooden bridges the trail loops back on itself and after about 1.6km (1 mile) reaches a **lookout point**, from where there are tree-framed views across the Bow Valley to the distant mountain peaks – look closely and you can even see the twisting outline of Hwy 1. From here the trail descends through switchbacks to the bike lock-up. Retrace your steps back to the start.

🚶 Johnson Lake

Duration 45 minutes round-trip

Distance 3km (1.9 miles)

Difficulty Easy

Start/Finish Johnson Lake parking lot

DURATION	DISTANCE	ELEVATION CHANGE	FEATURES	FACILITIES	PAGE
4-5hr	11.6km (7.2 miles)	725m (2379ft)	🦌	🏛️🍴	p62
3½hr	8.3km (5.1 miles)	negligible	👪	🚻🚌🍴	p58
6-7hr	18.4km (11.4 miles)	650m (2132ft)	🔭	🚻🚌🍴	p59
3 days	40.8km (25.4 miles)	up to 655m (2149ft)	🦌👪🐟	🥤🚌👤⛺🏕️	p68
3-4 days	55.7km (34.6 miles)	up to 695m (2280ft)	🦌	🚌👤⛺	p68

🔭 View	🧗 Rock Climbing	🚌 Public Transport to Trailhead	👤 Ranger Station

Elevation Change Negligible

Nearest Town Banff

Transportation Car, bike

Summary More an amble than a hike, this walk circles around the shore of a popular recreational lake, mixing wooded and open-air sections, with the option of a paddle in the water when the weather's warm.

Compared to nearby Lake Minnewanka, Johnson Lake is little more than a pond, but on warm summer days it's the nearest thing Banff has to a seaside getaway: sun-worshippers and beach bums throng to the lake to lounge around in the sunshine. The waters are also ideal for gentle kayaking and paddleboarding, although, with no lakeside boat concession, you'll need to bring your own craft (or rent one in Banff). Ringed by fir forest and encircled by an easy trail with views of Cascade Mountain, Johnson Lake makes a lovely place to combine a lakeside picnic with a leisurely stroll. To reach the lake, follow Lake Minnewanka Rd north of Hwy 1 and take the first right. The next junction is signposted right to Johnson Lake.

From the parking lot, follow the trail past a few picnic tables down to the lakeshore, and pick up the trail on the lake's right (southern side). Initially you'll pass through a grassy section overlooked by power lines from the nearby hydroelectric dam, but the dirt trail soon passes into the fir and spruce woods by the lakeshore.

The trail emerges at an earthen dike on the eastern edge of the lake after about 1.6km (1 mile). The forest to the east is one of the few areas of unmanaged woodland left in Banff National Park, with many old Douglas fir trees. Johnson Lake itself sits in the montane zone, a subalpine area that makes up just 3% of the park's landscape but provides a crucial, vegetation-rich habitat for wildlife. Look out for birds and insects as you walk, and see if you can spot any trout or spotted frogs in the water.

On the northern side of the lake the trail sticks close to the water and passes a small marshy section formed by a tributary off the main lake. Nearby is a shady area under the trees that makes an excellent spot to stop and tuck into your picnic. From here it's a short walk back to the parking lot.

🥾 Sulphur Mountain

Duration Four hours round-trip

Distance 11km (6.8 miles)

Difficulty Moderate

Start/Finish Banff Gondola terminal

Elevation Change 655m (2149ft)

Nearest Town Banff

Transportation Bus, bike

Summary Savor your superiority over the gondola-goers after climbing this challenging mountain, with outlooks on Banff Town and Mt Rundle.

If you want to test your calf muscles, this leg-sapping route up the side of Sulphur Mountain is just the ticket. While mere mortals ride to the top on the gondola (which you'll glimpse occasionally as you ascend the mountain), the sense of achievement you'll get by arriving on foot is worth the climb.

The trail starts at the northwest end of the gondola parking lot, near the Upper Hot Springs Pool. You start climbing almost immediately on the well-marked trail (a daily workout for some of Banff's fitter residents), with viewpoints of Mt Rundle and Banff as you ascend. Most of the trail is along well-graded switchbacks and becomes increasingly steep the further you go; the last section, where the trail arrows straight up the mountainside, is really tough going.

Once at the top, grab an ice cream at the gondola station as a reward and stroll along to Sanson Peak, where you'll find Norman Bethune Sanson's old weather station and great views over the whole valley.

Hikers used to get a free trip back down on the gondola, but now you'll have to pay half the standard fare, so you might as well just make the downhill trudge instead.

🏃 C-Level Cirque

Duration Four hours round-trip

Distance 8.8km (5.4 miles)

Difficulty Moderate

Start/Finish Upper Bankhead parking lot

Elevation Change 455m (1493ft)

Nearest Town Banff

Transportation Car, bike

Summary Throw your own echo into the silent peaks around a natural amphitheater – if you've still got the energy after the climb.

This popular trail starts out from the Upper Bankhead parking lot, 3.5km (2.2 miles) from Hwy 1 along Lake Minnewanka Rd. It's relatively short, but steep, and the cirque itself – a deep glacial bowl carved out by a long-gone glacier and surrounded by jagged mountaintops – makes a worthy reward for the climb. Snow lingers in the cirque well into summer; if you're hiking here in early spring, there is a danger of avalanches, so it's

worth checking at the park office on trail conditions before you set out.

The route starts from the west side of the parking lot and climbs for about 20 minutes through green forest, often sprinkled with violets, calypso orchids and clematis in summer, before reaching the first remains of the old anthracite coal mine of Lower Bankhead; the C-Level in the hike's name refers to the level where the miners once worked.

You'll pass more abandoned mine workings and capped-off shafts as the route climbs; if you're here alone, it can be a rather spooky place, even in blazing sunshine.

After around 45 minutes of climbing, the forest thins out and you'll begin to catch glimpses back toward Banff Town, Mt Rundle and the nearby lakes, and you'll pass through a few sections with steep drop-offs. A little over an hour into the hike, you'll emerge into the C-Level Cirque itself.

Pikas, golden-mantled ground squirrels and the occasional hoary marmot can often be seen scurrying beside the path as you continue along the rough trail along the edge of cirque, before joining up with the last steep, rubbly section up to the look-out knoll. Rest here and admire the fabulous views stretching back down the valley toward Banff and the Bow River, before retracing your steps.

🏃 Stewart Canyon

Duration 1½-2 hours round-trip

Distance 5.6km (3.5 miles)

Difficulty Easy

Start/Finish Lake Minnewanka parking lot

Elevation Change Negligible

Nearest Town Banff

Transportation Car, bike

Summary A level hike that takes in the north shore of Lake Minnewanka plus an impressive river canyon.

With several of the trails around Lake Minnewanka closed during buffalo-berry season due to grizzly bear activity – including the hike to Aylmer Lookout – the easy walk up to Stewart Canyon is the area's best option for a summer hike.

The trail starts from the recreational area near the boat ramp on the west side of the lake, and travels for a few hundred meters along a flat, paved section past picnic tables and barbecue shelters. The trailhead proper is marked by an information panel, where you'll find notices about trail closures during the buffalo-berry season.

From here the trail passes onto a wooded dirt track offering views of the turquoise lake; it's just about passable for sturdy wheelchairs, but becomes increasingly rooty and rocky the further you travel. The trail tracks into pleasant forest, heading over a wooden bridge above the Cascade River at the 1.6km (1-mile) mark. On the far side of the river, there's a fork in the trail: the right-hand branch leads up to Aylmer Pass, so take the left fork.

The trail follows the canyon side for another 1.2km (0.7 miles), before reaching another fork. The route to the right leads down into a river gully where you can clamber across boulders and rocks to the bottom of the canyon and the edge of the Cascade River. The canyon itself is named after George Stewart, first superintendent of Canada's first national park. The water level here has risen by about 25m (80ft) since Lake Minnewanka was last dammed in 1941.

Retrace your steps back to the Minnewanka parking lot.

🚶 Cascade Amphitheatre

Duration Six hours round-trip

Distance 15.4km (9.6 miles)

Difficulty Moderate-difficult

Start/Finish Mt Norquay parking lot

Elevation Change 640m (2100ft)

Nearest Town Banff

Transportation Car

Summary Huge views and a technical hike make this trail a good option if you're after something challenging.

You'll start out high and keep on getting higher on this mountain trail into a hanging valley beneath Cascade Mountain, carved out by glaciers that melted away long ago. It's a favored hangout for marmots and pikas, and a well-known spot for appreciating alpine wildflowers in late July and early August, but it's tough going and largely through forest, so you won't get too many views until the end. It might be a bit too much for younger walkers.

Head up Mt Norquay Rd from Banff Town all the way to the ski lodge parking lot; the trail starts near the entrance. You'll traverse a service road and pass the Mystic chairlift, then descend into lodgepole pine forest. Continue straight ahead at the Mystic Pass–Forty Mile Summit junction. After 3km (1.9 miles), you'll reach the banks of Forty Mile Creek; keep to the right and cross over the bridge.

From here the real climb begins as the trail continues through the forest to a junction with the Elk Lake Summit Trail at the 4.3km (2.7-mile) mark. Keep right and catch your breath ahead of a series of brutal switchbacks that carry you 2.3km (1.4 miles) up the pine-forested western slope of the mountain.

Just before arriving at the valley, the trail levels off and a number of faint paths head to the right. These lead to the summit ridge, which is suitable for mountaineers only, so stick to the main path until you emerge at a lovely alpine meadow, which is dotted with white anemone and yellow lilies in summer.

The trail becomes indistinct but continues for about 1km (0.6 miles) to the upper end of the amphitheater, where the vegetation thins out and boulders litter the ground. Rest here for a while and you'll be able to watch marmots and pikas scurrying between the rocks, before heading back.

🚶 Cory Pass Loop

Duration Five to six hours

Distance 13km (8.1 miles)

Difficulty Difficult

Start/Finish Fireside picnic area

Elevation Change 920m (3018ft)

Nearest Town Banff

Transportation Car, bike

Summary Banff's black-diamond hike incorporates mega-steep climbs, some rock-scrambling and a scree descent, but offers a thrilling white-knuckle ride for those fit enough to tackle it.

The trailhead for Cory Pass is at the Fireside picnic area at the southern end of the Bow Valley Pkwy just off Hwy 1. Although only 8km (5 miles) from Banff town centre, the trail's black (difficult) rating puts off many hikers, meaning splendid isolation is practically guaranteed.

The first part of the trail is deceptively flat, with Hwy 1 traffic noise reminding you of its presence below. After 1km (0.6 miles), the trail divides. Take the left fork and proceed steeply uphill. The next 1.5km (0.9 miles; it'll seem more like 4km!) climbs mercilessly upwards with almost no respite. When you reach the top of the crag, the path becomes less distinct and you have to undertake a short downhill rock-scramble to reach a dip below. Take extreme care in wet weather. Re-entering the forest briefly, the path flattens out, traversing a steep slope and climbing gradually toward Cory Pass. As the trees thin out, the path becomes increasingly narrow and a little exposed, requiring care and concentration. Cory Pass is visible long before you reach it. Stop briefly at the summit and admire your conquest. Rock pillars near the summit of Mt Edith tower above you and the Bow Valley sparkles below.

Snow cover and weather permitting, continue the loop by dropping over the other side of the pass. The path descends a loose scree slope steeply and then begins to traverse around the back of Mt Edith. It's tough going, but the sight of monolithic Mt Louis opposite stokes your inspiration. You'll eventually trade scree for a rockfall scattered with larger boulders. The path is less distinct here. A short ascent up a muddy slope brings you back into a dwarf forest bisected by avalanche chutes. Make plenty of noise – this is prime bear country. As the forest thickens and descends, you'll reach a junction with the Forty Mile Creek trail. Carry on down Edith Pass for 2.9km (1.8 miles) to the initial trail junction. From here, it's 1km (0.6 miles) back to the Fireside picnic area.

🏃 Johnston Canyon & the Inkpots

Duration Four hours round-trip

Distance 10.8km (6.7 miles)

Difficulty Moderate

Start/Finish Johnston Canyon parking lot

Elevation Change 215m (705ft) to Inkpots

Nearest Town Banff

Transportation Car

Summary A classic canyon hike past two of the park's most impressive waterfalls, with an optional add-on to five colorful springs in an alpine meadow.

The paved path through Johnston Canyon to its twin waterfalls is one of Banff's highlights, which means it's nearly always jammed with people – but don't let its popularity put you off. It's a must-see destination, and you can usually beat the worst of the crowds by turning up early – if you arrive before 9am you'll usually have the canyon practically to yourself.

The asphalt trail cuts through the center of the lush canyon, traversing several suspended catwalks high above the surging waters of Johnston Creek, which has carved out the canyon from the surrounding limestone rock. Shaded by trees, the towering canyon walls are covered with mosses, lichen and ferns, and black swifts can often be seen darting around the treetops during their nesting season from late June to September. It's also a great walk to do in the rain, as a downpour only adds to the spectacular force of the falls.

The first paved section (suitable for wheelchairs) leads to the Lower Falls after 30 minutes. Here you can duck through a natural cave right into the spray of the falls – be prepared to get wet, and bring a waterproof bag to protect your camera. The route to the Upper Falls (about 45 minutes from the Lower Falls) is steeper and crosses a few staircases, passing the mineral and algae-encrusted wall known as the Travertine Drape. You can descend to another platform viewpoint at the bottom of the Upper Falls, but it's worth continuing on up the trail for a reverse view of the falls as they plunge over the cliff edge into the canyon below.

Most people turn back at this point, but they're missing out on another nearby natural marvel: the colorful ponds known as the Inkpots (Map p94). From the Upper Falls, the trail climbs fairly steeply through the forest for 3km (1.9 miles) and then descends into a vast mountain meadow. Here you'll find the six Inkpots, encircled by snowcapped mountains; the pools get their name from the bright blue-green water that bubbles up from natural springs deep inside the mountain.

From the Inkpots, trails lead deep into the backcountry: northeast along Mystic Pass and Forty Mile Creek, and northwest along Johnston Creek (often used by bears as a drinking hole). Both are overnight trips, so you'll need proper supplies and a wilderness pass to tackle either trail.

🏃 Garden Path Trail & Twin Cairns Meadow

Duration 3½ hours round-trip

Distance 8.3km (5.1 miles)

Difficulty Easy

Start/Finish Sunshine Village ski area

Elevation Change Negligible from ski area, 655m (2149ft) from parking lot

Nearest Town Banff

Transportation Bus, car

Summary The easiest of the hikes from Sunshine Village takes in lakes, flowers and a viewpoint of Simpson Pass.

This might be the easiest option in Sunshine Meadows, but it's certainly not short on views. The flat, well-marked trail meanders past three glimmering alpine lakes and through lush meadows filled with summer wildflowers, leading to a grandstand lookout above the Continental Divide. Watch out for ground squirrels bounding around the pathway and take along a field guide to help you check off the summer blossoms.

Catch the bus from the parking lot to the Sunshine Village ski area. The trailhead starts on the southern side of the ski area, passing underneath the line of the main gondola up to Standish Ridge (look out for the log cabin at the start of the trail).

From here it's a gentle 10-minute climb up to the first fork, where you should stay right. At the top of the hill you enter the alpine meadows, sprinkled with mountain flowers and larch trees; you'll soon reach the summit of the Great Divide and cross over into British Columbia. At the next junction, keep right; the left fork leads to Quartz Hill and the soaring Citadel Pass.

Over the crest of the hill, the terrain rolls downward to **Rock Isle Lake**, so-called for the distinctive wooded islet that juts out from the middle of the water. Above the lake there's a good **lookout** with views of Standish Ridge to the right and Quartz Hill to the left, with a distant glimpse of the snowy pinnacle of Mt Assiniboine.

Rejoin the trail and head left at the next junction. The path winds through larch trees and past pebble-filled streams en route to the Grizzly and Larix Lakes Loop. Continue over the next junction for **Grizzly Lake**, and follow the lakeshore to the **Simpson Valley Lookout**. The pass is named after George Simpson, governor of the Hudson's Bay Company, who made the first foray along the valley in 1841. From the viewpoint, the trail loops around green-blue **Larix Lake** and rejoins the main Garden Path Trail.

You could return to Sunshine Village the way you came, but for better views head back via **Twin Cairns Meadow**. Turn left at the first junction after Rock Isle Lake, sign-posted to Standish Viewpoint. It's worth detouring 500m (0.3 miles) off the main trail to reach the **Standish Ridge Viewpoint**, which offers a 360-degree panorama encompassing Citadel Pass, Simpson Valley and Healy Pass.

Descend back to the main trail and turn right (north) across Twin Cairns Meadow. After 2km (1.2 miles) you reach a T-junction; take a detour left to **Monarch Viewpoint** (100m), which has excellent views of Mt Assiniboine on a clear day. Turn back from the viewpoint and follow the path back down to Sunshine Village, 1.6km (1 mile) away, via a winding trail through the woods.

🏃 Healy Pass & Simpson Pass

Duration Six to seven hours round-trip

Distance 18.4km (11.4 miles)

Difficulty Moderate-difficult

Start/Finish Sunshine Village parking lot

Elevation Change 650m (2132ft)

Nearest Town Banff

Transportation Bus, car

Summary Wildflowers, forest and lofty mountain ramparts combine on this varied hike, which ascends from the valley floor right onto the rooftop of Sunshine Meadows.

For an above-the-tree line Sunshine Meadows adventure, this challenging route up Healy Pass traverses lush meadows with an uninterrupted vista of peaks and lakes. It's ideally undertaken late in the season, when the weather's best.

The trailhead begins at the Sunshine Village parking lot, near the gondola base station. It leads up a rocky service road, passing into forest after 800m (0.5 miles). From here the trail crosses Sunshine Creek and ascends steadily along Healy Valley, canopied by spruce and fir trees. Look out for red squirrels, woodpeckers, chickadees and Clark's nutcrackers in the trees. The trail then leads along Healy Creek, reaching the Healy Creek Campground after 5.7km (3.5 miles).

From here the forest opens up and the trail levels off into a more gradual climb as it enters **Healy Meadows** by a gurgling stream. The meadows are alive with wildflowers throughout July and August. You'll pass the junction for Simpson Pass Trail on the left at the 7.7km (4.8-mile) mark, but press on to Healy Pass first, another 1.5km

(0.9 miles) further on through beautiful alpine terrain.

Perched at 2330m (7644ft) atop the escarpment of Monarch Ramparts, Healy Pass offers one of the Rockies' great views. It's only 1km (0.6 miles) from the Great Divide, and looks over some of the region's most dramatic sights, including the witch's-hat peak of Mt Assiniboine far to the southeast. To the west are Egypt, Mummy and Scarab Lakes, shining brightly beneath the Pharaoh Peaks, and to the north, the aptly named Massive Range broods along the horizon. You might even spy grizzlies and black bears on the open meadows around the pass.

Descend the way you came back to the Healy Meadows junction and take the trail toward Simpson Pass. Interspersing marshy meadows with stands of forest, the path passes a junction for Eohippus Lake before dropping down to Simpson Pass at 2135m (7004ft), a narrow meadow furnished by an isolated red bollard that marks the border between Alberta and British Columbia.

The path reenters forest traversing beneath a low escarpment before crossing a creek and climbing to Wawa Ridge. Views over meadows flecked with cotton grass and small ponds open out and you'll soon be delivered to the dramatic Monarch Viewpoint at the edge of Sunshine Meadows. From here its a 1.6km (1-mile) descent down to Sunshine Village where you can grab a snack in the Mad Trapper's Saloon, then catch a shuttle back to the parking lot.

Lake Louise & Around

🏃 Consolation Lakes Trail

Duration Two hours round-trip

Distance 6km (3.8 miles)

Difficulty Easy

Start/Finish Moraine Lake

Elevation Change 65m (213ft)

Nearest Town Lake Louise

Transportation Car

Summary It's only a short uphill stroll from Moraine Lake, but this trail still offers a taste of the wild Rockies.

Most people never get much further than the Moraine Lake shoreline, but to reach the real scenery you really do have to stretch your legs. This short trail winds through rocks and

boulders to a duo of sparkling mountain lakes backed by brooding cliffs. The walk is straightforward, although you will need proper hiking boots – the trail gets very muddy in spring and autumn, and traverses an area of rough, rocky boulders en route to the lakeshore. Note also that the Consolation Lakes are prime bear habitat, and fall under group access restrictions in summer.

Heading east from the parking lot, follow signs for the Consolation Lakes. You'll pass a small bridge and skirt the back of the rock-pile, crossing over a rocky moraine before ascending into pine forest. This section of the trail offers great views up the side of Mt Babel and back over the shoreline peaks of Moraine Lake.

For the next 1.6km (1 mile), the trail winds by the trees along the shores of the clattering Babel Creek. Some sections get very muddy after snowmelt and heavy rain, but try not to take any shortcuts off the main path, as it damages the fragile forest habitat.

You'll reach the Consolation Lakes after 3km (1.9 miles), tucked into the base of a distinctive U-shaped glacial valley dotted with rough boulders, scree and smashed rocks, which make for difficult walking. Take extra care as you cross the rocks toward the lakeshore. The valley is trammeled by Panorama Ridge to the east, Mt Bell to the southeast and the peaks of Mt Quadra and Bident Mountain at the northern side of the lake. The icy monsters to the west are Mt Fay and Mt Babel.

The trail to the Upper Lake crosses some treacherous areas of boulders and scree, so unless you're an experienced scrambler, it's best to settle for the views from the lower lake before heading for home.

🏃 Plain of Six Glaciers

Duration Four to five hours round-trip

Distance 13.5km (8.4 miles)

Difficulty Moderate

Start/Finish Fairmont Chateau Lake Louise

Elevation Change 365m (1198ft)

Nearest Town Lake Louise

Transportation Car

Summary One of the Lake Louise classics, ending at a historic teahouse with views across the Victoria and Lefroy Glaciers.

This perennially popular hike from Lake Louise punches up the rubble-strewn glacial

Lake Louise & Around – Day Hikes

Legend:
- Consolation Lakes Trail
- Lake Agnes & the Beehives
- Larch Valley & Sentinel Pass
- Paradise Valley & the Giant's Steps
- Plain of Six Glaciers
- Saddleback & Fairview

valley to the foot of Victoria and Lefroy Glaciers, twin tongues of glittering ice jammed between regal peaks. It's a jaw-dropper of a hike that'll leave you breathless in more ways than one. You'll need sturdy boots, warm layers and a good rain shell; walking poles are useful for keeping yourself upright on the shifting moraines. The trail is often one of the last to open after spring due to snow and avalanche danger; check trail conditions at the park office before you start out.

Follow the paved shoreline walk from the Fairmont Chateau Lake Louise for 2km (1.3 miles) to the lake's southwestern end, then head along the edge of the river flats, watching as the glacial creek feeding the lake becomes a torrent. The trail climbs steadily through forest, emerging occasionally to give you views of the glacial ravine. At the 3.3km (2-mile) mark and again at the 4km (2.5-mile) mark, you'll meet trails branching off to the right, leading to the

highline trail to the Big Beehive and Lake Agnes. Ignore these and press on up the valley, as the tree cover gradually thins out and you emerge onto switchbacks. You'll have plenty of opportunity to stop and catch your breath, as well as to gaze at the rapidly approaching glaciers to the southwest and the ice-strewn slopes of Mts Lefroy and Victoria. Keep your ears open for the rumble of avalanches crashing off the distant Victoria Glacier, especially late in the morning.

After two hours and 5.5km (3.4 miles) of climbing, you'll reach the **Plain of Six Glaciers Teahouse** (Map p94; snacks C$5-10; ⏰8am-6pm Jun–mid-Oct), constructed in 1927 as a way station for Swiss mountaineering guides leading clients up to the summit of Mt Victoria. Nestled in a quiet glade, the twin-level log chalet looks like something out of the pages of *Heidi*, and dishes up homemade sandwiches, cakes, gourmet teas and hot chocolates to a steady stream of puffed-out hikers.

Despite its allure, sensible walkers leave the treats of the teahouse for the return walk, as the main hike isn't over yet. From the clearing, the trail leads a further 1.6km (1 mile) uphill to the Plain of Six Glaciers itself, tracking a rubbly ridge that can be slippery in wet weather and is exposed to vicious winds funneled up the valley.

Although there's nothing to mark it, you'll know you've reached the lookout when you have a grandstand view of the front edge of the **Victoria Glacier** and can see back down the valley to Lake Louise and the chateau. In the 1800s the glacier covered most of the surrounding area. From the lookout, a path leads up the face of the moraine to the cliff edge and a small waterfall; it's very slippery, so only tackle it if you're a competent scrambler. You should see the cleft of Abbot Pass from the top. Once you've admired the views, retrace your steps down the moraine and visit the teahouse before heading back down the valley. If your legs are up to it, you could detour along the signposted highline trail, which links up with the route to Lake Agnes and the Big Beehive.

🥾 Larch Valley & Sentinel Pass

Duration Four to five hours round-trip

Distance 8.6km (5.3 miles) to Larch Valley, 11.6km (7.2 miles) to Sentinel Pass

Difficulty Moderate

Start/Finish Moraine Lake Trail

Elevation Change 535m (1755ft) to Larch Valley, 725m (2379ft) to Sentinel Pass

Nearest Town Lake Louise

Transportation Car

Summary A popular trail through larch forest and alpine meadows with wonderful views of the Wenkchemna Peaks.

Another of Lake Louise's quintessential hikes, this route offers one of the best outlooks of the Valley of the Ten Peaks and travels through some of the park's finest larch forests. Snow lingers at higher elevations well into spring, so it's best visited in fall when the valley turns into a sea of autumnal colors. Strong hikers can extend the walk for an impressive mountain panorama at Sentinel Pass.

Start on the Moraine Lake Trail and veer right at the signpost for Larch Valley into dense forest, traveling up a set of switchbacks that gain over 350m (1148ft) in 2.5km (1.6m miles).

At the first junction, the left trail leads to **Eiffel Lake** (another great destination that's often quieter than the Larch Valley trail). Follow the right-hand turn and climb further into the fragrant forest, emerging after about 3.5km (2.2 miles) into the wide-open spaces of **Larch Valley**. The meadows are famous for their wildflowers, but the high-alpine habitat is extremely fragile, so don't step off the main trail if you can possibly help it.

From here, the path breaks above the treeline and continues to the little **Minnestimma Lakes** at about the 4.5km (2.8-mile) mark. From here, there's an amazing view of eight of the 10 Wenkchemna Peaks, as well as the white mass of the **Fay Glacier**.

Most hikers end the walk here, but if the weather's good and your legs are feeling strong, you could continue up and over the 2611m (8566ft) **Sentinel Pass**, one of the highest maintained passes in the Canadian Rockies. It's a hard, tiring trail that crosses slippery areas of talus and scree; don't even think about tackling it in snow or heavy rain, as the weather can turn suddenly. Check the forecasts before you set out, and bring layers and waterproofs.

From the top of the pass, experienced hikers can make a truly epic circle down into the adjacent Paradise Valley, but you'll be stranded at the other end unless you've got two vehicles.

Note this route falls under group access restrictions.

🥾 Lake Agnes & the Beehives

Duration Four hours round-trip

Distance 10.8km (6.6 miles)

Difficulty Moderate to Lake Agnes, moderate-difficult to Big Beehive

Start/Finish Fairmont Chateau Lake Louise

Elevation Change 495m (1624ft)

Nearest Town Lake Louise

Transportation Car

Summary The walk that practically everyone who visits Lake Louise wants to do. It's crowded, but the sights are unmissable, visiting a historic teahouse, two mountain lakes, and a fantastic cloud-level lookout.

This is one of the most popular walks in the Lake Louise area, so it's worth doing early or late in the day to beat the crowds. It's a fine, well-marked route taking in forest trails, hidden lakes and scenic viewpoints, as well as a famous teahouse – but it is formidably steep (especially around the Big Beehive), so bring plenty of water and take regular rests. You can either make it a stand-alone hike or combine it with the Plain of Six Glaciers hike (p60).

Begin on the Lake Louise shoreline trail, and take the fork on the right after about 800m (0.5 miles) as it ascends into forest. The path zigzags through the trees for about 45 minutes, with occasional views back over the lake to Fairview Mountain, before emerging at the glassy surface of Mirror Lake, famous for its photogenic reflection of the Big Beehive. The lake makes a good place to refuel before continuing on the steep climb to Lake Agnes itself.

The trail divides at Mirror Lake. You can reach Lake Agnes via the right-hand trail, but the most straightforward route is to take a left from the lake and then an immediate right after about 100m for the direct climb to the teahouse (left here leads on to the Plain of Six Glaciers hike). It's a steep slog through the forest for a further 15 minutes, but you'll have good views of the mountains as the trees begin to thin out. The final section passes a waterfall and traverses a near-vertical set of wooden stairs before emerging at the lake and the teahouse.

Lake Agnes is named after Lady Susan Agnes Macdonald (wife of former prime minister Sir John Macdonald), who made the climb to the lake in 1890. There's been a teahouse (Map p94; snacks C$3-6; ⊙9am-6pm Jun-Aug, 10am-5:30pm Sep & Oct) here since 1901, but the present building is actually a replica built in 1981; it serves a huge selection of exotic teas ranging from golden monkey to 'Imperial Keernun' sacred blend, but tables can be scarce at peak times. Soups, cakes and sandwich platters are also available if you're after something more substantial.

Once you've fuelled up at the teahouse, you can take an optional detour to the top of the Little Beehive (105m/344ft elevation gain) before heading around the right side of the lake en route to its bigger brother, the Big Beehive (135m/442ft elevation gain), which you'll reach after 1.6km (1 mile) of relentless, leg-shredding switchbacks. Needless to say, the summit rewards the effort: you'll enjoy a sky-topping vantage of the entire Lake Louise area, with the Slate Range to the northeast, the Bow Valley southeast and Lake Louise

and its surrounding peaks way below. It's a truly unforgettable lookout, but you'll need a head for heights.

From the top, you can either retrace your steps to Lake Agnes, or descend south toward the Plain of Six Glaciers trail.

🏃 Saddleback & Fairview

Duration Five to six hours round-trip

Distance 7.4km (4.6 miles) to Saddleback, 10.2km (6.4 miles) to Fairview

Difficulty Moderate-difficult

Start/Finish Fairmont Chateau Lake Louise

Elevation Change 600m (1970ft) to Saddleback, 1013m (3323ft) to Fairview

Nearest Town Lake Louise

Transportation Car

Summary Big vistas from two of Lake Louise's most famous viewpoints, but tough going all the way to the top.

This hike starts out steep and just keeps getting steeper, climbing to a famous pass between Fairview and Saddle Mountain, and an even more famous summit lookout. There's no getting around the elevation gain, but at least you'll feel like you've earned the view.

Start at the viewpoint in front of the Fairmont Chateau Lake Louise, and follow signs pointing to Saddleback. After around 300m (0.2 miles), you'll reach a junction: the left fork joins up with the Moraine Lake Highline Trail, while the right fork emerges at a viewpoint above the lake. The main trail lies dead ahead. It climbs sharply along a snaking trail, ascending relentlessly through spruce and larch forest all the way to the Saddleback at the 3.7km (2.3-mile) mark.

The landscape of Lake Louise opens up like a panoramic picturebook once you finally reach the top of the pass. It's a superb place to tick off some of the main peaks around Lake Louise: south is Mt Temple, while southwest are Sheol Mountain and Haddo Peak. A compass and a topo map are useful to help identify each mountain.

Directly north of the pass is the trail to the top of Fairview, the craggy peak that dominates the southern side of Lake Louise. You don't necessarily have to tackle the path to the top, but it's worth the toil if you're up to it. Basic scrambling skills and sturdy boots with plenty of grip will come in handy, as some sections can be rocky and slippery.

Once you reach the top, you'll realize exactly how the mountain came by its name.

🚶 Paradise Valley & the Giant's Steps

Duration Six to seven hours round-trip

Distance 20.3km (12.6 miles)

Difficulty Difficult

Start/Finish Paradise Valley parking area, Moraine Lake Rd

Elevation Change 385m (1263ft)

Nearest Town Lake Louise

Transportation Car

Summary An unforgettable route along a remote mountain valley, rated by many seasoned hikers as one of their favorite destinations in the Canadian Rockies.

Paradise Valley goes head-to-head with Larch Valley in the scenic stakes. It's a showstopper, tracing a route past ice-crowned summits, delicate cornices, scree slopes and a natural rock cascade called the Giant's Steps. This is prime grizzly habitat, so group access restrictions may be in force – take care and make extra noise. Trails were rerouted in 2007 to reduce the risk of bear encounters. It's also a route for experienced hikers.

The trailhead starts at a small parking lot about 2.5km (1.6 miles) along Moraine Lake Rd. The first section travels gently through forest, tracking the course of Paradise Creek. At 1.1km (0.7 miles) from the trailhead, you'll cross the Moraine Lake Highline Trail between Lake Louise and Moraine Lake; turn right (north), then almost immediately left (west) for Paradise Valley.

The trail then crosses the creek a couple of times before passing the right-hand fork to Saddleback at the 4.2km (2.6-mile) mark. Ignore the junction and continue southwest toward Lake Annette, which you'll reach at around the 5.8km (3.6-mile) mark. This peaceful lake feels thrillingly remote, surrounded by lonely mountains and silent forest that remain snow-clad until well into July. It also offers soaring views of nearby Mt Temple, the highest peak around Lake Louise, and the third highest in Banff National Park.

From the lake, the trail rolls southwest toward the head of the valley, dominated by the dramatic Horseshoe Glacier and a cluster of impressive peaks. The tallest of all is Mt Hungabee, which means 'chieftain' in the Stoney language. As you continue southwest,

the specter of Pinnacle Mountain appears to the south, while to the northwest across the valley, the glacier-flanked slopes of Mt Lefroy loom above a sparkling blue glacial lake. This section is one of the most dramatic in the entire national park; take your time and don't forget to take plenty of pictures.

After 8.5km (5.2 miles), you'll reach a right-hand fork leading to the northwest. Take the turning and follow the path down toward a bridge over Paradise Creek. Soon afterwards, you'll reach another junction: straight ahead takes you to the little Paradise Valley Campground, while the right-hand fork leads to the tumble of rock slabs known as the Giant's Steps after about 300m (0.2 miles). Check ahead at the park office if you're planning on camping, as the campground is closed whenever there's bear activity in the valley.

From the Giant's Steps, you can either retrace your steps or make an optional loop around the edge of Horseshoe Meadow (keep an extra eye out for bears here). On the south side of the meadow, you'll pass the connector trail south to Sentinel Pass, while the main trail leads northeast back toward Lake Annette.

Icefields Parkway

🚶 Mistaya Canyon

Duration 30 minutes round-trip

Distance 1km (0.6 miles)

Difficulty Easy

Start/Finish Mistaya Canyon lay-by

Elevation Change Negligible

Nearest Town Saskatchewan Crossing

Transportation Car

Summary An easy walk to one of the park's most picturesque river canyons.

This short trail barely even qualifies as a hike, but it's well worth taking the detour from the Icefields Pkwy to discover this dramatic, potholed canyon. The level dirt track leads through forest for around 500m (0.3 miles) before emerging on the canyon wall high above the pounding swirl of the Mistaya River, which rises in Peyto Lake far to the south. From the bridge you can watch the river plunge impressively down into the curves and curls of the limestone ravine, and watch how the action of the water has carved out the canyon's tortuous shape.

Icefields Parkway – Day Hikes

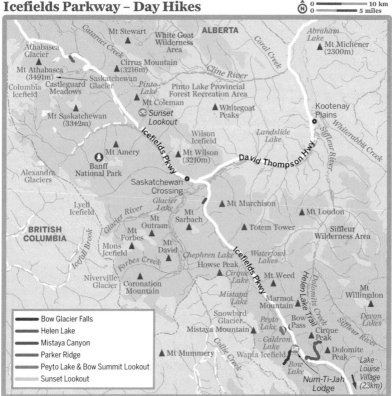

BANFF NATIONAL PARK DAY HIKES

From the far side of the bridge the path leads on to two much more challenging trails, including the long slog up to the disused Sarbach fire lookout, a 10.6km (6.6-mile) round-trip, and the historic route to Howse Pass, the first fur-trading route established through the Canadian Rockies. It's 4.3km (2.7 miles) to the Howse River.

🏃 Bow Glacier Falls

Duration Three hours round-trip

Distance 7.2km (4.4 miles)

Difficulty Easy-moderate

Start/Finish Num-Ti-Jah Lodge

Elevation Change 155m (509ft)

Nearest Town Lake Louise

Transportation Car

Summary Cross river flats and moraine

fields to reach an impressive glacier-fed waterfall.

When Jimmy Simpson used to lead his guests along this well-worn walk in the early 1900s, the Bow Glacier still filled much of the basin at the end of the trail. These days it has shrunk into the mountains, leaving a boulder-filled valley and the clattering Bow Glacier Falls in its wake. It's an easy and rewarding jaunt, with just one steep section and a fine finish as you cross the moraine moonscape up to the face of the falls. It's a good one to consider on rainy days, when the cascade is at its most powerful.

The trailhead starts just behind Jimmy Simpson's former hotel, Num-Ti-Jah Lodge (p106), 37km (23 miles) from the southern end of the Icefields Pkwy. The first section winds along the lakeshore, with views of Crowfoot Mountain and the Wapta Icefield. After 2km (1.2 miles) you reach the edge of the lake, and follow the path southwest across a rock bed. To your right are two narrow **waterfalls** streaming down the cliff face. Follow the cairns across the rocky terrain, heading for a distant staircase and the canyon mouth.

After 3.5km (2.2 miles) the steep staircase leads you up a forested ridge alongside the canyon; watch your step if it has been raining, as there are no handholds and there's a long drop to your left. About halfway up you'll pass a massive boulder jammed into the valley, which climbers have to cross in order to follow the route to the high-altitude Bow Hut, the starting point for many ascents.

After 10 minutes or so the staircase ends and the trail leads onto the edge of the huge moraine field, sprinkled with boulders, rocks and stones and backed by the distant crash of the **Bow Glacier Falls** plunging 100m (328ft) over the edge of the valley. Cairns mark the route across the valley to the falls themselves; walking poles will come in handy here, as it's usually slippery underfoot. Finish up with a drink and a picnic beside the cascade before retracing your steps back to the lodge.

🏃 Parker Ridge

Duration Two hours round-trip

Distance 4km (2.5 miles)

Difficulty Moderate

Start/Finish Parker Ridge parking lot

Elevation Change 250m (820ft)

Nearest Town Saskatchewan Crossing

Transportation Car

Summary If you want to see a glacier in all its glory, you can't beat this steep ascent onto the crest of an impossibly scenic ridge near the Banff–Jasper border.

If you only do one hike along the Icefields Pkwy, make it Parker Ridge. It's short enough to crack in an afternoon, but leads to one of the most impressive lookouts of any of Banff's day hikes, with a grandstand view of Mt Saskatchewan, Mt Athabasca and the gargantuan **Saskatchewan Glacier**. Bring warm clothing and a decent coat, as the wind on the ridge can be punishing.

The first part of the walk is pretty uneventful. From the parking lot the trail runs through a narrow wood before emerging on the hillside and entering a long series of switchbacks. As you climb, you look down onto the main road as it recedes into the distance, and every step improves the panorama

of mountains across the valley. Near the top, the trail turns briefly nasty, ascending sharply before you finally stumble over the crest of the ridge at the 2km (1.2-mile) mark, puffed out and panting, to be greeted by an arctic blast of wind and an explosive panorama of peaks and glaciers.

To the west loom Mts Athabasca and Andromeda, and just to their south is the gleaming bulk of the **Saskatchewan Glacier**, which lurks at the end of a deep valley. At almost 13km (8-miles) long, the glacier is one of the longest in the Rockies, but it's actually just a spur from the massive 230-sq-km (88-sq-mile) Columbia Icefield that lies to the north. For the best views, follow the trail southeast along the edge of the ridge and stop at one of the unmarked **viewpoints**.

On the way back down the trail, you can swing left onto a narrow spur trail, which climbs for 15 minutes to another ridge crest, marked by rough cairn shelters where you can escape the wind and look down over the parkway. Retrace your steps and rejoin the main trail for the descent to the parking lot.

🏃 Peyto Lake & Bow Summit Lookout

Duration Two hours round-trip

Distance 6.2km (3.8 miles)

Difficulty Moderate

Start/Finish Peyto Lake parking lot

Elevation Change 245m (803ft)

Nearest Town Saskatchewan Crossing

Transportation Car

Summary An old fire road passing the famous Peyto Lake viewpoint up to an abandoned fire lookout high above the Bow and Mistaya Valleys.

You'll have plenty of company along the first part of this trail; practically every visitor to the Icefields Pkwy stops to take in the sights from the **Peyto Lake Lookout**, which you'll reach after an easy 15 minutes through the forest from the main parking lot. Leave behind the crowds on the main wooden lookout and continue on to a three-way junction; left leads to the upper parking lot, while the right and middle trails continue on a forested loop with interpretive signs detailing various aspects of the alpine environment. Take the middle trail and look out for an unmarked dirt road on your left after about 1km (0.6 miles), zigzagging uphill toward the lookout. Soon you'll reach a plateau on the right with much better views across the lake than you'll get from the main viewpoint. Stop here for a while to appreciate the scenery, with mountain sentinels standing on either side of the glittering blue water and a string of smaller waterways leading off into the distance at the far end of the valley.

From here the trail continues to climb, with wildflowers replacing the increasingly scarce trees. At the 2.5km (1.5-mile) mark the road dips into a rocky bowl, often frequented by sunbathing marmots and bisected by a tinkling stream. Cross the bowl and set out on the last ascent of 500m (0.3 miles), crossing two hills to the Bow Summit Lookout. North is Mistaya Valley rising southwards up to Bow Pass, east is Cirque Peak, and southeast across the Bow Valley is the great sweep of Crowfoot Glacier.

🏃 Helen Lake

Duration Four hours round-trip

Distance 12km (7.5 miles)

Difficulty Moderate

Start/Finish Helen Lake parking lot

Elevation Change 455m (1493ft)

Nearest Town Lake Louise

Transportation Car

Summary Steep route leading up to a hidden valley renowned for its glorious display of summer wildflowers.

This is one of the most beautiful high-altitude valleys along the Icefields Pkwy and, in summer, it's one of the top places to see a display of Canadian wildflowers. You'll have a real sense of solitude at the top, and the mountain panoramas of Cirque Peak and Dolomite Peak are outstanding. It's best done in good weather; you're quite exposed on the trail and at the top, and the views are disappointing if it's sheeting with rain. The high mountain meadows also remain snowbound until well into July. Bears are fairly common visitors to the area, so hike in a group and make plenty of noise on the trail.

The trailhead is 33km (20.5 miles) along the parkway, near the turnoff to the Crowfoot Glacier viewpoint. From the Helen Lake parking lot, follow the dirt trail through spruce and fir for a 3km (1.9-mile) ascent. As the forest thins, you'll be treated to fine views of Crowfoot Glacier and Bow Lake across the valley.

Near the top of the ascent, an area of old burned forest slowly levels out into an ancient glacial valley, spotted with stands of pine and larch, and carpeted with vivid displays of wildflowers between July and August. The trail winds across a couple of creeks and leads past a massive rockslide, where you'll often be able to spot marmots squeaking among the rocks, before rising up and over a flat plateau of heather and alpine grass all the way to Helen Lake at the 6km (3.7-mile) mark.

The lake offers a superb viewpoint back down the valley. To the north is the lumpy prominence of Cirque Peak, and to the east are the chimneylike stacks of Dolomite Peak along the horizon, named by early explorers for its resemblance to the Dolomite Mountains of northern Italy. Break the hike here and savor the solitude; few hikes give you such a sense of the age and silent power of the country.

For a longer walk, strong hikers could continue northeast from the lake for the lonely lookout of Dolomite Pass, reached after another 2.9km.

🏃 Sunset Lookout

Duration Three hours round-trip

Distance 9.4km (5.8 miles)

Difficulty Moderate

Start/Finish Sunset Lookout parking lot

Elevation Change 250m (820ft)

Nearest Town Saskatchewan Crossing

Transportation Car

Summary An abandoned fire lookout commanding unbroken views of the North Saskatchewan Valley.

This remote trail is just a few kilometers inside the northern border of Banff National Park, and it feels a long way from anywhere. It's mainly used as an access route for backpackers on the way to Pinto Lake and the wilderness area beyond, but the first section gives you a sense of adventure without actually having to camp out overnight.

From the parking lot on the east side of the parkway, 16.5km north of Saskatchewan Crossing, the trail climbs sharply through lodgepole pine forest, roughly following the course of Norman Creek. In late July the forest is thick with buffalo-berry bushes, so it's a favorite feeding ground for hungry grizzlies – check for trail closures before you start out, and make noise to avoid surprise encounters. The path leads past a dramatic canyon carved out by Norman Creek, before zigzagging back into forest and reaching the left-hand junction for the lookout after around 2.9km (1.8 miles).

From here, it's another 1.8km (1.1 miles) to the lookout site, dangling high above the forest. Far below are the Graveyard Flats, crisscrossed by the neighboring Alexandra and North Saskatchewan Rivers. A roll call of remote mountains looms on each horizon, including Mt Saskatchewan to the west and faraway Bow Peak to the south. The fire lookout itself operated between 1943 and 1978; you can still make out its foundations and the remains of cables that were once connected to the lookout's lightning conductor.

Back at the main trail, you can either turn right back to the parking lot, or turn left and strike out for Sunset Pass, 7.6km (4.7 miles) from the trailhead. Beyond lies some of Banff's wildest backcountry, including Pinto Lake and the White Goat Wilderness Area.

🥾 OVERNIGHT HIKES

Banff's day hikes offer ample adventure for most people, but for a real appreciation of the park's wild side you've got to head into the backcountry. With a network of trails crisscrossing the high mountains, and a selection of routes ranging anywhere from two days to several weeks, there are enough backcountry trips here to satisfy the most mile-hungry hiker; the real challenge lies in choosing which one to do.

You don't necessarily have to submit a full trip itinerary when you purchase your wilderness pass, but it's often a good idea; if you're not back by the specified date, a search party will set out to look for you, so it's *vital* that you report back to park authorities once your trip is finished to avoid triggering a false alarm.

Wild camping is only permitted in certain remote areas – contact the Banff Visitor Centre (p112) for details. In the backcountry, you have to pack out all your garbage by law.

🥾 Egypt Lake & Gibbon Pass

Duration Three days round-trip; two days round-trip to Egypt Lake only

Distance 40.8km (25.4 miles); 24.8km (15.4 miles) round-trip to Egypt Lake only

Difficulty Moderate-difficult

🥾 Overnight Hike Mt Assiniboine

START SUNSHINE VILLAGE
END MT SHARK
LENGTH THREE TO FOUR DAYS; 55.7KM (34.6 MILES)

This multiday hike ventures into the heart of Mt Assiniboine Provincial Park, an area famous not just for its pyramidal mountain (Canada's Matterhorn), but also for its meadows, lakes and seemingly endless hiking options.

There are several routes into the park, including from Sunshine Village, from Kootenay National Park along the Simpson River Trail, and from Kananaskis Country along Bryant Creek (accessed near Mt Shark, about a 43km drive from Canmore along the gravel Smith-Dorrien/Spray Trail Rd). The best option is to combine the Sunshine Village and Bryant Creek trails, creating a stunning 55.7km (34.6-mile) route tracking the ridge of the Great Divide. You'll need a car at either end of the trail to avoid getting stranded; alternatively, leave your car at Mt Shark, catch a lift back to the Sunshine Village parking lot, then take the shuttle or hike up to Sunshine Meadows from the parking lot. If you're feeling really flush, you could even catch a helicopter into the park from Canmore, but that really would be cheating.

The following trip includes two days of hiking into the park and a one- or two-day hike back out to Mt Shark. There are possibilities for at least three days of side-trips at Lake Magog. Though popular, it's still proper backcountry: taking bear precautions and packing proper supplies are essential.

The hike officially starts at Sunshine Village, accessible from the Sunshine Village parking lot by a summer shuttle. Begin day one with the hike for the Garden Path Trail (p58). At the junction at the 1.3km (0.8-mile) mark, instead of continuing west toward Rock Isle and Grizzly Lake, turn south toward Citadel Pass. The trail crosses briefly into British Columbia, passing the Howard Douglas Lake and Campground en route to ❶ **Citadel Pass** at the 9.3km (5.8-mile) mark. If the weather's clear, from here you should have a great

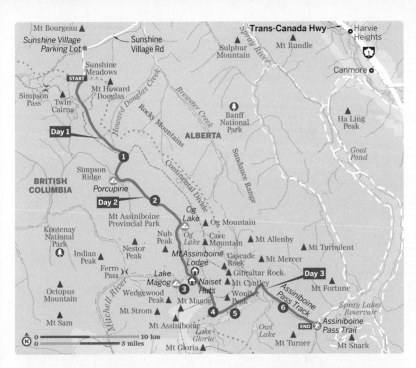

view of Mt Assiniboine spiking skywards, way off to the southeast.

After 12.3km (7.8 miles) the trail meets the junction to Porcupine Campground (where most hikers spend their first night). To reach the campground, head right (south) for another kilometer (0.6 miles).

On day two, head southeast from the campground for 3.5km (2.2 miles) to rejoin the main trail, which heads into the aptly named **2 Valley of the Rocks**. The enormous boulders that crowd this lengthy valley are left over from a long-ago rockslide, the largest anywhere in the Rockies; it feels wild and desolate at the best of times, but in bad weather seems positively unearthly. The valley runs southeast for around 6km (3.7 miles), but the rocky path makes it tough going. Also note that there is no water in the Valley of the Rocks, so make sure you're stocked up before you start out.

If the rocky traverse has worn you out, you could break overnight at Og Lake Campground, but if you feel up to it, it's worth continuing across Og Meadows for another 6km (3.7 miles) to reach **3 Lake Magog**, the main base for explorations around Mt Assiniboine.

There is a superb campground perched right beside the lakeshore, offering a grandstand viewpoint up the snowy slopes of Mt Assiniboine. There are also several rustic Naiset Huts and the wonderful Assiniboine Lodge (dating from 1928) situated near the lake; all are heavily oversubscribed in season, so book as early as possible to be sure of a place.

If you've managed to sort out transportation at the Mt Shark end, the best option for day three is to head out of the park via spectacular **4 Wonder Pass** (a hike of just over 25km/15 miles from Lake Magog). It's a wonderfully scenic walk in its own right, passing the shining expanse of **5 Marvel Lake**, the 6th-largest lake in Banff National Park, and **6 Bryant Creek**, site of an eponymous trail, warden's office and shelter. It's a long route to do in one day, so you might feel like breaking the walk in two; there are a couple of campgrounds near the lake's eastern end (McBride's Camp and Marvel Lake), which you'll reach around 12km (7.5 miles) from Lake Magog.

Alternatively, you could just visit Wonder Pass and Marvel Lake as a day hike before retracing your route back to the trailhead across Sunshine Meadows.

Egypt Lake & Gibbon Pass

Start Sunshine Village parking lot

Finish Vista Lake/Twin Lakes trailhead, Hwy 93

Elevation Change Up to 655m (2149ft)

Nearest Town Banff

Transportation Bus/car

Summary An ideal introduction to the world of the backcountry, crossing meadows and a mountain pass en route to a network of glittering lakes.

This backcountry classic starts out as a standard day hike to Healy Pass and just keeps on going. Rather than turning back once you've crossed the Continental Divide, you'll continue on for another 3km (1.9 miles) to reach the high mountain tarns around Egypt Lake. Time it right and you'll be greeted with a profusion of wonderful summer wildflowers or autumnal trees. Whenever you choose to come, you'll have a sweeping panorama of the

Monarch Ramparts, the Ball Range and the Alberta–British Columbia border. Best of all, it's relatively straightforward for a backcountry hike, which unfortunately also means it can get crowded in season.

DAY 1: SUNSHINE VILLAGE PARKING LOT TO EGYPT LAKE CAMPGROUND
4 HOURS / 12.4KM (7.7 MILES)

Start out on the Healy Pass hike (p59) from the Sunshine Village parking lot and, once you crest Healy Pass, continue northwest into forest, passing Pharaoh Creek after 3km (1.9 miles). A little further on, you pass a trail on the right to Egypt Lake Warden Cabin, then cross a bridged creek into a meadow, where you'll find your overnight spot of Egypt Lake Campground and Shelter. Book well ahead for both in season.

Several spur trails radiate out from the campground and provide excellent day-hike options, including the 4.2km (2.6 miles) to

Natalko (Talc) Lake and the 2.8km (1.7-mile) trail to Pharaoh and Black Rock Lakes.

DAY 2: EGYPT LAKE CAMPGROUND TO SHADOW LAKE
5-6 HOURS / 14.4KM (8.9 MILES)

Ringed by forest and the Pharaoh Peaks, **Egypt Lake** is one of the loveliest high-altitude lakes in the park. It shimmers a short 15-minute stroll from the Egypt Lake Campground. A couple of good side-trips beckon in the vicinity to **Scarab Lake** and **Mummy Lake**. To continue on the main hike, ascend **Whistling Pass**, supposedly named for the hooting hoary marmots that live there, although it could equally be named for the whistling wind that often whips across the top of the pass. From here, it's another 9km (5.6 miles) paralleling the Continental Divide to **Shadow Lake**, where you can overnight at the campground or backcountry lodge.

DAY 3: SHADOW LAKE TO VISTA LAKE TRAILHEAD
5-6 HOURS / 14KM (8.7 MILES)

From Shadow Lake, you have a choice of routes back to civilization. You could head northeast for 13.9km (8.6 miles) along **Redearth Creek**, but the more scenic option is the 14km (8.7-mile) route over **Gibbon Pass** via **Twin Lakes** and **Arnica Lake**, which ends at the Vista Lake/Twin Lakes trailhead on Hwy 93 in Kootenay National Park. Note that if you take this option, you'll need to arrange for someone to pick you up.

🥾 Skoki Valley

Duration Four days round-trip

Distance 50.4km (31.3 miles) round-trip

Difficulty Moderate-difficult

Start/Finish Fish Creek trailhead

Elevation Change Up to 1136m (3727ft)

Nearest Town Lake Louise

Skoki Valley

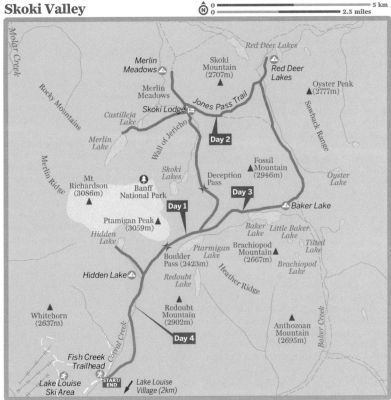

Transportation Bus/car

Summary A dreamy landscape of high mountains and lakes awaits around the Skoki Valley.

It might not have the lush greenery of some of Banff's other backcountry destinations, but for the desolate beauty of its high mountains and truly unparalleled views, Skoki Valley is a gem. The Skoki area has been a popular skiers' hangout since the 1930s, but these days it has also become a regular haunt of summer hikers, especially for those visitors itching to try out a night at Skoki Lodge, one of Banff's most historic ski lodges.

You can expect a mix of mountain landscapes en route – meadow, peaks, lakes and barren rock – and a massive sense of achievement once you're done.

DAY 1: FISH CREEK TRAILHEAD TO MERLIN MEADOWS
8 HOURS / 17.6KM (11 MILES)

The first day is a full-blown, hard mountain hike, so start as early as possible to be sure of camping in daylight. The trip starts out at an elevation of 1690m (5545ft), with the first steep, wooded section following Temple Fire Rd for 3.9km (2.4 miles). It reaches a trail lodge and crosses a ski slope before ascending to a meadowy area with great views of the Slate Range after around 6.5km (4 miles). At the 7.1km (4.4-mile) mark you'll pass Halfway Hut, a day shelter once used by skiers heading for Skoki Lodge, and the Hidden Lake Campground, where you can take an overnight break if you wish.

Most people push on to Boulder Pass, situated above Ptarmigan Lake with a view of Ptarmigan Peak, Redoubt Mountain and Mt Temple to the southwest. Take a break here and admire the vista, then continue north via Deception Pass, looking out for the Skoki Lakes on your left before reaching Skoki Lodge after 16.4km (10.2 miles). Base yourself at the lodge or the nearby Merlin Meadows Campground, another 1.2km northwest.

DAY 2: MERLIN MEADOWS TO RED DEER LAKES
6 HOURS / 11.4KM (7 MILES)

On the second day, backtrack the 1.2km (0.7-mile) trail and explore the high mountain scenery around Skoki Lodge, including the 6.2km (3.8-mile) round-trip to Merlin Lake. Back at the lodge, head south and take the left-hand (east) fork along the 'Jones Pass' Trail, which skirts past the southern flanks of Skoki Mountain.

Spend the night at Red Deer Lakes Campground, a walk of 4km (2.5 miles) from the lodge.

DAY 3: RED DEER LAKES TO HIDDEN LAKE CAMPGROUND
6-7 HOURS / 11.7KM (7.3 MILES)

On day three, head south through the alpine meadows around Oyster Creek and Cotton Grass Pass, before veering westwards along the northern shore of Baker Lake and rejoining the main Skoki trail just south of Deception Pass. On the way back down the valley, you'll have a fine outlook of Ptarmigan Peak (3059m/10,035ft) to the west and Redoubt Mountain (2902m/9520ft) to the south. Camp at the Hidden Lake Campground, near the Halfway Hut.

DAY 4: HIDDEN LAKE CAMPGROUND TO FISH CREEK TRAILHEAD
2-3 HOURS / 9.7KM (6 MILES)

On the final day, take an early-morning jaunt up to Hidden Lake itself (2.6km/1.6-mile round-trip), a classic glacial tarn nestled among craggy peaks. Rejoin the main trail and hike back to the start point at Fish Creek.

⚫ CYCLING

Cyclists fresh from sojourns in Jasper or Kananaskis Country will find Banff's trails a little more constricting. Many of the park's paths are designated 'hiking only,' but with a protected area this large there are still plenty of options to flick through your gears on a multifarious mixture of paved routes, fire roads and daring singletrack.

Road cyclists shouldn't overlook Banff's paved surfaces. The Bow Valley Pkwy makes for a bracing, but flat-ish ride, as does the mega-popular Legacy Trail into Canmore. More challenging is the undulating Lake Minnewanka Loop and the short but tough grunt up to the Sunshine Village base station. Another gradual, but unrelenting climb is the 11km-long Moraine Lake Rd near Lake Louise.

Two excellent off-road options are the Goat Creek Trail, a double tracked former fire road that's good for families (with confident kids aged eight and up) and the Rundle Riverside, a root-infested singletrack that will test more-experienced mountain bikers. Both trails run between Canmore and Banff. Backcountry cyclists can follow the 29.2km (18.1-mile) out-and-back Cascade Trail, an undulating old fire road that'll quickly get you away from civilization. The trail starts

To avoid complicated car pick-ups and key exchanges when cycling or hiking point-to-point trails, contact White Mountain Adventures who run a handy summer **Bike 'n' Hike Shuttle** (☑403-762-2282; www.bikeandhikeshuttle.com) that whisks tired cyclists and hikers back to their starting point on several popular trails in the Canmore and Banff area. The shuttle covers the Goat Creek Trail, the Rundle Riverside and the Legacy Trail (for cycling/hiking) and Ha Ling Peak trail (for hiking).

Fares are C$10/20 one way/return between Canmore and Banff, C$10 one-way from Canmore to the Nordic Centre, and C$15 one-way from Canmore to the Goat Creek/Ha Ling Peak trailheads. Reserve at least one day in advance.

Good hybrid bikes start at C$35 an hour (10% off if you pick up one of its ubiquitous discount leaflets). It also rents out other useful gear, including hiking boots, day packs and tents.

Soul Ski & Bike   BICYCLE RENTAL
(Map p88; ☑403-760-1650; www.theskistop.com; 203a Bear St, Banff Town; bikes per hour C$12-14, per day C$42-49; ◷10am-7pm) This is a good snowboard-cycling crossover. Hire bikes are mostly Trance models. Some of the ski equipment is positively deluxe.

Trail Sports   CYCLING
(☑403-678-6764; www.trailsports.ab.ca; Canmore Nordic Centre; bikes per hour/day C$15/45, kids' bikes C$5/15; ◷9am-7pm Mon-Fri, to 6pm Sat & Sun) If you're visiting Canmore's busy trail center, you don't even need to bring your own bike: Rocky Mountain rigs are available from Trail Sports, right across from the visitor office at the Canmore Nordic Centre (p117). It also runs guided tours around some of the center's trails.

from the Upper Bankhead car park, 3.5km (2.2 miles) from Banff Town on the Lake Minnewanka Loop.

The free *Mountain Biking and Cycling Guide,* available at park offices, details the most popular routes, most of which are shared-use trails with horseback riders and hikers.

Rentals

Wilson Mountain Sports (p111) is pretty much the only place to rent bikes in Lake Louise. Hardtails cost C$15/39 per hour/day. Kids' bikes, trail-a-bikes and chariot trailers cost C$10/20 per hour/day.

Gear Up   BICYCLE RENTAL
(Map p118; ☑403-678-1636; www.gearupsport.com; 1302 Bow Valley Pkwy, Canmore; bikes per day from C$45; ◷9am-5pm Mon-Thu, to 6pm Fri-Sun) This clean, easy-to-navigate Canmore rental shop is handy on account of its position within free-wheeling distance of the start of the Legacy Trail. This being Canmore, it's also got climbing gear and paddleboards (including blow-ups for easy transportation). Bikes come with a handy repair kit, plus helmet and lock.

Snowtips/Bactrax   BICYCLE RENTAL
(Map p88; www.snowtips-bactrax.com; 225 Bear St, Banff Town; bikes per hour/day from C$12/35; ◷8am-8pm) Banff's best-value bike rental can have you kitted out in a matter of minutes.

Legacy Trail

Duration 1½-2 hours one way

Distance 22km (13.7 miles)

Difficulty Easy

Start Alberta Visitor Information Centre, Canmore

Finish Banff Town

Nearest Towns Canmore & Banff

Transportation Bike

Summary Massively popular paved trail that parallels the Trans-Canada Hwy into Banff – good for a gentle meander or a brisk commute.

Though mainly flat, the Legacy Trail alongside Hwy 1 is best tackled starting out from Canmore, due to more favorable tailwinds and its slight overall descent into Banff. The trail first opened in 2010, with the final 4km (2.5-mile) section from the Banff National Park entrance into Canmore completed in 2013. The trail is paved throughout and split into two lanes; always cycle on the right. Although pedestrian traffic is light, there are cyclists a-plenty – over one thousand on a good day in summer.

The official starting point is on the Bow Valley Trail (Canmore's main through-road) on the northwest side of town opposite the Alberta Visitor Information Centre. An urban

Legacy Trail

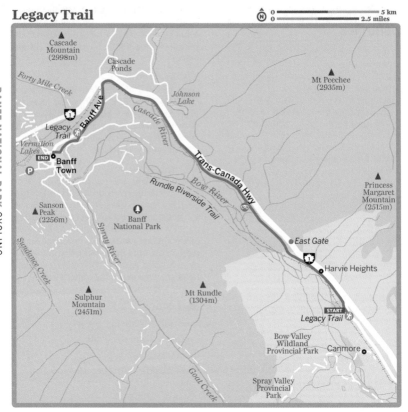

bike lane heads safely out here from the center of Canmore. The starting point is marked by a multicolored guidepost equipped with a count-o-meter detailing how many people have used the trail on any particular day/week/month.

The paved path parallels Hwy 1 and the railway line for most of its duration, dipping occasionally into small stands of trees. About 8km (5 miles) northwest of Canmore there is a picnic area where it is possible to stop and enjoy an unimpeded view of Mt Rundle.

As you approach Banff, another trail forks right under the highway. This leads to Cascade Ponds, a popular picnic area. Continue straight ahead for Banff. Soon after the fork, the trail curves west, veering away from Hwy 1 and joining the top end of Banff Ave. Here you'll encounter the only road crossing (Tunnel Mountain Rd) and pass the Banff Mountain Resort. Continue 3.5km (2.2 miles) along the paved path into downtown Banff.

Goat Creek Trail

Duration Two to three hours one way

Distance 19.1km (11.9 miles)

Difficulty Moderate

Start Whiteman's Gap, Canmore

Finish Banff Town

Nearest Towns Canmore & Banff

Transportation Car/minibus

Summary A great doubletrack between Banff and Canmore along an old fire road that's good for fit families or off-road cycling novices.

This much-recommended one-way route is best done starting from Canmore due to the favorable overall descent (1000m or 3280ft) into Banff. You can organize it with two vehicles, or use the Goat Creek Trail minibus (or an hourly Roam bus) to ferry you back to

Canmore. Alternatively, the energetic might consider cycling back along the easier Legacy Trail to make a challenging loop. Several bike shops offer a shuttle service to the trailhead.

It's a pretty easy ride along dirt and gravel doubletrack, with a few climbs and steep sections, as well as a fiddly bridge crossing and a few blind corners – watch out for other trail users, especially cyclists coming in the opposite direction.

The trailhead is high above Canmore at Whiteman's Gap, up the dirt Smith-Dorrien/Spray Trail Rd past Canmore Nordic Centre (a steep 5km (3.1-mile) climb out of town if you're not using a car or shuttle). The first section travels through pine and spruce forest along the course of Goat Creek, with the Goat Range to the south and Mt Rundle to the north. It feels wild and rewardingly remote and you can either roll along at a leisurely pace or pin back your ears and pick up the speed.

After 9.2km (5.7 miles) you'll reach a bridge over the Spray River near the old fire road. Turn right at the junction to begin the second section, which travels along the fire road all the way to the Fairmont Banff Springs parking lot.

۶&#x6;* Moraine Lake via Tramline

Duration Three to five hours round-trip

Distance 30km (17 miles)

Difficulty Difficult

Start/Finish Lake Louise Village

Nearest Town Lake Louise

Transportation Car

Summary Technically challenging, but rewarding; experienced mountain bikers rate this as the best trail in the Lake Louise area.

Goat Creek Trail

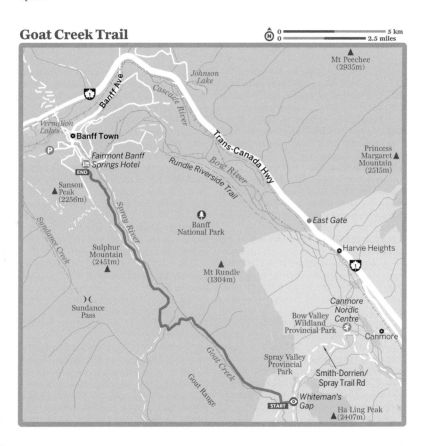

Moraine Lake via Tramline

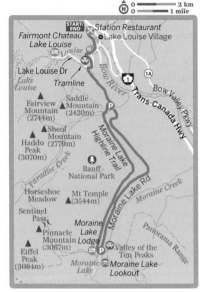

From here the views and the riding are fantastic as you follow the eastern flank of Mt Temple and encounter wonderful views over the Valley of the Ten Peaks, Moraine Lake and Consolation Valley. The route is rough, narrow and exposed in places – take it easy and admire the outlook. After around 10km (6.2 miles) you'll roll down to the shore of Moraine Lake.

You can retrace the route or head back along the paved (and steep) Moraine Lake Rd to complete the loop.

🚗 DRIVING

🚗 Minnewanka Loop

Duration 1-1½ hours round-trip

Distance 16.5km (10.2 miles)

Speed Limit 50km/h (31mph)

Start/Finish Banff

Nearest Town Banff

Summary A circular route taking in a trio of the park's loveliest lakes.

The trail to Moraine Lake begins outside the old Laggan station (now the Station Restaurant), and the first section follows the course of the old tramline that once ferried visitors up to Lake Louise in the early 1900s. If you want to avoid the uphill section, you could drive to the Paradise Valley parking lot and start the ride there.

If you're tackling the tramline, park opposite the Station Restaurant. Cross the bridge and set out along the broad trail, climbing steeply to **Louise Creek** and eventually linking up with busy Lake Louise Dr – take care crossing here, as traffic is fast and heavy.

Turn down Moraine Lake Rd. Look out for the Paradise Valley parking lot on the right, which also marks the start of the **Moraine Lake Highline Trail**. There's a junction about 1km (0.7 miles) from the Paradise Valley parking lot; turn left (south) to get onto the Highline.

Here's where the fun really starts: the trail zips into rocky, rooty singletrack that's tough and technical. Note this section is a grizzly favorite, and is sometimes closed during the peak buffalo-berry season from mid- to late summer – check with a park office before setting out, and make lots of noise at all times to avoid any bear-shaped surprises.

This loop makes a good morning or afternoon drive. There are great views of Cascade Mountain, the Palliser Range and the Fairholme Range and, if you wish, you can break up the drive with a hike to Stewart Canyon, Johnson Lake or C-Level Cirque. As with other high roads, this route is closed for snow cover from November to mid-April or May.

Heading northeast from Banff Town along Banff Ave, follow signs for Lake Minnewanka. You'll cross under Trans-Canada Hwy 1 and begin to climb along the lower flanks of Cascade Mountain; look out for waterfalls tumbling down the mountainside after heavy rain. On the right is **Cascade Ponds**, a picnic area around small pools of water.

Drive past the right-hand turn signed to Johnson Lake and continue north into the treeline, toward the stacked-up spires of the Palliser Range. At roughly the 3km (1.9-mile) mark, look out for the right-hand turn to **Lower Bankhead**, where you can wander around the ruins of an abandoned mining town constructed by the Canadian Pacific Railway (CPR) to exploit the rich coal deposits hidden deep beneath Cascade Mountain. Founded in 1903, Bankhead was once home to around 1000 people, and boasted electric power, running water, a school, a theater and even a couple of tennis courts. A disastrous

Minnewanka Loop

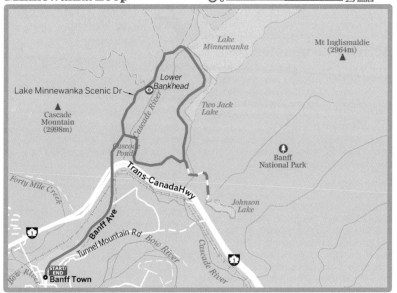

post-war collapse in coal prices and a series of costly labor strikes forced the closure of the mine in 1922. Many of the town's buildings were subsequently moved to Banff or Canmore, including the Bankhead train station, which can still be seen in Banff Town on Tunnel Mountain Dr.

Precious little now remains of this once-thriving industrial town, save for the old transformer house, the miners' lamp house and the footings of a few other key buildings. A self-guided trail winds its way around the ruins: look out for the huge slag-heaps of coal left behind after the mine's closure, spotted with wild rhubarb planted by the Chinese laborers who once lived nearby. The actual mine was located up the hill at Upper Bankhead, now the trailhead for C-Level Cirque (p56).

After 6km (3.7 miles) you'll arrive at Lake Minnewanka. Time your arrival right and you'll be able to jump on a boat for a trip around the lake (p91), otherwise just wander along the shoreline or stop for something cold from the lakeside snack shack.

From Lake Minnewanka, follow the road across the top of the lake dam toward Two Jack Lake, another popular spot with picnickers and sunbathers. The jagged mountain that looms up behind the lake is Mt Rundle, actually a crinkled ridge of peaks, which runs for 12km (7.5 miles) south all the way to Canmore. It's named after Robert Rundle, a Methodist missionary who spent much of his life working with First Nations tribes in the Bow Valley during the 1800s.

A little further on, 11km (6.8 miles) along the route, is the junction for Johnson Lake, another lakeside getaway for locals looking to escape the Banff bustle. If it's sunny, you can join people sunbathing around the lakeshore, or wander around the lake trail on cloudier days. Brave souls sometimes take the plunge into the lake's chilly waters, but you'll need a steely constitution (and preferably a wetsuit) to join them, as it stays chilly well into high summer.

From the junction the road trundles downhill and rejoins the main loop road. Turn left to head back to Banff.

⚓ OTHER ACTIVITIES

Although hiking and cycling are Banff's raison d'être and the best (and cheapest) way of experiencing the immense Rocky Mountain scenery, the park has other adventurous allures, from long-standing pursuits like horseback riding and fishing to the recent penchant for via ferratas (fixed-protection climbing routes). Unlike most other North American parks, Banff also has downhill ski areas (three of 'em), meaning it remains popular even in the frigid winter months.

Activity Companies

Banff has several agencies that can book a range of activity packages in and around the national park. Most have lots of experience with younger clients and people who are new to the sports, so they offer a great way to try out something different. If you're doing a lot of activities, booking through one agency can be very convenient, but you'll often get better deals by going direct to the provider.

Banff Adventures
Unlimited   ADVENTURE SPORTS
(Map p88; ☑ 403-762-4554; www.banffadventures. com; 211 Bear St, Bison Courtyard, Banff Town; ⊙ 7:30am-9pm Jun-Oct, 9am-9pm Nov-May) Banff's main activity booking company can organize a huge range of activities with experienced local operators, ranging from ATV tours to heli-hikes and rafting trips, and puts together its own combo packages (such as the 'Raft, Ride & Relax' tour). Its winter packages are equally comprehensive.

Inside Out Experience   ADVENTURE SPORTS
(☑ 403-949-3305; www.insideoutexperience.com) This good multi-activity provider offers mountain biking, white-water rafting, hiking and winter sports, as well as exciting combination tours involving several activities (ride and raft, saddle and paddle…you get the idea). Five-hour trips start at around C$165. The meet-up point for trips is on the Kananaskis River on Hwy 1X, just off Hwy 1 (exit 114), 30km east of Canmore.

White Mountain Adventures   ADVENTURE TOUR
(☑ 403-760-4403; www.whitemountainadventures. com; 120 Eagle Crescent, Banff Town; ⊙ 8am-5pm Mon-Fri) A well-regarded hiking and guiding service, with charter trips along popular Banff trails, covering nature spotting, local history and other points of interest – from easy strolls to heli-hiking. It also runs the ultra-helpful Sunshine Meadows shuttle in the summer.

Canoeing & Kayaking

Canoes and kayaks have played a pivotal role in Canada's history, particularly among the First Nations tribes. With numerous rivers and lakes (most of which are closed to

Driving Tour
Bow Valley Parkway

START BANFF TOWN
END LAKE LOUISE
LENGTH TWO TO 2½ HOURS ONE WAY / 52KM (32.2 MILES)

If you prefer scenery to speed, this leisurely drive between Banff Town and Lake Louise is a must-do. The Bow Valley Pkwy runs parallel to the Trans-Canada Hwy practically all the way to Lake Louise, but it's an altogether more tranquil drive. It's particularly well known for its wildlife; you'll have a great chance of spotting elk and bighorn sheep, especially early and late in the day, and if you're really lucky, you might even spot an elusive moose or black bear. Needless to say, this also makes the Bow Valley Pkwy a hot spot for collisions with animals, so keep your speed well down and keep your eyes peeled for wildlife on the edge of the road. The parkway's eastern end between the Fireside picnic area and Johnston Canyon is closed from 6pm to 9am during spring mating season (March to late June). The speed limit on the parkway is 60km/h (37mph), dropping to 30km/h (19mph) at certain points.

From Banff Town, head west on Trans-Canada Hwy 1 toward Lake Louise, taking the exit for Bow Valley Pkwy at the 5km (3.1-mile) mark. Soon after passing underneath the picturesque wooden archway that marks the parkway's start point, the road curves into forest, passing the ❶ **Muleshoe Wetlands** and the Sawback Range, which underwent a prescribed burn in 1993. Interpretive panels along the route explain the science behind forest fires.

After around 15km (9.3 miles) the road divides briefly (supposedly thanks to a lazy construction worker) before passing ❷ **Johnston Canyon** at the 18km (11.2-mile) mark. The smooth-sided limestone gorge through which Johnston Creek flows has been carved out by the river over the last 8000 years. You can walk upstream past two major waterfalls on walkways that occasionally dip beneath overhanging cliffs. Trees and moss cling to the canyon edges providing an ideal habitat for birds. Just west of the canyon is a viewpoint

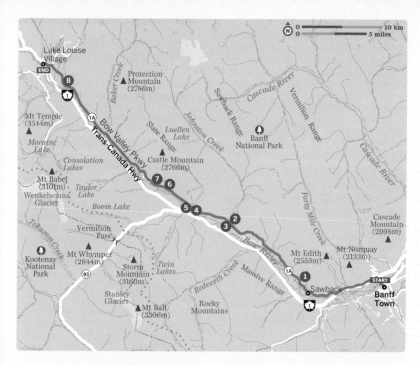

overlooking the grassy ③ **Moose Meadows**, once a favorite moose hangout, but now more often frequented by elk.

Around 5km (3.1 miles) further west, look out for a panel marking the site of ④ **Silver City**, one of several boom towns that briefly flourished around the Bow Valley during a series of mineral rushes in the 1880s and '90s. Silver City lasted barely two years – 3000 prospectors flocked to the site in 1883 after silver was said to have been found here, but the town collapsed in 1885 when it transpired that the discovery was nothing more than a moneymaking ruse propagated by unscrupulous entrepreneurs.

At the 24.5km (15.2-mile) mark you'll pass ⑤ **Castle Mountain Junction**, where a branch road heads over the Trans-Canada Hwy toward Kootenay National Park. There's a small gas station, general store and chalet complex next to the junction, which makes a good place to pick up drinks, snacks and ice creams.

North of the junction at the ⑥ **Castle Cliffs Viewpoint**, you can spy the craggy profile of Castle Mountain, so named for its castellated, fortress-like appearance, created by a combination of geological forces and natural erosion. After WWII the mountain was

briefly renamed Mt Eisenhower in honor of the US general, but locals were far from keen on the change and it was restored to Castle Mountain in 1979, although the stand-alone pillar at the southern end is still known as Eisenhower Peak.

Another 6km (3.7 miles) on, you'll pass a small ⑦ **Internment Camp Monument** that marks the site of a former prison camp that housed Ukrainian immigrants during WWI. Nearby is another pullout with grand views of Mt Whymper and the important wildlife corridor across the Vermilion Pass.

Continuing northwest toward Lake Louise, look out for a viewpoint looking southwest toward Storm Mountain, before crossing Baker Creek en route to the viewpoint at ⑧ **Morant's Curve**, a site much favored by the Canadian Pacific Railway and *National Geographic* photographer Nicholas Morant (1910–99), whose images helped publicize Banff during its early days as a national park.

The Bow Valley Pkwy ends after 47km (29.1 miles) at a T-junction. The right turn heads toward the Lake Louise Gondola, while the left turn heads toward Lake Louise and Trans-Canada Hwy 1.

motorboats) speckling the park, small human-powered boats remain popular with generations of tourists. You can hire (expensive) canoes from boathouses at Lake Louise and Moraine Lake, although the water is generally frozen from October to mid-May.

Stand-up paddleboarding has recently become popular on Banff's more sheltered lakes. Paddleboards (including more easily transported inflatable varieties) can be hired at the Banff Canoe Club in Banff Town and Gear Up (p73) in Canmore for around C$80 a day.

Banff Canoe Club   BOAT RENTAL
(Map p87; ☑ 403-762-5005; www.banffcanoeclub. com; cnr Wolf St & Bow Ave, Banff Town; canoes per hour C$36; ☻9am-9pm mid-May–mid-Sep) This new community resource rents boats from its river dock at the end of Wolf St. Grab a canoe or kayak and slide up the Bow River or the narrower, lazier Forty Mile Creek to Vermilion Lakes, where beavers will swim underneath your boat. Paddleboards are also available.

White-Water Rafting

The best rafting is outside the park (and province) on the Kicking Horse River in Yoho National Park, BC. There are class IV rapids here, meaning big waves, swirling pools and a guaranteed soaking. Lesser rapids are found on the Kananaskis River and the Horseshoe Canyon section of the Bow River. The Bow River around Banff is better for mellower float trips.

There are many companies to choose from, but it's always wise to go with a well-established operator, as white-water rafting is potentially a highly dangerous sport. Banff companies run trips to all of the above rivers.

Rapids are classed from I (easy) to V (expert) – the extreme class VI is for rapids that have rarely been completed successfully.

Hydra River Guides   RAFTING
(Map p88; ☑ 403-762-4554; www.raftbanff.com; 211 Bear St, Banff Town; ☻9am-7pm) Based in Bison Court, this well-regarded company offers three core trips along the Kicking Horse River. The most popular is the 20km (12.4-mile) Kicking Horse Classic (C$125), which tackles a varied range of rapids up to class IV, and includes a BBQ lunch. Hardier rafters could try the full-day trip (C$165), while novices might prefer the more sedate float trip (C$55). Hydra also offers combo packages including horseback riding, zip-lining and ATV driving.

Driving Tour
Into the Icefields

START LAKE LOUISE
END SUNWAPTA PASS
LENGTH FOUR HOURS ONE WAY /
230KM (143 MILES)

This once-in-a-lifetime road trip starts in Lake Louise and follows the southern section of the Icefields Pkwy to the Saskatchewan Crossing, near the border with Jasper National Park. It's a long route, so set out early and leave yourself plenty of time to enjoy the drive. Make sure you start out with a full tank, as the only gas stations en route are at Lake Louise or Saskatchewan Crossing. The road is officially open year-round, but is often closed due to snow between November and April. Note that the speed limit on this road is 90km/h (56mph). Large trucks are banned, making for a quieter, more pleasant journey.

Start at Lake Louise and head north along Hwy 1 to the signed turnoff to Jasper. You'll reach a parks tollbooth 2km (1.2 miles) north of the junction; as you'll already have your park pass, you can zip through without stopping.

To the west rises the Waputik Range, dominated by 2755m (9039ft) Waputik Peak, overlooking the winding Bow River. Around 16.1km (10 miles) from the start of the parkway you'll reach ❶ **Hector Lake**, named after James Hector, a geologist and naturalist who accompanied the historic Palliser Expedition to chart unexplored areas of western Canada between 1857 and 1860.

After 33km (20.5 miles), stop at the ❷ **Crowfoot Glacier lookout**, to see the icy behemoth nestled on the rocky flanks of Crowfoot Mountain above ice-blue Bow Lake. The glacier was named for its three clawlike 'toes,' but unfortunately its lowest toe had melted by the 1940s.

At the northern end of Bow Lake is ❸ **Num-Ti-Jah Lodge** (p109), built by the famous trailsman Jimmy Simpson, who was born in England in 1895 but went on to become one of the Rockies' best-known explorers, adventurers and guides. The lodge makes an ideal stop for lunch, and you can always burn off the calories by following the trail to Bow Falls.

From Bow Lake, the road climbs toward **4 Bow Pass**, which at 2069m (6788ft) is the highest point on the parkway. Nearby you'll find the turnoff to the busy **5 Peyto Lake & Bow Summit Lookout**, named after the park warden Bill Peyto. A 400m (0.2-mile) wooded trail leads from the parking lot to a decked viewpoint that looks out over the sapphire-blue lake. It's usually packed, but there's a quieter viewpoint further on, near the path to Bow Summit Lookout.

Back in the car, head 6km (3.7 miles) further north to a pullout overlooking Snowbird Glacier, which clings to the edge of Patterson Mountain like an avalanche frozen in mid-motion. Further north is the parking lot for **6 Mistaya Canyon** (p64), reached by a 500m (0.3-mile) walk from the pullout. Carved out by the Mistaya River, the curving limestone canyon is spanned by a wooden bridge from where you can look right down into the pounding white water.

A short drive northwest brings you to the **7 Saskatchewan River Crossing**, established by 19th-century fur trappers who crossed the North Saskatchewan River here on their way through the Rockies to British Columbia. Today, it marks the junction of Hwy 93 (the Icefields Pkwy) and Hwy 11 (the David Thompson Hwy). It is home to the only facilities between Lake Louise and the Columbia Icefield – a non-fancy motel, cafeteria-style restaurant and gas station.

From the crossing, the road traverses river flats (often frequented by elk and birdlife) en route to Cirrus Mountain, where snowmelt streams down the mountainside, creating a sheet of waterfalls known as the **8 Weeping Wall**, which freeze solid in winter. From here the road sweeps around a huge hairpin known as the **9 Big Bend** and climbs up the aptly named Big Hill; at the top there's a fantastic viewpoint that looks back down the North Saskatchewan Valley and to Mt Saskatchewan. Nearby are the aptly named Bridal Veil Falls, named for the interlaced pattern of their cascade.

At 230km (143 miles) into the trip, you'll reach the barren treeless **10 Sunwapta Pass**, 2023m (6637ft) above sea level and the most avalanche-prone section of the road in winter. The pass marks the boundary with Jasper National Park; you can either retrace your route back to Lake Louise, or continue on the Icefields Pkwy into Jasper.

Rainbow Riders   RAFTING

(☑ 403-678-7238; www.rainbowriders.com; cnr Hwy 1 & Hwy 1X) One of the best options for rafting on the Bow and Kananaskis Rivers. The introductory class (C$75) covers class I–III rapids through the Canoe Meadows on the Kananaskis. It also offers float trips (C$59) and riverboarding (C$98), which is a bit like bodyboarding on river rapids; you'll need to be a strong swimmer, but it's dangerously addictive.

Chinook Rafting   RAFTING

(Map p88; ☑ 866-330-7238; www.chinookrafting. com; 215 Banff Ave, Banff Town; ☉ 9am-5pm) A great company for families and groups, run jointly with Discover Banff Tours. Family-rated tours (adult/child C$89/59) are on the Kananaskis River, while Adventurous (C$92) and Wild (C$128) tours are on the Bow and Kicking Horse Rivers; kids need to be aged 12 or over for the more advanced trips. You can even train to be a river guide if you really catch the rafting bug.

Rocky Mountain Raft Tours   RAFTING

(☑ 403-762-3632; www.banffrafttours.com; Golf Course Loop Rd, Banff Town; ☉ mid-May–Sep) Banff's oldest rafting company sticks to what it knows best: easy excursions along the Bow River from their put-in point just below Bow Falls. Floats are reasonably priced and walk-ins are accepted. The one-hour Hoodoo Tour is C$50 and the 2½-hour Bow Safari is C$85.

Fishing

The fish in Banff might not be as plentiful as they were in the days of Bill Peyto and co, but angling is still a quintessential way to experience Banff's sedate side.

A fishing permit (per day/year C$9.80/34.30) is required for angling anywhere in the national parks, and can be purchased at visitor centers. The *Fishing Regulations* summary details current catch allowances; it is illegal to keep many endangered native species such as bull trout, kokanee salmon and cutthroat trout.

The most popular area to fish is the Bow River, which is open year-round (although ice fishing is always banned). Ghost Lake, Johnson Lake, Lake Minnewanka, Two Jack Lake and the Vermilion Lakes are usually open mid-May to mid-September.

Banff Fishing Unlimited   FISHING

(☑ 403-762-4936; www.banff-fishing.com) Year-round fly-fishing, spin-casting and lake fishing with experienced local guides. The full-day 'Walk and Wade' trips (from C$281 per person) combine guided hikes with some of the best fishing spots on the Bow River.

Tightline Adventures   FISHING

(Map p88; ☑ 403-762-4548; www.tightline adventures.com; trips for 2 people from C$225; ☉ May-Oct) Specializes in dry-fly fishing for rainbow and brook trout in the Bow River, and offers walk-and-wade packages to more remote river stretches.

Lake Minnewanka Guided Fishing   FISHING

(Map p87; www.brewster.ca/canadian-rockies/ destinations/banff/activities/guided-fishing-trips; half/full day for 2 adults C$425/550; ☉ Jun-Sep) Offers guided boat trips on Lake Minnewanka for lake trout and whitefish.

Climbing

Climbers have been flocking to Banff's sky-piercing peaks and finger-numbing rock faces since the sport first took off in the late 1800s. Yamnuska, Mt Rundle and Ha Ling Peak are just some of the best-known ascents, but there are hundreds more to discover. Unless you're an experienced climber, it's worth employing the services of a local guide to make sure you get the most out of your experience on the mountain and stay safe at the same time.

Canmore can validly claim to be the climbing capital of Canada and is the HQ of the legendary **Alpine Club of Canada** (☑ 403-678-3200; www.alpineclubofcanada.ca), founded by AO Wheeler in 1906. The organization can put you in touch with qualified guides across the Canadian Rockies.

Via Ferrata   ROCK CLIMBING

(☑ 844-667-7829; www.summer.banffnorquay.com; ☉ Jun-Oct) Part of the white-knuckle craze currently gripping Banff, these fixed-protection climbing routes on Mt Norquay offer three options to test your head for heights: namely, the Explorer (C$139; 2½ hours), the Ridgewalker (C$179; four hours) and the new-in-2015 Mountaineer (C$299; six hours). Prices include full safety kit, a guide and passage up the Norquay chairlift to the start point.

The latter trip includes passage over a three-wire suspension bridge (basically a

VIA FERRATAS

Banff's newest adventure activity was invented by the Italian military in WWI and has been popular in Italy for nearly a century. Engaged in a terrifying conflict with the Austrians in the Dolomites during the Great War, the Italians adapted ways of using ladders and ropes to build fixed-protection climbing paths known as *via ferratas* (iron roads) in order to ease the movement of troops and supplies across the rugged Alpine peaks. Upgraded with steel steps, narrow suspension bridges and heavy-duty wire after the war, the via ferratas became popular with tourists and were promoted as a cross between strenuous hiking and full-blown rock climbing. Suddenly, non-mountaineers were able to experience the kind of thrills normally reserved for skilled alpinists and given access to terrain that would have otherwise remained out of bounds.

Via ferratas in North America are a relatively new phenomenon. Banff's operation – which offers guided-only trips – opened with two routes in 2014, with a third route introduced in 2015. It is the first and – so far – only 'iron road' in a Canadian national park.

You don't need any mountaineering experience to use a via ferrata, just a reasonable level of fitness, a head for heights and a healthy sense of adventure. Safety is assured by using a standard via ferrata harness equipped with two carabiner clips. One carabiner clip is always attached to a ladder or cable, ensuring you don't fall off.

fixed-protection tightrope walk) to the top of Mt Norquay. Exhilarating is the word!

Yamnuska Mountain Adventures   ROCK CLIMBING
(☑ 403-678-4164; www.yamnuska.com; Suite 200, Summit Centre, 50 Lincoln Park, Canmore; ☺ 9am-5pm Mon-Fri, to 4pm Sat) This well-regarded company offers daily instruction courses, plus more challenging trips for intermediate and advanced climbers. From Tuesday to Saturday in July and August there's a daily climb for C$140 per person, including gear and transport. Just show up at Bow Falls in Banff at 8:30am.

On Top Mountaineering   ROCK CLIMBING
(☑ 800-506-7177; www.ontopmountaineering.com; 340 Canyon Close, Canmore) This locally run outfit offers five-day organized climbing courses in the Rockies throughout summer for C$830 per person, which provide an ideal introduction to the sport for new climbers, and help more experienced climbers hone their skills. Alternatively, you can devise your own custom route with a private guide from C$450 for two people.

Golf

With Kananaskis' golf course out of action indefinitely after damage sustained during the 2013 floods, you're better off heading into the national park.

Banff Springs Golf Course   GOLF
(Map p87; ☑ 403-762-6801; www.fairmont.com; ☺ May-Oct) Laid out in 1928 and impressively located in the shadow of Mt Rundle and Sulphur Mountain, this is one of the Rockies' most famous fairways. You'll need to dress up for the occasion – no denim, no sweats, dress shorts only and collared shirts required for men. Shoe and club rentals are available.

Even if you're not planning on a round, the road through the golf course makes a lovely bike ride, and is also a good place for spotting elk, especially at dawn and dusk.

Horseback Riding

Banff's first European explorers – fur traders and railway engineers – penetrated the region primarily on horseback. You can recreate their pioneering spirit on guided rides with a handful of well-established operators.

Banff Trail Riders   HORSEBACK RIDING
(Map p88; ☑ 403-762-4551; www.horseback.com; 132 Banff Ave, Banff Town; ☺ 9am-6pm) Trail Riders' two stables in Banff and Spray Creek run lots of horseback riding tours. Easy half-day trips are run regularly along the Bow River, Sundance Loop, Bow Valley and the Spray River, from C$54 to C$119 per person. For an authentic frontier experience, it also offers a breakfast and evening cookout (C$117).

For something more challenging, multiday expeditions to Trail Riders' backcountry lodges start at C$499 per person for a two-day trip. It also offers special trips geared toward photographers and wildlife enthusiasts.

Timberline Tours
HORSEBACK RIDING

(Map p94; ☎ 888-858-3388; www.timberlinetours. ca; St Piran Rd, Lake Louise) This outfitter has its corral near Lake Louise, and offers 1½-hour trips along the lake (C$80), half-day rides up to Lake Agnes Teahouse (C$125) and the Plain of Six Glaciers (C$145), and full-day rides to Paradise Valley, Skoki Lodge, Baker Lake and the Moraine Lake Highline Trail (C$199). Overnight trips and pony rides are also available.

Skiing & Snowboarding

Strange though it may seem, there are three ski areas in the national park (something almost unheard of in a US national park), two of them in the vicinity of Banff Town. Lofty, snowy Sunshine Village is considered world-class; Lake Louise has more skiable terrain than practically anywhere else in Canada; while Mt Norquay, 5km (3.1 miles) from downtown Banff, is your half-day family-friendly option.

You can get a collective ticket for all the Banff resorts with a **Big Three ski pass** (www. skibig3.com; 3-/7-day pass adult C$310/679), which allows you access to a combined area of 32.4 sq km (12.5 sq miles) and 290 runs.

Passes include gondolas, lifts and free shuttles to the ski domains, but as always you'll usually get better value if you buy them as part of an organized package tour, which includes accommodations at local hotels. The peak months are December and January, especially during the school holidays around Christmas and New Year. For the best deals, aim to ski early or late in the season; snow lingers at many of the highest runs until late April and even early May, and discounts are often substantial for off-season packages.

All the resorts have ski schools where you can pick up the basics or graduate to more advanced skills, as well as day-care facilities for younger kids. The websites for each resort have regular snow reports and piste webcams so you can check the snow before you go.

Mt Norquay
SKIING

(☎ 403-762-4421; www.banffnorquay.com; Mt Norquay Rd; day ski pass C$65; 👪) Mt Norquay is the nearest ski area to downtown Banff

---

WILDLIFE CROSSINGS

As you drive north from Banff toward Lake Louise along the Trans-Canada Hwy, look out for the six arched overpasses spanning the road. They're not for humans, but are actually wildlife crossings, which have been specially designed to allow Banff's animals to cross the road without fear of getting mown down by a passing truck or recreational vehicle (RV).

Trans-Canada Hwy 1 sits slap bang in the middle of several key 'wildlife corridors' (migratory routes between seasonal habitats) that crisscross the Bow Valley. Thousands of animals have been killed while trying to cross the highway over the years, especially since the road was twinned in 1981, and collisions with vehicles remain the number one cause of wildlife fatalities in the national park.

In order to reduce the risk of accidents and protect the park's increasingly fragile animal population, the wildlife crossings were built at a cost of around C$1 million each, alongside 38 other underpasses that tunnel beneath the road at various points.

They seem to be working: according to a park study, 11 different species of large mammals used the crossings in excess of 120,000 times between 1996 and 2012. Intriguingly, animals seem to have adapted to the crossings at different speeds: elk and deer began using them almost straightaway, while it took as long as five years for more wary species such as bears and wolves to adapt to them.

Different species also appear to have preferences for the types of bridges they like to use: elk, moose, wolves and grizzly bears seem to like crossings that are high, wide and short, while black bears and cougars prefer them long, low and narrow.

A new project is currently underway to monitor exactly which animals are using the crossings and how often, using DNA from barbed-wire fur traps positioned at the crossing entrances. Once the data has been collected and analyzed, it's very likely that there could be several more crossings built around the Lake Louise area over the next few years. Watch this space – or rather, watch this road.

(10 minutes by car or shuttle on the Mt Norquay Rd) and also the park's smallest. Dating back to 1926, it was the first ski resort in Canada to install a chairlift (in 1948). There are 77 hectares (190 acres) of skiable terrain, 33 trails and a drop of 503m (1650ft).

The limited runs and sometimes iffy snow has its advantages, keeping away the serious powder-hounds and providing a non-intimidating scene for families and beginners. However, unbeknownst to many, Norquay has a few steep double black diamond runs that will turn your hair whiter than the mountain snow. There's also a terrain park, ski school and night-skiing at weekends. The scenery is spectacular.

Sunshine Village   SKIING
(www.skibanff.com; day ski pass C$89) If restricted time or funds mean that you can only ski one resort in Banff, Sunshine Village is probably the best to choose. Sunshine's ski area is much larger than Norquay at a total of 13.6 sq km (5.3 sq miles), divided between 107 runs and the 6-hectare (15-acre) Rogers Terrain Park. With such a huge area, the resort can comfortably handle several thousand skiers and still feel relatively uncrowded.

All the runs are at high elevations (over 2133m/7000ft), so snow conditions are nearly always reliable on the three mountains (Lookout, Standish and Goat's Eye). It's also unusual in that it only needs to manufacture a small amount of snow every year: snowpack in good years can be up to 9m (29ft), most of which is captured naturally through an ingenious system of snow-fencing. The downside: it can be windy and cold.

Sunshine is only around 15km (9.3 miles) from downtown Banff, so many ski packages use off-mountain accommodations and employ shuttle buses to get you up to the resort. If you prefer to be closer to the snow, Sunshine also has Banff's only ski-in, ski-out hotel at the Sunshine Mountain Lodge.

Lake Louise Ski Area   SKIING
(Map p94; www.skilouise.com; day ski pass from C$89; [🚌]) The largest of the Big Three resorts is Lake Louise, offering a humungous skiable 17 sq km (6.5 sq miles), divided between 139 runs. It's probably the best for families, with a good spread of beginner-rated and intermediate-rated runs. The longest (8km/ 4.9 miles) is on the Larch Face, and there are lots of beginner runs on the Front Side/South Face, especially around the base area.

Lake Louise has plenty of powder and off-piste skiing for advanced riders too, as well as a snowboard park. However, its average snowfall is only around half that of Sunshine Village, meaning that snow machines are often used to supplement the natural snowpack.

Cross-Country Skiing

It might not have the adrenaline edge of downhilling, but cross-country skiing has a long mountain heritage and it's about the only way to explore the national park's trails in winter. It's one of Canada's fastest-growing sports.

Over 80km (50 miles) of trails are groomed by park authorities specifically for the use of cross-country skiers, including the Spray River Loop, Cave & Basin Trail, Cascade Fire Rd and the Golf Loop near Banff, and the Moraine Lake Rd and Lake Louise Shoreline Trail near Lake Louise Village.

Check with Parks Canada (www.parks canada.gc.ca/banff) to see which trails are open before you set out, as heavy snowfall means that trails are sometimes closed at short notice.

Cross-country gear can be rented at any of the ski stores in Banff, and most local activity agencies can help book taster sessions if you're a first-timer.

Other Winter Sports

Skiing isn't Banff's only winter activity. Ice-skating is often possible at various spots, depending on seasonal conditions. The Fairmont hotels in Lake Louise and Banff both maintain small skating areas, as does the Banff Recreation Centre. Vermilion Lakes, Johnson Lake and Lake Minnewanka often have skateable ice, but check with a park office first.

Another way to get out into the backcountry in winter is on showshoes, which are thought to have been used by First Nations people in the Rockies for hundreds of years. Most local mountaineering and activity companies offer taster sessions in both snowshoeing and ice-skating, and can also arrange guided ice-climbing trips for intermediate and advanced climbers.

◉ SIGHTS

Banff is a piece of history in itself. Founded in 1885, it is the world's third-oldest national park (and Canada's oldest). Cataloging past triumphs and tribulations, the townsite supports a healthy cache of four museums, virtually unprecedented for a 'natural' national park.

◉ Banff Town

Banff Town is something of an enigma. A resort town with souvenir shops, nightclubs and fancy restaurants is not something any national-park purist would want to claim credit for. But looks can be misleading. First, Banff is no ordinary town. It developed not as a residential district, but as a service center for the park that surrounds it. Second, the commercialism of Banff Ave is deceptive. Wander five minutes in either direction and (though you may not initially realize it) you're in wild country, a primeval food chain of bears, elk, wolves and bighorn sheep. Banff, civilized? It's just a rumor.

Banff Avenue STREET

(Map p88) A little over a century ago, Banff Ave *was* Banff. Initially, the central street was home to little more than a handful of hotels, homesteads and trail outfitters, but the town slowly began to develop following the arrival of the Canadian Pacific Railway (CPR) in 1885 and the opening of the landmark Banff Springs Hotel on the banks of the Bow River in 1888.

Though much of the architecture of Banff Ave is modern, it's still possible to make out a few of the historic buildings that would have greeted early visitors. The most obvious is the timber-framed **Banff Park Museum**, which has hardly changed since its construction in 1903. Further along the street, look out for the **Cascade Dance Hall** at number 120 (built in 1920), the original **Brewster Transportation Building** at number 202 (built in 1939, now occupied by the Rose & Crown pub), the **Banff School Auditorium** (built in 1939, now occupied by the Banff Information Centre) and St Paul's Presbyterian Church at number 230 (built in 1930).

There are several more historic houses around town that are worth seeking out – the Banff Information Centre can supply you with a free leaflet, *Walking Through Banff's History*, which points out the town's most important buildings. Alternatively, you can join one of the Whyte Museum's guided tours.

★ Whyte Museum of the Canadian Rockies MUSEUM

(Map p88; www.whyte.org; 111 Bear St; admission C$8; ⊙10am-5pm) The century-old Whyte Museum is more than just a rainy-day option. It boasts a beautiful gallery displaying some great pieces on an ever-changing basis, while the permanent collection tells the story of Banff and the hardy men and women who forged a home among the mountains.

Attached to the museum is an archive with thousands of photographs spanning the history of the town and park; these are available for reprint. The museum also gives out leaflets for a self-guided *Banff Culture Walk*.

Banff Park Museum MUSEUM

(Map p87; ☑403-762-1558; 93 Banff Ave; adult/child C$3.90/1.90; ⊙10am-5pm) Occupying an old wooden Canadian Pacific Railway building dating from 1903, this museum is a national historic site. Its exhibits – a taxidermic collection of animals found in the park, including grizzly and black bears, plus a tree carved with graffiti dating from 1841 – have changed little since the museum opened a century ago.

Bow Falls WATERFALL

(Map p87) About 500m (0.3 miles) south of town, just before the junction with Spray River, the Bow River plunges into a churning melee of white water at Bow Falls. Though the drop is relatively small – just 9m (30ft) at its highest point – Bow Falls is a dramatic sight, especially in spring following heavy snowmelt.

Paved trails run along both sides of the river, and make a lovely leisurely afternoon stroll from Banff; go early or late in the day in summer to avoid the endless procession of coach tours. The **west bank viewpoint** is the best place to watch the waterfall in full thundering flow, while the east bank trail leads to another famous viewpoint at **Surprise Corner** (Map p87), with a view across the falls toward the Fairmont Banff Springs hotel. It also marks the start of the Hoodoos Trail (p50), which leads along the Bow River to a landscape of bizarre rock pillars shaped by eons of natural erosion.

The river itself begins 100km upstream as meltwater from the Bow Glacier, flowing south through Banff en route to the prairies and Hudson Bay far beyond. The river has been known to First Nations people for well over 10,000 years; to the Cree Nation, it was known as *manachaban sipi* (literally 'the place from which bows are taken').

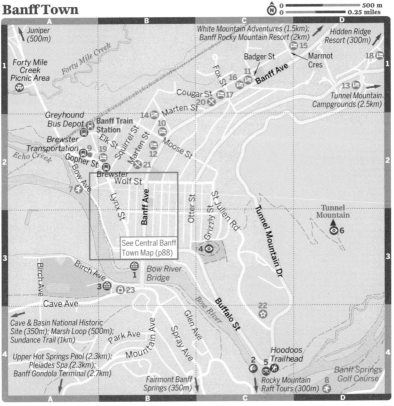

Banff Town

◎ Sights
1 Banff Park Museum	B3
2 Bow Falls	C4
3 Buffalo Nations Luxton Museum	B3
4 Old Banff Cemetery	C3
5 Surprise Corner Viewpoint	C4
6 Tunnel Mountain	D3

◎ Activities, Courses & Tours
7 Banff Canoe Club	A2
8 Banff Springs Golf Course	D4
9 Brewster	A2
Lake Minnewanka Guided Fishing	(see 9)

⊜ Sleeping
10 Banff Aspen Lodge	B2
11 Banff Caribou Lodge	C1
12 Banff Ptarmigan Inn	B2
13 Buffalo Mountain Lodge	D1
14 Buffaloberry	B2
15 Bumpers Inn	D1
16 Charlton's Cedar Court	C1
17 Fox Hotel & Suites	C1
18 HI-Banff Alpine Centre	D1
19 Poplar Inn	B2

⊗ Eating
20 Evergreen	C1
21 Safeway	B2

⊜ Drinking & Nightlife
Whitebark Cafe	(see 10)

⊛ Entertainment
22 Banff Centre	C4

⊝ Shopping
23 Banff Indian Trading Post	B3

Central Banff Town

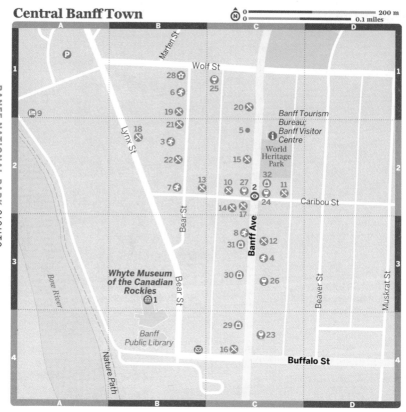

Banff Gondola CABLE CAR
(☎ 403-762-2523; Mountain Ave; adult/child C$40/20; ⊙ 8am-9pm) In summer or winter you can summit a peak near Banff thanks to the Banff Gondola, whose four-person enclosed cars glide up to the top of Sulphur Mountain in less than 10 minutes. Named for the thermal springs that emanate from its base, this peak is a perfect viewing point and a tick-box Banff attraction.

There are a couple of restaurants on top, plus an extended hike on boardwalks to Sanson Peak, an old weather station. Some people hike all the way up the mountain on a zigzagging 5.6km (3.5-mile) trail. You can travel back down on the gondola for half-price and recover in the hot springs.

The gondola is 4km south of central Banff. The easiest way to get there is to catch Route 1 on the Roam bus; alternatively, you can hunt for a spot in the enormous car park.

Upper Hot Springs Pool SPRING
(www.hotsprings.ca; Mountain Ave; adult/child/family C$7.30/6.30/22.50; ⊙ 9am-11pm mid-May–mid-Oct, 10am-10pm Sun-Thu, to 11pm Fri & Sat mid-Oct–mid-May) Banff quite literally wouldn't be Banff if it weren't for its hot springs, which gush out from 2.5km (1.5 miles) beneath Sulphur Mountain at a constant temperature of between 32°C (90°F) and 46°C (116°F). It was the hot springs that drew the first tourists to Banff, and you can still sample the soothing mineral waters at the Upper Hot Springs Pool, near the Banff Gondola.

Several hotels once occupied the site where the present-day Upper Hot Springs Pool stands – Dr RG Brett's Grand View Villa, built in 1886, was joined by the Hydro Hotel in 1890, but both establishments burnt down and were replaced in the 1930s by a new bathhouse in the fashionable art-deco style.

Renovations have since masked some of the bathhouse's period elegance, but the hot

Central Banff Town

◎ Top Sights
1 Whyte Museum of the Canadian
  Rockies.. B3

◎ Sights
2 Banff Avenue....................................... C2

◐ Activities, Courses & Tours
3 Banff Adventures Unlimited................ B2
4 Banff Trail Riders................................. C3
  Chinook Rafting ....(see 5)
5 Discover Banff Tours........................... C2
  GyPSy ....(see 5)
  Hydra River Guides..........................(see 3)
6 Snowtips/Bactrax................................ B1
7 Soul Ski & Bike B2
8 Tightline Adventures........................... C3

◉ Sleeping
9 Bow View Lodge................................... A1

✖ Eating
  Bear St Tavern ....(see 21)
  Bison Restaurant & Terrace.........(see 21)
10 Block Kitchen & Bar........................... C2
11 Bruno's Cafe & Grill C2
12 Cows... C3
13 Coyote's Deli & Grill........................... B2
14 Eddie Burger & Bar............................. C2

  Evelyn's Coffee Bar........................(see 5)
15 Grizzly House......................................C2
16 Le Beaujolais.......................................C4
17 Maple Leaf Grille................................C2
18 Melissa's Restaurant B2
19 Nourish B1
20 Park C1
21 Saltlik..B2
22 Wild Flour..B2

◉ Drinking & Nightlife
23 Banff Ave Brewing Co..........................C4
  Hoodoo Lounge ....(see 17)
24 Rose & Crown C2
25 St James's Gate Olde Irish Pub........... C1
26 Tommy's Neighbourhood Pub C3
27 Wild Bill's Legendary Saloon...............C2

◉ Entertainment
28 Lux Cinema Centre B1

◉ Shopping
29 All in the Wild Gallery & Gifts.............C4
30 Chocolaterie Bernard Callebaut...........C3
31 Monod Sports......................................C3
32 Rocky Mountain Soap Company..........C2
  Trail Rider Store ....(see 4)
  Viewpoint......................................(see 27)

springs still rank as one of those not-to-be-missed Banff experiences – there aren't many places in the world where you can take a hot bath with a mountain view as spectacular as this.

The pools get busy in season, so aim for a late dip if you prefer to have the water to yourself (alternatively, you can hire the whole place for C$270 per hour). Towels, lockers and swimsuits are available for hire, and the **Pleiades Spa** (per 30min/hour C$60/95) offers treatments such as shiatsu, hot-stone massage and reiki.

**Cave & Basin National
Historic Site**   HISTORIC SITE
(☑ 403-762-1557; Cave Ave; adult/child C$3.90/1.90; ◔10am-5pm daily mid-May–mid-Oct, noon-4pm Wed-Sun mid-Oct–mid-May) The Canadian national-park system was effectively born at these hot springs, discovered accidentally by three Canadian Pacific Railway employees on their day off in 1883, but known to Aboriginals for 10,000 years. Uncovering a thermal gold mine, the springs quickly became a bun fight for private businesses who offered facilities for bathers to enjoy the then-trendy thermal treatments.

To avert an environmental catastrophe, the government stepped in, deciding to declare Banff Canada's first national park in order to preserve the springs. You can't swim here any more, but the site reopened as an impressive museum in May 2013 after a two-year restoration. The original cave and the old outdoor springs and bathhouse (closed in 1971) can be viewed, alongside a lovingly curated cinematic exhibition of Parks Canada's cache of 44 national parks. Leading out from the complex are two trails: an interpretive walk along boardwalks to the cave vent; and the 2.3km (1.4 mile) **Marsh Loop** trail across the park's only natural river marsh.

Marsh Loop   NATURE RESERVE
This 2.3km (1.4 mile) loop trail begins near the Cave & Basin National Historic Site and meanders through one of Banff's most important areas of natural marshland. It's an excellent spot for bird-watching: keep your eyes peeled for red-winged blackbirds, green-winged teals and yellowthroats, as well as colorful butterflies and dragonflies. Part of the route follows a wooden boardwalk and leads to a **fish-viewing platform** and a **bird hide**. For a

THE BIRTH OF A NATIONAL PARK

Canada's present-day national-park system can trace its origins back to the discovery of three geothermally heated springs near Banff in the autumn of 1883. Although First Nations people had known about the hot springs around Banff for well over 10,000 years, the first white man to set eyes on them was James Hector, who recorded the springs on the Palliser Expedition of 1859, probably following the advice of local Stoneys. Two surveyors working for the Canadian Pacific Railway revisited the springs in 1874, but it was brothers Tom and William McCardell, and their partner Frank McCabe, that changed the history of the springs for good.

In the autumn of 1883, they crossed the marshy area to the west of present-day Banff and stumbled across a series of deep chambers filled with naturally hot water. When William was lowered by his companions into one of the caves, he's reported to have described it as being 'like some fantastic dream from a tale of *The Arabian Nights*.' The three companions smelled much more than just the odor of the sulfurous water – with the fashion for spa bathing still in full swing in Europe, and hot water on tap still an undreamt-of luxury, there was the whiff of money around the hot springs. Together they staked a claim on the area, though ownership soon degenerated into legal wranglings over mineral rights and land claims, forcing the government to step in and declare the springs the property of Canada – sowing the seeds for the birth of Banff National Park and the National Park Act, eventually enacted in 1930.

The springs themselves proved to be just the money-spinner the three men had hoped, although none of them saw any of the proceeds. Victorians and First Nations peoples alike believed the waters had healing properties (supposedly good for everything from arthritis to stinky feet) and within a few short years resort spas had sprung up all across the foot of Sulphur Mountain.

By the early 1900s, the precious water was being pumped to a health sanatorium on the site of present-day Canada Pl, while companies were bottling the water for export to the distant corners of Canada. There were even bars along Banff Ave where customers could take a tot of gin or rum along with a splash of mineral water. And though the medicinal properties of the waters have never quite been proven, there's no doubt that sinking into the hot waters with a view of the surrounding mountains is a fantastically soothing experience.

longer walk, you could continue on the trail to Sundance Canyon (p54).

South of the Marsh Loop, a band of forest on the flanks of Sulphur Mountain has been designated as the Middle Springs Wildlife Corridor to allow large mammals (including bears, wolves and cougars) to migrate across the valley without having to enter the townsite. The area is permanently off-limits to people, but animals don't always respect the boundaries, so look out for wildlife warnings and trail closures around Marsh Loop and Sundance Canyon.

Buffalo Nations Luxton Museum MUSEUM
(Map p87; ☎403-762-2388; www.buffalonations museum.net; 1 Birch Ave; adult/child C$10/5; ☺10am-7pm May-Sep, 11am-5pm Oct-Apr) The Luxton Museum is essentially the story of the Alberta Aboriginal people with a strong emphasis on the Cree, Blackfoot, Blood and Stoney peoples. The displays, though a bit dusty, are pretty informative and contain some impressive eagle-feather headdresses and a life-size replica of a rather macabre sun dance ceremony.

You'll probably learn an interesting fact or two here, but the museum won't delay you more than 30 minutes, making the C$10 entrance fee a little steep.

Vermilion Lakes NATURE RESERVE
Northwest of the townsite, this trio of tranquil lakes is a great place for wildlife spotting – elk, beavers, bald eagles and ospreys can often be seen around the lakeshore, especially at dawn and dusk. A paved driveway – part of the Legacy bike trail – runs along the lake's southern side for 4.5km (2.8 miles), but the proximity of the Trans-Canada Hwy means that it's not as peaceful as it could be.

Old Banff Cemetery CEMETERY
(Map p87; Buffalo St) Banff's shady cemetery is worth a visit, especially if you're interested in the town's history. Some of the gravestones

date back to the 1890s; among the famous folk buried here are the pioneering trail guides Tom Wilson (who discovered Lake Louise), Jim Brewster (the founder of Brewster Transportation) and Bill Peyto; the artists Peter and Catharine Whyte; and the frontierswoman, naturalist and writer Mary Schäffer-Warren, whose house can be seen just across the street from the cemetery.

Tunnel Mountain   MOUNTAIN

(Map p87) It might be Banff's smallest mountain (1692m/5551ft), but Tunnel Mountain is still one of the town's most recognizable landmarks. The mountain's distinctive rippled profile looms up to the east of town, and was known to the Stoney people as *tatanga* (buffalo), as it resembles a sleeping buffalo when seen from the north and east.

From the north side of St Julien Rd, a short trail (4.3 km/2.6 miles) switchbacks up the mountainside to the summit, offering an airy view over Banff Town.

The mountain gets its modern name courtesy of the Canadian Pacific Railway (CPR) surveyor Major AB Rogers who, while laying the groundwork for the arrival of the railway in Banff in 1882, devised a harebrained plan to blast a 275m (300yd) tunnel through the base of the mountain to avoid the twists and turns of the Bow River. Incensed at the projected cost, Rogers' superiors ordered him to find an alternative, and the railway was subsequently rerouted north of the mountain at a fraction of the original price.

Fairmont Banff Springs   LANDMARK

(www.fairmont.com/banffsprings;   Spray Ave) Looming up beside the Bow River, the Banff Springs is a local landmark in more ways than one. Originally built in 1888, and remodeled in 1928 to resemble a cross between a Scottish baronial castle and a European chateau, the turret-topped exterior conceals an eye-poppingly extravagant selection of ballrooms, lounges, dining rooms and balustraded staircases that would make William Randolph Hearst green with envy.

Highlights include an Arthurian great hall, an elegant wood-paneled bar, and the gorgeous hot-springs spa. Even if you're not staying here, you're welcome to wander around, and it's worth splashing out on a coffee or a cocktail in one of the four (count 'em!) lounges. The hotel is best seen in winter, when the lights of its 700-odd rooms twinkle out from under a thick crust of snow.

⊙ Around Banff Town

LAKE MINNEWANKA

Cradled high above town between the Palliser and Fairholme Ranges, Lake Minnewanka is the largest body of water in the national park – 24km (15 miles) long, 142m (465ft) deep and barely a few degrees above freezing. Known to Stoney people as *minn-waki* ('the lake of the spirits'), the lake was believed to be haunted by the spirits of the dead, perhaps explaining why early Europeans referred to it as Devil's Lake.

The lake has been dammed three times at its western end: in 1895, 1912 and finally in 1941, when the lake level was raised by around 30m, completely submerging the lively summer settlement of Minnewanka Landing, which had four avenues and three streets lined with hotels, shops and saloon bars. Today the drowned town is off-limits to everyone except scuba divers, so you'll have to content yourself with a picnic or a stroll along the lakeshore. There's a small seasonal cafe next to the car park that serves sandwiches, drinks, ice creams and other snacks. Bighorn sheep can often be seen grazing along the lakeshore.

Minnewanka is the only lake in Banff that allows motorboats. You can rent motor launches (boats per hour C$49, additional hours C$30; ⊙ Jun–mid-Oct) from the boathouse, or take a trip with Banff Lake Cruises (www.explorerockies.com/minnewanka; adult/child C$55/27.50; ⊙ hourly 10am-6pm mid-Jun–Sep), which offers 1½-hour cruises that include a commentary on the history, geology and mythology of the lake, and a visit to the glacial pass known as the Devil's Gap.

Minnewanka also marks the start of several hikes. The gentle trail to Stewart Canyon (p56) is a great family option, while hardier walkers might want to tackle Aylmer Lookout (11.8km/7.3 miles one way, 560m/1837ft elevation gain) or continue on to Aylmer Pass (13km/8 miles one way, 810m/2657ft elevation gain). Note that the Aylmer trails are closed during the buffalo-berry season between mid-July and September, as the area is a frequent hangout for grizzly bears.

MT NORQUAY

One of Banff's 'Big Three' ski resorts in the winter, Mt Norquay is named after John Norquay (premier of Manitoba from 1878 to 1887), who supposedly made the first summit ascent following the end of his premiership in 1887.

Norquay and its chairlift (www.summer. banffnorquay.com; adult/child C$20/10; ⊙9am-6pm Jun-Oct, to 4pm Nov-May) remain open year-round. When the snow melts people come up here to hike, visit the Cliffhouse Bistro at the top of the chairlift or engage in Banff's newest activity – the via ferrata (p82).

A free shuttle replaces the ski shuttle in the summer, allowing easy access from Banff Town. It stops just above the ski area parking lot at the base of the chairlift where you'll also find a small cafeteria-style eating joint. The ski area parking lot marks the start of two hikes: the long slog to Cascade Amphitheatre (p57), and the shorter trail to the wooded summit of Stoney Squaw Mountain (4.2km/2.6 miles round-trip, 190m/623ft elevation gain).

SUNSHINE MEADOWS

Straddling the Continental Divide and the border between Alberta and British Columbia, Sunshine Meadows is an expanse of high-alpine meadowland stretching for 15km (9.3 miles) between Citadel Pass and Healy Pass.

In winter, it's one of Banff's three ski areas, but in summer, once the snows thaw, it marks the start of several above-the-treeline hiking trails that are renowned for their placid lakes and impressionistic wildflowers.

The area known collectively as 'Sunshine' spins on two hubs. The base gondola station is located in a car park at the end of the Sunshine road, 15km from Banff Town. Here you'll find the year-round cafeteria-style Creekside Restaurant (www.skibanff.com/things-to-do/restaurants-eateries; sandwiches C$9-16; ⊙7:30am-5:30pm), plus all the usual ski facilities. At the far end of the car park is the trailhead for the summer-only hike to Healy Pass (p59).

Sunshine Village is situated at the top of the gondola and consists of a ski-season-only hotel, the Sunshine Mountain Lodge, along with several cafes and restaurants, only one of which, the Mad Trapper's Saloon (www.skibanff.com/things-to-do/restaurants-eateries; mains C$13-17; ⊙11am-5:30pm & 7pm-midnight Dec-May, 11am-5:30pm Jun-Oct) remains open in the summer. The village, at an altitude of about 2300m (7545ft), is on the cusp of several short alpine trails – including the Garden Path Trail (p58)– and a couple of longer ones, most notably the backcountry excursions to Egypt Lake (p68) and Mt Assiniboine Provincial Park (p68).

LOCAL KNOWLEDGE

SUMMER SUNSHINE

Sunshine Meadows is Banff's metaphoric rooftop. In the summer, it is one of the easiest places in the Rockies for back-of-the-pack hikers to get above the treeline to experience exuberant meadows, mirror-like lakes and hazy mountain views without the use of a helicopter or several pints of sweat.

Summer passage up to the meadows is handled, between mid-June and early October, by the White Mountain Adventures (p78) 'sunshine shuttle' (adult/child C$27/16), a yellow school bus that replaces the winter ski gondola. The shuttle runs from the gondola base station at the end of the Sunshine road up to the ski 'village' cutting out 6.5km (4 miles) of dull uphill hiking. It departs from the Sunshine parking lot eight times daily between 9am and 4:45pm and follows the resort's winter access road. It returns back down the mountain once hourly from 9:15am to 4:30pm. During July and August, there's an extra bus up the mountain at 8am and down at 5:30pm.

If you catch the 9am shuttle in July and August you'll qualify for a free 12km (7.5-mile) guided hike around the lakes and meadows on top. If you choose to go it alone, you can follow the trail to Garden Path and Twin Cairn Meadow (p58).

As an added bonus, White Mountain Adventures also runs a daily connection bus between Sunshine base station and Banff (adult/child C$55/30) in July and August. The bus leaves Banff between 8:15am and 8:30am and returns at 2:30pm and 5:30pm.

Hikers arriving at Sunshine Village fresh from a backcountry adventure can also purchase a one-way ticket back down the mountain for C$16, subject to availability.

Buy tickets in the Mad Trapper's Saloon at the top or the Creekside Restaurant at the base station. As places are limited, it's a good idea to reserve ahead online at www.sunshinemeadowsbanff.com or by calling ☎403-762-7889.

THE MOUNTAIN MAN

Driving into Banff you might notice a distinctive face staring at you from the town-limits sign, sporting a jaunty hat, a drooping meerschaum pipe and a rather splendid handle-bar moustache. Meet 'Wild' Bill Peyto, one of the great characters of the Canadian Rockies and the original wild man of the mountains.

Born in Kent, England, in 1869, young William was the third eldest of a family of nine children. Having left the cramped environs of the Peyto household at 17, Bill set out to find his fortune in Canada, arriving in Halifax in 1887, where he initially found work as a railway laborer, part-time rancher and government employee. But it wasn't long before Bill found his true calling – as a mountain guide working for the packing and outfitting business owned by Tom Wilson.

Over the next decade he proved himself a skilled trapper, huntsman and alpinist, exploring Mistaya Valley and Peyto Lake, making the first successful ascent of Bow Summit in 1894 and notching up the first (failed) attempt at Mt Assiniboine the following year (he eventually scaled it in 1902). He even found time for some book-larnin', schooling himself in paleontology and geology using secondhand textbooks. Within a matter of years he had become one of the most skilled amateur naturalists in the Rockies.

He was also a notorious showman with an eye for a natty outfit. One of his clients, Norman Collie, painted a vivid picture of Wild Bill: 'Peyto assumes a wild and picturesque though somewhat tattered attire. A sombrero, with a rakish tilt to one side, a blue shirt set off by a white kerchief (which may have served civilization for napkin), and a buckskin coat with a fringe border add to his cowboy appearance. A heavy belt containing a row of cartridges, hunting knife and six-shooter as well as the restless activity of his wicked blue eyes, give him an air of bravado...'

As his reputation grew, so did the stories that surrounded him. According to one famous legend, Bill once strolled into a saloon with a wild lynx strapped to his back to scare off the other punters (apparently he liked to drink in peace). Another tall tale maintains that he had a habit of setting man-traps inside his cabin in order to catch thieves helping themselves to his stores.

He was also a man with a conscience. He fought in the Boer War, became one of the very first park wardens in 1913, and later served with the 12th Mounted Regiment in WWI, sustaining wounds at Ypres in 1916 and enduring a long convalescence in England before returning to his park duties. He continued to serve as a warden until he retired in 1936 to care for his wife, Ethel Wells; she died in 1940, and Bill followed three years later.

You can still visit one of Bill's original log cabins on the grounds of the Whyte Museum in Banff (p86), and his action-packed diary – which is appropriately titled *Ain't It Hell: Bill Peyto's Mountain Journal* – is available from the museum shop.

BOW VALLEY PARKWAY

While most people zoom up busy Trans-Canada Hwy 1 with nothing but views of truck tailgates and overtaking automobiles, wiser souls swing over onto the quieter and much more scenic Hwy 1A, otherwise known as the Bow Valley Pkwy, which runs for 51km (31.6 miles) nearly all the way north to Lake Louise. The route is hemmed in by thick fir forest and mountains, with regular viewpoints looking out across the Bow Valley. It's a great route to look out for wildlife, especially elk, bighorn sheep and even the occasional moose, but take things slow: the regular speed limit is 60km/h (37mph), dropping down to 30km/h (19mph) at certain sections to avoid wildlife collisions.

If you're short on time, at the very least make sure to visit the thundering waterfalls of Johnston Canyon (p58), where a suspended catwalk tracks along the canyon wall to a series of viewpoints overlooking the Lower and Upper Falls. It's one of Banff's most popular sights, and the car park is often full by mid-morning; save it for an early morning or late-evening visit. A little further along the parkway is the lookout point at Castle Mountain, one of Banff's most recognizable mountain peaks.

The eastern section of the road between Fireside picnic area and Johnston Canyon is closed from 6pm to 9am during spring mating season (March to late June).

Banff National Park Region

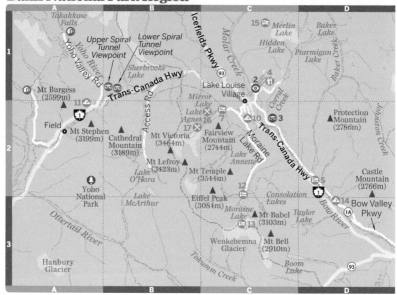

Banff National Park Region

⊙ Sights
1 Inkpots E3
2 Lake Louise Gondola...........................C1
3 Morant's Curve Viewpoint...................C2

⊕ Activities, Courses & Tours
Lake Louise Boathouse...................(see 7)
4 Lake Louise Ski Area.............................C1
Moraine Lake Canoe Hire.............(see 12)
Timberline Tours..............................(see 7)

🛏 Sleeping
5 Baker Creek Chalets............................D2
Castle Mountain Campground.......(see 6)
Castle Mountain Chalets...............(see 6)
6 Castle Mountain Wilderness Hostel......E3
Deer Lodge..(see 7)
7 Fairmont Chateau Lake Louise.............C2

8 Johnston Canyon Campground............E3
9 Johnston Canyon Resort.......................E3
Kicking Horse Campground..........(see 11)
10 Lake Louise Tent & Trailer
Campgrounds......................................C2
11 Monarch Campground...........................A2
12 Moraine Lake Lodge..............................C2
13 Neil Colgan Hut.....................................C3
14 Protection Mountain Campground.......D3
15 Skoki Lodge...C1

🍴 Eating
Baker Creek Bistro.........................(see 5)
Caribou Lounge...............................(see 7)
Fairview Lounge..............................(see 7)
16 Lake Agnes Teahouse...........................C2
17 Plain of Six Glaciers Teahouse.............B2

⊙ Lake Louise & Around

Famous for its teahouses, grizzly bears, grand hotel, Victoria Glacier, skiing, hiking and lakes (yes, plural), Lake Louise is what makes Banff National Park the phenomenon it is, an awe-inspiring natural feature that is impossible to describe without resorting to shameless clichés. Yes, there is a placid turquoise-tinted lake here; yes, the natural world feels (and is) tantalizingly close; and yes, the water is surrounded by an amphitheater of finely chiseled mountains that Michelangelo couldn't have made more aesthetically pleasing. Then there are the much commented-on 'crowds,' plus a strangely congruous (or incongruous – depending on your viewpoint) towering lump of bricks and mortar known as Chateau Lake Louise. But, frankly, who cares about the waterside claustrophobia?

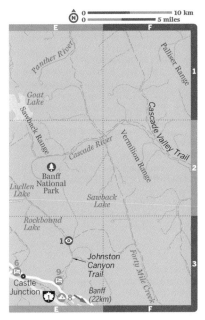

as Emerald Lake, it was later renamed in honor of Princess Louise Caroline Alberta, Queen Victoria's fourth daughter and wife of the then Canadian governor-general.

Roughly 2km (1.2 miles) end to end and 70m (230ft) deep, the lake is famous for its searingly blue water, caused by light reflecting off tiny particles of 'rock flour' (glacial silt) carried down from the mountain glaciers. On still days the lake becomes a shimmering mirror for the surrounding scenery; it's best seen early or late in the day, when the vibrant colors of the lake are strongest. In winter, the scene is transformed into a wonderland of powder-white ice and snow-cloaked peaks. The surface of the lake often freezes over and skaters glide across it, wrapped up tight against the biting mountain cold.

Since Tom's time, the lake has become one of Banff National Park's most famous (and busiest) attractions, and the lakeshore inevitably gets crushingly crowded on summer days. Visit as early as possible to avoid the squash, and spend the rest of the day exploring the nearby attractions of Moraine Lake and the Lake Louise Gondola.

You can usually escape the coachloads of sightseers milling around in front of the Fairmont Chateau Lake Louise by following the lakeshore trail, which tracks through forest along the northern side of the lake, offering fabulous vistas of Fairview Mountain and the Victoria Glacier. A spur trail leads steeply up the mountainside to the famous Lake Agnes Teahouse (p63) and the Big Beehive, but it's a long slog, so you'll need good shoes and plenty of water. Further along the lakeshore trail, you can continue up the valley on the Plain of Six Glaciers walk (p60). There are several more classic hikes leading off around Lake Louise, including the steep climbs up Saddleback (2330m/7644ft) and Fairview Mountain (2744m/9003ft), which both brood along the lake's southern shore.

For something more sedentary, you can hire canoes from the Lake Louise Boathouse (Map p94; 403-522-3511; canoes per hour C$65; 8am-8:30pm Jun-Oct). Once you've got over the shock of the price, you'll be rewarded with a sense of the silence and natural majesty that must have greeted Tom Wilson when he first laid eyes on the lake.

MORAINE LAKE

Reached by a twisting 13km (8-mile) road that's only open from June to October, the mountainous panoramas around Moraine Lake are arguably even more stunning than

Lake Louise isn't about dodging other tourists. It's about finding your own little nook and enjoying the sublime scenery.

When you're done with gawping, romancing or pledging undying love to your partner on the shimmering lakeshore, try hiking up into the mountainous landscape behind. Lake Louise also has a widely lauded ski resort and some equally enticing cross-country options. Thirteen kilometers (8 miles) to the southeast along a winding seasonal road is another spectacularly located body of water, Moraine Lake, which some heretics claim is even more beguiling than its famous sibling.

The village of Lake Louise, just off Hwy 1, is little more than an outdoor shopping mall, a gas station and a handful of hotels. The object of all your yearnings is 5km (3.1 miles) away by car or an equitable distance on foot along the pleasantly wooded Louise Creek trail, if the bears aren't out on patrol (check at the visitor center).

LAKE LOUISE

Stoney people knew about Lake Louise long before the first European settlers arrived, but the first white man to 'discover' it was the railway surveyor and pack guide Tom Wilson, who was taken to the 'Lake of Little Fishes' by Aboriginal guides in 1882. Originally known

DON'T MISS

LAKE LOUISE GONDOLA

For a bird's-eye view of the Lake Louise area – and a good chance of spotting grizzly bears on the avalanche slopes – climb aboard the Lake Louise Gondola (Map p94; 403-522-3555; www.lakelouisegondola.com; off Hwy 1A; adult/child C$32/16; 8:30am-6pm, with seasonal variation;), which crawls up the side of Whitehorn Mountain via an open ski lift or enclosed gondola to a dizzying viewpoint 2088m (6850ft) above the valley floor. Look out for the imposing fang of 3544m (11,626ft) Mt Temple piercing the skyline on the opposite side of the valley.

At the top of the mountain there are free hourly interpretive programs exploring grizzly bears and the history of the Lake Louise area, plus a 45-minute guided nature walk (tickets C$5.70; 11am, 1pm & 3pm), or you can wander around several short marked trails. Back at the bottom, snacks and light meals are available at the Lodge of the Ten Peaks (www.lakelouisegondola.com/dining.php; buffet lunch C$22; 8am-5:30pm mid-May–Sep). See the website for opening hours during the ski season.

The gondola is about 2km east of Lake Louise Village. Complimentary shuttle buses run several times daily from the Fairmont Chateau Lake Louise, Deer Lodge, Lake Louise Tent & Trailer Campgrounds and Samson Mall. For information on bus departure times, visit the Contact Us section of the gondola website.

those at Lake Louise. Backed by the dagger-point peaks of the Wenkchemna Range, all of which top out over 3000m (10,000ft), Moraine is another sparkling bluer-than-blue lake that's fed by glacial runoff from the surrounding mountains. It's one of the best-known views in the Rockies, and graced the back of the C$20 bill from 1969 to 1986.

The mountains were originally named in 1894 by the explorer Samuel Allen, using the numbers one to 10 in the Stoney language ('wenkchemna' means 10). All but two of the mountains have since been renamed, but you'll still see some guidebooks and maps using the original Stoney names.

At the eastern end of the lake is the Moraine Lake Rockpile, a massive heap of boulders of somewhat uncertain origin: some geologists think it was created by an ancient avalanche, while others believe it was formed by the long-gone glacier that carved out the rest of the valley. A paved trail leads up to a series of viewpoints at the top of the rockpile, offering a panoramic vista across the lake and the Wenkchemna Peaks beyond. On his first climb up the rockpile in 1899, early adventurer Walter Wilcox wrote: 'No scene has ever given me an equal impression of inspiring solitude and rugged grandeur.' It's hard to argue.

A part-paved trail leads off around the lake's northern shore, linking up with the branch trail to Larch Valley and Eiffel Lake (p62). Another trail leads southeast from the rockpile to Consolation Lakes (p60).

Alternatively, you can explore the lake in the manner of the old voyageurs by hiring a canoe (Map p94; 800-522-2777; canoes per hour C$55; 10am-6pm Jun-Sep) from the boathouse next to Moraine Lake Lodge.

Icefields Parkway

The Icefields Pkwy, the 'road to the clouds,' the Promenade des Glaciers...apply whichever sobriquet you wish; Canada's Hwy 93 is one of the most incredible roads in North America. Paralleling the Continental Divide for 230km (142.6 miles) between Lake Louise and Jasper Town, 122km (77 miles) of this precious parkway lies inside Banff National Park and is replete with fanning glaciers, teeming wildlife and gothic mountains. Miss it at your peril.

The Banff section of the parkway has accommodation at campgrounds at Rampart Creek, Mosquito Creek and Waterfowl Lakes; at the historic Num-Ti-Jah Lodge, which was established by the famous Rockies character Jimmy Simpson; and at a fairly dull motel at Saskatchewan Crossing. For the economy-minded there are two hostels at Mosquito Creek and Rampart Creek.

The speed limit on the parkway is 90km/h (56mph), with reduced speeds around Saskatchewan Crossing and the Columbia Icefield. The road often becomes impassable in winter due to heavy snow, and chains or all-season tires are advisable between October and May. Regardless of the time of year, you'll also need a valid National Park Pass for everyone in your vehicle in order to drive on the parkway. Sights on the parkway are covered in more detail in the 'Into the Icefields' driving tour (p80).

☞ TOURS

Unless you're really short on time or are traveling without your own vehicle, there's no real need to splash out on a guided tour – but if you prefer to let someone else do the organizing (and the driving), a minibus trip can be a good way of packing in the sights. Most companies offer pick-up and drop-off from your hotel, and include lunch in their full-day tours.

Brewster Tours

Founded way back in 1892 by the entrepreneurial Brewster brothers Bill and Jim, **Brewster** (Map p87; ☎ 403-762-6750; www. brewster.ca; 100 Gopher St, Banff Town) is one of Banff's oldest guiding firms and is still one of the town's busiest tour operators. Today, it also operates three of the park's most lucrative sights, including the Banff Gondola, Lake Minnewanka Boat Tours and the Columbia Icefield/Glacier Skywalk.

In the early days, visitors were ferried around by packhorse and mule train, but these days the transportation is rather plusher: Brewster's tours are run in large motor coaches, complete with air-con and guided commentary. The big buses feel a bit impersonal compared to smaller operators, and remember that stopping times (especially on the full-day tours) at the sights are whistle-stop brief.

Brewster offers a variety of combo packages to a cocktail of sights, which can save you money; see the website for details.

Evening Wildlife Safari   TOUR
(adult/child C$44/25) Two-hour wildlife-spotting tour around the Marsh Loop and Vermilion Lakes.

Discover Banff Tour   TOUR
(adult/child C$50/25) These three-hour tours stop at the Hoodoos, the Cave & Basin, Surprise Corner and Tunnel Mountain. Adding on the gondola costs an extra C$30/15 per adult/child.

Mountain Lakes & Waterfalls   TOUR
(adult/child C$123/62) This full-day tour (9½ hours) travels from Banff to Lake Louise for a picnic lunch and then on to Takakkaw Falls in Yoho National Park.

Explore Banff   TOUR
(adult/child C$131/68) Six-hour tour including Banff Gondola and a Lake Minnewanka Cruise.

THE SWISS GUIDES IN CANADA

Following the death of Philip Abbot on Mt Lefroy in 1896, the Canadian Pacific Railway (CPR) knew it had to do something to keep mountaineering enthusiasts boarding its trains for the Rockies.

In order to reassure investors' nerves and ensure the safety of their clients in the mountains, the CPR decided to hire the services of some of Switzerland's top alpine guides, shipping them over at considerable expense with the promise of accommodations, attractive pay and – most importantly – the opportunity to be the first to claim some of the Rockies' numerous unclimbed peaks.

First to arrive in 1899 were Edward Feuz Sr and Christian Haesler, two of Switzerland's most renowned guides, followed a few seasons later by another handful of skilled alpinists, including Edward's trio of mountain-climbing sons, Ernest, Edward Feuz Jr and Walter. In order to help their new employees feel more at home, in 1911 the CPR constructed a small settlement of Swiss-style timber chalets just outside Golden, which became known to locals as the 'Swiss Village' or 'Edelweiss.' Many of the original buildings are still standing.

The Swiss guides played an important role in the development of Canadian mountaineering, and were instrumental in the formation of the Alpine Club of Canada, which was based in Golden during its early years.

Though Feuz Sr never permanently settled in Canada, he continued to visit most summers until his death in 1965, leading over 100 new routes and becoming the first man to climb 78 Canadian peaks. During his 50-year career, he never lost a client.

Columbia Icefield Discovery TOUR
(adult/child C$206/104) From Banff to Columbia Icefield and the new Glacier Skywalk; 9½-hour tour includes hot lunch and Snocoach ticket.

Explore Lake Louise TOUR
(adult/child C$83/42) From Banff to Lake Louise via Johnston Canyon and Castle Mountain; includes lunch and free time at Lake Louise.

Discover Banff Tours

Besides Brewster, Discover Banff Tours (Map p88; ☑ 403-760-5007; www.banfftours.com; Sundance Mall, 215 Banff Ave, Banff Town) is the other big tour operator located in Banff. It runs smaller buses than Brewster, so things feel a bit less regimented – you can even hire your own personal guide (half-/full day C$325/450).

Discover Banff & Its Wildlife TOUR
(adult/child C$56/30) A great three-hour tour for wildlife, with stops around Banff, Vermilion Lakes and the Bow Valley Pkwy. Special morning and evening wildlife safaris are also available.

Explore Lake Louise TOUR
(adult/child C$72/40) This full-day (10-hour) tour includes a commentated bus ride to Lake Louise, with seven hours to spend exploring the lake. Shorter tours to Lake Louise and Moraine Lake are also available.

Columbia Icefields Parkway Tour TOUR
(adult/child C$174/93) This 10-hour trip stops at Lake Louise en route to the Icefields Pkwy, with a trip onto the Columbia Icefield included.

★ **Discover Grizzly Bears** TOUR
(adult/child C$169/89) Travel via Yoho National Park to the Kicking Horse Resort grizzly center near Golden, BC. A gourmet lunch is included on this 10-hour tour.

Other Tours

GyPSy TOUR
(Map p88; ☑ 866-477-4171; www.gypsyguide.com/canada; 215 Banff Ave, Banff Town) These audioguides offer GPS-based tours to sights across the Rockies and western Canada. They're a good option if you prefer to devise your own route, but the commentary is fairly basic.

🛏 SLEEPING

Despite having enough hotel rooms to rival a town three times its size, finding a place to sleep in Banff Town can be a tricky proposition. Sitting in a protected park, the town has strict laws surrounding its development. New hotels can't just be wantonly built. Book several months in advance, especially if you're coming in June, July or August, and especially if you want to save money. Banff's room rates are notoriously expensive and take a hefty upward hike in peak season.

One option to consider is to stay just outside the park in Canmore, where rooms are usually slightly cheaper. Canmore is easily accessible due to a good hourly public bus service into Banff.

Many visitors choose to cut costs by camping or hiring recreational vehicles (RVs). Renting a condo or vacation apartment can be another good way to keep costs down. However, even with condos and camping, it's wise to book well ahead.

🛏 Banff

Camping

Tunnel Mountain CAMPGROUND $
(Tunnel Mountain Dr; tent & RV sites C$28-39; ☺ kiosk 7am-midnight) Banff's massive main campground is split over three separate 'villages' halfway up the slope of Tunnel Mountain. All told, the combined area offers over 1000 sites, but still manages to fill to capacity in summer thanks to its convenient location just a quick drive from downtown Banff.

All three areas have flush toilets, proper showers and wheelchair-accessible sites, making them suitable for pretty much everyone – but you might be better off elsewhere if you're looking for tranquil camping.

Lodging

If you're looking to save some cash, staying in local B&Bs is usually much cheaper than an equivalent hotel room; ask about weekly rates, and check policies on kids and pets before booking. Contact the Banff Visitor Centre for a full list. If you're stuck for a place to sleep, Banff Central Reservations (☑ 403-277-7669; www.banffinfo.com) and Banff Tourism Bureau (p112) can help find available rooms.

BANFF CAMPGROUNDS

Banff has 13 frontcountry campgrounds catering for tents, recreational vehicles (RVs) and camper vans. Most are open from around June to mid-September, although Tunnel Mountain Village Two and Lake Louise Trailer campgrounds are open year-round.

Advance reservations are currently only available at four campgrounds: Tunnel Mountain, Two Jack, Johnston Canyon and Lake Louise; contact the **Parks Canada campground reservation service** (☑ 877-737-3783; www.reservation.parkscanada.gc.ca; ⊙ 7am-7pm), which books sites up to 24 hours in advance for a fee of C$10.80 in addition to regular camping fees.

Sites at all other campgrounds are allocated on a first-come, first-served basis, so the best way to claim a spot is to turn up early (by official checkout time at 11am) or check with parks staff about which campgrounds currently have availability. Banff Park Radio (101.1FM) also releases regular bulletins on campgrounds with available sites. It's a good idea to stay in one place over weekends; sites are generally easier to come by on Thursday and Friday.

Checkout at all campgrounds is 11am and there's a maximum stay of 14 nights. You can have one tent and up to two vehicles at one campsite. At larger campgrounds you'll need to pay fees at the entry kiosk, but at smaller campgrounds, you'll have to self-register: find a vacant site first, then go to the self-registration shelter, remembering to enter your name, site number, license plate and duration of stay on the envelope along with the relevant fees. If it's late when you arrive, you can do this in the morning, or sometimes staff will come around and collect your fees in person in the morning.

Fires are usually allowed at campsites where there's a fire pit – you'll need to buy a fire permit (C$8.80, including wood) from the campground entrance. Watch for fire restrictions during dry periods.

HI-Banff Alpine Centre HOSTEL $
(Map p87; ☑ 403-762-4122; www.hihostels.ca; 801 Hidden Ridge Way; dm/d from C$44/118; P @ 🛜) Banff's best hostel is near the top of Tunnel Mountain and well away from the madness of Banff Ave. Walkers will find the commute a good workout, and their efforts will not go unrewarded; the buildings are finished in classic mountain-lodge style, but without classic mountain-lodge prices.

★ **Banff Ptarmigan Inn** HOTEL $$
(Map p87; ☑ 403-762-2207; www.bestofbanff.com; 337 Banff Ave; d C$179; P 🛜 🐾) It lacks the wow factor of Banff's top-end hotels, but for value the Ptarmigan Inn is a top choice. There's little to choose between the standard, superior and premium rooms (floral throws, framed watercolors and beige shades are standard throughout), though extra cash buys extra space and perhaps a mountain view. Facilities include whirlpools, sauna and steam room, and breakfast is included.

Banff Rocky Mountain Resort HOTEL $$
(☑ 403-762-5531; www.bestofbanff.com; 1029 Banff Ave; r from C$159; P 🛜 🐾) Being 4km out of town at the far, far end of Banff Ave is a small price to pay for the preferential prices and excellent all-round facilities here (in-cluding a hot tub, pool, tennis courts and cafe-restaurant).

Added to this is the greater sense of de-tachment, quiet tree-filled grounds (it never feels like a 'resort') and generously sized bedrooms with sofas, desks and extra beds. There's a free shuttle into town (hourly) or you can walk or cycle along the Legacy Trail.

Banff Caribou Lodge HOTEL $$
(Map p87; ☑ 403-762-5887; www.bestofbanff.com; 521 Banff Ave; d from C$234; P @ 🛜) One of the posher places in the locally run Banff Lodging Co empire (which tags it at 3½ stars), the Caribou fits the classic stereotype of a mountain lodge, with its log-and-stone exterior, giant lobby fireplace and general alpine coziness.

Charlton's Cedar Court MOTEL $$
(Map p87; ☑ 403-762-4485; www.charltonscedar court.com; 513 Banff Ave; d C$159; ste C$169-185; P ❄ 🛜 🐾) Yes, it's a bit old-fashioned, but this motel complex on Banff Ave has some of the most consistent rates in town. Cheaper rooms are dowdy, so better to opt for one of the larger split-level suites, some of which have kitchenettes and mezzanine sleeping areas. Luxury it ain't, but it's a reasonable downtown base.

BANFF NATIONAL PARK CAMPGROUNDS

CAMPGROUND	LOCATION	DESCRIPTION	NO OF SITES
Tunnel Mountain Trailer Court	Banff Town	Dedicated RV and trailer site with full hookups	321
Tunnel Mountain Village One	Banff Town	Large, forested, tent-only campground, popular with families, but can get over-crowded	618
Tunnel Mountain Village Two	Banff Town	Mixed-use campground that's handy for Banff Town, but feels a little exposed to the elements	188
Castle Mountain	Bow Valley Parkway	Small woodland campground that's handily located near a grocery store	43
Johnston Canyon	Bow Valley Parkway	One of the park's most scenic and best-equipped campgrounds, with lots of day hikes on its doorstep	132
Protection Mountain	Bow Valley Parkway	Popular with hikers thanks to its proximity to trailheads; amenities include recycling and kitchen shelters	89
Mosquito Creek	Icefields Parkway	Very basic, tree-lined campground in the shadow of Mt Hector, at the southern end of the Icefields Pkwy	32
Rampart Creek	Icefields Parkway	The last frontcountry campground south of the Jasper border; rudimentary, but peaceful	50
Waterfowl Lakes	Icefields Parkway	The best equipped of the Icefields Pkwy campgrounds, with recycling bins, piped water and food storage	116
Lake Louise Tent Campgrounds	Lake Louise	Tent campground next door to the RV campground, protected by an electric bear-proof fence	206
Lake Louise Trailer Campgrounds	Lake Louise	RV-friendly campground that keeps 30 sites open in winter	189
Two Jack Lakeside	Lake Minnewanka	Beautiful and very popular lakeside campground with private, secluded sites	74
Two Jack Main	Lake Minnewanka	Scattered pleasantly under the trees, but the lack of shower facilities is a drawback	380

 Drinking Water   *Flush Toilets*   *Great for Families*   *Grocery Store Nearby*

Poplar Inn B&B $$

(Map p87; ☑ 403-760-8688; www.thepoplarinn.ca; 316 Lynx St; d C$185; P) Two sweet rooms in a heritage home just steps from Banff Ave. Both have luxury touches such as Egyptian cotton sheets and sliding doors onto private garden patios. The lovely breakfast of muffins, cinnamon buns and chocolate croissants is served in one of the house's turrets.

Juniper HOTEL $$

(☑ 403-762-2281; www.thejuniper.com; 1 Juniper Way; r C$169-229; P❄☎) Purpose-built, pet-friendly hotel with modern rooms and a decent restaurant. It's perched above the Trans-Canada Hwy at the bottom of the Mt Norquay road just outside town, so it gets a bit of traffic noise.

ELEVATION	OPEN	RESERVATION REQUIRED?	DAILY FEE	FACILITIES	PAGE
1440m (4725ft)	May-Oct	yes	C$39		p98
1440m (4725ft)	May-Oct	yes	C$28		p98
1450m (4760ft)	year-round	yes	C$33		p98
1450m (4760ft)	May-Sep	no	C$22		p104
1430m (4700ft)	May-Sep	no	C$28		p103
1450m (4760ft)	Jun-Sep	no	C$22		p104
1850m (6070ft)	Jun-Oct	no	C$18		p106
1450m (4760ft)	Jun-Oct	no	C$16		p106
1650m (5410ft)	Jun-Sep	no	C$22		p106
1540m (5050ft)	May-Sep	yes	C$28		p104
1540m (5050ft)	year-round	yes	C$33		p104
1460m (4790ft)	May-Oct	no	C$28		p103
1460m (4790ft)	Jun-Sep	no	C$22		p103

 Restaurant Nearby   *Payphone*   *Summertime Campfire Program*   *RV Dump Station*

Bow View Lodge HOTEL **$$**
(Map p88; ☑ 403-762-2261; www.bowview.com; 228 Bow Ave; r from C$144; P ❄ 🛜 🛥) The Bow View is a workaday Banff option – older than most of the attractive log inns that line Banff Ave, but neat and tidy all the same. Without any surcharge you can use the fitness facilities and pool in the huge Banff Park Lodge next door.

Bumpers Inn MOTEL **$$**
(Map p87; ☑ 403-762-3386; www.bumpersinn.com; 603 Banff Ave; r from C$159; P 🛜 🛥) Banff provides a rare no-frills motel in bog-standard Bumpers, which offers zero pretension but plenty of financial savings. The check-in is at Inns of Banff across the road, but you can also use their pool and hot tub.

STAYING IN THE BACKCOUNTRY

Camping

There are over 50 campgrounds dotted around the Banff backcountry, but they're generally a lot more basic than the national park's other camping areas. Cleared sites, tent pads and pit toilets pretty much sum up the facilities; some also have bear-proof bins or food storage cables. You'll need to pack in everything else (including food, fuel, water-treatment equipment and other supplies). You'll also need to pack everything out again once your trip is finished (including all your rubbish).

All overnight stays in the backcountry require a wilderness pass (per day/year C$9.80/68.70), available from park visitor centers. You'll need to indicate which camp-grounds you intend to use when you purchase your pass; reservations are accepted up to three months in advance for a C$11.70 fee, and you *must* stick to these campgrounds once you've booked them. Trail and campground numbers are strictly limited, so you might well find your route is booked out unless you plan ahead, especially in July and August. The maximum stay at any one site is three days.

Beyond the backcountry, wild camping is permitted in some areas. Make sure your campsite is 5km (3.1 miles) from any trailhead, 50m (164ft) off the trail and 70m (229ft) from any water source, and take the usual precautions against bears and forest fires.

Shelters

Parks Canada operates two backcountry trail shelters, one at Egypt Lake and another at Bryant Creek. Both are extremely rustic and offer little more than a roof over your head. You'll need to be completely self-sufficient, with your own bedding, food and cooking equipment. You can book spaces at the shelters when you purchase your wilderness pass.

Alpine Club of Canada Huts

The Alpine Club of Canada operates several remote huts for climbers and mountaineers that are also open to backcountry walkers. They range from basic portacabins to historic log huts. Most have mattresses, cooking stoves and utensils, but you'll need your own sleeping bag, food and other supplies (including toilet paper and matches).

Reservations are required at all huts and can be made through the **Alpine Clubhouse** (403-678-3200; www.alpineclubofcanada.ca; Indian Flats Rd, Canmore) up to a month in advance. Key Alpine Club of Canada huts include **Abbot Pass Hut** (www.alpineclubof canada.ca; member/non-member C$25/36; summer), which sleeps 24 and is perched atop a difficult glacier climb at the end of the Plain of Six Glaciers, and **Castle Mountain Hut** (www.alpineclubofcanada.ca; member/non-member C$25/36; summer), which sleeps six, is located halfway up Castle Mountain and is mainly used by rock climbers.

There's also a string of huts along the Wapta Icefield, allowing adventurers to com-plete the so-called Wapta Traverse. These include **Peyto Hut** (summer & winter), which sleeps 18 in summer and 16 in winter; **Bow Hut** (summer & winter), sleeping 30; and **Neil Colgan Hut** (Map p94; summer & winter), the highest habitable structure in Canada, sleeping up to 18 in summer.

Lodges

For a bit of extra comfort in the backcountry, there are two historic mountain lodges at Skoki (p106) and Shadow Lake (p107).

⭐**Fairmont Banff Springs** HOTEL **$$$**
(403-762-2211; www.fairmont.com/banffsprings; 405 Spray Ave; r from C$589; P @ 🛜 🏊) Sitting at the top end of the 'lost for words' category comes this exquisite beauty. Imagine cross-ing a Scottish castle with a French chateau and then plonking it in the middle of one of the world's most spectacular (and accessible) wilderness areas.

Rising like a Gaelic Balmoral above the trees at the base of Sulphur Mountain and visible from miles away, the Banff Springs is a wonder of early 1920s revivalist architecture and one of Canada's most iconic buildings. Wandering around its museum-like interior, it's easy to forget that it's also a hotel.

Fox Hotel & Suites
HOTEL $$$

(Map p87; ☎ 800-760-8500; www.bestofbanff.com; 461 Banff Ave; d from C$279; P @ 🛜 ⛄) One of Banff's more modern options, the Fox justifies its four-star billing with an eye for the aesthetic and great attention to detail. Bright, modern rooms have retro-patterned wallpaper and unique, interesting artworks, while the reception has enough trickling water to invoke flashbacks of Rome.

The highlight is the inspired re-creation of the Cave & Basin springs in the hot-tub area, with an open hole in the roof that gives out to the sky. The bar-restaurant is called Chilis and serves, among other things, excellent margaritas. The town centre is a 10-minute walk away.

Buffalo Mountain Lodge
HOTEL $$$

(Map p87; ☎ 800-661-1367; www.crmr.com/buffalo; 700 Tunnel Mountain Dr; r C$279-339; 🛜) Three hectares (9 acres) of private grounds make this lodge-hotel complex on Tunnel Mountain one of Banff's most pleasant mountain retreats. The lodge-style rooms combine rustic-chic with mod-cons: timber beams, clawfoot tubs, fieldstone log fires, and underfloor heating in the bathrooms. You don't even have to go into town for dinner thanks to the in-house restaurant Cilantro.

Banff Aspen Lodge
HOTEL $$$

(Map p87; ☎ 403-762-4401; www.banffaspenlodge. com; 401 Banff Ave; r C$289-329; P 🛜) Despite its boxy exterior and equally boxy rooms, the Banff Aspen is still worth investigating. Inside it feels up-to-date and uncluttered: rooms are finished in slate grays and sharp pine, and most have a balcony overlooking Banff Ave. Economy rooms are on the ground floor; bumping up to superior buys more space, but won't shut out the constant thrum of traffic noise. A couple of hot tubs are available downstairs for guests' use.

Buffaloberry
B&B $$$

(Map p87; ☎ 403-762-3750; www.buffaloberry.com; 417 Marten St; r C$365; P ❄ 🛜) This premium B&B makes a comfortable place to stay, but you'll have to pay for the privilege. The four bedrooms are heavy on homey charm and country fabrics, and under floor heating and nightly turn-down treats keep the pamper factor high, but it's pricey for what you get.

Hidden Ridge Resort
RESORT $$$

(☎ 403-762-3544; www.bestofbanff.com; 901 Coyote Dr; 1-bedroom condo C$299; P ❄ 🛜 ⛄) Half hotel, half self-catering resort, the Hidden Ridge is a great option for families, with modern condos and A-frame chalets available in multiple configurations. The basic chalets boast wood-burning stoves, galley kitchens and mountain-view porches, while at the top end you can splash out on Jacuzzis and cozy loft bedrooms for the kids.

There's even a forest hot tub if you're valiant enough to brave the mountain air.

🛏 Lake Minnewanka

The twin campgrounds around Lake Minnewanka are perennially popular thanks to their peaceful wooded setting.

Two Jack Lakeside
CAMPGROUND $

(Minnewanka Loop Dr; tent & RV sites C$28; ☺ May-Oct; P) Right on Two Jack Lake, and the most scenic of the Banff area campgrounds, Lakeside fills its 74 nonreservable sites quickly.

You can now 'glamp' at Two Jack in one of 10 oTENTiks, fully serviced A-frame 'tents' with hot showers and electricity. They sleep up to six people and cost a thoroughly reasonable C$120 per night.

Two Jack Main
CAMPGROUND $

(Minnewanka Loop Dr; tent & RV sites C$22; ☺ Jun-Sep) If the lakeside campground is full (and it probably will be), Two Jack's main campground is a very pleasant fallback. The 380 pitches are spread out spaciously under the trees just up the road from the lakeside campground, but the lack of showers and laundry facilities is a big drawback.

🛏 Bow Valley

Set midway between Banff Town and Lake Louise Village, the Bow Valley gives you a chance to experience the wilderness and is also handy for an early start on day hikes.

The only negative to staying in the Bow Valley is the proximity of the CPR train line, which runs right along the length of the valley all the way to Lake Louise. The melancholy blast of a distant train horn sounds romantic around a campfire at dusk, but you might not feel quite so charitable when it wakes you up at 3am.

Camping

Johnston Canyon Campground
CAMPGROUND $

(Map p94; Bow Valley Pkwy; tent & RV sites C$28; ☺ May-Sep) For that authentic backwoods camping feel, this lovely creekside campground opposite the parking lot for Johnston Canyon is tough to top. It strikes just the right balance between facilities and camper freedom. The 132 sites are spacious and fairly private, and you won't feel nearly as hemmed in as at some of Banff's bigger campgrounds.

Flush toilets and hot and cold water are available at all of the five washroom blocks, but only two have showers. Most sites are suitable for RVs.

Castle Mountain
Campground
CAMPGROUND $

(Map p94; Bow Valley Pkwy; tent & RV sites C$22; ☺May-Sep) A small self-registration campground of only 43 sites, handily placed among pine forest near the Castle Mountain store. It's beautifully secluded, with sites arranged around one long woodland loop, but there's only one washblock and annoyingly it doesn't have any showers. Nevertheless, the lovely surroundings and limited sites means it fills up fast.

Protection Mountain
Campground
CAMPGROUND $

(Map p94; Bow Valley Pkwy; tent & RV sites C$22; ☺Jun-Sep) A basic site further up the Bow Valley Pkwy from Castle Mountain. With 89 sites, no hookups, showers or laundry facilities, and a relatively long journey to Banff and Lake Louise, it's often quieter than the other Bow Valley campgrounds, and you can usually find a spot even at the busiest times.

Lodging

Castle Mountain Wilderness
Hostel
HOSTEL $

(Map p94; ☑403-670-7580; www.hihostels.ca; Castle Junction; dm C$28; ☺year-round, closed Mon Oct-Apr) This 'wilderness hostel' is more a backcountry cabin than a facility-packed backpackers. There's a simple kitchen, a couple of gender-sorted dorms and a snug common room set around a log-burning stove, with large windows looking out onto mountainous countryside. Don't be surprised if you spy an elk or two grazing outside – it's all part of the backwoods vibe.

Johnston Canyon Resort
CABINS $$

(Map p94; ☑403-762-0868; www.johnstoncanyon. com; Bow Valley Pkwy; cabins C$169-289; ☺May-Oct) Built in the late 1920s to accompany the nearby teahouse (now a restaurant), these dinky log cabins trade heavily on their proximity to Johnston Canyon. Despite their heritage appearance (complete with porch and smoking chimneys), the interior decor wouldn't look out of place in a modern motel.

Bear in mind that the Canyon is a major tour-bus stop, though things settle down at night. There's a restaurant on-site.

Castle Mountain Chalets
CABINS $$

(Map p94; ☑403-762-3868; www.castlemountain. com; Castle Junction; chalets C$149-239) Right next door to the Castle Mountain store, these log chalets are plain inside but offer a surprising number of mod-cons, including DVD players, dishwashers, wood-burning stoves and even iPod clock-radios. At C$239, the top double-room chalets are great value for families or two couples, but work out expensive for solo or duo travelers.

Baker Creek Chalets
CABINS $$$

(Map p94; ☑403-522-3761; www.bakercreek.com; Bow Valley Pkwy; cabins C$295-335) Set on a quiet glade near Baker Creek, this cabin complex has a choice of single-story chalets, deluxe twin-level loft cabins, or suites inside the main lodge. The style is deliberately old country – wood panels, porches, stoves – but the rates are quite pricey for what you get. Still, kids will absolutely love the wooden ladders up to the loft beds in the twin-level cabins.

🛌 Lake Louise

Beautiful as it is, staying around Lake Louise will make a hefty dent in your wallet. The premium location means local hotels can charge ludicrously inflated prices – and they do, especially in summer. Unless there's a really good reason to stay here, you're better off basing yourself in Banff or Yoho and visiting on a day trip.

Camping

Lake Louise Tent & Trailer
Campgrounds
CAMPGROUND $

(Map p94; Lake Louise Village; tent sites C$28, RV sites C$33; ☺tent park May-Sep, trailer park year-round) Lake Louise's huge campground (actually separate tent and RV sites with one access gate) is over 4km (2.5 miles) from the lake and 1km (0.6 miles) from the village, but as it's the only place for campers and RVs nearby, it's nearly always busy.

It's certainly not as pretty or private as some of Banff's other campgrounds, and nearly all the sites suffer from constant traffic noise thanks to the nearby highway. Online

booking is available at www.reservation.
parkscanada.gc.ca.

Lodging

HI-Lake Louise Alpine Centre
HOSTEL $

(☑ 403-522-2200; www.hihostels.ca; Village Rd; dm/d from C$42/115; P) This is what a hostel should be – clean, friendly, affordable and full of interesting travelers. The building itself is a stunning example of Rockies architecture, with raw timber and stone melding into a rustic aesthetic masterpiece. The dorm rooms are fairly standard; the private rooms are small and a bit overpriced. Don't miss the on-site Bill Peyto's Café (p109).

Deer Lodge
HOTEL $$

(Map p94; ☑ 403-410-7417; www.crmr.com; 109 Lake Louise Dr; r from C$175; P 🛜) Tucked demurely behind the Chateau Lake Louise, the Deer Lodge is a historic throwback dating from the 1920s. But, although the rustic exterior and creaky corridors can't have changed much since the days of bobbed hair and F Scott Fitzgerald, the refurbished rooms are another matter, replete with new comfy beds and smart boutique-like furnishings. TV addicts, beware – there aren't any.

Lake Louise Inn
HOTEL $$

(☑ 403-522-3791; www.lakelouiseinn.com; 210 Village Rd; d from C$199; P @ 🛜 🛏 🐾) A large, sprawling resort close to the village that has its merits, including a pool, a restaurant and a tiny historic ice-cream chalet. Room quality is variable, with some of the older wings more downbeat and motel-like.

★ Fairmont Chateau Lake Louise
HOTEL $$$

(Map p94; ☑ 403-522-3511; www.fairmont.com/lake-louise; Lake Louise Dr; d from C$450; P @ 🛜 🛏) This opulent Fairmont enjoys one of the world's most enviable locations, on the shores of Lake Louise. Originally built by the Canadian Pacific Railway in the 1890s, the hotel was added to in 1925 and 2004.

While opinions differ on its architectural merits, few deny the luxury and romance of its facilities, which include a spa, fine dining, a mini-museum, fork-dropping views, and unforgettably grandiose decor. Rooms are comfortable, if a little generic.

Moraine Lake Lodge
HOTEL $$$

(Map p94; ☑ 800-522-2777; www.morainelakelodge.com; d C$345-599; ⏱ Jun-Sep; P) Few people would shirk at an opportunity to hang around Moraine Lake for a day or three – and here's your chance. The experience here is intimate, personal and private, and the service is famously good.

Post Hotel
HOTEL $$$

(☑ 403-522-3989; www.posthotel.com; Village Rd; r C$385-850; P ✱ 🛜) You may need a second mortgage to afford a mountain view at this modern hotel in Lake Louise Village, though it's admittedly beautiful, with a gurgling river running through well-tended gardens.

HIKING RESTRICTIONS AROUND LAKE LOUISE

The Lake Louise area is one of three key grizzly bear habitats in Banff National Park, and supports a number of grizzly sows and their cubs. To avoid bear encounters, park authorities often impose group access restrictions in summer on several trails around Lake Louise, including the Consolation Lakes Trail, Larch Valley, Sentinel Pass, Paradise Valley and Wenkchemna Pass.

Under the rules, hikers are required by law to travel in tight groups of at least four people, and take the usual precautions to avoid bear encounters (make noise on the trail, carry bear spray etc). Other routes (including the Moraine Lake Highline Trail) may also be closed according to bear activity – check ahead with park staff. If you're caught breaching the 'group of four' rule, you'll be up for a hefty fine, so stick to the rules: they're there for your own safety.

The timetable varies every year according to bear activity and the berry season, but usually begins around mid-July and lasts until early September. Restrictions are clearly posted in park offices and at trailheads.

If your group is short, the Lake Louise Visitor Centre keeps a logbook where you can leave your details to get in touch with other hikers to make up the required numbers. Alternatively, leave your details at one of the local hostels or just hang around the trailheads at the start of the day – you're bound to find another group who won't mind you tagging along.

🛏 Icefields Parkway

Camping

The campgrounds along the Icefields Pkwy are a lot more basic than many in Banff, but they're ideal if you want to escape the campfire smoke and crowds of the busier sites.

Mosquito Creek

Campground CAMPGROUND $

(tent sites C$18; ☺ Jun-Oct) Tucked under Mt Hector in a wooded creekside setting, this tiny 32-site campground is about as simple as they come – pit toilets and a hand pump for water just about sum up the facilities – but it's a wonderful spot for those who are seeking seclusion. And, despite the name, mosquitoes don't seem to be too much of a problem.

Rampart Creek Campground CAMPGROUND $

(tent sites C$16; ☺ Jun-Oct) The northernmost campground in Banff is a primitive affair, but handy for the Columbia Icefield. The mountain views are particularly grand and it's often a good spot for wildlife – don't be surprised if the odd elk or bighorn sheep putters past your tent. There's well water, dry privies and kitchen shelters on-site, plus a fire-free loop if you're sick of smelling other people's smoke.

Waterfowl Lakes

Campground CAMPGROUND $

(tent & RV sites C$22; ☺ Jun-Sep) The best serviced of the parkway campgrounds, Waterfowl Lakes is situated at the head of the lake and has lots of large, wooded, wheelchair-accessible sites and surprisingly fancy facilities, including flush toilets and BBQ shelters.

Lodging

Mosquito Creek Wilderness

Hostel HOSTEL $

(☑ 403-670-7580; www.hihostels.ca; dm/d C$25/62; ☺ year-round) Tucked away under trees near the campground, this small 34-bed HI hostel was built to house German POWs during WWII, and these days makes a charming backcountry hostel. There's a rustic sauna, a stove-lit lounge and a pocket-sized (propane-powered) kitchen where you can cook up communal grub. Dorms are single-gender.

Rampart Creek Wilderness Hostel HOSTEL $

(☑ 403-670-7580; www.hihostels.ca; dm C$25; ☺ closed Thu Oct-Apr) These 12 gingerbread cabins collected around a wood clearing are much loved by climbers and hikers looking to get out into the real backwoods. Facilities include plain dorm cabins, a shared lounge, a wood-fired sauna and a lively communal kitchen.

Crossing MOTEL $$

(☑ 403-761-7000; www.thecrossingresort.com; cnr Hwy 11 & Icefields Pkwy; d C$173-183, tr C$188-204, q C$203-219; ☺ mid-Mar–Nov; P ☎) This dull motel is one of only a handful of accommodations options on the Icefields Pkwy. The bog-standard units are arranged around a central courtyard, which is also home to the only cafe, pub and shop for kilometers around.

★ Num-Ti-Jah Lodge INN $$$

(☑ 403-522-2167; www.sntj.ca; d from C$247; ☺ mid-May–mid-Oct; P ☎) Standing like a guardian of Bow Lake, the historic Num-Ti-Jah Lodge is full to the brim with character and backcountry nostalgia. Built by pioneering backwoodsman Jimmy Simpson in 1923 (12 years before the highway), the carved-wood interior displays animal heads and photos from the golden age of travel.

The rooms are tidy, if a little small, and there's an on-site restaurant with an extensive wine list.

🛏 Backcountry

Traveling in the backcountry doesn't necessarily have to mean roughing it. In the early days of Banff's history, the only people who could afford to explore the national park were wealthy adventurers, and they often expected a bit more comfort than a pup tent and an open campfire. Consequently, a number of backcountry lodges were built by the early trail guides to cater for their guests, a couple of which are still in use today.

Skoki Lodge HOTEL $$$

(Map p94; ☑ 403-522-3555; www.skoki.com; r per person C$195-225, 2-night minimum stay) The first ski lodge ever built in the Canadian Rockies remains one of the most atmospheric places to stay in the whole national park. Built in 1931 overlooking a glorious high mountain valley, and briefly managed by Peter and Catharine Whyte (who founded Banff's Whyte Museum), the lodge is reached after an 11km (6.8-mile) climb from Lake Louise via Deception Pass.

As you'd expect, the decor is rough and ready – log walls, rustic bunks, kerosene lamps, and water jugs for washing – but that's all part of Skoki's special charm. Rates include meals cooked up by the lodge chef. If you really want an adventure, you can even snowshoe or ski to the lodge in midwinter.

Shadow Lake Lodge
CABINS $$$

(☎ 403-762-0116; www.shadowlakelodge.com; cabins per person C$205-225, 2-night minimum stay; ☺ Jun-Sep, Jan-Mar) This lodge offers 12 sweet timber cabins just a stone's throw from Shadow Lake, 13.2km (8.2 miles) from the Red Earth Creek trailhead. Though it lacks the heritage kick of Skoki, Banff's other backcountry lodge, the cabins are a little roomier and more private (complete with solar-powered lighting and propane heating).

You'll even be treated to afternoon tea and a glass of champagne during your stay, as three gourmet meals are included in the price. The lodge is open June to September. It reopens January to March for cross-country skiers.

✖ EATING

Banff dining is more than just hiker food. Sushi and foie gras have long embellished the restaurants of Banff Ave, and some of the more elegant places will inspire dirty hikers to return to their hotel rooms to take a shower before pulling up a chair. Aside from the establishments listed here, many of Banff's hotels have their own excellent on-site restaurants that welcome nonguests. AAA Alberta beef makes an appearance on even the most exotic à la carte menu.

✖ Banff Town

★ Cows
ICE CREAM $

(Map p88; ☎ 403-760-3493; www.cows.ca; 134 Banff Ave; ice cream C$3.50-5; ☺ 10am-9pm) Banff Ave isn't Banff Ave without an omnipresent queue snaking out of Cows, purveyors of what is possibly the best ice cream in Canada. A product of Prince Edward Island, Cows' 30-plus flavors are topped by the epic 'moo crunch', an extra-creamy melange of chocolate and peanut butter cups, and well worth the 20-minute wait.

Bruno's Cafe & Grill
BREAKFAST, BURGERS $

(Map p88; ☎ 403-762-8115; www.brunosbanff.com; 304 Caribou St; mains C$10-16; ☺ 8am-10pm) While other joints stop serving breakfast at 11am, Bruno's keeps going all day, replenishing the appetites of mountain men and women as it once replenished its one-time Swiss-guide owner, Bruno Engler. It's a kind of greasy-spoon-meets-pub. The walls are decorated with antique ski gear, and the crowd at the next table could well be last night's live band refueling for tonight's gig.

The formidable Mountain Breakfast (C$17) is served in a basket and requires a Mt Rundle–sized appetite.

Evelyn's Coffee Bar
CAFE $

(Map p88; ☎ 403-762-0352; www.evelynscoffeebar. com; 215 Banff Ave; mains C$6-10; ☺ 6:30am-11pm; ☎) Pushing Starbucks onto the periphery, Evelyn's parades two downtown locations, both on Banff Ave. Dive into either one of them for wraps, pies and – best of all – its own selection of giant homemade cookies. The second branch is a block further south at 119 Banff Ave.

Wild Flour
CAFE $

(Map p88; ☎ 403-760-5074; www.wildflourbakery. ca; 211 Bear St; mains C$5-10; ☺ 7am-7pm; ☎ ☑) 🍃 Banff's antidote to Tim Hortons is heavy on organic, vegan and frankly strange-looking cakes, pastries and cinnamon buns backed up with free-trade, organic coffee. It also bakes its own bread.

Safeway
SUPERMARKET $

(Map p87; cnr Elk & Marten Sts; ☺ 8am-11pm) Banff's largest supermarket has the best selection for campers and self-caterers.

Saltlik
STEAK $$

(Map p88; ☎ 403-762-2467; www.saltliksteakhouse. com; 221 Bear St; mains C$16-27; ☺ 11am-2am) With rib eye in citrus-rosemary butter and peppercorn New York striploin on the menu, Saltlik is clearly not a 'plain Jane' steakhouse knocking out flavorless T-bones. No, this polished dining room abounds with rustic elegance and a list of steaks the length of many establishments' entire menu. In a town not short on steak-providers, this could be number one.

Coyote's Deli & Grill
FUSION $$

(Map p88; ☎ 403-762-3963; www.coyotesbanff. com; 206 Caribou St; mains C$20; ☺ 7:30am-10:30pm) Coyote's is best at lunchtime, when you can bunk off hiking and choose a treat from the deli and grill menu, which is inflected with a strong southwestern slant. Perch on a stool and listen to the behind-the-bar banter as you order up flatbreads, seafood cakes, quesadillas or some interesting soups (try the sweet potato and corn chowder).

Block Kitchen & Bar
TAPAS $$

(Map p88; ☑ 403-985-2887; www.banffblock.com; 201 Banff Ave; tapas C$7-26; ☺ 11am-10pm) An interesting new restaurant that has broken the mold in Banff, marrying a casual atmosphere with sophisticated food – the menu is heavy with Asian and Mediterranean influences. The small but creative tapas plates might not satisfy truly ravenous post-hiking appetites, but if you're taking a day off physical activity or are on a romantic getaway, this place ought to impress.

Eddie Burger & Bar
BURGERS $$

(Map p88; ☑ 403-762-2230; www.eddieburgerbar.ca; 6/137 Banff Ave; burgers C$12-20; ☺ 11am-2am) Sometimes nothing hits the spot like a burger, and the Eddie serves up some of the best in town. It's decked out in authentic diner style and, as you'd expect, all the classics are on the menu. If you're feeling a bit more adventurous, you might like to try one of the 'Signature' burgers, such as elk burger with avocado, Gouda cheese and pesto mayo.

Bear St Tavern
PUB FOOD $$

(Map p88; www.bearstreettavern.ca; 211 Bear St; mains C$15-18; ☺ 11:30am-late) Run by the owners of the Bison, this gastro-pub hits a double whammy: ingeniously flavored pizzas washed down with locally brewed pints. Banffites head here in their droves for a plate of pulled-pork nachos or a bison-and-onion pizza, accompanied by pitchers of hoppy ale. The patio overlooking Bison Courtyard is the best place to linger if the weather cooperates.

Melissa's Restaurant
STEAK $$

(Map p88; ☑ 403-762-5511; www.melissasrestaurant. com; 218 Lynx St; mains C$17-27; ☺ 7am-10pm; ☝) Melissa's is a casual ketchup-on-the-table type of place in a 1928 heritage building. It's huge in the local community and has an equally huge selection of food and price ranges. Nonetheless, its brunch, dinnertime steaks and deep-dish pizzas are probably its most defining dishes.

Nourish
VEGETARIAN $$

(Map p88; ☑ 403-760-3933; www.nourishbistro. com; 215 Bear St; mains C$10-18; ☺ 11:30am-10pm; ☝) Nourish has carved out a devoted following in Banff thanks to its vegetarian and vegan food. The menu revolves around fairly conventional standards such as portobello-mushroom melts and oven-baked falafels.

★ Park
MODERN CANADIAN $$$

(Map p88; ☑ 403-762-5114; www.parkdistillery.com; 219 Banff Ave; mains C$17-44; ☺ 11am-late) Banff gets hip with a microdistillery to complement its microbrewery, plying various drinks and cocktails mixed with spirits (gin, vodka and whiskey) that are made on the premises. Park also does good food and offers a trendy and boisterous space in which to enjoy it.

Weather permitting, you can decamp to a roped-off street-side patio or Banff Ave's finest 1st-floor deck. It's huge, but popular. Try the pork-filled hoagie bun.

Bison Restaurant & Terrace
CANADIAN, FUSION $$$

(Map p88; ☑ 403-762-5550; www.thebison.ca; 211 Bear St; mains C$29-45; ☺ 5pm-late) The Bison might look like it's full of trendy, well-off Calgarians dressed in expensive hiking gear, but its a two-level affair, with a rustically elegant restaurant upstairs sporting a menu saturated with meat, and the cheaper, more casual Bear St Tavern on the terrace below.

Maple Leaf Grille
CANADIAN $$$

(Map p88; ☑ 403-762-7680; www.banffmapleleaf. com; 137 Banff Ave; mains C$20-40; ☺ 11am-10pm) With plenty of local and foreign plaudits, the Maple Leaf eschews all other pretensions in favor of one defining word: 'Canadian.' Hence, the menu is anchored by BC salmon, east coast cod, Albertan beef and Okanagan Wine Country salad... you get the drift.

Le Beaujolais
FRENCH $$$

(Map p88; ☑ 403-762-2712; www.lebeaujolaisbanff. com; cnr Banff Ave & Buffalo St; 3-/6-course meals C$68/95; ☺ 6-10pm) Stick the word 'French' in the marketing lingo and out come the ironed napkins, waiters in ties, and elevated prices. True, Beaujolais might not serve up your standard post-hiking dinner spread, but if you've spent the last few days feasting on pot noodles, menu items like beef tartar and lobster salad could start to look very appetizing.

Evergreen
CANADIAN $$$

(Map p87; ☑ 403-762-3307; www.theevergreen.ca; 459 Banff Ave; mains C$26-40; ☺ 6:30am-10:30pm) Hotel restaurants can be hit-and-miss, but the Evergreen inside the Delta Banff Royal Canadian Lodge is consistently good – provided you like formal fine-dining and can look past the rather dated decor. The Michelin-trained chef's modus operandi is to combine classic French dishes with Canadian produce to create such enticing hybrids as braised

Alberta bison short-ribs bourguignonne and elk medallions.

Grizzly House
EUROPEAN $$$

(Map p88; ☑ 403-762-4055; www.banffgrizzly house.com; 207 Banff Ave; fondues per person C$27-80; ⊙ 11:30am-midnight) This odd restaurant specializes in exotic meats, from beef and buffalo to shark and rattlesnake, cooked fondue-style at your table, either in hot oil or on a hot rock. It's dark, dingy and gets very smoky when everyone's sizzling, but at the very least it'll be an experience to tell your friends about. Check out the working phone beside your table, left over from the restaurant's days as a disco in the 1970s.

✖ Bow Valley Parkway

Baker Creek Bistro
EUROPEAN $$$

(Map p94; ☑ 403-522-2182; www.bakercreekbistro. net; Bow Valley Pkwy; mains C$18-40; ⊙ 8:30am-10am, 11:30am-4pm & 5-10pm) This attractive cabin restaurant is located inside the Baker Creek Chalet complex and is one of the few places to eat on the Bow Valley Pkwy. Good thing it's decent, with such exotic lures as bison stroganoff fettuccine and coffee beer-braised short-ribs. There's also a cheaper lounge selling burgers and the like, and a breezy patio.

✖ Lake Louise

Trailhead Café
SANDWICHES $

(Samson Mall; sandwiches C$6-10; ⊙ 8am-5:30pm) Join the queue for trail supplies at this bustling coffee and sandwich bar in Lake Louise Village. Sandwiches, bagels and wraps are made to order, and there's a selection of juices, cakes and pastries on the counter.

Bill Peyto's Café
CAFE $

(Village Rd; mains C$5-12; ⊙ 7am-10pm May-Sep, to 9pm Oct-Apr) You can fill up for next to nothing at the HI's in-house cafe, so expect queues when the hostel's full. The menu is certainly nothing fancy, but if a bowl of chili or a baked potato is all you're after, Peyto's definitely hits the spot.

Laggan's Bakery
BAKERY $

(☑ 403-522-2017; Samson Mall; mains C$5-10; ⊙ 6am-8pm) Laggan's (named after Lake Louise's original settlement) is a cafeteria-bakery with limited seating that's famously busy in the summer. The pastries and savories aren't legendary, but they're handy hiking snacks

and tend to taste better the hungrier you get. The pizza bagels are worth a special mention.

Village Market
SUPERMARKET $

(Samson Mall; ⊙ 6am-8pm) Supermarket selling general groceries and food supplies.

Lake Louise Station Restaurant
CANADIAN $$

(☑ 403-522-2600; www.lakelouisestation.com; 200 Sentinel Rd; mains C$15-25; ⊙ 11:30am-9:30pm) Restaurants with a theme have to be handled so carefully, and thankfully this railway-inspired eatery, at the end of Sentinel Rd, does it just right. You can either dine in the station among the discarded luggage or in one of the dining cars, which are nothing short of elegant. The food is simple, yet effective. A must-stop for train-spotters.

Caribou Lounge
INTERNATIONAL $$

(Map p94; ☑ 403-522-3991; www.crmr.com; 109 Lake Louise Dr; mains C$15-22; ⊙ 11am-10pm) The more relaxed of the two restaurants at the Deer Lodge is one of the nicest places for lunch around Lake Louise, with a selection of light dishes such as flatbread pizzas, salmon linguine and burgers, and proper afternoon tea served with dainty cakes. The lounge has the same heritage feel as the rest of the lodge, but the real selling point is the grand view of Victoria Glacier from the outside patio.

★ Fairview Lounge
BRITISH $$$

(Map p94; ☑ 403-522-1601; www.fairmont.com/ lake-louise; Lake Louise Dr; afternoon tea C$43; ⊙ noon-3pm) File it under 'part of the experience.' Rarely will you get afternoon tea served up with these kind of views. Showing off its British credentials (Lake Louise is, after all, named after Queen Victoria's daughter), the Chateau Lake Louise's expensive spread includes finger sandwiches, India's best orange pekoe, and scones with real Devonshire cream. It's all served up in an atmosphere heavy with *Downton Abbey*–era nostalgia.

✖ Icefields Parkway

Num-Ti-Jah Lodge
CANADIAN $$

(☑ 403-522-2167; www.num-ti-jah.com; Icefields Pkwy; mains C$18-40; ⊙ 5-10pm) The Num-Ti-Jah's delightfully down-home Elkhorn dining room serves hale and hearty food (steaks, pastas, fish and game) in a gorgeous log room overlooked by the requisite moose heads and elk horns. Priority goes to guests, so if you're staying elsewhere make sure you reserve ahead.

🍷 DRINKING & NIGHTLIFE

Throw a stone in Banff Ave and you're more likely to hit a gap-year Australian than a local. For drinking and entertainment, follow the Sydney accents to local watering holes or look through the listings in the 'Summit Up' section of the weekly Banff *Crag & Canyon* newspaper.

★ Banff Ave Brewing Co   MICROBREWERY
(Map p88; www.banffavebrewingco.ca; 110 Banff Ave; ⊙11:30am-2am) An offshoot of the excellent Jasper Brewing Co, this brewpub opened in Banff in 2010. It's best for a drink of craft beer, brewed on the premises and infused with Saskatoon berries and the like.

★ Whitebark Cafe   CAFE
(Map p87; ☑403-760-7298; www.whitebarkcafe.com; 401 Banff Ave; ⊙6:30am-7pm) Coffee in Banff recently got a wake-up call thanks to this new cafe that shares digs with the Aspen Lodge on Banff Ave. What it lacks in indoor seating space, the Whitebark makes up for in the excellence of its java, expertly confected by a team of friendly baristas. Snacks and sandwiches provide added fuel, but this place is primarily about the high-quality brews.

Rose & Crown   PUB
(Map p88; ☑403-762-2121; www.roseandcrown.ca; 202 Banff Ave; ⊙11am-2am) Banff's oldest pub (since 1985!) is a fairly standard British-style boozer with pool tables and a rooftop patio. Out of all of the town's drinking houses, it is best known for its live music, which raises the rafters seven nights a week – everything from communal singalongs to Seattle grunge.

Wild Bill's Legendary Saloon   BAR
(Map p88; ☑403-762-0333; www.wildbillsbanff.com; 201 Banff Ave; ⊙11am-late) Cowboys – where would Alberta be without them? Check this bar out if you're into line dancing, calf-roping, karaoke and live music of the twangy Willy Nelson variety. The saloon is named after Wild Bill Peyto, a colorful 'local' character who was actually born and raised in that not-so-famous cowboy county of Kent in England.

Tommy's Neighbourhood Pub   PUB
(Map p88; ☑403-762-8888; www.tommysneighbourhoodpub.com; 120 Banff Ave; ⊙11am-11pm) Tommy's pub-grub menu stretches to crab cakes and spinach-artichoke dip. More importantly for traditionalists, there's good draft beer, a dartboard, and plenty of opportunity

to meet the kind of globe-trotting mavericks who have made Banff their temporary home.

St James's Gate Olde Irish Pub   PUB
(Map p88; ☑403-762-9355; www.stjamesgatebanff.com; 205 Wolf St; ⊙11am-1am Sun-Thu, to 2am Fri & Sat) As Celts pretty much opened up western Canada and gave their name to the town of Banff, it's hardly surprising to find an Irish pub in the park, and a rather good one at that. Aside from stout on tap and a healthy selection of malts, St James's offers classic pub grub including an epic beef-and-ale pie.

Hoodoo Lounge   CLUB
(Map p88; www.hoodoolounge.com; 137 Banff Ave; ⊙9pm-3am Mon-Sat) If you came to Banff to go nightclubbing (silly you!) look no further than this joint, where you can drink, pose and dance in your sexy fleece not a mile from where wild animals roam.

☆ ENTERTAINMENT

Banff Centre   CONCERT VENUE
(Map p87; ☑403-762-6301; www.banffcentre.ca; 107 Tunnel Mountain Dr; tickets C$10-25) Perched on the side of Tunnel Mountain, Banff's flagship arts venue hosts a varied program of concerts, lectures, exhibitions and events throughout the year. It's also the main focus for big cultural events, including the Banff Summer Arts Festival in July, the Banff International String Quartet Competition in August, and the Banff Mountain Film Festival in November.

Lux Cinema Centre   CINEMA
(Map p88; www.luxbanff.com; 229 Bear St; tickets C$9-11) The local movie house screens first-run films.

🔒 SHOPPING

🔒 Banff Town

Banff Indian Trading Post   GIFTS
(Map p87; www.banffindiantradingpost.com; cnr Cave & Birch Aves; ⊙9am-9pm) Established by Norman Luxton, the old Sign of the Goat store is still the first place to head if you're after some First Nations crafts, including beadwork, deer-hide gloves, antler-handled hunting knives and 'dreamcatchers.' Some of the stuff is pretty tacky and of dubious provenance, so choose carefully.

Busy shopping area, Banff Town

All in the Wild Gallery & Gifts ARTS
(Map p88; ☎ 403-760-3141; www.banffphoto.com;
105 Banff Ave; ⊗10am-8pm Mon-Wed, to 9pm Thu-
Sun) Among the jokey trinket outlets on Banff
Ave, this place stands out. It exhibits and sells
the work of the superb wildlife photographer,
Jason Leo Bantle. If your budget doesn't
stretch to a framed blow-up, there are also
coffee-table spreads and even an illustrated
children's wildlife book.

Monod Sports OUTDOOR EQUIPMENT
(Map p88; www.monodsports.com; 129 Banff Ave;
⊗10am-9pm) This is Banff's oldest outdoor-
equipment supplier, and still the best.
Women's and men's clothing from big brands
such as Patagonia, Arc'teryx, Icebreaker, Columbia and North Face, are supplemented by
dedicated sections for rucksacks, equipment
and footwear.

Trail Rider Store CLOTHING
(Map p88; www.horseback.com/about-us/our-store;
132 Banff Ave; ⊗9am-6pm) Pick up all the cowboy fashion you'll ever need for looking the
part in the saddle, from Stetsons and plaid
shirts to handmade leather cowboy boots.

Viewpoint BOOKS, GIFTS
(Map p88; www.theviewpoint.ca; 201 Caribou St;
⊗9am-5pm) Sells glossy photo books, books

on Banff's local history, geology and wildlife,
and a good stash of local park maps.

Rocky Mountain Soap Company BEAUTY
(Map p88; www.rockymountainsoap.com; 204 Banff
Ave; ⊗10am-9:30pm Sun-Thu, to 10pm Fri & Sat)
Banff branch of the Canmore-based beauty
company, selling natural soaps, lotions and
creams.

Chocolaterie Bernard Callebaut FOOD
(Map p88; www.bernardcallebaut.com; 111 Banff
Ave; ⊗10am-7pm Mon & Wed-Fri, to 5pm Tue, 11am-
7pm Sat & Sun) Gourmet chocolate-maker
with over 48 flavors to choose from.

🛍 Lake Louise

Wilson Mountain Sports OUTDOOR EQUIPMENT
(www.wmsll.com; Samson Mall; ⊗9am-7pm) This
outdoors shop is pretty much the only place
to rent bikes in Lake Louise. Hardtails cost
C$15/39 per hour/day, while kids' bikes, trail-
a-bikes and chariot trailers cost C$10/20.

ℹ Information

DANGERS & ANNOYANCES
Banff is generally one of the safest of the national
parks, but as always, you should take the necessary precautions to avoid unexpected wildlife

ℹ️ USEFUL NUMBERS

The following telephone numbers might come in useful during your stay:

Avalanche Hazards (📞403-762-1460) Recorded message detailing areas at high risk of avalanche.

Banff Weather Office (📞403-762-2088) For the latest weather forecast and warnings.

Road Conditions (📞403-762-1450) Provided by Rocky Mountain National Parks.

Trail Conditions (📞403-760-1305) Trail reports, wildlife warnings and closures (recorded message).

encounters. Carry bear spray, make noise on the trail and hike in groups wherever possible. Pay attention to trail closures and group access restrictions, especially around the Lake Louise area in summer.

It's also important to take extra care on the road, as road and railway collisions are still the number one cause of death for wildlife in Banff.

If you're hiking and leaving your vehicle at a trailhead (especially overnight), make sure you don't leave any valuables on display. If you're cycling, use a lock.

EMERGENCY

For fire, mountain rescue and other emergencies, call 📞911.

Park Warden Office (emergencies 📞403-762-4506, nonemergencies 📞403-762-1470) For park-related matters and to report wildlife sightings (especially bears, cougars, wolverines and lynx).

MEDIA

Crag & Canyon (www.banffcragandcanyon.com) Free local newspaper published Tuesday.

Park Radio (www.friendsofbanff.com/park-radio) Not-for-profit radio station (101.1/103.3FM) with regular trail reports, weather bulletins and other park news.

Rocky Mountain Outlook (www.rmoutlook.com) Canmore-based paper that covers general Banff news. Published Thursday.

MEDICAL SERVICES

Mineral Springs Hospital (📞403-762-2222; 305 Lynx St, Banff Town; ⊙24hr) Emergency medical treatment.

MONEY

Bank of Montreal (107 Banff Ave, Banff Town; ⊙9:30am-5pm Mon-Sat)

CIBC (98 Banff Ave, Banff Town; ⊙9:30am-5pm Mon-Fri, to 4pm Sat)

POST

Banff Post Office (Map p88; 204 Buffalo St, Banff Town; ⊙8:30am-5:30pm Mon-Fri, 11am-3:30pm Sat)

TOURIST INFORMATION

Banff Tourism Bureau (Map p88; 📞403-762-8421; www.banfflakelouise.com; 224 Banff Ave, Banff Town; ⊙9am-7pm mid-Jun–Aug, to 5pm Sep–mid-Jun) Opposite the Parks Canada desks in the Banff Visitor Centre, this info desk provides advice on accommodations, activities and attractions.

Banff Visitor Centre (Map p88; www.pc.gc.ca/banff; 224 Banff Ave, Banff Town; ⊙9am-7pm mid-Jun–Aug, to 5pm Sep–mid-Jun) Offices for Parks Canada.

Lake Louise Backcountry Trails Office (📞403-522-1264; Lake Louise Visitor Centre, Lake Louise Village; ⊙9am-7pm mid-Jun–Aug, to 5pm May–mid-Jun & Sep–mid-Oct, 9am-4:30pm Thu-Sun mid-Oct–Apr) Specialist advice on exploring the backcountry area around Lake Louise.

Lake Louise Tourism Bureau (📞403-762-8421; Lake Louise Visitor Centre, Lake Louise Village; ⊙9am-7pm mid-Jun–Aug, to 5pm May–mid-Jun & Sep–mid-Oct, 9am-4:30pm Thu-Sun mid-Oct–Apr) Information on activities and accommodations in Lake Louise Village.

Lake Louise Visitors Centre (Samson Mall, Lake Louise Village; ⊙9am-7pm mid-Jun–Aug, to 5pm May–mid-Jun & Sep–mid-Oct, 9am-4:30pm Thu-Sun mid-Oct–Apr) Has some good geological displays, a Parks Canada desk, and a small film theater.

ℹ️ Getting There & Away

Most visitors arrive in the park by car, although regular shuttle services travel to Banff and Lake Louise from the airport.

BUS

The Banff Airporter (www.banffairporter.com) airport shuttle bus runs nine times daily from Calgary airport to Banff (one way adult/child C$59/29.50). Buses provide door-to-door service to/from Banff hotels and also stop in Canmore.

The Brewster Airport Shuttle (www.explorerockies.com/airport-shuttles) has seven daily buses from Calgary airport to Banff (one way adult/child $57/27.50) and Lake Louise (C$78/39). One bus continues to Jasper (C$128/64). Free wi-fi is available on board.

Greyhound (📞800-661-8747; www.greyhound.ca) offers a long-distance bus service five times daily to/from Calgary via Canmore and Banff, and four times daily to/from Banff via Lake Louise, Golden and Vancouver. There's also a once-daily service to Radium Hot Springs (for Kootenay). Buses stop at Canmore Visitor Centre, Banff train station, and Samson Mall in Lake Louise. A surcharge of C$3 is added to all routes on weekends, and discounts are available online.

Note that Greyhound buses do not currently stop at Calgary airport. You can get from the airport to Calgary bus depot with a combination of bus and C-train.

Sample Greyhound fares:

DESTINATION	ADULT ONE-WAY FARE
Banff–Calgary	C$25.50
Banff–Canmore	C$5.70
Banff–Lake Louise	C$16
Banff–Radium Hot Springs	C$29.30
Banff–Vancouver	C$93.50

CAR

If you're arriving by air, the easiest option is to rent a car at either Calgary or Edmonton airports (but note that airport rentals incur a surcharge). A few of the major car-hire companies have offices in Banff:

Avis (☑ 403-762-3222; cnr Wolf St & Banff Ave; ☺ 8am-4:30pm Mon-Sat, to noon Sun)

Budget (☑ 403-226-1550; 202 Bear St; ☺ 8am-5pm Mon-Fri, to 3pm Sat, to 2pm Sun)

Enterprise (☑ 403-762-2688; cnr Lynx & Caribou Sts; ☺ 8am-5pm Mon-Fri)

TRAIN

Banff's historic train station is just outside town on Railway Ave. The only passenger train that stops there is the luxurious, but expensive, *Rocky Mountaineer* (www.rockymountaineer.com), which is essentially a tourist train selling travel packages for trips between Banff, Lake Louise, Kamloops and Vancouver, BC.

❶ Getting Around

Unlike Glacier in the US, Banff National Park has no free hikers' shuttle. There are limited private shuttles to some trailheads.

BICYCLE

Banff is well geared for cyclists, with plenty of bike shops and rental companies dotted around the main town. Very few trailheads have cycle racks, but some rental companies offer shuttle services to main trails.

BUS

Roam (☑ 403-762-1215; www.roamtransit.com) buses serve sights around Banff Town, plus there's an hourly bus to Canmore. Tickets are C$2 for local buses and C$6 for the Canmore run.

Route 1 Banff Ave to Sulphur Mountain and the Banff Gondola.

Route 2 Tunnel Mountain campgrounds to the Fairmont Banff Springs hotel via Banff Ave.

Route 3 Banff to Canmore

Route 4 Banff Ave to the Cave & Basin springs.

All three ski resorts run shuttles to their base gondolas in the winter. The free Mt Norquay shuttle (www.summer.banffnorquay.com/plan-your-visit/shuttle-information) also runs in the summer, picking up along Banff Ave. **White Mountain Adventures** (p78) runs a summer shuttle to Sunshine Meadows.

CAR

Trans-Canada Hwy 1 runs straight through the center of the park via Canmore, Banff Town and Lake Louise Village. The single-lane Bow Valley Pkwy (Hwy 1A) runs parallel to Hwy 1, and is closed in spring from 6pm to 9am to protect wildlife.

➜ Speed limits are usually 90km/h (56mph) for major roads, and 60km/h (37mph) on secondary roads, unless otherwise indicated.

➜ Outside Banff and Lake Louise, the only gas stations are at Castle Mountain Junction and Saskatchewan Crossing.

➜ Most parking lots at trailheads and in Lake Louise Village and Banff Town are free.

TAXI

Due to the distances between sights, taxis aren't a very practical way of getting around, although they can make an economical way of getting to trailheads for families and groups of more than three people. A fare between Banff and Canmore is approximately C$50.

Banff Taxi (☑ 403-762-4444)
Lake Louise Taxi (☑ 403-522-2020)

JEAN-PIERRE LESCOURRET / GETTY IMAGES ©

1. Lake Louise Gondola (p96)
This gondola takes you 2088m (6850ft) above the valley floor to offer a bird's-eye view of the Lake Louise area.

2. Lake Louise (p95)
One of Banff National Park's most famous attractions, Lake Louise is known for its searingly blue water, which often mirrors the surrounding scenery.

3. Winter in the Canadian Rocky Mountains
Many hiking and biking paths are given over to cross-country skiing and snowshoeing in winter.

4. Yoho National Park (p124)
Hikers looking for fossils at the Burgess Shale formation.

VICKI MAR PHOTOGRAPHY / GETTY IMAGES ©

Around Banff National Park

Includes ➡

Canmore 117
Kananaskis
Country 121
Yoho National Park . . 124
Lake O'Hara. 127
Mt Assiniboine
Provincial Park 127
Kootenay National
Park & Radium Hot
Springs. 128
Golden 131

Best Places to Stay

➡ Paintbox Lodge (p119)

➡ Sundance Lodges (p122)

➡ Assiniboine Lodge (p128)

➡ Kicking Horse Mountain Resort (p133)

Best Places to Eat

➡ Rocky Mountain Bagel Co (p120)

➡ Trough (p121)

➡ Truffle Pigs (p127)

➡ Eleven22 (p133)

Why Go?

Although many visitors never venture much beyond Banff, it's well worth taking the time to explore outside the park's borders. Banff is buffered by numerous other spectacular national and provincial parks, all blessed with the same kind of sky-high scenery, but with the added advantages of having far fewer visitors and quieter trails. Kananaskis and Yoho are the locals' tips for hiking, while Golden is the center for adventure sports. Backcountry walkers head for the remote trails in British Columbia's roadless Mt Assiniboine Provincial Park.

When to Go

Banff National Park

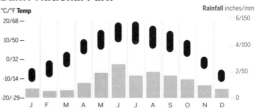

Jul Warm, settled weather makes this the prime month for hiking and sightseeing.

Late Sep The summer crowds die down and the forests are at their most colorful.

Nov The winter season begins and outdoor activities are plentiful.

Canmore

Canmore is Banff for locals, a former coal-mining town that reinvented itself during the 1988 Winter Olympics (when it hosted the cross-country skiing events) into an outdoor activity center extraordinaire. Spend time sitting in a downtown bar or cafe and you'll quickly ascertain that most of the population lives here because they love it – and no wonder! The hiking, cycling, skiing and spiky mountain vistas are magnificent, and the rock climbing – Canmore acts as HQ for the Alpine Club of Canada – is world-class.

Quieter, cheaper and more chilled than Banff, Canmore's small, but still growing, hub makes a good launching pad for the national park or the more hidden pleasures of Kananaskis Country to the south. There are plenty of hotels scattered around town, and reasonable transport links connecting to both Banff and Calgary, including the bike-friendly Legacy Trail, which is heavily used by both locals and tourists.

In June 2013, Canmore was temporarily cut off when catastrophic flooding closed Hwy 1 and destroyed a number of local homes. A state of emergency was declared and massive damage to infrastructure ensued. All told, it was the costliest natural disaster in Canadian history. Most of the visible damage in Canmore has now been repaired.

Canmore is 24km (15 miles) southeast of Banff Town and 7km (4.3 miles) from the park's East Gate along Hwy 1. Most shops, services and restaurants are along Main St (8th St), which runs west from Railway Ave.

◉ Sights

Big Head SCULPTURE
At the end of Main St, half-buried in gravel by the Bow River, sits the impressive sculpture known as the Big Head (for reasons that will soon become obvious once you see it). Created by the artist Al Henderson, the sculpture was inspired by Canmore's name; the original town of Canmore in northwest Scotland was called *ceann mór,* a Gaelic word meaning great head or chief.

The sculpture has become a much-loved landmark, and the head's shiny pate is sometimes adorned to mark town festivities. It occasionally even gets its very own woolly toque in winter.

Canmore Museum & Geoscience Centre MUSEUM
(www.cmags.org; 907 7th Ave; adult/child C$5/3; ☺noon-5pm Mon-Fri, 11am-5pm Sat & Sun May-Sep, 1-4pm Fri-Mon Oct-Apr) The town's small museum has an intriguing collection of exhibits and photographs relating to Canmore's coal-mining history, the story of the 1988 Olympics and, more recently, the devastating 2013 floods.

🏃 Activities

★**Canmore Nordic Centre** MOUNTAIN BIKING
(www.canmorenordiccentre.ca; Olympic Way) Nestled in the hills to the west of town on the way to the Spray Lakes Reservoir, this huge trail center was originally developed for the Nordic events of the 1988 Winter Olympics. It's now one of the best mountainbike parks in western Canada, with over 65km (40 miles) of groomed trails developed by some of the nation's top pedal-heads and trail designers.

There are graded routes to suit all abilities, from easy rides to technical singletracks and full-on downhills. You can bring your own bike, or hire one from Trail Sports (p73), opposite the center's day lodge. The center also offers guided rides and skills clinics (C$60 for 1½ hours) with certified instructors.

If mountain biking is not your thing, most of the center's trails are also open to walkers, orienteers and roller-skiers, and in winter some are specially groomed for cross-country skiers. Whatever the time of year, take precautions to avoid wildlife encounters, as the trails cross through areas of backcountry that form part of the Bow Valley Wildlife Corridor, and you might find that grizzlies, black bears and ungulates have decided to use the trails, too.

The center is a 3.6km (2.2-mile) drive from Canmore on Spray Lakes Rd. Across the river take Rundle Dr, continue south along Three Sisters Dr and follow signs to the Canmore Nordic Centre.

Elevation Place HEALTH & FITNESS
(☎403-678-8920; www.elevationplace.ca; 700 Railway Ave; ☺6am-9pm Mon-Fri, 8am-9pm Sat & Sun; ♿) Canmore's spanking new sports center replicates many of the activities you can do outdoors, so if the weather's not cooperating, this is a good place to hang out. The kid-friendly swimming pool is excellent, and the huge indoor climbing wall is an ideal place to get to grip with the basics before you tackle a real crag.

Canmore

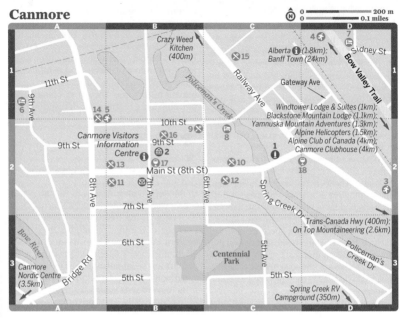

Canmore

◎ Sights
1 Big Head...C2
2 Canmore Museum & Geoscience
  Centre..B2

◎ Activities, Courses & Tours
3 Elevation Place...................................D2
4 Gear Up...D1
5 Snowy Owl Tours...............................B1

◎ Sleeping
6 Canadian Artisans..............................A1
7 Lady Macdonald Country Inn.............D1
8 Paintbox Lodge...................................C2

◎ Eating
9 Communitea...B2
10 Grizzly Paw...C2
11 Mountain Mercato...............................B2
12 Old School Bus....................................C2
13 Rocky Mountain Bagel Co...................B2
14 Rocky Mountain Flatbread Co.............A1
15 Safeway..C1
16 Trough...B2

◎ Drinking & Nightlife
17 Canmore Hotel....................................B2
18 Rose & Crown.....................................D2

Grassi Lakes Trail   HIKING

There are plenty of trails within easy reach of town, including the popular 3.8km (2.4-mile) round-trip to Grassi Lakes, named after Lawrence Grassi, one of Canmore's founding fathers.

Other options include trails to Cougar Creek and Grotto Canyon (both around 4km/2.5 miles), the sky-high ascent of Ha Ling Peak (5.6km/3.5 miles) and an airy scramble to the mountain of Lady Macdonald (8km/5 miles), which passes an abandoned teahouse en route. Trail maps and route advice are available from the Canmore Visitors Information Centre.

Alpine Helicopters   SCENIC FLIGHTS

(☏403-678-4802; www.alpinehelicopters.com; 91 Bow Valley Trail) Canmore is a busy base for scenic chopper flights over Spray Lakes (12 minutes; C$124 per person) and Mt Assiniboine (30 minutes; C$289). It also offers heli-hiking and heli-skiing. Flights are weather dependent, so it's always best to have a backup plan in case the clouds roll in. The heliport is just south of town on the Bow Valley Trail.

Canmore Cave Tours   ADVENTURE SPORTS

(☏403-678-8819; www.canmorecavetours.com) Buried deep beneath the Grotto Mountain near Canmore is a system of deep caves known as the **Rat's Nest**. Canmore Cave Tours runs guided trips into the maze of twisting passageways and claustrophobic caverns.

There are two core trips: the Explorer Tour (adult/child C$125/105), a 4½-hour trip that involves around two hours underground; and the longer Adventure Tour (adult/child C$155/145), a six-hour trip that features an 18m (15ft) abseil and ends at the Grotto, a stalactite-filled chamber with a crystal-clear underground pool.

Young kids are permitted on the shorter Discovery Tour (adult/child C$45/35). Be prepared to get very wet and muddy, and brace yourself for chilly temperatures, as the caves stay at a constant 5°C (41°F) year-round.

Dogsledding

Following recent controversy over dogsledding and its treatment of animals, it's become doubly important to make sure that dogsledding companies treat their dogs with respect and dignity.

Snowy Owl Tours DOGSLEDDING
(✆ 403-678-9588; www.snowyowltours.com; 829 10th St; 2hr tour adult/child C$159/85) Dogsledding has been a traditional mode of travel in the Canadian Rockies for centuries, and it's a wonderful way to see the wilderness. Snowy Owl Tours offers sled trips on custom-built sleighs pulled by your own well-cared-for team of Siberian and Alaskan huskies.

The sledding season is usually from November to April; if you're here in summer, you can meet the dogs on a kennel tour (adult/child under 11 years C$45/35).

🛏 Sleeping

Canmore's hotels and B&Bs generally offer better value than most places inside the park. The **Canmore Bow Valley B&B Association** (✆ 403-609-7224; www.bbcanmore.com) keeps a comprehensive list of all the local B&Bs, and you'll find lots of motels and hotels along the Bow Valley Trail.

There is also a large number of apartment and condo rentals in Canmore, many of which are advertised online at B&B and holiday accommodations sites. Good places to start include Rentals in the Rockies (www.rentalsintherockies.com) and Canmore Holiday Accommodation (www.canmoreholiday accommodation.com).

Booking and information for all the main campgrounds around Canmore is handled by **Bow Valley Park Campgrounds** (✆ 403-673-2163; www.bowvalleycampgrounds.com).

Canmore Clubhouse HOSTEL $
(✆ 403-678-3200; www.alpineclubofcanada.ca; Indian Flats Rd; dm from $36; 🅿) 🧺 Steeped in climbing history and mountain mystique, the Alpine Club of Canada's beautiful hostel sits on a rise overlooking the valley. You'll find all of the usual hostel amenities here, along with a sauna. The Alpine Club offers classes in mountaineering and maintains several backcountry huts.

Three Sisters Campground CAMPGROUND $
(✆ 403-673-2163; www.bowvalleycampgrounds.com; Hwy 1; tent & RV sites C$23; ⊘ mid-Apr–Nov) For pretty sites and a relatively peaceful atmosphere, head to this campground in the satellite town of Three Sisters, 16km (10 miles) east of Canmore. The tent spaces furthest from the highway are generally the quietest and you're handily positioned near plenty of hiking trails. RVs are welcome.

Bow River Campground CAMPGROUND $
(✆ 403-673-2163; www.bowvalleycampgrounds.com; Hwy 1; tent & RV sites C$23; ⊘ May-Sep) The municipal campground in Canmore is very basic, so the best option if you want to camp close to town is this riverside site 1.6km (1 mile) down Hwy 1. It's sandwiched between the river and the highway, so it's not as peaceful as it could be, but it's pleasant enough if you can bag a spot by the water. Basic facilities include non-flush toilets and RV-accessible sites, but there are no hookups.

Spring Creek RV Campground CAMPGROUND $
(✆ 403-678-5111; www.springcreekrv.ca; 1 Spring Creek Gate; RV sites C$38-49; ⊘ mid-Apr–mid-Oct) Dedicated entirely to motor-homers, this open-meadow RV ground has fantastic mountain views, despite the total lack of privacy between the pitches. Nevertheless, full hookups and the handy town-edge location ensure it's usually busy.

⭐Paintbox Lodge B&B $$
(✆ 403-609-0482; www.paintboxlodge.com; 629 10th St; r C$147-279, 2-night minimum mid-Jun–mid-Sep & Christmas; 🅿 🛜) Run by ex-Olympic skiers Thomas Grandi and Sarah Renner, this truly lavish B&B fully deserves its boutique tagline. The five suites are a super mix of country chic and luxury comfort. For maximum space ask for the Loft Suite, which sleeps four and features beamed ceilings, mountain-view balcony and sexy corner tub. All rooms share use of the mountain kitchen, kitted out with top-of-the-range Miele appliances (including an espresso machine).

Blackstone Mountain Lodge   HOTEL $$

(☑ 888-830-8883; www.blackstonecanmore.ca; 170 Kananaskis Way; d C$139-249; ⊡※⊛☑) The pick of several Bellstar properties around Canmore, the Blackstone is located a quick drive out of town on the Bow Valley Trail. It's a purpose-built hotel with a choice of traditional rooms or suites that come with their own fully equipped kitchen (complete with oven, dishwasher and washing machine), making them ideal for families. The rates are very reasonable, even in summer, and there's a hot tub and outdoor pool to boot.

Lady Macdonald Country Inn   GUESTHOUSE $$

(☑ 800-567-3919; www.ladymacdonald.com; 1201 Bow Valley Trail; r C$125-199, ste C$200-250; ⊡�☑) This frilly little inn wouldn't look out of place in small-town Connecticut, with its elegant verandas, turrets and wooden cladding. The rooms are dinky, each with their own style: Vermilion has views of Ha Ling and a Jacuzzi; Cascade has a gas fireplace and turret outlook; and the top Three Sisters Suite has wall-to-wall mountain views. Breakfast is included.

Windtower Lodge & Suites   HOTEL $$

(☑ 403-609-6600; www.windtower.ca; 160 Kananaskis Way; d/ste C$139/239; ⊡@☑) Named for the stunning rock feature only a few kilometers to the east, this modern and well-appointed hotel is a good option. The rooms are a bit small, so spending more on a suite is a good idea. Some rooms have fine views of the Three Sisters, and all have access to an outdoor hot tub. Breakfast is included.

Canadian Artisans   B&B $$

(☑ 403-678-4138; www.canadianartisans.ca; 1016 9th Ave; ste C$180-210; ⊡☑) This oddball B&B is tucked away in forest on the edge of Canmore. The two wood-lined suites are detached from the main house. The best is the Treehouse Suite, which has picture windows, stained-glass door panels, a futuristic shower pod and a lovely vaulted roof. The Foresthouse is a bit more cramped (especially in the bathroom-cum-bedroom department).

✖ Eating

For such a small town, Canmore has a surprising number of great places to dine – so many, in fact, that people often drive over from Banff solely for the pleasure of eating here.

Safeway (1200 Railway Ave; ⊗8am-11pm). Good for self-catering supplies.

★ Rocky Mountain Bagel Co   CAFE $

(☑ 403-678-9978; www.thebagel.ca; 829 8th St; bagels C$6-8; ⊗6am-6pm; ☑) ✎ Is there anything better in life than sitting under the flower baskets at Rocky Mountain Bagel Co, studying the morning shadows on the Three Sisters peaks while enjoying a toasted maple bagel and a latte? Possibly not.

Communitea   CAFE $

(www.thecommunitea.com; 1001 6th Ave; lunch mains C$6-10; ⊗9am-5pm; ☑⊞) ✎ In a perfect world, this is what all cafes would be like. Locally run, ethically aware and all organic, this sweet little community cafe has become a Canmore institution since it opened in 2008. Homey veggie food, fresh-pressed juices and great coffee pack in the daytime punters, and the cafe hosts regular gigs, readings and discussions at weekends.

Mountain Mercato   COFFEE, DELI $

(www.mountainmercato.com; 817 8th St; lunch mains C$8-12; ⊗9am-6pm Mon-Fri, 10am-7pm Sat & Sun) ✎ If you're looking for the best coffee in Canmore, this lovely deli is where you'll find it. The Americanos and macchiatos are rich, strong and beautifully brewed; while you're waiting, you can browse the shelves for posh goodies, including organic fruit juices, handmade chocolates and other luxury items.

Old School Bus   ICE CREAM $

(8th St; 1/2 scoops C$3.75/4.75, kid's scoop C$2.50; ⊗9am-5:30pm; ⊞) Permanently parked just off Main St, this converted school bus is the place for ice cream in Canmore. The chalkboard's full of unusual flavors, including white chocolate, blackberry, and peanut butter, and the milkshakes are heavenly, too.

★ Rocky Mountain Flatbread Co   ITALIAN $$

(www.rockymountainflatbread.ca; 838 10th St; pizza C$16-28; ⊗11:30am-9pm Sun-Thu, to 10pm Fri & Sat; ☑) ✎ In a town where, by the nature of your outdoor activities, you end up craving plenty of pizza, Rocky Mountain Flatbread Co is a pleasant apparition. This is the real McCoy Italian-style, although you can rev things up a bit with pizza flavors like fig and Brie cheese or lemon chicken and apple. The pasta is equally good – homemade, with different toppings displayed on a daily specials board.

Grizzly Paw   PUB FOOD $$

(☑ 403-678-9983; www.thegrizzlypaw.com; 622 8th St; mains C$13-20; ⊗11am-midnight) ✎ Shock, horror exclusive: Alberta's best microbrewery (offering six year-round beers) is hiding in the mountains of Canmore. The veterans of Raspberry Ale and Grumpy Bear beer recently built a new brewery to support their legendary brewpub (tours and tasters are available). There's also a microdistillery on the way. And, yes, the pub serves grub.

★ **Trough** CANADIAN $$$
(☑ 403-678-2820; www.thetrough.ca; 725 9th St; mains C$32-38; ⊙ 5:30pm-late Tue-Sun) Canmore's slinkiest bistro is tucked away on 9th St, but it's absolutely worth the effort to find. It regularly features in the Rockies' top restaurant lists, and with good reason: the food is about the best anywhere in town, mixing modern Canadian flavors with inspiration from fusion, Asian and Mediterranean cuisines.

Crazy Weed Kitchen INTERNATIONAL $$$
(☑ 403-609-2530; www.crazyweed.ca; 1600 Railway Ave; mains C$22-38; ⊙ 5-9:30pm Mon-Wed, 11:30am-3pm & 5-10pm Thu-Sun) This flashy new bistro on the edge of Railway Ave feels more big city than small town, with its sharp designer lines, funky artwork and globetrotting menu that takes in everything from wood-fired pizza to short ribs in *massaman* curry to Kashmiri lamb balls. It has earned a devoted following, so book ahead.

Drinking & Nightlife

Rose & Crown PUB
(749 Railway Ave; ⊙ 11am-2am) This spit-and-sawdust British pub at the northern end of Main St looks dingy from outside, but things feel a lot more welcoming once you get out onto the riverside patio. Plentiful beers on tap make it a good place to rub shoulders with the locals, and it's also one of Canmore's main venues for live music.

Canmore Hotel PUB
(738 8th St; ⊙ 11am-midnight) A (very) old-school boozer where the beer slips down nicely with a burger and fries. The building is historic, but raffishly unrestored, and most of the 'locals' look like they've been coming here since the 1970s. Touring bands provide noise.

❶ Information

Alberta Visitor Information Centre (☑ 403-678-5277; www.travelalberta.com; 2801 Bow Valley Trail; ⊙ 8am-8pm May-Oct, to 6pm Nov-Apr) Regional visitor center just off the Trans-Canada Hwy northwest of town.

Canmore General Hospital (☑ 403-678-5536; 1100 Hospital Pl; ⊙ 24hr)

Canmore Visitors Information Centre (www.tourismcanmore.com; 907a 7th Ave; ⊙ 9am-5pm) Just off the main drag.

Post Office (801 8th St; ⊙ 9am-5pm Mon-Fri, to noon Sat)

❶ Getting There & Away

Canmore is easily accessible by car from Banff and Calgary along Trans-Canada Hwy 1. Brewster (www.brewster.ca/transportation) buses and the Banff Airporter (www.banffairporter.com) shuttle link several times daily to Calgary airport, Banff and Lake Louise.

Roam (www.roamtransit.com) The number 3 bus (C$6, 24 minutes, hourly) runs between Canmore and Banff, 6am to 9pm weekdays, and 9am to 7pm weekends and holidays.

Greyhound (www.greyhound.ca) Buses head to Calgary (C$24.50, 1¼ hours, five daily), Banff (C$5.70, 25 minutes, five daily) and points beyond.

Kananaskis Country

The area collectively known as Kananaskis Country (or K-Country to the locals) covers a vast area to the south and east of Banff National Park, comprising several side-by-side provincial parks and protected areas, including Peter Lougheed Provincial Park, Elbow Valley, Sheep Valley, Ghost River Wilderness Area and Don Getty Wildland Provincial Park.

While visitors and tourists make a beeline for Banff's trails, many Albertans prefer to hike in K-Country, where the routes are quieter, the scenery is just as impressive and that all-important sense of wilderness is much easier to come by. It's less well-known than Banff, but with a bit of research you'll find some fantastic hikes and trails, as well as plenty of sky-topping peaks, mountain lakes and outdoor pursuits.

⭐ Activities

There are two main roads through the area, which link up near the Kananaskis Lakes to form a convenient loop. The main Kananaskis Trail (Hwy 40) travels through the center of Kananaskis Valley from Barrier Lake, while the unpaved gravel Spray Lakes Trail (Hwy 742) heads northwest from the junction near Lower Kananaskis Lake all the way back to Canmore.

The best facilities in the area are around Kananaskis Village, which consists primarily of the Delta Lodge at Kananaskis. Numerous walking trails, as well as the paved Bill Milne bike path, lead out from here. The 'village' also has several restaurants and a useful outdoor shop, **Kananaskis Outfitters** (www.kananaskis outfitters.com; Kananaskis Village; bikes per day C$45; ☑10am-6pm), which rents bikes.

Boundary Ranch   HORSEBACK RIDING
(☑403-591-7171; www.boundaryranch.com; Hwy 40; rides from C$43.50; ☑May-Oct) This experienced trail-riding ranch offers lots of options for day rides and longer pack trips, some of which also feature white-water rafting and backcountry hikes. The ranch is also home to the popular Rick Guinn's Steakhouse.

Nakiska   SKIING
(www.skinakiska.com; Hwy 40; day lift pass C$74.95) The K-Country's only ski resort was one of the main venues for the 1988 Winter Olympics, and it's still a popular place to hit the slopes, although the facilities and runs are a lot less developed than in Banff. Shuttle buses run throughout the winter season from Canmore and Banff, making Nakiska a credible (and often quieter) alternative to the Big Three.

There are around 30 groomed runs spread out over 413 hectares (1021 acres), with plenty of scope for off-piste riding on the slopes of Mt Allan. Over two-thirds of the runs are rated intermediate, so Nakiska is a good all-round resort for most mid-level skiers. Snowboarders can also tackle the challenging Najibska Rail Park. The resort also has some of the Rockies' only accessible areas for glade skiing.

Peter Lougheed Provincial Park   HIKING
The quiet trails and backcountry areas of K-Country are superb for hikers, especially around Peter Lougheed Provincial Park, situated on the west side of Kananaskis Valley. Named after the premier of Alberta from 1971 to 1985, this remote park covers an area of 304 sq km (117 sq miles), including the **Upper** and **Lower Kananaskis Lakes** and the **Highwood Pass**, the highest-navigable road pass in Canada at 2350m (7710ft; usually open from June to October). It's an excellent area for wildlife spotting, as it's an important wildlife corridor and the valley has been subjected to very little development.

Recommended half-day hikes include the 3km (1.9-mile) trail to **Boulton Creek** (one hour) and the 5km (3.1-mile) hike to the natural bowl of **Ptarmigan Cirque** (three hours). Longer day routes include the 7.2km (4.5-mile) hike to **Mt Indefatigable** (four hours) and the 16km (10-mile) **Upper Kananaskis Lake Circuit** (five hours). Trail leaflets and information on conditions are available from the park visitor center near Kananaskis Lakes.

🛏 Sleeping & Eating

Outside the business-oriented Delta Lodge at Kananaskis, hotels are thin on the ground. As a result, those not up for camping often base themselves in Canmore and visit Kananaskis on day trips.

Kananaskis' campgrounds, however, when compared to Banff, are a haven of peace and tranquility. Book well ahead, as K-Country's backcountry trails are very popular.

There's a full listing of all the main K-Country campgrounds at www.kananaskis countrycampgrounds.com. Reservations for most sites can be made online through the new Alberta Campgrounds (www.reserve. albertaparks.ca) reservation service. You'll need a wilderness permit (C$8.80) if you're planning to stay anywhere in the backcountry.

Self-catering supplies for campers are available from the small stores at Fortress Junction, Mt Kidd RV Park, Boulton Creek Trading Post and Kananaskis Village.

★ **Sundance Lodges**   CAMPGROUND $
(☑403-591-7122; www.sundancelodges.com; Kananaskis Trail; campsites C$32, teepees C$65-90, trappers' tents C$90; ☑mid-May–Oct) For that authentic Canadian experience, try the hand-painted teepees and old-timey trappers' tents at this privately run campground. As you'd expect, facilities are basic – sleeping platforms and a kerosene lantern are about all you'll find inside – so you'll need the usual camping gear, but kids are bound to lap up the John Muir vibe.

Mt Kidd RV Park   CAMPGROUND $
(☑403-591-7700; www.mountkiddrv.com; Mt Kidd Dr; RV sites with/without hookups C$48/33; ☑year-round) Halfway along the Kananaskis Valley, and handily placed for the facilities around Kananaskis Village, this place is the best option for trailer and RV campers, with full hookups and over 200 sites, plus comprehensive facilities, including tennis courts, a laundry, a grocery store, games rooms and even a sauna.

Canyon Camping   CAMPGROUND $
(☑866-366-2267; Kananaskis Lakes Rd; campsites C$26; ☑May-Oct) Just a few steps from Lower Kananaskis Lake and a gorgeous little picnic area, this is a lovely mountain-view campground. Loop A has just a few sites, while Loop C is furthest from the lakeshore, but usually the quietest. There are horse pits, trailer pull-throughs and a bike trail that's handy to the visitor center.

THE SMITH-DORRIEN/SPRAY TRAIL ROAD

The Smith-Dorrien/Spray Trail Rd (or Hwy 742 to give it its official title) is a dirt and gravel highway that runs for around 62km (38.5 miles) from the Kananaskis Lakes to Canmore. Named after a British commander of WWI, Horace Smith-Dorrien, the rough, unsealed trail passes through some of the wildest areas of the Peter Lougheed, Spray Valley and Bow Valley Wildland Provincial Parks.

The scenery is stunning, but the road is tough going, especially after heavy rain: be prepared for plenty of ruts and potholes, and go slow unless you want to wreck your rental car's suspension. There are several lakeside picnic areas en route where you can break the journey and drink in the mountain scenery. The northern section of the road into Canmore beyond Goat Creek is extremely steep, so take extra care here.

For much of its length, the road tracks the western edge of the **Spray Lakes Reservoir**, which provides much of Canmore's power through a hydro-electric dam built in 1950. Apart from the dam, the valley is almost entirely unpopulated, so it's a brilliant area for wildlife spotting: Rocky Mountain sheep, mountain goats, elk, moose and even bears can often be seen along the sides of the road, especially early or late in the day (take things slow if you want to have a chance of actually seeing anything). After dark you might even be lucky enough to hear the ghostly howl of a wolf echoing around the mountains, as the Spray Valley is a seasonal hunting ground for one of the Bow Valley's last remaining wild wolf packs.

The road also provides access to some of the K-Country's most remote trails, including the stunning **Bryant Creek route** into Mt Assiniboine Provincial Park from the Mt Shark parking lot, the 10km (6.4-mile) **Chester Lake Trail**, and the arduous 15km (9.3-mile) hike to **Burstall Pass** (five hours).

HI Kananaskis Wilderness Hostel   HOSTEL **$**
(☑ 403-521-8421; www.hihostels.ca; Kananaskis Village; dm/d C$27/66; ☺ reception 5-11pm) The rustic exterior might fool you into thinking you'll be roughing it at this backwoods hostel, but, fear not, inside you'll find shiny pine floors, plush sofas, a fire-lit lounge and a kingly kitchen. The large bunk-bed dorms are a bit institutional, but there are private-room options, too.

William Watson Lodge   CABINS **$**
(☑ 403-591-7227; Kananaskis Lakes Rd; cabins C$30-40; ☺ year-round) This subsidized cabin complex is specially designed for visitors with disabilities, with fully accessible lodges in a quiet wood, as well as organized activities to help guests get out and explore. You'll need your own food and bedding.

Delta Lodge at Kananaskis   HOTEL **$$**
(☑ 403-591-7711; www.deltahotels.com; 1 Centennial Dr, Kananaskis Village; r from $189; ▣ ▤ @ ᯤ ⛱) Kananaskis 'village' effectively consists of this sprawling lodge and its outbuildings, which include half-a-dozen restaurants and an outfitters. The lodge gained international fame when it hosted the 2008 G8 summit (with Bush II, Putin, Blair et al), an event that helped put K-Country on the map.

These days it's a comfortable if slightly institutional place that sits on the cusp of some truly amazing countryside; well-marked trails fan out directly from the complex. Staff are highly professional.

Mt Engadine Lodge   LODGE **$$$**
(☑ 403-678-4080; www.mountengadine.com; Mt Shark Rd; s/d/4-person chalet C$220/460/795; ▣ ᯤ) You can't get much more rural – or more peaceful – than this remote mountain lodge, situated about 30km along the Smith-Dorrien/Spray Trail Rd from Kananaskis Lakes. The lodge has a selection of peaceful rooms and family suites (the latter complete with balcony and sitting room), as well as detached cabins large enough for several people, all overlooking unspoiled meadows. Lodge rates include four hearty meals, including a build-your-own lunch and afternoon tea.

Rick Guinn's Steakhouse   STEAK **$$**
(☑ 403-591-7171; Hwy 40; mains C$10-20; ☺ 11am-7pm mid-May–mid-Oct) Boundary Ranch is home to this steakhouse, which turns out flame-grilled burgers, inch-thick steaks and smoked pork chops for its hungry horseback-riding guests (and anyone else who happens to be passing through).

ℹ Information

There are several visitor centers where you can pick up brochures, trail maps and wilderness passes.

Barrier Lake Information Centre (☎403-673-3985; www.tpr.alberta.ca/parks; Hwy 40; ⏱9am-5pm) Located 6.5km south of the junction on Hwy 1.

Elbow Valley Visitor Centre (☎403-949-2461; ⏱10:30am-2pm & 3-6pm Fri, 9am-12:30pm & 1:30-4:30pm Sat & Sun May-Oct) Just west of Bragg Creek.

Peter Lougheed Information Centre (☎403-591-6322; Kananaskis Lakes Rd; ⏱9am-9pm Jul & Aug, 9:30am-4pm Apr-Jun, Sep & Oct) Near the junction with Hwy 742, north of Kananaskis Lakes.

ℹ Getting There & Away

Kananaskis Country can be reached off Trans-Canada Hwy 1 on the Kananaskis Trail (Hwy 40), east of Canmore. From southern Alberta, you can reach the area in summer along Hwy 40 via the Highwood Pass.

Brewster (p276) buses running between Calgary and Banff stop at the Stoney Nakoda Resort at the junction of Hwy 1 and Hwy 40. From here a shuttle from the Delta Lodge at Kananaskis can whisk you down to Kananaskis Village (note: there's a surcharge for non-lodge guests).

Yoho National Park

To the west of Lake Louise, the Kicking Horse River bucks and surges into the wild, ice-crowned mountains of Yoho National Park, which is located across the Alberta border in the neighboring province of British Columbia. Though much smaller than Banff at around 1313 sq km (506 sq miles), Yoho (from a Cree word denoting awe or amazement) is every bit as spectacular as its neighbor: hulking peaks brood along either side of the plunging Kicking Horse Valley, and spur roads twist and turn to the area's most renowned attractions, including the crashing cascade of Takakkaw Falls and the glittering, green-blue pool of Emerald Lake.

Yoho is considered valuable to science for its Burgess Shale formation, first discovered by Charles Walcott in 1909. Its ancient rocks contain well-preserved fossils of sea creatures over 500 million years old.

Away from arterial Hwy 1, which cuts through the middle of the park, Yoho is still wild, remote country, and you'll find little in the way of visitor facilities. The only real settlement is the old railway service town of Field, just off Hwy 1, 27km (16.7 miles) to the west of Lake Louise, a quaint little town that has retained many of its original 19th-century clapboard buildings.

◎ Sights & Activities

★ Takakkaw Falls   WATERFALL
Yoho has several impressive waterfalls, but none are quite as grand as Takakkaw. A thundering torrent of water tumbles from its source in the nearby Daly Glacier over a sheer cliff face for 255m (836ft), making it the second-highest waterfall in Canada. The name comes from the Cree language, and roughly translates as 'it is magnificent.' The total base-to-top height of the falls is actually 384m (1259ft), but it is split into two tiers of freefall.

Takakkaw is equally impressive seen in rain or shine, and the noise at any time is quite deafening. The falls are reached via a snaking 13km (8-mile) spur road leading off Hwy 1; en route you'll pass a couple of interesting viewpoints, including the Meeting of the Waters, where the Yoho and Kicking Horse Rivers join into one mighty torrent. The road is steep and traverses a couple of punishing sections of switchbacks that can be extremely challenging for nervous drivers, especially if you're in an RV; be prepared to stop and let traffic pass when necessary.

At the end of the road, a trail leads for around 800m (0.5 miles) from the Takakkaw parking lot to the base of the falls. Looking back down the valley, you'll also have a grand view of the surrounding mountains, including the Vice President, Michael Peak and Wapta Mountain.

Emerald Lake   LAKE
For most visitors, this vividly colored lake is Yoho's most unmissable sight. Like its sister lakes of Peyto, Moraine and Lake Louise, Emerald Lake gains its otherworldly color from sunlight bouncing off rock particles suspended in the water – the brighter the light, the more vivid the color. Ringed by forest and silhouetted by impressive mountains, including the iconic profile of Mt Burgess to the southeast, it's a truly beautiful – if busy – spot.

The lake also marks the start of several hikes, including the easy 800m (0.5-mile) jaunt from the parking lot to Hamilton Falls, and the much tougher high-level hike via the Wapta Highline.

Canoes can be rented from the lakeside Emerald Sports & Gifts, and fishing is permitted from July to November.

The lake road is signed off Hwy 1 just to the southwest of Field and continues for 10km (6.2 miles) to the lakeshore. You can stop for a peek at a natural rock bridge over the Kicking Horse River just after the turnoff.

Kicking Horse Pass & Spiral Tunnels   VIEWPOINT

The historic Kicking Horse Pass between Banff and Yoho is one of the most important passes in the Rockies. It was discovered in 1858 by the Palliser Expedition, which was tasked with discovering a possible route across the Rockies for the Canadian Pacific Railway (CPR).

The first steam trains finally steamed across the pass in 1885, but the steep gradient was an enormous technical challenge: the very first train to attempt the new railway careered out of control, killing three workers, and wrecks and runaways continued to plague the railway during its first years of operation. To cut down on accidents, an ingenious system of underground passages known as the Spiral Tunnels was subsequently devised by one of the CPR's assistant chief engineers, JE Schwitzer, modeled on designs he had seen pioneered in the Swiss Alps. Snaking beneath the roots of Mt Ogden and Cathedral Mountain, the tunnels allowed trains to tackle the extreme gradient in stages rather than in one nightmare plunge, and drastically improved the railway's safety and reliability after they were opened in 1909. They are still in use to this day.

The main viewing platform (the Upper Lookout) is off Hwy 1, 8km (5 miles) east of Field. If you time it right, you can see a train exiting from the top of the tunnel while its final cars are still entering at the bottom.

Wapta Falls   WATERFALL

They might not be quite as high as Takakkaw, but what they lack in stature, Wapta Falls more than make up for in noise. They are the largest set of falls anywhere on the Kicking Horse River, measuring 150m (490ft) across and 30m (98ft) high.

They're also famous as the supposed spot where, during the historic Palliser Expedition of 1858, the geologist James Hector was kicked in the chest while trying to recover a runaway horse – an event that apparently inspired the name of one of the Rocky Mountains' most famous rivers.

The falls are reached after a gentle half-hour walk from the trailhead near the western border of Yoho. They are clearly signed off Hwy 1.

Iceline Trail   HIKING

For truly unbelievable views, Yoho's infamous Iceline Trail has attained legendary status among hikers, following an airy ridgeline for 12.8km (8 miles; elevation gain 710m/2330ft) across barren extraterrestrial rock that was covered by glacial ice as recently as the turn of the 20th century.

The trail affords a mind-blowing outlook of Takakkaw Falls and the Yoho Valley peaks, as well as a superb panorama over the glittering Emerald Glacier. It's a hard trail and can feel very exposed in bad weather, so save it for a settled day.

The route can be done as an out-and-back hike, but many people turn it into an overnight trip by linking up with the Yoho Valley Loop for a 21.1km (13.1-mile) round-trip, overnighting at one of the backcountry campgrounds at Little Yoho, Twin Falls or Laughing Falls.

Yoho Lake & Wapta Highline   HIKING

This strenuous route ranks among the finest (and hardest) day hikes in the Rockies. The route starts at the Whiskey Jack trailhead near Takakkaw Falls, and climbs to Yoho Lake before ascending onto the sky-top flanks of Wapta Mountain.

The route descends through forest and ends on Hwy 1, around 1.3km east of Field. In total it's a route of 18.3km (11.4 miles), with an elevation gain of 1010m (3314ft).

Twin Falls & the Whaleback   HIKING

If waterfalls are your thing, this moderate 8.2km (5.1-mile) route from Takakkaw Falls parking lot through pine forest takes in four lovely cascades: the Angel's Staircase, Point Lace Falls, Laughing Falls and the double-tiered Twin Falls.

It's a round-trip of around seven hours, or you can extend it into an overnight trip by camping at Twin Falls Campground and following the Whaleback ridgeline back down the valley. The Whaleback crosses a seasonal bridge across the upper falls; it's sometimes swamped by snow or snowmelt, so check at the park office before setting out. The Whaleback adds on around 5km (3.1 miles) to the Twin Falls hike.

Burgess Shale Geoscience Foundation   HIKING

(☑800-343-3006; www.burgess-shale.bc.ca; 200 Kicking Horse Ave, Field; tours adult/child from C$94/44; ☉Jul-Sep) Yoho's Burgess Shale fossil fields, displaying imprints of 505-million-year-old sea creatures, have been protected as a World Heritage site since 1981, and due to their delicate nature can now only be visited on a guided hike provided by the Burgess Shale Geoscience Foundation.

There are two core hikes, one to the original Walcott Quarry and another to the adjacent fossil fields on Mt Stephen. Both are strenuous full-day trips with plenty of elevation gain, so you'll need to be fit and wear proper footwear.

🛏 Sleeping

The best place to base yourself in Yoho is in its sole settlement, Field, which has lots of private B&Bs and rooms for rent. The visitor center keeps a comprehensive list.

Yoho's four campgrounds have only 197 sites between them, all of which are first-come, first-served. Arrive early!

Fireweed Hostel HOSTEL $

(☑ 250-343-6999; www.fireweedhostel.com; 313 Stephen Ave, Field; dm/d/ste $40/125/170; 🛜) This small hostel in Field is a real find, beautifully finished in rustic pine, complete with snowshoes above the hearth and hiking books for perusal. The dorms are small but smart; each room has two pine bunk beds and a shared bathroom off the hallway, and all have full use of a lovely kitchen and sitting room.

Kicking Horse Campground CAMPGROUND $

(Map p94; Yoho Valley Rd; tent & RV sites C$28; ⊗May-Oct; 🛜) This is probably the most popular campground in Yoho, in a nice forested location with plenty of space between sites, as well as all the deluxe facilities (hookups, flush toilets and wheelchair-accessible showers). The riverside sites (especially 68 to 74) are the pick of the bunch.

Monarch Campground CAMPGROUND $

(Map p94; Yoho Valley Rd; campsites C$18; ⊗May-Sep) Around 3km east of Field, and a stone's throw from Kicking Horse Campground, this basic site is situated in an open meadow. Water is sourced from an on-site well and there's an outdoor BBQ shelter for alfresco cookouts.

Whiskey Jack International Hostel HOSTEL $

(☑ 866-762-4122; www.hihostels.ca; Yoho Valley Rd; dm C$28; ⊗late Jun-Sep) You can almost feel the spray from Takakkaw Falls at Yoho's HI hostel – you can actually see the falls from the hostel's timber deck – but the accommodations are simple, bordering on spartan. Three nine-bed dorms and a basic kitchen are about all that's on offer, but despite the rudimentary facilities, it's usually booked out in summer.

Kicking Horse Lodge HOTEL $$

(☑ 250-343-6303; www.trufflepigs.com; 100 Centre Street, Field; d/ste C$115/200; ⊗Jun-Sep; 🅿❄🛜) Run by the owners of the Truffle Pigs bistro, this is Field's only hotel, and it's a decent bolthole as long as you're not too fussy about five-star luxury. The timber building has heritage charm, but the rooms are fairly simply decked out in cappuccino and cream hues. There are 'hikers' suites' with kitchenettes, and a family room.

Canadian Rockies Inn GUESTHOUSE $$

(☑ 250-343-6046; www.canadianrockiesinn.com; Stephen Ave, Field; r C$125-185; 🅿🛜) Run by jovial owners Luc and Kim, who also own the shop next door, this attractive Field house has several spacious rooms for rent. Spotless rooms and enormous beds are the main attractions, and all the rooms have microwaves, kettles and fridges; shame they don't have proper kitchens, too.

Emerald Lake Lodge LODGE $$$

(☑ 403-410-7417; www.crmr.com/emerald; lodges C$375-440; 🛜❄) Commanding a picture-perfect 5-hectare (13-acre) site right beside the tranquil shores of Emerald Lake, and accessed by its own romantic bridge – you really couldn't ask for a better position. But these pricey lodges don't really live up to first billing. The interiors feel disappointingly old-fashioned, heavy on the frills and floral motifs, but this is pretty much the only option in Yoho if you simply can't live without a lake view.

🍴 Eating

Siding CAFE, STORE $

(☑ 250-343-6002; www.sidingcafe.ca; 318 Stephen Ave, Field; snacks C$5-8; ⊗10am-5pm) Field's general store has been the hub of the community since the early days of the railway. It's chaotically but engagingly run, with shelves stacked high with supplies, and a small cafe on the side that dishes up homemade sandwiches and fresh-baked muffins to a steady local clientele.

Cilantro INTERNATIONAL $$

(☑ 250-343-6321; Emerald Lake; mains C$12-20; ⊗11am-10pm) Once the crowds disperse, this lakeside restaurant beside the bridge to Emerald Lake Lodge makes a pleasant detour for supper. The feel is more down-to-earth bistro than fine-dining emporium, and it's all the better for it: aim for a table on the lake-view deck and tuck into seared salmon, crispy tortillas and chargrilled steaks.

★**Truffle Pigs** FUSION **$$$**
(☑250-343-6303; www.trufflepigs.com; 100 Centre St, Field; dinner mains C$21-29; ☺11am-3pm & 5-9pm Mon-Fri, 8am-3pm & 5-9pm Sat & Sun) It's the only place to eat out in Field after dark, but thankfully the Truffle Pigs shows no sign of resting on its laurels. It offers just the right blend of culinary creativity and down-home charm, with a cute cabin-like dining room that looks out across the CPR railtracks, and an offbeat menu that veers from snow crab and stick ribs to truffled potato pierogi.

ⓘ Information

Yoho National Park Information Centre
(☑250-343-6783; off Hwy 1, Field; ☺9am-7pm May-Oct) Pick up maps and trail descriptions. Rangers can advise on itineraries and conditions. Alberta Tourism staffs a desk here in summer and Friends of Yoho also maintains a bookshop.

ⓘ Getting There & Away

Inexplicably, the Greyhound buses passing through Yoho on their way between Golden and Lake Louise don't stop in Field, leaving Yoho off the regular public-transportation network.

If you're car-less, the only options are periodic winter ski shuttles or pricey summer guided tours.

Lake O'Hara

Hiking destinations don't get much more exclusive than Lake O'Hara. Hidden away among a glorious amphitheater of mountains in the eastern part of Yoho National Park, the area is home to some of the park's most picturesque wildflower meadows and backcountry trails.

The only way into the Lake O'Hara area is via the 11km (6.8-mile) access road from the parking lot just off Hwy 1. The road is closed to public vehicles, so you'll either have to hike in on foot or try for a spot on one of the hugely oversubscribed **shuttle buses** (adult/child return C$15/8; ☺mid-Jun–Sep) from Field. The four daily buses have a total of 42 places and are always full, so you'll need to book way in advance; you'll also need to reserve well ahead to be sure of a place at Lake O'Hara's hugely popular 30-pitch **campground** (☑250-343-6433; tent site C$12; ☺Apr-Oct).

Reservations for the shuttle bus and campsites at the campground can be made up to three months in advance for a C$11.70 fee by calling the Lake O'Hara reservation line (☑250-343-6344). Facilities in the area are very limited, although hot snacks and drinks are sold at Le Relais day shelter in season (cash only). You'll also need a valid wilderness pass to visit the Lake O'Hara area; camping fees are included if you already hold an annual wilderness pass.

If you want to stay overnight and can't get a spot at the campground, there are also two **Alpine Club of Canada Huts** (☑reservations 403-678-3200, ext 1; per person per night C$36) in Lake O'Hara: the Abbot and Elizabeth Parker. Reservations are mandatory, and include a seat on one of the inbound buses.

Even better, book into one of the gorgeously old-world cabins at **Lake O'Hara Lodge** (☑250-343-6418; www.lakeohara.com; r/cabin C$650/920; ☺Jan-Apr & Jun-Oct) ⚑, where you'll be treated to home-cooked meals, afternoon tea and hot tubs, despite the fact that you're kilometers away from the outside world. Prices include bus transportation.

For a really exclusive experience, Lake O'Hara also provides access to the remote and fantastically wild **McArthur Valley**, which is strictly off-limits to people until August 15 to protect grizzly habitat. To visit the valley, you need to be granted one of the limited number of hiking permits that are made available each year. Phone the Yoho National Park Information Centre for more information.

Mt Assiniboine Provincial Park

If it's a real wilderness hit you're craving, Mt Assiniboine Provincial Park is the place. With its ice-encrusted slopes and distinctive skyrocket profile, the pointy pinnacle of **Mt Assiniboine** is one of the most recognizable landmarks of the Canadian Rockies, and at 3618m (11,870ft) is the highest peak in the southern ranges.

Dubbed the Matterhorn of Canada thanks to its distinctive pyramidal shape, the mountain and the surrounding 390-sq-km (150-sq-mile) provincial park can only be reached on foot (or, if you flash the cash, by chartered chopper). But you won't regret the effort it takes to get there: the high-altitude trails around the mountain and nearby Lake Magog are some of the most exquisite in the Canadian Rockies. Civilization has never felt so far away.

Most people make the trip into Assiniboine in three to five days; one in, one out, and between one and three to explore the trails and mountain country around Lake Magog.

Note that most of Mt Assiniboine Provincial Park is across the British Columbia border, so you'll need a valid British Columbia backcountry permit for every night you intend to stay (C$10). If you're overnighting at a campground across the Alberta border (such as Marvel Lake on Bryant Creek), you'll also need a Banff wilderness pass, plus a reservation at the relevant campground. If in doubt, check with staff at one of the park visitor centers before you set out.

You'll find general information on Assiniboine at www.env.gov.bc.ca/bcparks/explore/parkpgs/mt_assiniboine.

Activities

Needless to say, it's the trails that draw everyone to Mt Assiniboine. The core area centers on **Lake Magog**, with easy day hikes nearby.

Rock climbing and **mountaineering** are for experienced alpinists only. The routes are challenging and the drops are very, very long, so you need to know what you're doing. The mountain was first climbed in 1901 by a trio of mountaineers including James Outram, Christian Hasler and Christian Bohren, but the first man to conquer it solo was Lawrence Grassi in 1925.

Cross-country skiing is another way to explore the park in winter; telemarkers mostly arrive via Assiniboine Pass and need to be prepared for emergency camping and carry an avalanche beacon.

Sleeping

There are several backcountry campgrounds in Assiniboine, but most people end up pitching at either Lake Magog or Og Lake. All campsites are allocated on a first-come, first-served basis, and cost C$10 per person. Fires aren't permitted anywhere in the park.

If you're camping in Assiniboine, it's extremely important to take precautions against bears: grizzlies and black bears often trundle through the area, so make use of the bear-proof bins at Lake Magog, Og Lake and Porcupine.

For a bit more shelter you can book a bunk in one of four **Naiset Huts** (per person from C$20), which offer simple wooden beds, mattresses and a woodstove, as well as a cooking shelter with propane lights and a stove. Reservations (C$5 per night) are a good idea in summer and mandatory in winter. There's also a 15-person climbing shelter called the RC Hind Hut nestled near the northern face

of Mt Assiniboine. Reservations for all huts are made through Assiniboine Lodge.

⭐ **Assiniboine Lodge**   LODGE $$$
(☎ 403-678-2883; www.assiniboinelodge.com; r lodge per person C$300, shared/private cabin per person C$300/370; ☺ Feb-Mar, Jun-Oct) The only lodge in Assiniboine is also the oldest ski lodge in the Canadian Rockies, and is surrounded by mountain meadows and gloriously backed by Mt Assiniboine. The rustic lodge rooms sleep one or two people (solo travelers are usually required to share), plus there are shared (three to five people) or private cabins. Rates include communal meals and hiking guide service.

ℹ Getting There & Away

Forget public transportation – your only chance of a lift into Assiniboine is aboard a helicopter from the Mt Shark heliport (C$155) or Canmore (C$175), booked through Assiniboine Lodge.

Kootenay National Park & Radium Hot Springs

Stretching for just 8km (5 miles) on either side of Hwy 93 (sometimes known locally as the Kootenay Hwy or the Banff–Windermere Rd), Kootenay was founded in 1920 as a by-product of the construction of the first automobile highway across the Canadian Rockies. In exchange for helping out with the financial costs of building the road, the Canadian government claimed the slender sliver of land that now makes up the national park. Hwy 93 is the only road through the park, running for 94km (58.3 miles) from just west of Castle Junction across the Alberta–British Columbia border to Radium Hot Springs.

Due to its unusual geography, Kootenay is one of the most fire-prone areas in the Canadian Rockies; the southern section of the park toward Radium Hot Springs has been dubbed 'lightning alley' thanks to its frequent summer thunderstorms. In 2003, 174.1 sq km (67.2 sq miles) of forest in the northern part of the park were damaged by a huge wildfire sparked by lightning. The scars left by the blaze are still plain to see, and while it looks severe, it's worth remembering that wildfires are an essential part of the forest ecosystem, killing off disease and pests, clearing underbrush and weak trees and stimulating fresh growth.

◉ Sights

Marble Canyon   CANYON

In northern Kootenay, several kilometers southwest of the Stanley Glacier trailhead, the popular trail around Marble Canyon has been reincarnated since the 2003 fire. The easy 1.6km (1-mile) loop crosses Tokumm Creek and offers great views down into the plunging limestone canyon, sculpted and shaped by the surging force of the river.

Paint Pots   SPRING

Three kilometers southwest of Marble Canyon (and linked by a trail), a short wheelchair-friendly trail leads from Hwy 93 to the rust-red ochre ponds, once used by First Nation tribes including the Ktunaxa (Kootenay), Stoney and Blackfoot as a source of decorative paint for adorning teepees, clothing and bodies.

European settlers later used the ochre as a base for paint manufacture and a thriving mining operation was in full swing here in the early 1900s; you can still see bits of machinery scattered around the mineral beds. The Paint Pots themselves are three cold mineral springs with blue-green water that contrasts with the crimson crust of iron oxide decorating their edges.

Simpson Monument   VIEWPOINT

Hwy 93 crosses the Vermilion River around 31km (19.3 miles) from the Alberta border. Shortly afterward, look out for the Simpson Monument and viewpoint on the left, which commemorates the trailblazing explorer George Simpson, who pioneered the first trail over the mountains to Banff in 1841 and later went on to run the Hudsons Bay Trading Company. The historic route he followed heads west from here along the Simpson River, and now makes a popular route into the west side of Mt Assiniboine Provincial Park.

Look out for elk, moose and mountain goats at the Mt Wardle Animal Lick, just south of the viewpoint. There's another animal lick near Hector Gorge, about 17km southwest of the Simpson Monument.

🏃 Activities

Radium Hot Springs   HOT SPRING

(📞250-347-9485; www.pc.gc.ca/hotsprings; off Hwy 93; adult/child C$6.30/5.40; ⊙9am-11pm) Like its sister resort in Banff, Radium was put on the map in the late 19th century by its natural hot springs, which bubble out from beneath the mountains at a constant temperature of 44°C (111°F), cooling to a balmy 39°C (102°F) once the water reaches the 'hot' pool, and 29°C (84°F) once the water gets to the 'cool' pool.

Initially, the interest in the springs was medicinal: traces of radium dissolved from the surrounding rocks mean that the water is very faintly radioactive, and it was thought to have therapeutic value for curing everything from upset stomachs to gout. A scheme to bottle the water in the early 1900s failed, however, and the springs were subsequently developed as a spa resort. Don't fret too much about the radium in the water – it's about as radioactive as a luminous watch dial.

The twin pools themselves are pleasantly positioned beneath sheer rock faces, although the constant buzz of traffic from the nearby highway is a bit of a letdown. With a bit of luck, you might even glimpse a bighorn sheep or two while you take your dip.

Fireweed Trail   HIKING

The Vermilion Pass area, right on the edge of the Continental Divide, was the scene of a devastating fire in 1968 and you can now take a scenic 15-minute, wheelchair-accessible walk around the Fireweed Trail, with explanatory signs detailing the role that fires play in the life of the forest.

Far more evident is the starkly visible legacy of the 2003 forest fire viewable from Hwy 93 throughout most of northern Kootenay. Blackened trunks and ash-gray land coat the mountainsides on either side of the road, dotted with lush green patches where the forest has started to regenerate.

Stanley Glacier   HIKING

Located on arterial Hwy 93 is the trailhead to Stanley Glacier, by far the most interesting day hike anywhere in Kootenay. It's an 11km (6.8-mile) round-trip that takes in fire, forest and ice, and allows you to get right up close to one of the park's largest glaciers.

The first section of the trail winds up through burned pine forest, where you can see spectacular displays of wildflowers in summer, particularly arnica, paintbrush and fireweed. At the top of the climb, you pass into an area of old woodland that escaped the 2003 fire, before ascending into an impressive hanging valley overlooked by the crests of Storm Mountain, Stanley Peak and the sheer rock face known as the Guardwall.

On the right side of the valley, a slippery trail winds up across the boulder-strewn moraines to a fine viewpoint right beneath Stanley Glacier. It's best left for late summer, as the danger of avalanches remains high until the end of seasonal snowmelt.

Kootenay River Runners   RAFTING
(☑ 800-599-4399; www.raftingtherockies.com; Hwy 93; rafting trips C$52-115) Based just outside Radium, this rafting company offers several trips on class I–III rapids on both the Kootenay and Kicking Horse Rivers and nearby Toby Creek, as well as atmospheric trips in modern 'voyageur' canoes, the multi-person vessels used by early explorers.

Tours

Toby Creek Adventures   ADVENTURE TOURS
(☑ 250-342-5047; www.tobycreekadventures.com; Panorama; ATV trips C$99-274) Located 32km (19.8 miles) from Radium, this company offers daily ATV tours around local trails and the abandoned Paradise Silver Mine, as well as snowmobile trips in winter. The evening wildlife tours are great for photographers, too.

Sleeping

Apart from the campgrounds along Hwy 93, most of Kootenay's accommodations are in Radium, and are of the unfussy motel variety.

The three campgrounds have a communal capacity of 383 sites (far, far less than neighboring Banff). Redstreak is the only one that accepts reservations.

Cedar Motel   MOTEL $
(☑ 250-347-9463; www.cedarmotel.ca; 7593 Main St W, Radium Hot Springs; r C$85-92; P 🛜) Clean, cheap and (as its name suggests) cedar-clad, this Swiss-run place is one of the more attractive motels in Radium. The rooms are boxy but bright, with large beds and Technicolor bedspreads. Some have teeny kitchenettes and interjoining doorways, useful for families.

Redstreak Campground   CAMPGROUND $
(☑ 877-737-378; Stanley St E, Radium Hot Springs; tent & RV sites C$28-39; ⊙ May-Oct) Kootenay's largest campground with 242 sites tops the list for facilities, with everything from flush toilets and hot-and-cold running water to full hookup sites, a kids' playground and a small theater. It's a big, busy site, partially wooded, but crisscrossed by lots of access roads; it's probably not the place if you're looking for peace and quiet, but it's only a 30-minute walk from Radium *and* the hot springs.

There are 10 new oTENTiks (A-frame tents) with electricity and hot water for 'glampers'.

McLeod Meadows
Campground   CAMPGROUND $
(Hwy 93; tent & RV sites C$21.50; ⊙ Jun-Sep) You'll find plenty of natural splendor at this 80-pitch campground, peacefully located on

the banks of the Kootenay River just a 2.6km (1.6-mile) walk to the shores of pretty Dog Lake. Plentiful trees and spacious, grassy sites make this a fine place to pitch your canvas, especially since there are only 10 sites to each loop. Flush toilets, bear-proof bins, fire rings, cooking shelters and RV dumps are all on-site.

Marble Canyon Campground   CAMPGROUND $
(Hwy 93; tent & RV sites C$21.50; ⊙ Jul-Sep) This high-country 61-pitch campground is situated near the Marble Canyon trail, and has flush toilets but no showers. Most sites have tree cover to keep you out of the wind. The eastern side has the best views.

Kootenay Park Lodge   CABINS $$
(☑ 403-762-9196; www.kootenayparklodge.com; Hwy 93, Vermilion Crossing; d cabins C$135-200; ⊙ mid-May–late Sep; P) The pick of the places to stay inside the park, with a range of cute log cabins complete with verandas, fridges and two-burner hot plates to warm your beans and trail stews. The general vibe is rusticity rather than refinement, but it makes a way nicer place to sleep than Radium.

Village Country Inn   GUESTHOUSE $$
(☑ 250-347-9392; www.villagecountryinn.bc.ca; 7557 Canyon Ave, Radium Hot Springs; r C$119-139, ste C$129-175; P 🛜) If you really have to stay in Radium, take our advice and head for this cute gabled house just off the main drag. All the rooms are decked out in country fashion with plenty of plump pillows, frilly pelmets and potted plants. The same folksy feel runs into the downstairs tearoom, where afternoon tea is served on bone china and frilly doilies.

Storm Mountain Lodge   LODGE $$$
(☑ 403-762-4155; www.stormmountainlodge.com; Hwy 93; r C$239-299; P) Just inside the border of Kootenay National Park and set amid the forest, these luxury cabins were built in 1922 and have been gorgeously restored right down to the copper piping in the bathroom. They're cozy and romantic, with a big wooden bed, fireplace and claw-foot bathtub. Meals in the equally enchanting lodge are gourmet.

Eating

Radium's dining scene isn't going to rock your world, but there are a couple of passable places on the main highway into town.

Meet on Higher Ground
Coffee House   CAFE $
(☑ 250-347-6567; www.meetonhigherground.com; 7527 Main St, Radium Hot Springs; snacks C$3-10;

⊙6am-5pm; 📶) An ideal road-trip stop where you can refuel with coffee and a cinnamon bun or something more savory alongside other road-trippers and a few Radium regulars.

Old Salzburg Restaurant   AUSTRIAN $$
(📞250-347-6553; www.oldsalzburgrestaurant.com; Hwy 93; mains C$19-27; ⊙11:30am-10pm Apr-Oct, 5-10pm Nov-Mar) Pretty much everything is Austrian in this Radium restaurant, from the gabled roof to the homemade *spaetzle* (a kind of soft egg noodle or dumpling) to the garb worn by the waitstaff. For a break from steak and burgers, it's a fine choice perched handily at the jaws of Sinclair Canyon with a lovely outdoor patio should the weather cooperate.

ℹ Information

Kootenay National Park Visitor Centre
(📞250-347-9505; 7556 Main St E, Radium Hot Springs; ⊙9am-7pm mid-Jun–Sep, to 5pm Oct–mid-Jun) Main visitor center on the main highway through Radium Hot Springs.
Kootenay Park Lodge Visitor Centre (📞403-762-9196; info@kootenayparklodge.com; ⊙9am-6pm Jul-Sep, to 4pm or 5pm Oct-Jun) Located at Vermilion Crossing, 68km north of Radium Hot Springs.

ℹ Getting There & Away

From Banff, head south along Hwy 93 from Castle Junction. You can also reach the park from the south by heading north from Cranbrook on Hwy 93 to Radium Hot Springs.
   Greyhound (www.greyhound.ca) buses head up through Kootenay National Park to Banff (C$30, 1¾ hours, daily). In Radium they stop at a gas station on Hwy 93, near the junction with Hwy 98.
   Sun City Coachlines (www.suncity.bc.ca) heads from Radium north to Golden (C$19, 1¼ hours, daily) and south to Cranbrook (C$29, 2½ hours, two daily). Book through Greyhound.

Golden

The little community of Golden might be a long way from Banff's big mountains and sky-high scenery, but what it lacks in good looks it makes up for in adrenaline. It has become a popular center for outdoor activities, with everything from downhill mountain biking to white-water rafting on its doorstep, and though the town itself might not have much charm, it makes a convenient (and cheap) base for exploring Yoho to the east and the small national parks of Glacier and Mt Revelstoke to the west.

Traveling on Hwy 1, Golden is 58km (36 miles) west of Field, and 87km (54 miles) west of Lake Louise.

⊙ Sights & Activities

Kicking Horse Pedestrian Bridge   BRIDGE
Originally established as a logging town and supply station for the Canadian Pacific Railway (when the town was simply known as 'the Cache'), Golden is split in two by the Kicking Horse River. Just north of the main shopping thoroughfare of 9th Ave is the town's much-loved landmark, the Kicking Horse Pedestrian Bridge, which locals proudly trumpet as the longest freestanding timber bridge anywhere in Canada. Built in 2001 mainly by community volunteers, the bridge spans an impressive 46m (150ft).

★**Grizzly Bear Interpretive Centre**   WILDLIFE RESERVE
(www.kickinghorseresort.com; adult/child/family C$25/14/71; ⊙10am-5pm Jun-Sep) Coming face-to-face with a fully grown grizzly bear might not seem like a good idea to anyone who values their life, unless the bear happens to be Boo, Kicking Horse Mountain Resort's (p133) resident critter, who's lived on a large mountainside refuge since arriving as an orphaned cub in 2003 (his companion bear, Cari, sadly died shortly after arrival).
   While zoos and wildlife parks might not be everyone's cup of tea, the ethics of Boo's captivity are a little different. Following his instincts during mating season, the playful grizzly has escaped a number of times in the past, but has always voluntarily returned to his 'home.' On top of this, his refuge is run and maintained by highly professional wardens who talk with enthusiasm and authority about Boo and other ursine matters. Although a new tour leaves every hour, visitors are encouraged to dip in and out as they wish and ask all manner of questions.
   To visit the refuge, purchase tickets at the Kicking Horse gondola base station. Access is via the Catamount Chairlift. Tours run hourly from 9am to 5pm, with an hour's break for lunch at 1pm. A better deal is the Adventure Pass (adult/child C$39/30), which allows you to also travel on the gondola to the top of the mountain for hiking and sightseeing.
   For a more up-close introduction to Boo with one of his keepers, join the Ranger Assistant Tour (📞866-754-5425; adult/child/family C$30/20/80). The visits run at 9am and 4pm; numbers are limited to five per visit, so book ahead.

Northern Lights Wolf Centre   NATURE PARK
([📞]250-344-6798; www.northernlightswildlife.com; 1745 Short Rd; adult/child C$12/6; ⊙9am-7pm) This small wildlife center is dedicated to the welfare and preservation of Canada's native wolves, and houses a small pack of gray wolves and wolf-husky crosses, all born and bred in captivity. Visits include a guided tour of the wildlife facility and an introduction to the resident wolves – although most of the viewing is done through wire-frame pens.

The center is about a 14km (8.7-mile) drive north of Golden. Head north on Hwy 1, turn right onto Moberly Branch Rd for 2km (1.2 miles), then left onto Upper Donald Rd and follow the signs.

White-Water Sports

With the Kicking Horse River running right through the middle of town, it's hardly surprising that Golden is a center for white-water sports. As usual, all the local operators offer a variety of runs to suit all abilities, ranging from sedate floats to heart-stopping roller-coaster rides down the rapids. All equipment, including helmets and paddles, is provided. Many operators also offer canoe trips onto the Blaeberry, Kicking Horse, Blue Water and Spillimacheen Rivers.

Alpine Rafting ([📞]250-344-6778; www.alpine rafting.com; 101 Golden Donald Upper Rd; ⊙Jun-Sep; 🚌) Offers some good family rafting options, including a family white-water run for kids aged four and up (adult/child C$65/35), right up to the more mental class IV+ 'Kicking Horse Challenge' (C$165 – adults only!).

Wet & Wild ([📞]800-668-9119; www.wetnwild. bc.ca; 1509 Lafontaine Rd; rafting trips C$60-145) Offers several trips on the Kicking Horse, including two-day packages with overnight accommodations at McLaren Lodge in Golden. Also offers skidoo trips in winter.

Winter Activities

In addition to the many ski runs at Kicking Horse Mountain Resort, the slopes around Golden provide perfect territory for many other winter sports. **Chatter Creek** ([📞]877-311-7199; www.chattercreek.ca) is a ski area north of Golden that specializes in cat- and heli-skiing in the remote high country around the Chatter Creek, while **Snowpeak Rentals** ([📞]250-344-8385; www.snowpeakrentals.com; 1025 10th Ave N; full-day tours C$345-395) organizes snowmobile and skidoo tours.

🛏 Sleeping

Dull motels and chain hotels abound in downtown Golden, but there are some lovely B&Bs and lodges within easy reach.

Golden Eco-Adventure Ranch   CAMPGROUND $
([📞]250-344-6825; www.goldenadventurepark. com; 872 MacBeath Rd; tent & RV sites C$35, yurts C$52; ⊙early Apr–late Sep) Spread over 160 hectares (395 acres) of mountain meadow 5km (3.1 miles) south of Golden on Hwy 95, this great campground-cum-outdoors-center feels a world away from the cramped confines of municipal camping. Sites are spacious, there are full RV hookups, and you can even kip in a Mongolian yurt if you're tired of your tent.

Vagabond Lodge   LODGE $$
([📞]250-344-2622; www.vagabondlodge.ca; 158 Cache Close; d from C$180-250; [P][📶]) The best value of the accommodations at the Kicking Horse Mountain Resort, this is a mountain mansion with boutique pretensions. Six of the rooms have balconies overlooking the mountains, but the best are the two split-level rooms with their own snug sleeping lofts.

Kicking Horse Canyon B&B   GUESTHOUSE $$
([📞]250-344-6848; www.kickinghorsecanyonbb.com; 644 Lapp Rd; d C$125-145; [P][📶]) Hidden away among the hills to the east of Golden (phone for directions), this endearingly offbeat B&B takes you into the bosom of the family the minute you cross the threshold. Run by genial host Jeannie Cook and her husband Jerry, it's a real alpine home-away-from-home, surrounded by private grassy grounds with views across the mountains.

Canyon Ridge Lodge   GUESTHOUSE $$
([📞]250-344-9876; www.canyonridgelodge.com; 1392 Pine Dr; d C$109-119; [P][📶]) Three gleaming white rooms and a high-ceilinged studio suite are on offer at this timber-frame home, 1km (0.6 miles) from Golden's visitor center just off Golden Donald Upper Rd. It's beautifully finished (underfloor heating, slate-tiled private bathrooms) and there's a communal hot tub across the garden where you can soothe your aches after a day of exploring.

Copper Horse Lodge   BOUTIQUE HOTEL $$
([📞]250-344-7644; www.copperhorselodge.com; Cache Close; ste C$180-245; [P][❄][📶]) Part of the Kicking Horse complex, this groovy little number combines the ambience of a ski lodge with the amenities of an upmarket hotel; expect luxurious fabrics, huge beds and sexy bathrooms with multi-jet showers.

KICKING HORSE MOUNTAIN RESORT

Kicking Horse Mountain Resort (www.kickinghorseresort.com; day ski pass C$79) A four-season destination extraordinaire, the Rocky Mountains' newest ski resort (established on the site of the smaller Whitettooth resort in 2000) is a jack-of-many-trades and a master of quite a few. If you like uninterrupted downhill mountain biking, daredevil ski runs, assisted rock climbing, up-close bear viewing, or even fine dining, this could be your nirvana.

All of the facilities are easily navigable thanks to the year-round **Golden Eye Gondola**, which whisks visitors up to 2450m (8033ft) for grand views over Golden, the Rockies and the Columbia Wetlands.

With around 11.1 skiable sq kilometers (4.3 sq miles) covered each winter in a carpet of beautiful dry powder, Kicking Horse is revered for its steep expert skiing terrain and refreshing lack of crowds. Its vertical drop is 1260m (4133ft) – the fourth longest in North America. In summer, the same trails are used by mountain bikers when the mountain metamorphoses into the longest cycling descent in Canada. Basic bikes can be rented at the gondola base station for C$38 a day. For a full-suspension bike, plus body armor and a gondola day pass, you're looking at C$160.

Other attractions on Kicking Horse include the Grizzly Bear Interpretive Centre (p131), summit hiking trails, and the **Eagle's Eye Restaurant** (☎250-439-5400; mains C$30-44; ⏱11:30am-2pm May-Jun, to 4pm Jul-Sep), a gourmet establishment at the top of the gondola. There are other, more casual eating options at the gondola base station, including the **Double Black Cafe** (☎250-344-2214; www.doubleblackcafe.com; lunch C$10; ⏱8am-4pm). In summer, hikers can walk down the mountain on a fairly gentle doubletrack path (shared with cyclists) called 'It's a 10' (because it's 10km!). In winter, skiers use the same route.

The resort is 14km (8.7 miles) west of Golden in the Dogtooth Range and fairly well-signed. Public transport is non-existent in the summer (taxis from Golden cost C$50 one way). However, in the ski season there's a thrice-weekly shuttle linking to Banff and Calgary Airport run by **Discover Banff Tours** (p98).

✗ Eating

Bacchus Cafe CAFE $
(www.bacchusbooks.ca; 409 9th Ave N; mains C$6-12; ⏱9am-5:30pm Mon-Sat, 10am-4pm Sun) This bohemian hideaway at the end of 8th St is a favorite haunt for Golden's artsy crowd. Browse for books (new and secondhand) in the downstairs bookstore, then head upstairs to find a table for tea. Sandwiches, salads and cakes are all made on the premises, and the coffee is as good as you'll find in Golden.

★ Eleven22 FUSION $$
(☎250-344-2443; www.eleven22.ca; 1122 10th Ave S; mains $11-24; ⏱5-10pm; 🍴) A cross between a restaurant and a dinner party, this appealing option has art on the walls of the small dining rooms and all the stars you can count out on the patio. Watch the kitchen action from the lounge area while sharing small plates. Ingredients are mostly sourced locally.

Island Restaurant INTERNATIONAL $$
(☎250-344-2400; www.islandrestaurant.ca; 101 Gould's Island; mains C$12-23; ⏱9am-9pm) Location is the big deal here (on a small river island in the middle of Golden), followed by decor (especially the riverside patio). The food wears many hats, from a Jamaican jerk chicken sandwich to full-on Mexican nights on Mondays and Tuesdays. All in all, a well-priced, extremely varied downtown bet.

ℹ Information

Golden Visitor Information Centre (☎250-344-7125; www.tourismgolden.com; 500 N 10th Ave; ⏱9am-5pm May-Sep, to 4pm Tue-Fri Oct-Apr) In a purpose-built building on the main highway into town.

ℹ Getting There & Away

About 25km (15.5 miles) west of Yoho National Park, Golden is situated next to the Trans-Canada Hwy, at the junction of Hwy 95 south.

Greyhound (☎800-661-8747; www.greyhound.ca) buses pass through town heading west to Kamloops (C$56, four to five hours, five daily) and Vancouver (C$112, 10 to 12 hours, five daily), and east to Lake Louise (C$17, 1¼ hours, four daily) and Banff (C$22, two hours, four daily).

Sun City Coachlines (☎250-417-3117; www.suncity.bc.ca) runs daily minibuses south to Radium Hot Springs (C$19, 1¼ hours, daily).

Jasper National Park

Includes ➡

Day Hikes 138
Overnight Hikes 146
Cycling 149
Driving 152
Other Activities. 152
Sights. 156
Sleeping. 163
Eating. 169
Drinking &
Nightlife 170
Shopping 171
Around Jasper
National Park 172

Best Hikes

➡ Skyline Trail (p146)
➡ Tonquin Valley (p148)
➡ Path of the Glacier Trail (p138)
➡ Bald Hills Loop (p145)

Best Post-Hike Refreshment Spots

➡ Bear's Paw Bakery (p169)
➡ SnowDome Coffee Bar (p170)
➡ Jasper Brewing Co (p170)
➡ View Restaurant (p170)

Why Go?

In a modern world of clamorous cities and ubiquitous social media, Jasper seems like the perfect antidote. Who needs a shrink when you've got Maligne Lake? What use is Facebook when you're two days by foot from the nearest road? And, how can you possibly describe the Athabasca Glacier in a 140-character tweet? Filled with the kind of immense scenery that has turned the monosyllabic into romantic poets, Jasper is a rugged beauty; more raw and less tourist-pampering than its southern cousin Banff, and hence host to a more ambitious, adventurous visitor. Its tour de force is its extensive multipurpose trail network, much of it instantly accessible from the park's compact townsite. Backing it up is abundant wildlife, colossal icefields and – for the brave – the kind of desolate backcountry that makes you feel as though you're a good few kilometers (and centuries) from anything resembling civilization.

Road Distance (KM)

	Columbia Icefield Centre	Jasper	Maligne Lake	Mt Robson (Visitor Centre)
Jasper	105			
Maligne Lake	150	50		
Mt Robson (Visitor Centre)	185	85	135	
Pocahontas	150	45	85	130

Note: Distances are approximate

Entrances

There are three main road entrances to Jasper National Park. The East Park Entrance is on Hwy 16 between Jasper and Hinton, just east of Pocahontas. The West Park Entrance is on the same highway, 24km (15 miles) west of Jasper Town, near Yellowhead Pass and the border with British Columbia and Mt Robson Provincial Park. The Icefields Parkway Entrance is south of Jasper Town on Hwy 93, on the way to Lake Louise. You must either buy or show a park pass at all entry gates.

DON'T MISS

Unlike Banff, most of Jasper's trails are 'multi-use', open to hikers, horseback riders and cyclists. Thanks to this liberal sharing policy, the park is able to offer what is the best network of off-road cycling trails in Canada – and they're not just for daredevils. They're rated green (easy), blue (moderate) or black (difficult), so pretty much everyone is catered for, including kids or parents towing chariots.

An added bonus is that many of Jasper's trails start directly from the townsite, meaning you don't need to lug your bike around in a car or bus. Using a special cycling trail map (free from the info office), numerous loops can be plotted from your hotel or campground, with time to incorporate hiking, swimming, canoeing or grabbing a cup of coffee along the way.

When You Arrive

➡ All visitors intending to stop off in Jasper National Park must purchase a park pass (adult/youth/senior/family day pass C$9.80/4.90/8.30/19.60), even if just for a picnic or short leg-stretch.

➡ Passes can be procured at the Jasper Information Centre or at one of three different road entrances.

➡ If you're spending a week, an annual pass (C$67.70) works out cheaper and can be used in all national parks across Canada, including Banff, Kootenay and Yoho.

➡ The park is open year-round, though many activities and services are closed during winter.

PLANNING TIP

Overnight stays in the backcountry require a wilderness pass (per person per night C$9.80); pick it up from the park office within 24 hours of heading out.

Fast Facts

➡ **Area** 11,228 sq km (4335 sq miles)

➡ **Highest elevation** 3782m (12,408ft)

➡ **Lowest elevation** 985m (3232ft)

Reservations

You can make reservations at four of Jasper's 10 campgrounds: Whistlers, Wapiti, Wabasso and Pocahontas. Reservations are recommended for backcountry camping, as Parks Canada limits the number of hikers on each trail; these can be made up to three months in advance and cost C$11.70.

Resources

➡ **Jasper National Park** (www.jaspernationalpark. com)

➡ **Parks Canada** (www. pc.gc.ca/eng/pn-np/ab/ jasper/index.aspx)

JASPER NATIONAL PARK

Jasper National Park

0 5 miles
0 10 km

MIETTE HOT SPRINGS

The springs are a starting point for various trails, most notably the hugely rewarding and spectacular Sulphur Skyline and the more protracted Fiddle River Trail, which plunges quickly into backcountry. (p163)

PYRAMID BENCH

The low tree-covered plateau that rises directly above Jasper Town is filled with meandering trails good for hikes, bikes and horseback riding. Look out for wildlife around the many small lakes and ponds. (p138)

NORTH BOUNDARY

Jasper's most remote corner is the domain of adventurous backcountry hikers following an epic multiday trek all the way to Mt Robson in British Columbia. (p162)

Grande Cache/Willmore Wilderness Park (190km); Edmonton (332km)

East Park Gate

Fiddle Range

Ashlar Ridge

Miette Hot Springs Rd

Roche Miette (2278m)

Pocahontas

Bosche Range

Beaver Bluffs

Princess Lake
Celestine Lake

North Boundary Trail

Snake Indian River

Talbot Lake

Devona Flats

Jasper Lake

De Smet Range

Snaring

Celestine Lake Rd

Grassy Ridge

Snaring River

ALBERTA

Pyramid Mountain (2719m)

Saturday Night Lake Loop

Pyramid Lake

Patricia Lake

The Palisade

Yellowhead Hwy

Overlander Trail

Miette Hot Springs

Sulphur Lookout

Fiddle River Trail

Miette Range

Utopia Mountain (2521m)

Makwa Creek

Makwa Ridge

Nashan Creek

Jacques Range

Fiddle Valley

Fiddle Pass

Nikanassin Range

Whitehorse Wildland Provincial Park

Jasper National Park

Beaver, Summit & Jacques Lakes Trail

Jacques Lake

Sirdar Mountain (2804m)

Colin Range

Roche Bonhomme (2459m)

Maligne

Lake

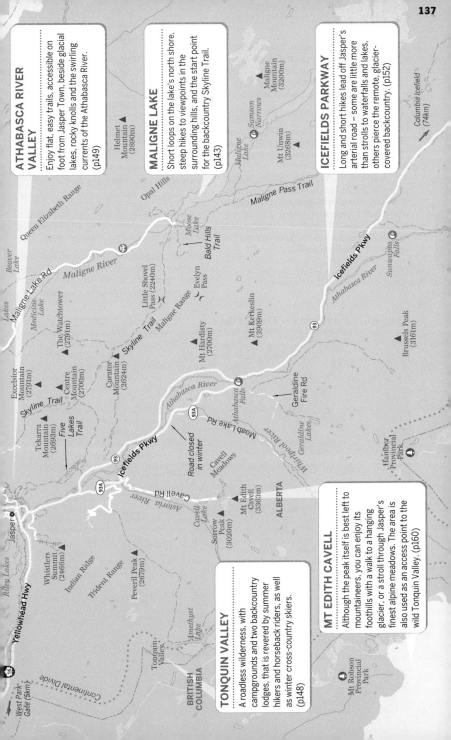

ATHABASCA RIVER VALLEY

Enjoy flat, easy trails, accessible on foot from Jasper Town, beside glacial lakes, rocky knolls and the swirling currents of the Athabasca River. (p149)

MALIGNE LAKE

Short loops on the lake's north shore, steep hikes to viewpoints in the surrounding hills, and the start point for the backcountry Skyline Trail. (p143)

ICEFIELDS PARKWAY

Long and short hikes lead off Jasper's arterial road – some are little more than strolls to waterfalls and lakes, others pierce the remote, glacier-covered backcountry. (p152)

TONQUIN VALLEY

A roadless wilderness, with campgrounds and two backcountry lodges, that is revered by summer hikers and horseback riders, as well as winter cross-country skiers. (p148)

MT EDITH CAVELL

Although the peak itself is best left to mountaineers, you can enjoy its foothills with a walk to a hanging glacier, or a stroll through Jasper's finest alpine meadows. The area is also used as an access point to the wild Tonquin Valley. (p160)

🥾 DAY HIKES

Even when judged against other Canadian national parks, Jasper's trail network is mighty and, with comparatively fewer people than its sister park, Banff, to the south, you've a better chance of seeing more wildlife and fewer people.

The park claims to have 1200km (660 miles) of hiking trails, many of which are shared with horseback riders and off-road cyclists. It is rightly famous for the abundance of trails leaving directly from its urban hub, Jasper Town, meaning shuttles or time-consuming drives to trailheads are not always necessary. Many of these trails crisscross the tree-covered plateau situated immediately behind the townsite known as the **Pyramid Bench**. Others track the Athabasca River Valley and its numerous small lakes.

Icefields Parkway

🥾 Path of the Glacier & Cavell Meadows Trails

Duration Three hours round-trip

Distance 9.1km (5.6 miles)

Difficulty Moderate-difficult

Start/Finish Cavell Meadows parking lot

Elevation Change 400m (1300ft)

Nearest Facilities Icefields Parkway

Transportation Private

Summary Angelic glaciers and heavenly scenery give this recently restored mountain trail a distinctly ethereal quality.

With its wings spread celestially between Mt Edith Cavell and Sorrow Peak, Angel Glacier gives the appearance of hovering over a small sapphire lake that is afloat with

Icefields Parkway – Day Hikes

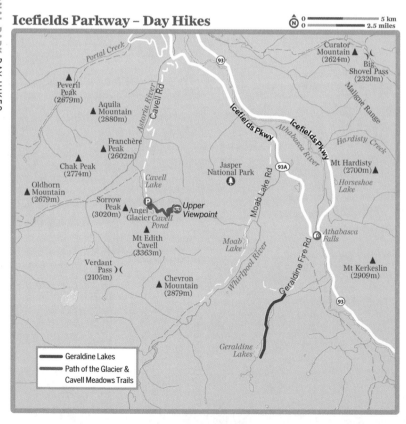

icebergs. The lake's ice-blue sheen is made all the more dramatic for the barren, stony surroundings that were created by the glacier's not-so-long-ago flight across the valley.

The Path of the Glacier Loop is the most popular hike in the area, but, for greater solitude and a brilliant wildflower display (in July), head further up the peak to Cavell Meadows.

To reach the trailhead from Jasper, follow Hwy 93A south to Cavell Rd and then drive 12km (7.4 miles) to a parking lot. Interpretive signs along the route tell the story of both Edith Cavell and the glacier.

Beginning with a climb through rocky moraine you'll pass the Cavell Meadows Trail turnoff after 0.5km (0.3 miles). The Path of the Glacier Trail continues ascending another 1km (0.6 miles) to a fantastic viewpoint of Angel Glacier, reflected in tiny Cavell Pond. Although the trail descends to the water, approaching the famous ice caves here is extremely hazardous. Keep your distance from the caves and beware of falling ice.

From the lake, the path levels out and loops back to the parking lot. This area was covered by the glacier until the 1950s, and small trees and plants are only just beginning to reappear.

A loop around Cavell Meadows will treat you to fantastic views and an even better workout. Take the left turn off the Path of the Glacier Trail at 0.5km (0.3 miles) and begin a steep ascent north. The trail soon levels off with clear views of the glacier to the right. This area is strewn with boulders up to 4m (13ft) high, left behind by the glacier. After crossing a stream, switchbacks take you north into the forest; keep right at the junction – 2.2km (1.4 miles) – crossing two more streams before entering an open, flowery meadow. At 3km (1.9 miles) a side trail branches right to the Lower Viewpoint.

Returning to the main trail, a brief climb brings you to another junction. If you've had enough, head left to meet up with the Path of the Glacier Trail; if you've still got some energy and a penchant for climbs, turn right for the Upper Viewpoint.

The way is steep, and the rock-strewn trail becomes fainter and slippery. Continuing uphill to the right brings you to a high subalpine meadow with an explosion of flowers. The path runs along a bank of loose shale with a steep drop on the left; then it turns right, where it becomes incredibly steep and rather treacherous.

You'll know you've reached the Upper Viewpoint by the yellow marker; the views are also something of a giveaway. Southwest is Mt Edith Cavell; Pyramid Mountain lies to the north and Roche Bonhomme to the northeast. Angel Glacier is suspended to the west; from this height you have an impressive view of its wings and upper half.

Heading back, the descent along the loose shale is tricky. At the junction, turn right to return through lush meadows to the Path of the Glacier Trail.

🏃 Geraldine Lakes

Duration Three to four hours round-trip

Distance 10km (6.3 miles)

Difficulty Moderate-difficult

Start/Finish End of Geraldine Fire Rd

Elevation Change 407m (1335ft)

Nearest Town Jasper

Transportation Private

Summary A rocky scramble through a staircase-like valley replete with lakes and waterfalls.

Geraldine Lakes is a hike of two different halves. The first part to Lake No 1 is easy; beyond that you'd better have strong ankles, a head for heights and a penchant for scrambling over bare, sometimes slippery, rock.

The hike starts at a parking lot at the end of Geraldine Fire Rd, an unpaved track that branches off Hwy 93A. Take the obvious trail through the trees and ascend moderately to Geraldine Creek at 1.5km (0.9 miles). In another 300m (0.2 miles) you'll spy the first Geraldine Lake through the trees – so far, so easy.

The going gets tougher as you skirt the north shore of the lake on a rougher trail and come up against your first obstacle, a large waterfall at the lake's far end. The trail (no longer obvious) climbs steeply up to the right of the waterfall for 100m (109yd), requiring scrambling skills and a firm footing. The path reappears briefly at the top and then disappears again in another rock field. Watch carefully for small cairns and a yellow marker here that will direct you across the small valley (over the now underground creek), and into some trees on the other side where the trail materializes once again. Coming out of the trees, you'll approach a photogenic second waterfall and another rocky climb and scramble up to Lake No 2, which lies a good 400m (0.25-mile) rock-hop from the summit.

HIKING IN JASPER NATIONAL PARK

REGION	NAME	DESCRIPTION
Icefields Parkway	Path of the Glacier & Cavell Meadows Trails	See Angel Glacier resting atop a lake and the finest alpine meadows in Jasper
Icefields Parkway	Geraldine Lakes	A rocky scramble through a staircase-like valley replete with lakes and waterfalls
Icefields Parkway	Tonquin Valley	Wildlife, lush meadows and sparkling lakes, all in the shadow of the Ramparts
Jasper Town & Around	Mina & Riley Lakes Loop	Burrow into the woods near town to a couple of placid lakes
Jasper Town & Around	Old Fort Point Loop	A short, steep climb to a stellar view over Jasper Town and surroundings
Jasper Town & Around	Whistlers Summit	A long walk up a steep hill through three different life zones
Maligne Lake Area	Mary Schäffer Loop	Holds the famous Lake Maligne view first seen by Mary Schäffer in the 1900s
Maligne Lake Area	Moose Lake Loop	Offers a peaceful, verdant forest and the chance to spot a moose
Maligne Lake Area	Beaver, Summit & Jacques Lakes	One of the park's simplest 'long' hikes with wide paths and peek-a-boo mountain views
Maligne Lake Area	Skyline Trail	The Rockies' premier backcountry trail, offering infinite views across the mountains
Maligne Lake Area	Bald Hills Loop	A steep grunt up to flower-filled meadows above Maligne Lake
North of Jasper Town	Sulphur Skyline	A short sharp hike up to a lofty ridge with spectacular views

 Drinking Water   Restrooms   Ranger Station Nearby   Great for Families   Fishing

By now you'll have ascertained the unique staircase design of the valley. There are actually two more Geraldine Lakes above Lake No 2, but the trail to reach them is practically nonexistent. Most hikers are satisfied with turning round at the second lake, though a 1.2km (0.7-mile) trail that tracks its southern shore leads to a backcountry campground at the far end.

Jasper Town & Around

🚶 Mina & Riley Lakes Loop

Duration Three hours round-trip

Distance 9km (5.6 miles)

Difficulty Easy-moderate

Start/Finish Jasper-Yellowhead Museum parking lot

Elevation Change 160m (525ft)

Nearest Town Jasper

Transportation Bus/train

Summary A straightforward tramp to a trio of peaceful lakes that will give you a tantalizing taste of the scope of Jasper's surrounding wilderness.

A whole network of trails heads west from Jasper Town into the forest-covered foothills of the Athabasca Valley. Venture less than 1km (0.6 miles) into this lake-speckled mini-wilderness and you'll quickly leave the hustle and bustle of the townsite behind.

Considered a good first-day orientation hike, the Mina & Riley Lakes Loop leaves from the northwest corner of the Jasper-Yellowhead Museum parking lot. Following trail No 8, climb gently up behind the town before turning rather abruptly into the forest.

DIFFICULTY	DURATION	DISTANCE	ELEVATION CHANGE	FEATURES	FACILITIES	PAGE
moderate-difficult	3hr	9.1km (5.6 miles)	400m (1300ft)			p138
moderate-difficult	3-4hr	10km (6.3 miles)	407m (1335ft)			p139
difficult	2-3 days	53.2km (33 miles)	710m (2329ft)			p148
easy-moderate	3hr	9km (5.6 miles)	160m (525ft)			p140
easy-moderate	1-2hr	4km (2.5 miles)	130m (427ft)			p141
difficult	3½hr	7.9km (4.9 miles)	1280m (4125ft)			p143
easy	45min	3.2km (2 miles)	negligible			p143
easy	45min	2.6km (1.6 miles)	negligible			p143
easy-moderate	6-7hr	24km (15 miles)	90m (300ft)			p144
moderate-difficult	2-3 days	45.8km (28.5 miles)	1400m (4526ft)			p146
difficult	4-6hr	10.4km (6.5 miles)	500m (1640ft)			p145
moderate-difficult	3hr	8km (5 miles)	700m (2297ft)			p145

Backcountry Campsite   View   Restaurant Nearby   Transportation to Trailhead   Wildlife Watching

Keep to the right at the next three junctions, heading west through a mixture of pine, fir and spruce trees until the path widens out into a man-made meadow and fire break.

After crossing the gravel Cabin Creek Rd, the route plunges quickly back into a thick forest sprinkled with stands of closely packed birch trees. Swampy Lower Mina Lake will appear within minutes on your left-hand side, a large pond guarded by ptarmigan and Barrow's goldeneye ducks. Just beyond is the larger Upper Mina Lake, where you'll often spot loons gliding across the green surface.

At the western edge of the lake, turn right and climb up and down some gentle hills to a second junction. Footsore first-timers can shortcut back to town here via trail No 8c. Old stalwarts, meanwhile, can descend the long hill down to Riley Lake, which glimmers ethereally with Pyramid Mountain framed behind it. The trail briefly skirts the moss-green edge of the lake before tracking back into the forest. Take a right at the next junction and ascend to Cottonwood Slough, which has open views over to the Roche Bonhomme. Continue east to the road, from where trail No 2 returns south to the museum parking lot.

🏃 Old Fort Point Loop

Duration One to two hours

Distance 4km (2.5 miles)

Difficulty Easy-moderate

Start/Finish Old Fort Point parking lot

Elevation Change 130m (427ft)

Nearest Town Jasper

Transportation Car/walk

Summary For a small effort, get big views atop this glacial *roche moutonnée* near

Jasper Town & Around – Day Hikes

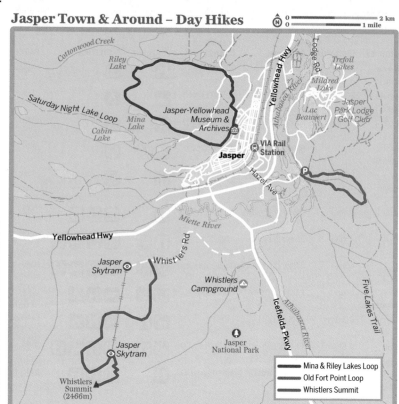

Jasper Town, the site of a long-abandoned trading post.

One of Jasper Town's most accessible and instantly rewarding trails is this short, steep climb up to a nearby *roche moutonnée* – a bedrock knob shaped by glaciers – known as Old Fort Point. Unfortunately, you won't find an old fort here. Instead, the name refers to the likely site of a one-time fur-trading post known as Henry House, which was built near here in 1811 by William Henry, a colleague of Canadian-British explorer David Thompson.

The official start point for the Old Fort Point trail (marked trail #1) is at a small parking lot next to a bridge over the Athabasca River. You can reach the parking lot on foot from Jasper Town by following the Wapiti Trail to where it crosses Hwy 16, and then branching left onto the Red Squirrel Trail. the total distance from town to trailhead is 1.6km (1 mile).

From the parking lot, a wooden stairway ascends a tall riverside crag. At the top, next to a monument honoring the natural wonder of the Athabasca River, a short steep slope leads upwards to the hike's summit. You'll need to scramble up another small crag to reach the true summit, but the views of Jasper Town, the Athabasca River Valley and the surrounding peaks are stupendous. On a clear day, count on seeing Mt Edith Cavell, the Whistlers, Pyramid Mountain and the mountains of the Continental Divide bordering British Columbia.

Beyond the summit, the trail dips down with easy gradient into aspen forest. You'll soon come to a four-way junction where the trail becomes open to cyclists, who use it to access the Valley of the Five Lakes (the right-hand fork). Trail No 1a, an easier alternative to trail No 1 used mainly by horses and bikes, goes straight ahead here (take this if you don't like steep slopes). Trail No 1 goes left and descends a steepish gully down to a flat forest path. After 500m (0.3 miles) trail No 1a rejoins on the right. Follow the main trail through a small open meadow and dip back into trees. You'll pass a junction with trail No 7a on the right and then start a short descent back towards the parking lot and the finish.

🚶 Whistlers Summit

Duration 3½ hours one-way

Distance 7.9km (4.9 miles)

Difficulty Difficult

Start Trailhead on Whistlers Rd

Finish Summit of Whistlers Mountain

Elevation Change 1280m (4125ft)

Nearest Town Jasper

Transportation Jasper Skytram Shuttle

Summary A long walk up a steep hill – with a wicked 360-degree view at the top.

If you're a peak-bagger, this arduous climb through three different life zones to the top of Jasper's most visited summit – and a handy energy-refueling café – could be the lung-bursting wake-up call you've been waiting for. While most sane people get the Skytram, there are always one or two masochistic maniacs punishing themselves on this 7.9km (4.9-mile) uphill slog.

To get to the trailhead, proceed 2.8km (1.7 miles) down Whistlers Rd to a short, unpaved spur road on the left, which dead-ends in a small parking lot. The hike begins in what is known as the montane life zone of the mountain, consisting of thick forest and healthy aspen growth but, within 2km (1.2 miles), your uphill endeavors will be rewarded with a rich display of colorful wildflowers. Progressing up toward the treeline, the crippling switchbacks ease momentarily as you pass underneath the midpoint tower of the Jasper Skytram at approximately 1640m (5380ft) of elevation.

Above the treeline the landscape becomes ever more stony and barren, with eagle-eye views of the Athabasca Valley and Jasper Town unfolding like a satellite map beneath you. For the final 1.5km (0.9 miles), from the Skytram's upper terminal to the top, you should have plenty of company, as annoyingly fresh Skytram riders join in for the relatively undemanding dash for the 2466m (8088ft) summit. The stupendous views of lake-speckled valleys and row after row of endless snow-coated peaks are spellbinding.

Maligne Lake Area

🚶 Mary Schäffer Loop

Duration 45 minutes round-trip

Distance 3.2km (2 miles)

Difficulty Easy

Start/Finish Maligne Lake parking lot

Elevation Change Negligible

Nearest Facilities Maligne Lake area

Transportation Maligne Lake Shuttle

Summary View the lake through the eyes of one of Jasper's earliest 'tourists' on this easy waterside ramble.

Following the eastern shoreline of Maligne Lake before dipping into the surrounding forest, this trail gives you a chance to take in the view seen by the first European explorer to cross this body of water. When Mary Schäffer stepped off her raft in 1908, she wrote, 'There burst upon us...the finest view any of us had ever beheld in the Rockies.'

To reach the Mary Schäffer Lookout, follow a paved, wheelchair-accessible path past Curly's historic boathouse for about 800m (0.5 miles) to where a quartet of informative signs tells the story of the lake's early-20th-century 'discovery'. Beyond the lookout, the trail continues inland through a spruce, pine and fir forest, with copious roots underfoot barring any further access to wheelchairs and strollers. After passing through a meadow, stay left at two junctions.

Along this path you'll see kettles, which are giant depressions left by glacial ice trapped beneath sand and silt. At the third junction, head right to return to the boathouse.

🚶 Moose Lake Loop

Duration 45 minutes round-trip

Distance 2.6km (1.6 miles)

Difficulty Easy

Start/Finish Maligne Lake parking lot

Elevation Change Negligible

Nearest Facilities Maligne Lake area

Transportation Maligne Lake Shuttle

Summary Escape from the crowds on this short, but surprisingly untrampled path, which leads to a tranquil lake renowned for its moose sightings.

JASPER NATIONAL PARK DAY HIKES

Maligne Lake Area – Day Hikes

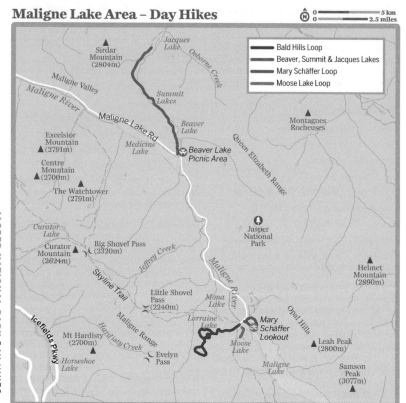

Offering a quick escape from the Maligne Lake hordes, this short, easy loop delivers you to a gorgeously placid lake framed by craning trees and embellished by the glacier-chiseled summit of Samson Peak. A moose sighting along the trail is another distinct possibility.

The trail starts in the parking lot at the end of the Maligne Lake Rd and follows the Bald Hills fire road for the first few hundred meters (approximately 100yd). Turn left at the first signpost and you'll quickly enter dense forest, with the lake and its attendant boat cruisers a distant memory.

This new path is the Maligne Pass Trail, but a left at the second junction will divert you in the direction of Moose Lake and, if you're extremely lucky, a glimpse of one of those giants of the forest swimming, foraging or hanging out near the shoreline. Moose or no moose, the scenery here is lovely.

With your curiosity satisfied, head north through the woods to the western shore of Maligne Lake and back to the trailhead parking lot.

Beaver, Summit & Jacques Lakes

Duration Six to seven hours

Distance 24km (15 miles) round-trip

Difficulty Easy-moderate

Start/Finish Beaver Lake Picnic Area

Elevation Change 90m (300ft)

Nearest Facilities Maligne Lake area

Transportation Maligne Lake Shuttle

Summary This is one of the simplest 'long' hikes in the park, thanks to its wide paths and minimal elevation gain, but the peek-a-boo views of nearby mountains are immense.

Three lakes and three turnaround options; this popular trail is flat (the elevation gain is negligible) but scenic with decent views of the Colin and Queen Elizabeth mountain ranges opening out around the lakes. The hike is also notable for its accessibility year-round; in winter it becomes a cross-country ski trail, and in autumn, thanks to its lower altitude, it remains doable long after other paths have been snowed-under.

From the start point at the southern end of Medicine Lake, the trail progresses along a wide dirt track (an old fire road), past some horse stables, to Beaver Lake at the 1.6km (1-mile) mark, a small body of water popular with fishermen and bird-watchers. Hike along the lake's west shore with views of the craggy limestone cliffs of the Queen Elizabeth Range to your right. The foot traffic drops off noticeably as you approach the First Summit Lake at 4.8km (3 miles). Follow the eastern shore and in 1.2km (0.8 miles) you'll reach Second Summit Lake, where the trail can be muddy after rain, due to heavy horse traffic. The valley swings due east at this point and the path enters denser forest on its journey to Jacques Lake, 5.2km (3.3 miles) away. This lake is the turnaround point for most day-hikers, although there is a campground at its eastern end. Fishing is not permitted. Beyond here, the path continues along the epic Southern Boundary Trail, 164 more kilometers (102 miles) of eerie isolation.

🚶 Bald Hills Loop

Duration Four to six hours

Distance 10.4km (6.5 miles)

Difficulty Difficult

Start/Finish Maligne Lake parking lot

Elevation Change 500m (1640ft)

Nearest Facilities Maligne Lake area

Transportation Maligne Lake Shuttle

Summary Get above the treeline on the north shore of Maligne Lake with this steep but worthwhile climb to a bald (read: unimpeded vistas) 360-degree viewpoint.

The road from Jasper dead-ends on the north shore of Maligne Lake, which is home to a chalet, restaurant, boat dock and parking lot. A handful of hikes converge here, all of them well signposted. The Bald Hills trail starts near the parking lot at the northwest corner of the lake on a wide fire road that leads steadily uphill – get used to it; 'uphill' is the central theme of the hike. The more altitude you gain, the more the trees diminish in both density and stature. After 3.2km (2 miles), the trail splits. The easier fire road continues following a gradual and circuitous ascent, while a rougher, much steeper trail takes a more direct path. Opting for the steeper route will save you 1.5km (0.9 miles) in distance, but cost a lot more sweat. The paths converge again on the upper cusp of the treeline at the top of the old fire road close to the site of a demolished fire lookout tower.

Here, the trail flattens out momentarily, traversing the mountain at the top of the tree line, before reaching another path junction. This is the start of the Bald Hills summit loop. Branch right here and a steep, clearly visible path takes you up a treeless slope to the rocky summit. Some hikers rest here before descending the way they came, but, for the sake of some more fantastic views, it's worth carrying on. Weather permitting, the full loop is clearly visible from the summit. First you track down to an astounding viewpoint over the uninhabited Evelyn Creek Valley. From here the path briefly climbs a rocky ridge, before descending and looping through alpine meadows (at their best in July and August) back to the trail junction just below the summit. From here you can retrace your steps to Maligne Lake.

North of Jasper Town

🚶 Sulphur Skyline

Duration Three hours round-trip

Distance 8km (5 miles) round-trip

Difficulty Moderate-difficult

Start/Finish Miette Hot Springs parking lot

Elevation Change 700m (2297ft)

Nearest Facilities Miette Hot Springs

Transportation Private

Summary A short, rarely dull hike that delivers spectacular views from a ridge high over one of Jasper's more remote corners.

Two hikes lead out from Miette Hot Springs: a pleasant ramble along the Sulphur River to Sulphur Pass at the start of the backcountry Fiddle River Trail, or this energetic scramble up to the 2050m (6724ft) Sulphur Skyline.

The fickle weather on this hike is notorious and hot sun and thunderstorms can hit in the same afternoon; be prepared for

Sulphur Skyline

either eventuality. The hike starts innocuously enough at Miette Hot Springs on a wide, paved, sometimes crowded, path, which is also the start of a longer hike to Mystery Lake. Ascend gradually and watch as the path narrows to a single track within 1km (0.6 miles). At the 2.2km (1.4-mile) mark at the Shuey Pass Junction, turn right and begin the real climb. Over the next 1.8km (1.1 miles) you'll gain 400m (1312ft) of elevation as the trail switchbacks through scattered forest and grassy slopes. Miraculously, the earlier crowds drop off to just a handful. At the treeline look out for a giant white boulder left over from an erstwhile glacier. From here it's not far to the summit (4km, or 2.4 miles, from the start), where a sea of mountaintops awaits. Look out for Utopia Mountain due west and the distinctive shape of Pyramid Mountain to the northwest. To the south lies the Fiddle River, gradually disappearing off into remote backcountry.

🚶 OVERNIGHT HIKES

Jasper has a huge backcountry, most of it pretty lightly trodden even in peak season, and the most popular multiday hike – the Skyline Trail – is considered one of the best in the nation. If the park has a weakness, it's the lack of overnight trips starting and finishing at the same point. The Saturday Night Lake Loop (described as a bike trip on p150) is one of the better options on this score and can easily be hiked over two days, overnighting at one of three backcountry campgrounds.

🚶 Skyline Trail

Duration Two days

Distance 45.8km (28.5 miles)

Difficulty Moderate-difficult

Elevation Change 1400m (4526ft)

Start Maligne Lake

Finish Maligne Canyon

Summary The crème de la crème of backcountry hiking in the Canadian Rockies, the Skyline Trail is a North American classic that hovers on or above the treeline for roughly 25 of its 45.8 serendipitous kilometers (28.5 miles).

Some hikers spread the expedition over three days, others tackle it in two, while the odd gung-ho trail runner has been known to knock it out in just one. But don't get too ambitious. With a notable lack of trees and little natural shelter en route, the Skyline is notoriously open to the elements, and fickle weather has taken the wind out of many an experienced hiker's sails.

A good, comfortable overnight option for two-day hikes is to reserve a room at the historic Shovel Pass Lodge (p168) at the halfway point. Alternatively, there are half-a-dozen backcountry campgrounds en route (campfires are prohibited, though), and for a comfortable three-day outing you could camp at Snowbowl and Tekarra Campgrounds, leaving the final descent for the third morning. Transportation to both trailheads is easy, via the Maligne Lake Shuttle. Most people leave their car at Maligne Canyon and catch the bus for an early start at Maligne Lake.

DAY 1: MALIGNE LAKE TRAILHEAD TO SHOVEL PASS LODGE

7 HOURS / 20.4KM (12.6 MILES)

Starting at the Maligne Lake trailhead, follow the Lorraine and Mona Lakes Trail through the woods for the first 5km (3.1 miles). Beyond the turnoff for Mona Lake, switchbacks leave the trees behind, passing Evelyn Creek Campground – keep right at the junction – and bringing you into meadows. Upon the slopes of Maligne Range, Little Shovel Pass, at 10.2km (6.3 miles), gives you views back over Maligne Lake and to the gray Queen Elizabeth Range, to the east. The pass was named by Mary Schäffer in 1911, when she and her guides were forced to dig their way through the snow with shovels hastily fashioned out of nearby trees.

From here the trail dips down into the Snowbowl, a lush if somewhat boggy meadow crisscrossed with streams and stretching 7.3km (4.5 miles) along the Maligne Range between Little Shovel Pass and Big Shovel

Pass. Snowbowl Campground is at 11.8km (7.3 miles).

At the end of the Snowbowl, a short climb brings you up to Big Shovel Pass at the 17km/10.5-mile point, which has more great views. Soon after, the Skyline passes two main trail intersections. The first is the junction with the Watchtower trail, which branches off to the east where it ultimately connects with the Maligne Lake Rd. The second is the intersection with the Wabasso trail that branches west at the 19km/11.9-mile mark toward the Icefields Pkwy. Take this trail if you are overnighting at the Curator Campground or the Shovel Pass Lodge. Both places are located on the Wabasso trail just over 1km (0.6 miles) west of the main Skyline Trail.

DAY 2: SHOVEL PASS LODGE TO MALIGNE CANYON HOSTEL

8 HOURS / 25.2KM (15.6 MILES)

Begin the day with a brisk climb up to tiny Curator Lake, which is surrounded by vast,

JASPER NATIONAL PARK OVERNIGHT HIKES

Skyline Trail

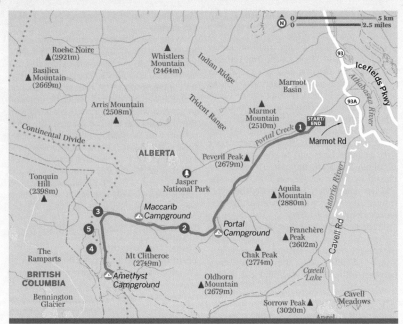

Overnight Hike
Tonquin Valley

START/END MARMOT BASIN ROAD
LENGTH 2-3 DAYS ROUND-TRIP / 53.2KM
(33 MILES)

Wildlife, lush meadows, sparkling lakes and gorgeous views make roadless Tonquin Valley a mecca for hikers and horseback-riders alike. The valley's crowning glory is the Ramparts, a collection of 10 peaks towering like Gothic fortresses over the network of backcountry trails. According to First Nations people, they harbor supernatural spirits.

The trail begins from Marmot Basin Rd, off Hwy 93A and about 16km (10 miles) south of Jasper Town. While there is a shorter, less-grueling approach to Amethyst Lake from the south, this route is far more scenic.

The hike to Amethyst Campground is a full day's hike; you can break the journey by staying at one of the two campgrounds en route, or stretch it to a three- or four-day trip by continuing along one of the trails from Amethyst Lake. Campfires are not permitted at any of the campgrounds.

From Marmot Basin Rd, the trail follows **❶ Portal Creek** southwest and climbs into the Portal, a narrow canyon amid the Trident Range. The path crosses large rockslides beneath Peveril Peak and then descends into a forested valley. A gradual climb takes you past Portal Campground and up toward **❷ Maccarib Pass** at 11.7km (7.3 miles). As you ascend above the treeline, you can't help but notice Oldhorn Mountain to the south.

Beyond the pass, begin your descent into the meadowland of **❸ Tonquin Valley** with impressive views of the Ramparts to the west. Maccarib Campground is next to a small creek at 17.8km (11 miles). The trail heads southwest for 6km (3.7 miles) to the northern shore of glistening **❹ Amethyst Lake**. At the junction, head right if you have reservations at **❺ Tonquin Valley Backcountry Lodge**, or continue along the shoreline to Amethyst Campground at 26.6km (16.5 miles). On still days, the water reflects the snow-cloaked Ramparts like a mirror.

Either pack up camp the following day and make the return journey along the same route or, if you have time, spend a day exploring around Amethyst Lake before heading back to the trailhead on the third day.

windswept terrain. The trail becomes steep as it climbs to **The Notch**. At 2510m (8733ft), this is the high point of the trail, with breathtaking views along the Athabasca Valley and, if you're lucky, all the way to Mt Robson in the northeast. Continue on to the summit of **Amber Mountain**, below which the trail switchbacks down to **Centre Lakes**, with the sentinel Centre Mountain to the northeast. The trail heads through a small valley to **Tekarra Lake** and then follows around the north side of Tekarra Mountain, amid the first trees you'll have seen all day. Tekarra Campground lies at 11.3km (7 miles), between the peaks of its namesake and Excelsior Mountain.

Coming back out of the trees, you'll have views of Pyramid Mountain to the northwest and the Roche Bonhomme to the north. It's worth taking the short detour left at 16.2km (10.1 miles) to **Signal Lookout** for even better views. Signal Campground is just beyond this junction. From here it's all downhill – 800m (2624ft) of descent over 9km (5.6 miles) – through forest down an old fire road (which is also used by mountain bikers). You'll come in via a small car park on the Maligne Lake Rd close to the Maligne Canyon Hostel.

◌ CYCLING

Jasper is well known for its extensive network of multipurpose trails fanning out from the central hub of Jasper Town, including some fantastic singletracks. Cyclists experience few limitations here – in contrast to more rule-ridden US national parks – resulting in some of the most scenic, varied and technically challenging rides in North America. An excellent trail map highlighting cycling routes is available from the Jasper Information Centre (p171) and most hotels. Bears are prevalent in the park, so ride with caution (and bear spray). The season runs from May to October.

Rentals

If you didn't bring your own bike, you can easily rent a top-notch machine from a number of different outlets. Prices start at C$12/24/32 per hour/three hours/day for front-suspension mountain bikes.

Freewheel Cycle   BICYCLE RENTAL
(Map p160; www.freewheeljasper.com; 618 Patricia St; bikes per day C$40; ⊙ 9am-10pm) Freewheel rents and sells cycling gear. This is a good

place for children, with kids' bikes and chariots for hire (C$24 per day).

Vicious Cycle   BICYCLE RENTAL
(Map p160; ☑ 780-852-1111; www.viciouscyclecanada. com; 630 Connaught Dr; per day from C$32; ⊙ 9am-6pm) Super-cool cycling shop rents bikes in summer and snowboards in the winter.

◌ Athabasca River Valley Loop

Duration Three hours round-trip

Distance 18km (11.2 miles)

Difficulty Easy

Start/Finish Jasper

Nearest Town Jasper

Summary A paved (but light on traffic) sojourn around the verdant Athabasca River Valley that should whet your appetite for further biking adventures elsewhere.

If you're looking for a safe, flat family bike ride, or just prefer the certainty of a paved road to singletrack, this 18km (11.2-mile) spin around three luminous lakes on the southeast side of the Athabasca River Valley is an ideal option.

Start by tracking south from Jasper Town on the Wapiti Trail alongside Hwy 93A, crossing both the railway line and busy Hwy 16.

Athabasca River Valley Loop

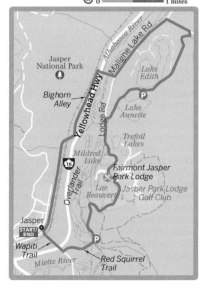

On the other side of the highway turn left onto the Red Squirrel Trail, which will quickly deposit you on a narrow bridge across the Athabasca River next to the step crags of Old Fort Point. Another 1km (0.6 miles) further on, you'll come to the shores of beautiful Lac Beauvert with the Fairmont Jasper Park Lodge perched on its opposite shoreline. Circumnavigate the lake via the scenic golf course – listening out for shouts of 'fore!' – to the lodge itself, which is well worth closer inspection, before proceeding past the entrance gate and branching off onto the Lake Annette road. With its picnic tables, small beach and paved lake loop, this is a great place for lunch and/or a glacier-fed bath (in summer). Almost adjacent to Lake Annette is Lake Edith, and an old road, now closed to cars, leads along its south shore. Ultimately, this will bring you out onto the busier Maligne Lake Rd. Turn left here and pedal a couple of kilometers to an attractive bridge across the Athabasca River and the junction with Hwy 16. On the west side of the bridge, cross Hwy 16 and pick up the Bighorn Alley Trail on the other side. This smooth singletrack path leads through scattered forest and past the town graveyard back to the north end of Jasper Town.

᚛ Saturday Night Lake Loop

Duration Three to four hours

Distance 27.4km (17 miles)

Difficulty Moderate-difficult

Start/Finish Jasper

Nearest Town Jasper

Summary An interesting technical ride through a root-ridden and sometimes swampy forest, with plenty of nature-watching opportunities and half-a-dozen quiet, unspoiled lakes.

If Jasper lacks one thing, it is long-distance loop trails, which makes this roller-coaster jaunt all the more satisfying. Even better, it begins and ends in the townsite, yet never feels particularly close to civilization. Sometimes erroneously called the 20-mile Loop (it's nearer 17 miles), the trail is numbered 3, gains 540m (1771ft) in elevation and never rises above the timberline. There are some tough technical stretches in the middle part of the ride involving mud, roots and short, steep descents.

From the center of Jasper follow Patricia St southwest to Patricia Cres. Turn right at the T-junction and the trailhead is on your left. Proceeding counterclockwise around the loop means you save the best descents till last, so take the right-hand No 3 option and follow the switchbacks out of town up onto the Pyramid Bench. A little over 1km (0.6 miles) of climbing brings you to the end of the dirt Cabin Lake Rd at the eastern end of Cabin Lake. From here take the singletrack along the lake's northeast shore and begin a gradual wooded ascent to smaller Saturday Night Lake, 4.3km (2.7 miles) distant (a 400m/437yd spur trail leads off the main trail to the lake and its campground). The going gets tougher for the next 9km to 10km (5 to 6 miles) with muddy, swampy sections along the base of the Victoria Cross Range, interspersed with some narrow creek crossings and plenty of tree roots. The trail begins to loop back east at the 11.5km (7.2-mile) mark at a log bridge at the bottom of a waterfall. Just beyond here is High Lakes and the second campground (the trail is also a popular two- to three-day hike). You'll be descending now over roots and rocks past Minnow Lake, where things settle down to a smoother pace to Caledonia Lake, a peaceful pond amid the trees. Fork left at the trail junction just past the lake and continue for 4km (2.4 miles; passing Marjorie Lake) back to the start point in Jasper Town.

᚛ Valley of the Five Lakes

Duration Three hours round-trip

Distance 27km (17 miles)

Difficulty Difficult

Start/Finish Jasper

Nearest Town Jasper

Summary The holy grail for Jasper cyclists. Riders travel from far and wide to test out this tough but scenic two-wheeled odyssey.

A hair-raising but gloriously scenic spin through the attractive Athabasca Valley to five turquoise mountain lakes, this trail has it *all,* including sweeping singletrack, bone-rattling rocks and roots, sudden downhills and tough, technical inclines. No wonder serious cycling junkies rate it as one of the best off-road rides in North America.

Accessible via trail No 1, which cuts around the back of Old Fort Point, Valley of the Five Lakes is popularly tackled as an out-and-back

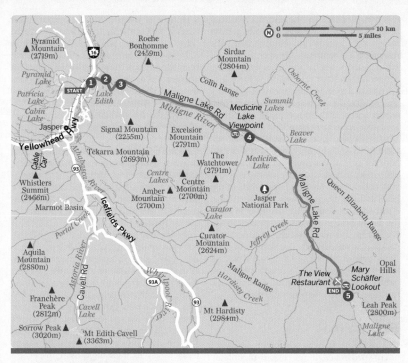

Driving Tour
Maligne Lake Road

START MALIGNE LAKE ROAD TURNOFF ON HWY 16
END MALIGNE LAKE
LENGTH 45 MINUTES / 46KM (28.5 MILES)

The Maligne Lake Rd is as scenic as the destination. Wildlife is rife and with luck you'll spot a wolf, a bear or a moose. Obey speed restrictions and watch for animals bounding across the road.

Begin the tour 2km (1.2 miles) north of Jasper Town; follow Hwy 16 to the turnoff for Maligne Lake Rd, crossing the **1 Athabasca River** and following the road left. Ahead are views of Roche Bonhomme, with its Old Man summit, and to the west lies the rust-colored Pyramid Mountain. At 3km (1.9 miles), the **2 Fifth Bridge** crosses the powerful Maligne River; if you're feeling ambitious, you can head over this suspension bridge and climb the trail into **3 Maligne Canyon**, one of the deepest in the Rockies. An easier way to see this dramatic canyon is via the Upper Canyon Trail; the trailhead is 7km (4.3 miles) along the route.

The road continues east between the Colin Range to the north and the Maligne Range to the south. At 22km (13.6 miles) there's a pull-out to Maligne River, though it only carries water here if Medicine Lake floods. Instead, the water flows downstream in an underground waterway. Aboriginals in the area believed the water was whisked away by magic (or bad medicine) and feared it.

The next turnoff, on the northwest corner of **4 Medicine Lake**, offers superb views across the water. Along the north side of the lake, the craggy Colin Range leans flat-faced toward the road, and a delta on the far eastern side of the lake often hosts caribou in early spring and late fall.

At 32km (19.8 miles), look up. Above, you'll see limestone arches cut into the summit of the Queen Elizabeth Range, caused by water that's freezing in the crevices, expanding and shattering the rock. If you've brought a picnic and are hoping for a little peace, try the rest stop at 40km (24.8 miles), where you can relax beside the river before reaching the more hectic **5 Maligne Lake**, 6km (3.7 miles) up the road.

trip from Jasper Town. Linking up with trail No 9 after 2km (1.2 miles), the ride gathers pace with a narrow but nontechnical path meandering seamlessly through tracts of sun-dappled forest to the lakes themselves, approximately 10km (6.2 miles) to the south. With Lake 1 in sight, things start to get hairy and, if you can make it around all five of these watery havens without getting off to push (at least once), consider yourself an aficionado.

After looping around Lake 4 with its resident loons and shimmering emerald coloration, the trail winds up at a crossroads that offers bikers three distinct options. The first is to double back on the opposite side of the lakes and link up again with trail No 9 for a return ride to Jasper. The second is to cross the plank bridge over the Wabasso Creek Wetlands and make for the trailhead and parking lot on Hwy 93. The third is to head south toward Wabasso Lake and a second Hwy 93 trailhead 9km (5.6 miles) away. Look out for wildlife if you elect to follow this last trail, and be aware of bears and deer.

🚗 DRIVING

Driving along Jasper's well-maintained and uncrowded roads, amid rugged mountains and seemingly endless forests, is one of life's simple pleasures. Keep your eyes peeled for wildlife foraging by the roadside.

🚗 Icefields Parkway

Duration Two hours

Distance 103km (64 miles)

Start Jasper

Finish Columbia Icefield Centre

Nearest Town Jasper

Summary Considered one of the most scenic drives in North America, the Icefields Pkwy is a mélange of cascading waterfalls and spectacularly carved peaks, whose crowning glory is the glistening Columbia Icefield on the park's southern limits.

It measures 230km (144 miles) from Jasper Town down to Lake Louise; a 108km (67-mile) segment of the route traverses Jasper National Park, incorporating some of the region's star attractions.

Driving south out of Jasper, the first highlight is Mt Edith Cavell, the town's snow-capped guardian, accessible via a winding spur road off Hwy 93A. Stop here to stroll through flower-filled meadows and catch a glimpse of the peak's wing-shaped Angel Glacier. Rejoin the main parkway for 20km (12.4 miles) and you'll pass Horseshoe Lake, with its steep-sided cliffs and clear, bracing waters, followed quickly by the Athabasca Falls, the park's most voluminous waterfall, which throws its glacial meltwater over a 21m (70ft) limestone cliff.

Look out for wildlife on the next section of the route as you head south through a wide corridor of mountains that parallels the Continental Divide. At Honeymoon Lake there's a viewpoint over the Athabasca River, while 2km (1.2 miles) further on, at Sunwapta Falls, you can refuel at the restaurant or stretch your legs on the short hike to the waterfall. This is also the start of a wilderness hike to Fortress Lake.

As the tree cover thins and the river becomes a confusing maze of different channels, you'll start to notice the glaciers. Stop at the Stutfield Glacier Viewpoint, just past Beauty Creek, to admire this outlying tentacle of the Columbia Icefield; 2km (1.2 miles) further on you'll pass Tangle Falls and the start of the scenic Wilcox Pass Trail. The drive's apex is the green-roofed Columbia Icefield Centre and the world-famous Athabasca Glacier. Stop here for interpretive displays, a walk around the Forefield Trail and an excursion on one of the unique Snocoaches or to the new Glacier Skywalk.

⚡ OTHER ACTIVITIES

Got any energy left, tired hiker/biker/driver? Thought so! Read on...

White-Water Rafting & Float Trips

Charging rivers course their way through Jasper National Park. The Athabasca and Sunwapta Rivers are the two most utilized by rafters, who travel mainly on organized trips. The Athabasca has class II rapids, meaning it's considered family-friendly and will give you more enjoyment than stress. The word 'Sunwapta' means 'turbulent river' in the Stony First Nations language, hinting at tougher challenges. The rapids are rated III here (on a scale of I to VI), meaning some previous experience is recommended. The rafting season is from mid-May to the end of September. Prices are around C$59/94 for the Athabasca/Sunwapta Rivers for three- to four-hour trips, transportation included.

Icefields Parkway

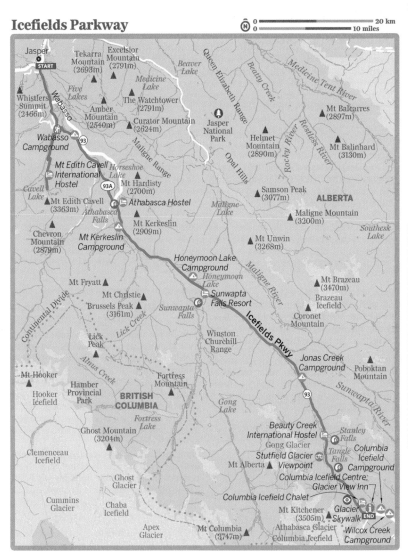

Maligne Rafting Adventures RAFTING
(Map p160; ☎780-852-3370; www.raftjasper.com;
616 Patricia St; trips from C$59) Everything from
float trips to grade II and III adventures, plus
overnight trips.

Jasper Raft Tours RAFTING
(Map p160; ☎780-852-2665; www.jasperrafttours.
com; 611 Patricia St; adult/child C$65/20; ⋒)
Specializes in family-orientated trips (with
favorable rates for kids) on the milder Athabasca River.

Boating

The Athabasca Valley is speckled with hidden
lakes and misty ponds, most of which allow
rowboats, kayaks, canoes and – more recently – stand-up paddleboards. Of the bodies of
water around Jasper Town, Pyramid Lake is
the most popular spot, an oasis of tranquility
caught in the distinctive shadow of Pyramid
Mountain. As the largest lake in the Canadian
Rockies, Maligne Lake (p162) offers visitors
the archetypal Jasper experience.

LOCAL KNOWLEDGE

BACKCOUNTRY KAYAKING

Paddling off into the sunset will never seem as alluring as it does on Maligne Lake, where wispy clouds share watery reflections with sugar-colored glaciers. Serviced by Curly Phillips' historic Maligne Lake Boathouse, the lake has long been popular with kayakers and canoeists, though few paddlers venture beyond shouting distance of the tourist-heavy north shore. However, for more solitude and a full-on backcountry kayaking adventure, it's possible to explore Maligne Lake's uninhabited shorelines by taking advantage of three paddle-in campgrounds. Newly opened Hidden Cove is 5km (3.1 miles) south of the north shore bustle on the lake's west side; Fisherman's Bay is 8km (5 miles) further south on the east shore; while Coronet Creek is a kilometer shy of the 22km-long (13.7 miles) lake's southern tip. True to Jasper's backcountry ethos, all the lakeside campgrounds are basic, with boat docks, tent pads, fire pits and picnic tables. As space is limited (up to 10 tents per campground), you must book ahead. There's a two-night maximum stay in peak season.

Tour boats ply Maligne Lake daily between 9am and 6pm as far south as Spirit Island (14km/8.7 miles from the boathouse). To avoid their foamy wake and other fickle weather conditions, it is best to set out early. Beyond the north shore, Maligne is a wilderness lake with no access roads or services. Be prepared for wildlife encounters, bad weather and backcountry emergencies, but be equally prepared to have a stunningly good time!

Pyramid Lake Boat Rentals BOATING
(Map p158; www.pyramidlakeresort.com; Pyramid Lake Rd; boats per hr C$25) Pyramid Lake Boat Rentals has canoes, rowboats, kayaks and paddleboats for hire on the eponymous lake.

Maligne Lake Boathouse BOATING
(Map p158; ☑780-852-3370; boats per hr/day C$30/90) The historic Curly Phillips Boathouse (dating from 1928) rents canoes for a paddle around the lake.

Fishing

Fishing is popular throughout the park, with both locals and visitors. Waters frequented by anglers include Celestine, Princess, Maligne and Pyramid Lakes – though there are many smaller nooks.

Fishing is permitted in these lakes as well as many of the park's other lakes and rivers, including parts of the Athabasca, Maligne and Miette Rivers, as long as you are in possession of a valid permit (day/year C$9.80/34.30). Most of these waters are only open for short seasons, and many others are closed throughout the year. Visit the Parks Canada website or drop into one of its offices for opening dates and fishing restrictions.

On-Line Sport & Tackle FISHING
(Map p160; ☑780-852-3630; www.fishonlinejasper. com; 600 Patricia St; half-/full day trip C$199/299) Rents gear, teaches fly-fishing and runs lots of fishing trips, including 10-hour marathons.

Climbing

Because of its preponderance of sedimentary rock, Jasper doesn't draw as many ambitious rock climbers as other Rockies hot spots, such as Canmore. The advantage of this is relative solitude.

Located up the trail from Fifth Bridge, off Maligne Lake Rd, Rock Gardens is the most popular crag and has the easiest approach. A more recent addition is Lost Boys, 'discovered' in 1994 and situated 25km (15.5 miles) south on Hwy 93A from the junction with Hwy 93. From the parking spot it's a 20-minute hike in to the quartzite crag. For climbers with experience (and preferably a guide), Mt Edith Cavell offers incredible vistas, while Ashlar Ridge and Morro Ridge are strictly the terrain of experts.

Rockaboo Adventures ROCK CLIMBING
(Map p160; ☑780-820-0092; www.rockaboo.ca; 807 Tonquin St) Jasper's most comprehensive year-round climbing guides offer everything from a four-hour Experience Rock Climbing course (C$125) good for kids aged six and up, to ascents of lofty Mt Edith Cavell. It also arranges rappelling (C$79).

Horseback Riding

With horseback riders sharing trails with hikers and bikers, Jasper trumps most other parks when it comes to equestrian adventures.

Rival stables on either side of the Athabasca Valley ply routes around Lakes Patricia and Annette, while further afield stunning backcountry trips can be organized in the Tonquin Valley, Maligne Pass, Jacques Lake and Bald Hills. Permits and regulations apply.

Tonquin Valley Adventures HORSEBACK RIDING
(☑780-852-1188; www.tonquinadventures.com; 3-/4-/5-day trips C$795/1050/1295) The owners of the backcountry Tonquin Amethyst Lake Lodge can organize memorable three- to five-day pack trips.

Jasper Riding Stables HORSEBACK RIDING
(Map p158; ☑780-852-7433; Pyramid Lake Rd; 1-/2-hour rides C$42/72) For gentle horseback riding on the 'bench' behind Jasper Town, call in here.

Wildlife Watching

With 69 different mammals, 277 species of bird and 16 amphibians and reptiles, your chances of spotting wildlife in Jasper National Park are pretty high. A trip down Maligne Rd or Miette Hot Springs Rd may score you a bear, wolf or mountain-goat sighting, and elk tend to linger just south of Jasper Town, at the end of Hwy 93. About 0.5km (0.3 miles) north of Jasper Town, on the eastern side of the road, a salt lick is frequented by goats and sheep in summer.

Alpine Art-Eco Tours WILDLIFE WATCHING
(Map p160; ☑780-852-3709; www.alpineart.ca; 500 Pyramid Lake Rd; half-day per person C$69) A locally own certified guiding company that runs year-round safaris in search of elk, grizzlies, moose and the like. In summer, it takes in the wildflowers, and in winter you can hike along on snowshoes.

Jasper Adventure Centre TOUR
(Map p160; ☑780-852-5595; www.jasperadventure centre.com; 611 Patricia St; tour adult/child C$65/35) Offers a daily summer Wildlife Discovery tour at 5:30pm.

Jasper Walks & Talks HIKING
(Map p160; ☑780-852-4994; www.walksntalks. com; 626 Connaught Dr) Walks & Talks leads small groups of people on personalized tours that include a morning Birding and Wildlife Adventure (C$70) at 6:45am from June to October, and Mount Edith Cavell Meadows picnics (C$90), departing at 9am from June to October.

Ranger Programs

Whistlers Outdoor Theatre INTERPRETIVE PROGRAM
(Map p158; Whistlers Campground; ☑) Each summer, Parks Canada sponsors live theater and free family-geared interpretive programs at 9pm nightly at Whistlers Outdoor Theatre, 3km (1.8 miles) south of Jasper Town. Non-campers are welcome. Topics vary from bear tips to park history.

Friends of Jasper WALKING TOUR
(Map p160; ☑780-852-4767; www.friendsofjasper. com; 500 Connaught Dr; ☑) Friends of Jasper hosts a nightly historical walking tour at 7:30pm throughout the summer, leaving from the Jasper Information Centre. Groups are limited to 30 and tickets are available in advance from the information center. Other interpretive walks include a junior naturalist program for kids aged six to 10 at the Whistlers Campground.

Golf

Fairmont Jasper Park Lodge Golf Club GOLF
(Map p158; www.fairmontgolf.com/jasper; green fees from C$129; ☑mid-May–mid-Oct) Overlooking the beautiful green shores of shimmering Lac Beauvert are several more greens – 18 to be precise. Designed in 1925 by Stanley Thompson, Jasper's golf course is as stunning as it is challenging. There's also a driving range, and you can rent shoes and clubs. Try not to hit a bear.

Skiing & Snowboarding

Marmot Basin SKIING
(Map p158; www.skimarmot.com; Marmot Basin Rd; day pass adult/child C$88/70) Jasper's only ski area is 19km (11.8 miles) southwest of the townsite. A daily shuttle (C$7 one way) connects the two during the season.

Although not legendary, the presence of 86 runs and the longest high-speed quad chair in the Rockies means Marmot is no pushover, and its relative isolation compared to the trio of ski areas in Banff means shorter lift lines. The cons: it can get cold, and there's no overnight accommodations on-site.

Cross-Country Skiing & Snowshoeing

True to its ethos of multipurpose trails for all, many of Jasper's hiking and biking paths are given over to cross-country skiing and snowshoeing in winter. Trails track-set for classic and skate skiing are centered on three main areas. Close to Jasper Town you can try the 4.5km (2.8-mile) Whistlers Campground Loop or the 10km (6.2-mile) there-and-back Pipeline Trail, sandwiched between Hwy 16 and the Miette River. Near Maligne Lake is the 10km (6.2-mile) round-trip Beaver and Summit Lakes Trail, following a scenic summer hiking route with little gradient; and the easy 2.3km (1.4-mile) Moose Lake Loop.

The third and most comprehensive track-set skiing area can be found on and around Hwy 93A, which is left unplowed in winter for 10.5km (6.5 miles) between the Meeting of the Waters picnic area and Athabasca Falls. Branching off this road is a trail to Moab Lake, or further north you can tackle the steep 11km (6.8-mile) unplowed Edith Cavell Rd skiable as far as Cavell Meadows. For the more adventurous, there's cross-country skiing to the remote Tonquin Valley.

Other Winter Activities

Half of Jasper shuts down in winter; the other half just adapts and metamorphoses into something just as good (if not better) than its summertime equivalent. Lakes become skating rinks, hiking and biking routes become cross-country skiing trails, waterfalls become ice climbs, wildlife migrates to lower climes, and – last but by no means least – prices become far more reasonable.

There are two hot spots for outdoor skating. The Fairmont Jasper Park Lodge clears an area on Lac Beauvert in front of the hotel and it is floodlit after dark. Another, far better, Zamboni-cleared oval is maintained on Mildred Lake, on the other side of the hotel. Benches are set out here, spontaneous hockey games often erupt, and free hot chocolate revives shivering bystanders. For a quieter, more romantic skate, head up to Pyramid Lake, 6km (3.7 miles) northeast of the townsite. You can rent skates at Jasper Source for Sports (www.jaspersports.com; 406 Patricia St).

The area around Pyramid Bench is maintained for winter hiking (weather permitting). Along these trails you'll be sheltered

BACKCOUNTRY SKIING THE TONQUIN VALLEY

Want a white-knuckle backcountry adventure without heart-stopping risks? Look no further than the Tonquin Valley in winter, when you can ski up frozen Portal Creek to Maccarib Pass before descending into a rampart-guarded wilderness for a couple of nights at the cozy backcountry Tonquin Amethyst Lake Lodge. By February, the Tonquin trail has been 'broken in' by other skiers, yet remains inspiringly remote. Pushing the stress levels down further is the low avalanche risk (though it *always* pays to check ahead) and minimal bear paranoia (they're asleep). It's 22km (13.7 miles) from the Portal Creek trailhead to the lodge and then another 29km (18.1 miles) out again via the gorgeous Astoria River/Cavell Rd route. You can go it alone, or join a guided group with Tonquin Valley Adventures (www.tonquinadventures.com). The lodge has a two-night minimum stay in the winter – ideal for less frenetic sidetrips.

by the woods and have a good chance of spotting wildlife. The Mina and Riley Lakes Loop (p140) is well trodden most of the year by locals, who include it in their early-morning jogs.

Slightly less athletic is the three-hour Maligne Canyon Icewalk offered by Jasper Adventure Centre (p155). It's a walk through a series of frozen waterfalls, viewable from December to April. Extremists tackle these slippery behemoths with rappels and ice axes. Gravity Gear (Map p160; 852-3155; www.gravitygearjasper.com; 618 Patricia St) can rent equipment.

◎ SIGHTS

◎ Icefields Parkway

Paralleling the Continental Divide for 230km (143 miles) between Lake Louise and Jasper Town, plain old Hwy 93 is usually branded as the Icefields Pkwy (or the slightly more romantic 'Promenade des Glaciers' in French) as a means of somehow preparing people for the majesty of its surroundings. And what majesty! The Parkway's highlight is undoubtedly the humungous Columbia Icefield and its numerous fanning glaciers, and this dynamic lesson in erosive geography is complemented by weeping waterfalls, aquamarine lakes, dramatic mountains and the sudden dart of a bear, an elk, or was it a caribou?

Most people ply the Parkway's asphalt by car, meaning it can get busy in July and August. For a clearer vision, consider taking a bus or, even better, tackling it on a bike – the road is wide, never prohibitively steep, and sprinkled with plenty of strategically spaced campgrounds, hostels and hotels.

Columbia Icefield Centre   MUSEUM, LANDMARK

(Icefields Pkwy; ⊙ early May–mid-Oct) FREE Situated on the Icefields Pkwy, close to the toe of the Athabasca Glacier, the green-roofed Icefield Centre contains a hotel, cafeteria, restaurant, gift shop, Snocoach ticket booth and Parks Canada information desk. It's a bit of a human zoo in summer, with tour coaches cramming the parking lot. Purchase tickets and board buses for the Snocoaches and Glacier Skywalk here. A subterranean museum area was being renovated at last visit, with new exhibits promised.

Athabasca Glacier   GLACIER

The tongue of the Athabasca Glacier runs from the Columbia Icefield almost down to the road opposite the Icefield Centre and can be visited on foot or in specially designed buses. The glacier has retreated about 1.6km (1 mile) in the last 150 years. To reach its toe (bottom edge), you can walk directly from the Icefield Centre on the 1.8km **Forefield Trail** and then join the 1km **Toe of the Athabasca Glacier Trail**.

While it is permitted to stand on a small roped section of the ice, do not attempt to cross the warning tape. Many do, but the glacier is riddled with crevasses and there have been fatalities.

To walk safely on the Columbia Icefield, you'll need to enlist the help of **Athabasca Glacier Icewalks** (☏ 780-852-5595; www.icewalks.com; Icefield Centre; 3/5hr tours C$85/105), which supplies all the gear you'll need and a guide to show you the ropes. It offers a three-hour tour (departing 10am or 1:30pm daily June to September), and a five-hour option (Sunday and Thursday) for those wanting to venture further out on the glacier.

The other far easier (and more popular) way to get on the glacier is via a **Snocoach** (www.columbiaicefield.com; tours adult/child C$55/27.50; ⊙ 9am-6pm Apr-Oct) ice tour offered by Brewster. For many people this is the defining experience of their Columbia Icefield visit. The large hybrid bus-truck grinds a track onto the ice where it stops to allow you to go for a short walk in a controlled area on

JASPER NATIONAL PARK SIGHTS

STARGAZING

Stargazing probably isn't the first activity one associates with the dramatic mountain-scaling scenery of Jasper, but interest in the the night sky and its innumerable galaxies is growing in popularity. It harks back to a tradition long practiced by the First Nations and 19th-century European explorers. David Thompson, one of the Jasper area's earliest pioneers, was an expert surveyor and astronomer nicknamed Koo-Koo-Sint, or 'stargazer', by the indigenous people.

Interest in outer space was reignited in 2011 when Jasper was named a 'Dark Sky Preserve' by the Royal Astronomical Society of Canada, earmarking it as an area where light pollution is measured and controlled in order to enhance Milky Way vistas and promote astronomical study.

Every year since 2011, Jasper has held a **Dark Sky Festival** (www.jasperdarksky. travel) in the traditionally quiet month of October, putting on a multitude of diverse events, including visits from well-known astronauts and astronomers and classical concerts under the stars.

More interest was added in June 2015 when a small, but expertly curated **planetarium** (Map p158; ☏ 780-852-4056; www.jasperplanetarium.ca; 86 Connaught Dr; adult/child C$29/12.50; ⊙ shows 9pm & 9:45pm) was rigged up in the Marmot Lodge courtyard. The 35-capacity auditorium is encased in an ingenious inflatable structure protected by a tent and runs 35-minute audiovisual shows about Jasper's night sky. There's also the opportunity to take a peep through the largest telescope in the Rockies and perhaps see the rings of Saturn.

Other easily accessible places to go stargazing year-round are the small island on Pyramid Lake, 5km (3.1 miles) northeast of Jasper Town, the north shore of Maligne Lake, and the Athabasca Glacier.

Jasper National Park Region

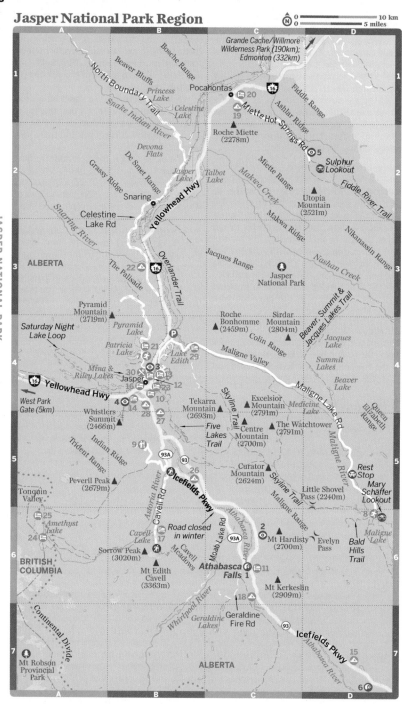

N 0 — 10 km
0 — 5 miles

Grande Cache/Willmore
Wilderness Park (190km);
Edmonton (332km)

Pocahontas
20
19
Miette Hot Springs Rd
Roche Miette
(2278m)
5 Sulphur
Lookout

Bosche Range
Beaver Bluffs
Princess
Lake
Celestine
Lake
North Boundary Trail
Snake Indian River
De Smet Range
Devona Flats
Grassy Ridge Rd
Snaring
Jasper
Lake
Talbot
Lake
Makwa Creek
Miette Range
Utopia
Mountain
(2521m)
Fiddle Range
Ashlar Ridge
Fiddle River Trail
Nikanassin Range

Yellowhead Hwy

ALBERTA

Snaring River
The Palisade
22
16
Overlander Trail
Jacques Range
Makwa Ridge
Nashan Creek
Jasper
National Park

Pyramid
Mountain
(2719m)
Pyramid
Lake
Roche
Bonhomme
(2459m)
Sirdar
Mountain
(2804m)
Colin Range
Beaver, Summit &
Jacques Lakes Trail
Jacques
Lake

Saturday Night
Lake Loop
Patricia
Lake
Lake
Edith
29
Maligne Valley
Summit
Lakes

Mina &
Riley Lakes
21
7
3
Jasper
16
23
12
30
Beaver
Lake

16 Yellowhead Hwy
4
14
10
28
27
Tekarra
Mountain
(2693m)
Skyline Trail
Excelsior
Mountain
(2791m)
Medicine
Lake
Maligne Lake Rd
Maligne River
Queen
Elizabeth
Range

West Park
Gate (5km)
Whistlers
Summit
(2466m)
Five
Lakes
Trail
Centre
Mountain
(2700m)
The Watchtower
(2791m)

Trident Range
Indian Ridge
9
93A
93
26
Curator
Mountain
(2624m)
Skyline Trail
Little Shovel
Pass (2240m)
Rest
Stop
Mary
Schäffer
Lookout
8

Peveril Peak
(2679m)
Icefields Pkwy
Astoria River
Maligne Range
Maligne
Lake
Bald
Hills
Trail

Tonquin
Valley
25
Amethyst
Lake
24
17
Road closed
in winter
Cavell Rd
Cavell
Lake
Moab Lake Rd
Athabasca River
2
Mt Hardisty
(2700m)
Evelyn
Pass

BRITISH
COLUMBIA
Sorrow Peak
(3020m)
Mt Edith
Cavell
(3363m)
Cavell
Meadows
93A
Athabasca
Falls 1
11
Mt Kerkeslin
(2909m)

Continental Divide
Whirlpool River
Geraldine
Lakes
18
Geraldine
Fire Rd
93
Icefields Pkwy
Athabasca River

Mt Robson
Provincial
Park
ALBERTA
15
6

Jasper National Park Region

◎ Top Sights
1 Athabasca Falls.....................................C6

◎ Sights
2 Horseshoe Lake.....................................C6
3 Jasper Planetarium...............................B4
4 Jasper Skytram.....................................B4
5 Miette Hot Springs................................D2
6 Sunwapta Falls.....................................D7

◉ Activities, Courses & Tours
Fairmont Jasper Park Lodge
Golf Club......................................(see 13)
7 Jasper Riding Stables..........................B4
8 Maligne Lake Boathouse......................D6
9 Marmot Basin.......................................B5
Pyramid Lake Boat Rentals..........(see 21)
Whistlers Outdoor Theatre..........(see 28)

◎ Sleeping
10 Alpine Village...B4
11 Athabasca Falls International
Hostel...C6
12 Crimson..B4
13 Fairmont Jasper Park Lodge................B4

14 HI-Jasper...B4
15 Honeymoon Lake Campground............D7
Miette Hot Springs Resort.............(see 5)
16 Mount Robson Inn.................................B4
17 Mt Edith Cavell International Hostel.....B6
18 Mt Kerkeslin Campground....................C6
19 Pocahontas..C1
20 Pocahontas Cabins..............................C1
21 Pyramid Lake Resort............................B4
Sawridge Inn & Conference
Centre.......................................(see 3)
22 Snaring River Campground..................B3
Sunwapta Falls Resort..................(see 6)
23 Tekarra Lodge.......................................B4
24 Tonquin Amethyst Lake Lodge.............A6
25 Tonquin Valley Backcountry Lodge......A6
26 Wabasso..B5
27 Wapiti Campground..............................B5
28 Whistlers Campground.........................B4
29 YHA Maligne Canyon............................B4

◎ Eating
30 The Inn Restaurant...............................B4
View Restaurant.............................(see 8)

the glacier. Dress warmly and wear solid shoes. Tickets can be bought at the Icefield Centre or online; tours depart every 15 to 30 minutes.

Glacier Skywalk
VIEWPOINT
(adult/child C$30/15; ⊙10am-5pm Apr-Oct) Opened in May 2014, the Glacier Skywalk is a cleverly designed interpretive lookout and walkway (with a glass floor) suspended high above the Sunwapta River opposite Mt Kitchener. While it has collected a number of architectural awards since its inception, the Skywalk has left some visitors questioning whether it really adds anything to the park and its already spectacular scenery.

The only way to visit the Skywalk (which is run by Brewster) is via bus from the Columbia Icefield Centre. Casual drivers along the Icefields Pkwy are not permitted to stop at the sight, presumably to avoid overcrowding.

The experience itself takes you on a short interpretive walk along the top of the river canyon that abuts the main road and then out onto the Skywalk itself. Vertigo-sufferers, hold your breath.

An audioguide is included in the price of a ticket.

★ Athabasca Falls
WATERFALL
(Map p158) A deafening combination of sound, spray and water, Athabasca Falls is Jasper's most dramatic and voluminous waterfall. Copious visitors crowd the large parking lot and short access trail to catch a glimpse of this enduring park emblem, which is just off the Icefields Pkwy, 28km (17 miles) south of Jasper Town, and at its most ferocious during summer.

Despite being only 23m (75ft) high, the heavy flow volume of the Athabasca River has cut deeply into the soft limestone rock, carving potholes, canyons and various water channels. Interpretive signs explain the basics of the local geology.

Sunwapta Falls
WATERFALL
(Map p158) Meaning 'turbulent water' in the Stoney language, 18m-high (60ft) Sunwapta Falls formed when the glacial meltwater of the Sunwapta River began falling from a hanging valley into the deeper U-shaped Athabasca Valley. Close to the Icefields Pkwy and the Sunwapta Falls Resort and restaurant, the falls are a popular stop for travelers plying the scenic highway. They're also the start of a 25km (15.5-mile) biking and hiking trail to remote Fortress Lake in Hamber Provincial Park.

Horseshoe Lake
LAKE
(Map p158) This idyllic blue-green horseshoe-shaped lake just off the Icefields Pkwy is missed by many visitors, making a stopover

Jasper Town

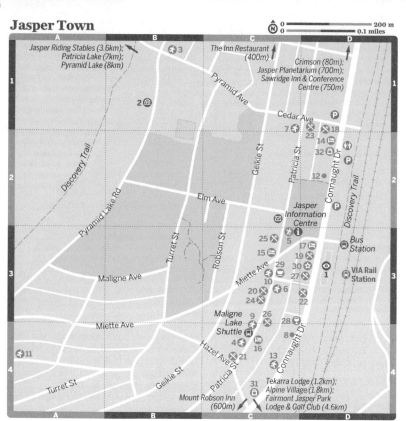

here all the more alluring. A choice spot for a bracing summer swim or a short stroll around the perimeter, the lake is surrounded by steep cliffs and is hence frequented by cliff divers. It's probably safer to watch than join in.

Mt Edith Cavell   MOUNTAIN
Rising like a snowy sentinel over Jasper Town, 3363m (11,033ft) Mt Edith Cavell is one of the park's most distinctive and physically arresting peaks. What it lacks in height it makes up for in stark, ethereal beauty. Accessed via a winding, precipitous road that branches off the Icefields Pkwy 6km (3.7 miles) south of Jasper, the mountain is famous for its flower meadows and its wing-shaped Angel Glacier.

First climbed in 1915, it was named the following year in honor of a humanitarian British nurse executed by a German firing squad during WWI, after helping to smuggle over 200 wounded Allied soldiers into neutral Holland.

⊙ Jasper Town & Around

Built in the early 1900s at the confluence of three river valleys, Jasper Town (originally known as Fitzhugh) is surrounded by mountains and blessed with one of the most easily accessible trail systems in North America. Characterized by a mishmash of low-rise shops and residential properties – not all of which are attractive – the town these days maintains strict development laws, meaning its tenure as an expanding urban hub is well and truly over. While the main sights lie outside the town, it makes a good evening base and, should the weather turn ugly, you can linger in an excellent museum, and ponder some interesting railway memorabilia.

Jasper Skytram   CABLE CAR
(Map p158; ☎ 780-852-3093; www.jaspertramway. com; Whistlers Mountain Rd; adult/child C$37/18.50; ☺ 9am-8pm Apr-Oct) If the views from Jasper

Jasper Town

◉ Sights
1 Jasper Train Station...............................D3
2 Jasper-Yellowhead Museum &
   Archives..B1

✚ Activities, Courses & Tours
3 Alpine Art-Eco Tours............................B1
4 Freewheel Cycle..................................C4
5 Friends of Jasper................................C3
   Gravity Gear...............................(see 4)
   Jasper Adventure Centre..............(see 6)
6 Jasper Raft Tours................................C3
7 Jasper Source for Sports.....................C1
8 Jasper Walks & Talks..........................C4
9 Maligne Rafting Adventures................C4
   Maligne Tours.............................(see 9)
10 On-Line Sport & Tackle......................C3
11 Rockaboo Adventures.........................A4
12 SunDog Tour Company.......................D2
13 Vicious Cycle...................................C4

⊨ Sleeping
14 Astoria Hotel....................................D2
15 Athabasca Hotel................................C3
16 Park Place Inn..................................C4
17 Whistlers Inn....................................D3

⊗ Eating
18 Bear's Paw Bakery.............................D1
19 Cassio's Trattoria..............................D3
20 Coco's Cafe......................................C3
21 Evil Dave's Grill.................................C4
22 Fiddle River Seafood Co.....................D3
23 Olive Bistro.......................................D1
   Papa George's..........................(see 14)
24 Patricia Street Deli............................C3
25 Raven Bistro.....................................C3
26 Something Else..................................C3
27 The Other Paw Bakery........................D3

◉ Drinking & Nightlife
   Atha-B Nightclub.......................(see 15)
   Downstream Bar.......................(see 22)
28 Jasper Brewing Co.............................C3
29 SnowDome Coffee Bar.......................C3
   Whistle Stop Pub......................(see 17)

◉ Entertainment
30 Chaba Cinema...................................D3

⊕ Shopping
31 Tangle Creek Gifts.............................C4
32 Totem Ski Shop.................................D2

simply aren't blowing your hair back, go for a ride up this sightseeing gondola. The journey zips up through through various mountain life zones to the high barren slopes of the Whistlers, where there's a small but pricey cafe. From the top of the gondola you can take the steep 1.5km (0.9-mile) hike to the mountain's true summit, where views stretch for 75km (47 miles).

The Skytram is about 7km (4.3 miles) south of Jasper Town along Whistlers Mountain Rd, off the Icefields Pkwy.

Discovery Trail   HERITAGE TRAIL
An interesting mix of interpretive walk, heritage trail and outdoor museum, the Jasper Discovery Trail completely circumnavigates the town via an 8km (5-mile) part-paved, part-unpaved pathway. Split into three sections highlighting the town's natural, historical and railroad legacies, the trail makes a worthwhile evening stroll or bracing early-morning jog.

Interpretive boards en route provide an educational introduction to both town and park and, on the northwestern side, the trail dips in and out of montane forest, offering excellent views over the surrounding mountains. The train station is a good place to start the trail.

Patricia & Pyramid Lakes   LAKES
These two lakes, less than 10km (6.2 miles) from town, offer abundant water activities. Patricia Lake contains the wreck of a WWII boat called *Habbakuk* which sunk after a secret wartime mission. Experienced divers can examine it in close-up with **Jasper Dive Adventures** (☑780-852-3560; www.jasperdive adventures.com; dives per person C$75). Pyramid Lake, overlooked by an eponymous resort, is popular with canoeists and kayakers in the summer and ice-skaters in the winter. It has a lovely island, popular with nighttime stargazers, accessible by a bridge.

Lakes Annette & Edith   LAKES
On the opposite side of the highway to the town, Lakes Annette and Edith are popular for water activities in the summer, as both have small beach areas. If you're brave and it's very hot, Annette is good for a quick summer dip – just remember the water was in a glacier not too long ago! Edith is more frequented by kayakers and boaters. Both are ringed by cycling/hiking trails and picnic areas. The trail that circumnavigates Lake Annette is wheelchair-accessible.

Lac Beauvert   LAKE

Dominated by the Fairmont Jasper Park Lodge and golf course, crystal-clear Lac Beauvert (literally 'beautiful green' in French) is another Athabasca Valley glacier-fed lake. It's a popular place for boating during summer and ice-skating in winter and has a more pastoral feel than other local bodies of water.

**Jasper-Yellowhead Museum
& Archives**   MUSEUM

(Map p160; ☎780-852-3013; www.jaspermuseum. org; 400 Pyramid Lake Rd; admission C$6; ☺10am-5pm) Poke your head into this museum if it's raining, snowing or too hot. Even if the weather is nice, it does an ample job of telling the Jasper story and the tales of the larger-than-life characters who arrived here to make it into the town it is today.

Jasper Train Station   LANDMARK

(Map p160; 607 Connaught Dr) Jasper grew up as a railway town and the train station, constructed by the Canadian National Railway (CNR), is one of its oldest and most attractive buildings. Designed in an unusual arts-and-crafts meets national-park architectural style, it was completed in 1925 to blend into its rustic surroundings. The interior has been upgraded, but remains sympathetic to the golden railroad era, with heavy wooden benches and art-deco travel posters from the 1940s and '50s.

◉ Maligne Lake Area

Maligne Canyon   CANYON

A steep, narrow gorge shaped by a river flowing at its base, this canyon at its narrowest is only a few meters wide and drops a stomach-turning 50m (164ft) beneath your feet. Crossed by six bridges, various trails lead out from the parking area on Maligne Lake Rd where there's also a quaint (if basic) teahouse. In the winter, waterfalls freeze solid into sheets of white ice and are popular with ice climbers.

Maligne Lake   LAKE

Almost 50km (31 miles) from Jasper at the end of the road that bears its name, 22km-long (13.7-mile) Maligne Lake is the recipient of a lot of hype. It is billed as one of the most beautiful lakes within the park and there's no denying its appeal: the baby-blue water and a craning circle of rocky, photogenic peaks are a feast for the eyes.

Although the north end of the lake is heavy with the summer tour-bus brigade, most of the rest of the shoreline is accessible only by foot or boat – hence it's quieter. Numerous campgrounds are available lakeside and are ideal for adventurous kayakers and

---

WORTH A TRIP

THE DESOLATE NORTH

Steal a glance at a map of Jasper National Park and you'll see that the whole area to the north of east–west Hwy 16 is almost blank. Although this extensive zone comprises over one-third of the park's total area, it contains no roads, no facilities and warrants virtually no mention at all in any of the standard park literature. So, what's the story?

Covered in a dense mountainscape, Jasper's north is a rugged pastiche of bugs, bogs and roaming caribou, where the infrastructure begins and ends in a handful of primitive campgrounds. For the curious and brave, this is backcountry of the highest order, where you're often three or four days' walk from civilization, and a week or more can pass without seeing another hiker. The only serviceable path through the region is the mythical North Boundary Trail, 192km (120 miles) of brooding backcountry speckled with 20 primitive campgrounds. Long stretches of shadowy forests and mosquito-infested marshes are juxtaposed with reaffirming highlights, such as misty Snake Indian Falls, the glacial intensity of Berg Lake and the meadowed magnificence of Snake Indian Pass. If you hike east–west starting at Celestine Lake, 53km (33 miles) northeast of Jasper Town, you'll save the best part until last: the dramatic north face of Mt Robson rising like an impregnable wall above Berg Lake.

Although lightly trafficked, the North Boundary Trail is well maintained and all river crossings have rudimentary bridges. The hike is unusual in that it runs east–west rather than tracking the Continental Divide. It is generally tackled over eight to 12 days ending near Mt Robson on Hwy 16, 88km (55 miles) west of Jasper Town. Call in at the Jasper Information Centre for trail conditions and maps.

backcountry hikers. Moose and grizzly bears are also sometimes seen here.

The Maligne Lake Boathouse (p154) rents canoes for a paddle around the lake. Not many people paddle all the way to Spirit Island (the lake's most classic view), as it would take you all day. Most people take it in on the classic and riotously popular boat trip with Maligne Tours (Map p160; ☑780-852-3370; www.malignelake.com; 616 Patricia St; adult/child C$67/33.50). The trips leave the boat dock up to eight times daily and last 1½ hours.

Medicine Lake LAKE

A geological rarity, Medicine Lake is perhaps best described as a sinking lake that has holes in the bottom and functions rather like a plugless bathtub. In summer, when the run-off is high, the lake fills more quickly than it can drain away and the body of water appears deep and expansive. In winter, as the run-off slows, the water empties, causing the lake to shrink to the size of a small stream.

What bewildered Aboriginals and other early visitors was the apparent lack of any water outlet. In fact, the water actually flows out of the lake via a series of small holes on its floor, before passing into a complex underground cave system. The river then re-emerges 16km (10 miles) downstream near Maligne Canyon. In the 1950s, a ferry service across the lake was briefly attempted, but efforts to plug the holes with sandbags, mattresses and even bundles of magazines all proved futile.

◉ North of Jasper Town

Pocahontas HISTORIC SITE

A one-time mining community that produced heaps of poor-quality smokeless coal for the Allied war effort during WWI, Pocahontas was once the largest settlement in Jasper National Park and home to hundreds of miners. When the market price for coal fell in 1921, the town slipped into a rapid decline, becoming a veritable ghost town nine years later when the 1930 National Parks Act banned mining in the park for good.

All that remains of Pocahontas today are some overgrown ruins, an antiquated superintendent's home and a set of rather plush tourist facilities, otherwise known as the Pocahontas Cabins (p169).

Visitors can amuse themselves on a 1km (0.6-mile) wheelchair-accessible interpretive trail that meanders around the old mining site, re-creating the days when the government encouraged resource extraction from the park in return for handsome royalties. To get here take the Miette Hot Springs Rd off Hwy 16 and turn at the first right into the parking lot.

Miette Hot Springs SPRING

(Map p158; www.parkscanada.gc.ca/hotsprings; Miette Rd; adult/child/family $6/5/18.50; ☺8:30am-10:30pm) More remote than Banff's historic springs, Miette Hot Springs, 'discovered' in 1909, are 61km (37.9 miles) northeast of Jasper off Hwy 16, near the park boundary. The soothing waters are kept at a pleasant 39°C (102°F) and are especially enjoyable when the fall snow is falling on your head and steam envelops the crowd.

There are a couple of hot pools and a cold one too – just to get the heart going – so it's best to stick a toe in before doing your cannonball.

☞ TOURS

SunDog Tour Company GUIDED TOUR

(Map p160; ☑780-852-4056; www.sundogtours.com; 414 Connaught Dr) SunDog Tour Company is one of many tour companies and booking centers in Jasper. It runs a whole host of tours, including trips to the icefields, train rides, boat rides, wildlife viewing, rafting, horseback riding and more.

⛏ SLEEPING

Aside from its one historic lodge, Jasper has a varied stash of hotels, motels, hostels, cabins, B&Bs and campgrounds. Notwithstanding, in July and August you'd be wise to make reservations way in advance.

Jasper Town is the operations center for the park's various accommodation establishments, with a handful of economical hotels and a good smattering of privately run B&Bs. The park's biggest campground, Whistlers, is a veritable giant situated 3.5km (2.2 miles) to the south of town, while the region's rustic quintet of HI hostels provides cheap beds for travelers on a budget.

Reservations (☑877-737-3783; www.reservation.parkscanada.gc.ca) are taken for four Jasper campgrounds: Whistlers, Pocahontas, Wabasso and Wapiti. All other campgrounds operate on a first-come, first-served basis.

🛏 Icefields Parkway

Camping

Wabasso
CAMPGROUND $
(Map p158; Hwy 93A; tent & RV sites C$21.50-32.50; ⊘ Jun-Sep) Peaceful and remote, this campground is nevertheless located relatively near to sights and Jasper Town on quiet Hwy 93A. Despite having 228 sites (51 of these have electricity), the grounds are spread out and fairly private. Walk-in tent sites along the river are wooded and lovely. Amenities include hot water and flush toilets as well as wheelchair-accessible sites.

Honeymoon Lake Campground
CAMPGROUND $
(Map p158; tent & RV sites C$15.70; ⊘ Jun-Sep) With lake access, these rustic sites are fairly popular. Sites 26 to 28 are right next to the water, and the rest of the 35 sites are wooded and fairly large. Dry toilets and a water pump are the only home comforts, but the Sunwapta Falls Resort restaurant is only 4km (2.4 miles) to the south.

Wilcox Creek Campground
CAMPGROUND $
(tent & RV sites C$9.80-15.70; ⊘ year-round) Located at the park's southern tip on the Icefields Pkwy beside the Wilcox Pass trailhead, this 46-site campground has trees and privacy. Facilities are minimal with dry toilet, a water pump and payphones, but it is one of only two park campgrounds that are open year-round.

Columbia Icefield Campground
CAMPGROUND $
(tent sites C$15.70; ⊘ May-Oct) While somewhat exposed to the elements, its 33 sites are relatively secluded from the Parkway yet afford excellent glacier views. Facilities are limited to dry toilets and a water pump. This is Jasper's sole tent-only campground.

Jonas Creek Campground
CAMPGROUND $
(tent & RV sites C$15.70; ⊘ May-Sep) The park's smallest campground has 25 sites. Unserviced and with no electricity or dump station, the place has a real backcountry feel, despite its location just off the Icefields Pkwy.

Mt Kerkeslin Campground
CAMPGROUND $
(Map p158; tent & RV sites C$15.70; ⊘ Jun-Sep) Across from its towering namesake, this campground has 42 sheltered sites and is routinely overlooked. Facilities are limited to dry toilets and a water pump.

Lodging

Athabasca Falls International Hostel
HOSTEL $
(Map p158; ☎780-852-3215; www.hihostels.ca; Icefields Pkwy; dm/d C$24.20/63.60; ⊘ closed Tue Oct-Apr) 🍴 A super-friendly hostel in the woods with an ingenious watering-can shower (summer only), a big, alpine-style kitchen-sitting area, table tennis and heated dorms in separate wooden cabins. There's no running water (just an outdoor pump) and the toilets are in outhouses, earning the place a 'rustic' tag.

Mt Edith Cavell International Hostel
HOSTEL $
(Map p158; ☎780-852-3215; www.hihostels.ca; Cavell Rd; dm C$25.15; ⊘ mid-May–mid-Oct) 🍴 Don't expect basic luxuries such as flush toilets, running water or electricity here. However, you can draw strength from the knowledge that your small but congenial communal dorm sits pretty in the foothills of one of the Rockies' most sublime mountain peaks. Enjoy the scenery from the deck or the outdoor fire pit. The hostel is open for cross-country skiers from February to May on a key-collect system.

Beauty Creek International Hostel
HOSTEL $
(☎780-852-3215; www.hihostels.ca; Icefields Pkwy; dm C$25.15; ⊘ mid-May–mid-Oct) 🍴 Forget the lack of electricity. Forget the propane-powered lights, outdoor loos and well-drawn water. Home in on the all-you-can-eat pancake breakfast and poetry-inspiring scenery.

Sunwapta Falls Resort
HOTEL $$
(☎888-828-5777; www.sunwapta.com; Icefields Pkwy; r from C$209; 🅿 @) A handy Icefields pit stop 53km (33 miles) south of Jasper Town, Sunwapta offers a comfortable mix of suites and lodge rooms cocooned in pleasant natural surroundings. It has a home-style restaurant and gift shop that are popular with the tour-bus crowd.

Glacier View Inn
HOTEL $$
(☎877-423-7433; Icefield Centre, Icefields Parkway; r from C$249; ⊘ May-Oct; 🅿) Panoramic glacier views are unbelievable at this chalet – if only the windows were a bit bigger. It's in the same complex as the Icefield Centre, so there are times when you may feel like you're in a shopping mall, but once the buses go away, you're left in one of the most spectacular places around. A nothing-to-write-home-about cafeteria shares the complex.

🛏 Jasper Town & Around

Camping

⭐ Wapiti Campground
CAMPGROUND $

(Map p158; Hwy 93; tent/RV sites C$27.40/32.30; ⊙year-round) Jasper's second-biggest campground (362 sites) is located close to its largest (the Whistlers) with a handy bike/hike trail linking them and continuing on to Jasper Town (5km/3.1 miles). Clean and well-maintained shower and toilet blocks are a given here, but Wapiti's main draw is its location on the banks of the Athabasca River. The campsite is unique in that it operates year-round; in the winter 93 sites are kept open.

Whistlers Campground
CAMPGROUND $

(Map p158; ☑780-852-6177; Whistlers Rd; tent/RV sites C$22.50/38.30; ⊙May-Oct; P) The Whistlers, with 781 mainly wooded sites and plenty of amenities (showers, wheelchair access, playground and an interpretive program) is one of North America's largest campgrounds. It's 3.5km south of Jasper Town and linked by a well-used bike/hike path. Elk sightings are common. 'Glamping' options include 21 oTENTiks: canvas-walled six-person 'cottage tents' (C$70), with kitchen facilities, beds and electricity.

Lodging

HI-Jasper
HOSTEL $

(Map p158; ☑780-852-3215; www.hihostels.ca; Whistlers Mountain Rd; dm/d C$26.25/68.65; P@🛜) 🍃 It would be easy not to like this hostel. With dorm rooms that sleep upward of 40 people (meaning you're pretty much guaranteed some midnight snoring) and a location just far enough from town that the walk is a killer, it's already two strikes down. Despite all of this, though, it's a great place to stay.

Park Place Inn
BOUTIQUE HOTEL $$

(Map p160; ☑780-852-9970; www.parkplaceinn. com; 623 Patricia St; r from C$229; @🛜) Giving nothing away behind its rather ordinary exterior among a parade of downtown shops, the Park Place is a head-turner as soon as you ascend the stairs to its plush open lobby. The 14 self-proclaimed heritage rooms are well deserving of their superior status, with marble surfaces, fine local art, claw-foot baths and a general air of refinement and luxury. The service is equally professional.

Tekarra Lodge
HOTEL $$

(Map p158; ☑780-852-3058; www.tekarralodge. com; Hwy 93A; d from C$188; ⊙May-Oct; P🛜🐾) The most atmospheric cabins in the park are set next to the Athabasca River amid tall trees and tranquility. Hardwood floors, wood-paneled walls plus fireplaces and kitchenettes inspire coziness. It's only 1km from the town, but has a distinct backcountry feel. The on-site restaurant is fine dining by Jasper standards.

Athabasca Hotel
HOTEL $$

(Map p160; ☑780-852-3386; www.athabascahotel. com; 510 Patricia St; r without/with bath C$99/175; P@🛜) If you can take the stuffed moose-heads, noisy downstairs bar-nightclub and service that's sometimes as fickle as the mountain weather, you'll have no problems at the Athabasca (or Atha-B, as it's known). Centrally located with an attached restaurant and small, but comfortable, rooms (many with shared bath), it's been around since 1929 and is the best bargain in town.

Whistlers Inn
HOTEL $$

(Map p160; ☑780-852-9919; www.whistlersinn.com; cnr Connaught Dr & Miette Ave; r C$195; @🛜🥘) A central location and above-standard rooms give Whistlers an edge over many of its rivals. The rooftop hot tub alone is worth spending the night for – watch the sun dip behind the hills as the recuperative waters soak away the stress of the day.

> ### ⓘ WHEN THERE'S NO ROOM AT THE INN
>
> Jasper gets seriously busy in July and August, and finding a room on the spur of the moment can be extremely difficult. Fortunately, aside from the standard clutch of hotels, motels and campgrounds, Jasper Town – which has a permanent population of 4500 – has over 100 B&Bs in private houses. The **Jasper Home Accommodation Association** (www.stayinjasper.com) maintains an excellent website of inspected B&Bs inside the park, complete with descriptions, contact details and web links. Prices range from C$60 to C$200 in high season and facilities often include kitchenettes, private entrances and cable TV.

JASPER NATIONAL PARK SLEEPING

JASPER NATIONAL PARK CAMPGROUNDS

CAMPGROUND	LOCATION	DESCRIPTION	NO OF SITES
Columbia Icefield	Icefields Parkway	Tents only and basic facilities, but campground is secluded and views are tremendous	33
Honeymoon Lake	Icefields Parkway	Small and quiet, with some sites on lakeshore	35
Jonas Creek	Icefields Parkway	Close to highway with some seclusion if you choose the right site	25
Mt Kerkeslin	Icefields Parkway	Basic campground with sheltered sites close to Athabasca Falls	42
Wabasso	Icefields Parkway	Well-serviced but relatively remote campground off main highway and close to Mt Edith Cavell hikes	228
Wilcox Creek	Icefields Parkway	Close to Columbia Icefield Centre and Wilcox Pass trailhead	46
Wapiti	Jasper Town & Around	Offers 40 serviced sites and showers; numbers limited in winter	362
Whistlers	Jasper Town & Around	A mini-town with every facility imaginable; great for families	781
Pocahontas	North of Jasper Town	Quiet and wooded; close to eastern park entrance	140
Snaring River	North of Jasper Town	Rustic with no RVs; situated off highway 15km (9.5 miles) north of Jasper Town	66

[icon] Drinking Water   [icon] Flush Toilets   [icon] Great for Families   [icon] RV Dump Station

Astoria Hotel
HOTEL $$
(Map p160; ☑ 780-852-3351; www.astoriahotel.com; 404 Connaught Dr; d from C$199; ☎) With its gabled Bavarian roof, the Astoria is one of the town's most distinctive pieces of architecture and one of an original trio of Jasper hotels that has been owned by the same family since the 1920s. Journeyman rooms are functional and comfortable, and are bolstered by the presence of a downstairs bar (De'd Dog) and restaurant (Papa George's).

★ Alpine Village
CABIN $$$
(Map p158; ☑ 780-852-3285; www.alpinevillage jasper.com; d C$195-480; ☺ May-Oct; P ☎) Regular renovations – the last in 2012 – keep this discreet but deluxe cabin complex a cut above the rest. The location, flush against the Athabasca River, allows you to enjoy the tranquility (the nearest neighbors are usually elk), but you're close enough to walk to town. The cabins themselves have plush country-style adornments with mezzanine bedrooms and stone fireplaces.

Crimson
HOTEL $$$
(Map p158; ☑ 780-852-3394; www.mpjasper.com; 200 Connaught Ave; r C$280-320; P ❄ ☎ ☎) The newest addition to Jasper's hotel scene is one of six hotels owned by Mountain Park Lodges and aims to satisfy the deluxe market. It's centrally located, although its position just across from the railway tracks is unlikely to excite insomniacs. Rooms are big, there's a pool and gym, and the restaurant (named C200) is one of Jasper's finer eating options.

Mount Robson Inn
MOTEL $$$
(Map p158; ☑ 780-852-3327; www.mountrobsoninn. com; 902 Connaught Dr; r from C$255; P ❄ @ ☎) A clean, plush place laid out motel-style that offers hot tubs, an on-site restaurant and a substantial complimentary breakfast. Find it on the edge of Jasper Town.

ELEVATION	OPEN	RESERVATION NEEDED?	DAILY FEE	FACILITIES	PAGE
2012m (6600ft)	May-Oct	no	C$15.70		p164
1310m (4300ft)	Jun-Sep	no	C$15.70		p164
1500m (4920ft)	May-Sep	no	C$15.70		p164
1200m (3936ft)	Jun-Sep	no	C$15.70		p164
1125m (3690ft)	Jun-Sep	advisable Jul-Aug	C$21.50-32.30		p164
2012m (6600ft)	year-round	no	C$9.80-15.70		p164
1070m (3510ft)	year-round	advisable Jul-Aug	C$27.40-32.30		p165
1070m (3510ft)	May-Oct	advisable Jul-Aug	C$22.50-38.30		p165
1200m (3936ft)	May-Sep	advisable Jul-Aug	C$21.50		p168
1050m (3445ft)	May-Sep	no	C$15.70		p168

Grocery Store Nearby   Restaurant Nearby   Payphone   Summertime Campfire Program

Fairmont Jasper Park Lodge   HOTEL **$$$**
(Map p158; ☎780-852-3301; www.fairmont.com/jasper; 1 Old Lodge Rd; r from C$450; P@🛜) Sitting on the shore of Lac Beauvert and surrounded by manicured grounds and mountain peaks, this classic old lodge can't quite match the panache of the Banff and Lake Louise Fairmonts, although you'll bump into fewer afternoon-tea-seeking tourists. With a country-club meets 1950s-holiday-camp air, the amenity-filled cabins and chalets are a throwback to a more opulent era.

The lodge's highlight is its main lounge, open to the public, with stupendous lake views. It's filled with log furniture, chandeliers and fireplaces and is the best place in town to write a postcard over a quiet cocktail. There are often off-season discounts.

Pyramid Lake Resort   HOTEL **$$$**
(Map p158; ☎780-852-4900; www.mpljasper.com; Pyramid Lake Rd; d C$202-289; P🛜🏊) A former Coast hotel now in the hands of Mountain Park Lodges, this refined 'resort' has fantastic views of the lake and great access to it. The design is a bit strange, with a huge swath of concrete driveway bisecting the hotel, but most of the chalet-style rooms enjoy an unencumbered view of the lake.

Ample opportunities for lake fun abound, with canoes for rent and a small beach to hang out on. There's also a fitness room, hot tub, shop and restaurant. The town is a 5km (3.1-mile) downhill hike or bike away.

Sawridge Inn & Conference Centre   HOTEL **$$$**
(Map p158; ☎780-852-6590; www.sawridgejasper.com; 76 Connaught Dr; d from C$286; P✳@🛜🏊) Yes, it's large and a little bit corporate but, on the face of it, Jasper (and the Sawridge) isn't such a bad place to organize a business conference – and many businesses do. For all its slickness, the hotel has plenty of nooks to escape to, plus an impressive plant-filled central atrium for more social animals.

🛏 Maligne Lake Area

YHA Maligne Canyon   HOSTEL **$**
(Map p158; ☎1-877-852-0781; www.hihostels.ca;
Maligne Lake Rd; dm $24.20; 🅿) 🍂 Well posi-
tioned for winter cross-country skiing and
summer sorties along the Skyline Trail, this
very basic hostel is poised a little too close to
the road to merit a proper 'rustic' tag. Die-
hards can get back to nature with six-bed
dorms, outhouse toilets and regular visits to
the water pump.

🛏 North of Jasper Town

Camping

Pocahontas   CAMPGROUND **$**
(Map p158; Miette Hot Springs Rd; tent & RV sites
C$21.50; ☺May-Sep) It's spacious and densely
wooded, so you'd never know this place has
140 sites. Facilities are minimal, albeit with
flush toilets and wheelchair-accessible sites,
and it's very well maintained.

Snaring River Campground   CAMPGROUND **$**
(Map p158; Hwy 16; tent sites C$15.70; ☺May-Sep;
🅿) Situated 15km (9.5 miles) north of Jasper
Town, this basic campground – the park's

BACKCOUNTRY HUTS & LODGES

Jasper offers half-a-dozen-or-so huts and lodges modeled on the European alpine tradition.
All situated a good day's hike from the nearest road, these venerable backcountry retreats
offer a unique wilderness experience without the hassle of tent erection or listening to things
that go 'bump' in the night.

Huts

The Alpine Club of Canada maintains three rustic backcountry huts in Jasper National
Park. For each hut, you must bring your own bedding, food, matches, toilet paper and
dishcloth, and must pack out all of your garbage. Reservations (C$36) are required and
can be made through the Canmore Clubhouse (p119). You are also required to have
a Parks Canada wilderness pass.

Wates-Gibson Hut (Tonquin Valley) This hut is a beautiful log cabin built in 1959 with a
wood-burning stove, sleeping mattresses (C$30/24 in summer/winter) and a propane-
powered cooking system (utensils available). In summer, you can hike here via the 18km
(11.2-mile) Astoria River Trail from the Mt Edith Cavell International Hostel. Add on another
12km (7.5 miles) in winter when the Mt Edith Cavell Rd is closed.

Mt Colin Centennial Hut (Colin Range) Used mainly by climbers, this six-bed hut is
accessed by a demanding six- to eight-hour hike off the Overlander Trail. It has a Coleman
stove, mattresses and cooking utensils, and is closed in winter.

Sydney Vallance (Fryatt) Hut This 12-bed hut, situated 24km (15 miles) up the Fryatt
Valley from the Icefields Pkwy, is perhaps the most isolated hut and was given a complete
renovation in 1999. It's open year-round and facilities include propane cooking and lighting
and a wood-heating stove.

Lodges

In Tonquin Valley, the Tonquin Amethyst Lake Lodge (Map p158; ☎780-852-1188; www.
tonquinadventures.com; r per person C$195, incl meals) and Tonquin Valley Backcountry
Lodge (Map p158; ☎780-852-3909; www.tonquinvalley.com; r per person C$205, incl meals) pro-
vide rustic accommodations in historic cabins with views of the lake and Ramparts, approximately 24km (15 miles) from the nearest road. Both lodges run multiday horseback-riding
treks in summer; in winter you can cross-country ski to the lodges.

Built in 1921 and rebuilt in 1991, the Shovel Pass Lodge (☎780-852-4215; www.sky
linetrail.com; r per person C$195, incl meals), situated halfway along the emblematic Skyline
Trail, is the oldest lodge in the park. With seven guest cabins plus a main chalet and dining
room, the lodge can accommodate up to 18 people. Meals, bed linen and propane lights and
heating are provided, though you'll have to bring your own towel. The price includes accommodations, three meals, and transportation of up to 6.8kg (15lb) of gear (by horse). Three-
day horseback-riding treks are also available. It's open June to September.

most primitive and isolated – is the perfect antidote to the busy campgrounds elsewhere in the park.

Lodging

Pocahontas Cabins — RESORT $$

(Map p158; ☑ 780-866-3732; www.mpljasper.com; cnr Hwy 16 & Miette Hot Springs Rd; cabins C$180-254; 🅿🐾) Once a mining community, Pocahontas now consists of this cabin resort, equipped with a restaurant, hot tub, outdoor swimming pool and small grocery store. One- and two-bedroom cabins are relatively plush by park standards, with a clean refurbished feel. You can go up a notch by nabbing the luxury Cedar Lodge (private balcony and gas fireplace).

Miette Hot Springs Resort — MOTEL, CABIN $$

(Map p158; ☑ 780-866-3750; www.mhresort.com; Miette Hot Springs Rd; motel/bungalows/cabins C$97/120/167; 🅿) Right next to the bathhouse, wood is the binding theme at this low-key 're-sort' situated in a collection of old-fashioned but charming cabins, bungalows and motel rooms dating from 1938 to the 1970s. Bunga-lows and cabins sleep up to six and some of the 17 motel rooms have kitchenettes.

✖ EATING

While Jasper's culinary scene is a long way from the bright lights of Calgary and Edmon-ton, budding gastronomes needn't starve. Outside of the small cluster of fast-food fran-chises and the usual cache of post-hike refue-ling joints, fine diners can travel the world in refined Patricia St, touching down in such ex-otic locales as Japan, Korea, Italy and Greece.

✖ Icefields Parkway

Columbia Icefield Centre

Dining Room — CAFETERIA $

(Columbia Icefield Centre, Icefields Pkwy; snacks C$8-10, mains C$20; ☺8-10am & 6-9pm May-Oct) Fantastic views of Athabasca Glacier will likely keep you from noticing the lack of at-mosphere in the Columbia Icefield Centre's eateries. The 2nd-floor dining room does breakfast, dinner and a buffet lunch. Handier is the hectic canteen (open 9am to 6pm April to October), good for quick bites to eat.

Sunwapta Falls Resort — AMERICAN $$

(Map p158; Icefields Parkway; lunch/dinner C$12/25; ☺deli 11am-6pm, dining room 6-9pm May-Nov) One of the better tourist-orientated restaurant-

gift-shop combos on the Icefields Pkwy, the Sunwapta does familiar ranch-style break-fasts and tasty salads, sandwiches and soups. Arrive early for lunch before the daily tour-bus crowds arrive.

✖ Jasper Town & Around

★ Bear's Paw Bakery — BAKERY, CAFE $

(Map p160; www.bearspawbakery.com; 4 Cedar Ave; pastries C$3-5; ☺6am-6pm) The Bear's Paw is one of the best bakery-cafes west of Winnipeg, so thank your lucky stars it's just where you need it most at the end of an energy-sapping hike/bike/ski. Try any of the insanely addictive scones, cookies, muffins and focaccia-like breads. The coffee's equally gratifying. A better-positioned branch called The Other Paw Bakery (Map p160; 610 Con-naught Dr; snacks C$2-6; ☺7am-6pm) is opposite the train station.

Patricia Street Deli — SANDWICHES $

(Map p160; 610 Patricia St; sandwiches C$5-9; ☺10am-5pm) The rule of thumb in a national park is simple no-nonsense North American food with minimal embellishment, which accounts in many ways for the continuing success of this deli, where homemade bread is made into generously filled sandwiches by people who are just as generous with their hiking tips. Join the queue and satiate your ravenous backcountry appetite.

Coco's Cafe — CAFE $

(Map p160; ☑780-852-4550; 608 Patricia St; mains C$5-10; ☺8am-4pm) 🍃 Rating Jasper's overall cafe is a toss-up for some, but few dis-agree that Coco's usually comes out on top on the breakfast front. There's not much room inside, but plenty of bodies are content to cram in to plan hikes or trade bear sightings. Ethical eaters are well catered for, with tofu scrambles and fair trade coffee.

Olive Bistro — MEDITERRANEAN $$

(Map p160; ☑780-852-5222; www.olivebistro.ca; 401 Patricia St; mains C$16-25; ☺5-11pm; 🍴) For an away-day from Alberta beef, hit Olive Bistro, whose Mediterranean leanings stretch to an unusual vegetable strudel, tasty enough to tempt the most avowed carnivores from their default steak. The restaurant also doubles up as one of Jasper's live-music venues.

Cassio's Trattoria — ITALIAN $$

(Map p160; 602 Connaught Dr; meals C$14-30; ☺7:30am-11pm; 🚫) In the long-standing Whis-tlers Inn, the Cassio family concentrates on presenting *real* Italian fare – gnocchi, meatballs, pasta marinara and a well-stuffed antipasto plate.

The Inn Restaurant
MODERN AMERICAN $$

(Map p158; ☑ 780-852-3232; 98 Geikie St; mains C$13-28; ☺ 6:30am-11pm) The local Best Western Hotel is not always the most obvious stop for fine dining, but Jasper's has established an eating offshoot regularly touted by locals as one of the best in town, That said, it'll take a long hike to justify the rich but satisfying butter chicken, and an even longer one to bag the lobster mac and cheese (with pancetta).

Papa George's
AMERICAN $$

(Map p160; www.papageorgesrestaurant.com; 404 Connaught Dr; meals C$12-30; ☺ 7am-2pm & 5-10pm; ☑) Almost as old as the park, this stalwart has been in business since 1925 and something about the original rock fireplace, reliable service and know-what-you're-getting food still rings true. The menu takes the word local seriously with elk striploin and wild boar chops.

Something Else
MEDITERRANEAN, STEAKHOUSE $$

(Map p160; 621 Patricia St; mains C$13-24; ☺ 11am-11pm; ☐) Essentially a Greek restaurant, Something Else wears many hats (American, Italian, Cajun) and doesn't always succeed. What it *is* good for is space (even on a Saturday night), decent beer, menu variety, copious kids' options and the good old homemade Greek stuff. Try the lamb or chicken souvlaki.

★ Raven Bistro
MEDITERRANEAN $$$

(Map p160; ☑ 780-852-5151; www.theravenbistro.com; 504 Patricia St; mains C$21-32; ☺ 5-10pm; ☑) It's not every day that Jasper sprouts a new business, especially a restaurant, so make the most of this small, tastefully designed bistro that pushes vegetarian dishes and encourages shared plates.

Evil Dave's Grill
CANADIAN, FUSION $$$

(Map p160; ☑ 780-852-3323; www.evildaves.com; 622 Patricia St; mains C$22-35; ☺ 4-11pm) There's nothing evil about Dave's, one of a handful of local attempts to bury Jasper's dodgy image as a bastion of family-friendly, post-hiking grub that fills stomachs rather than excites taste buds. The excellent fusion food is all over the map, with Caribbean, Middle Eastern and Japanese influences lighting up the fish and beef.

Fiddle River Seafood Co
SEAFOOD $$$

(Map p160; ☑ 780-852-3032; 620 Connaught Dr; mains C$22-32; ☺ 5-10pm) Being almost 1600km from the sea makes some customers understandably leery, but Jasper's premier seafood joint is no slouch. Pull up a seat near the window and tuck into one of the innovative creations, such as pumpkin-seed-crusted trout.

✖ Maligne Lake Area

View Restaurant
FAST FOOD $

(Map p158; Maligne Lake Lodge; snacks C$4-10; ☺ 9am-7pm) On first impressions this aptly named restaurant at the head of Maligne Lake is just another overpriced cafeteria for tourists. But, beyond the sandwiches and soups, this place serves up some of the best pastries, muffins and cinnamon buns in the park.

🍷 DRINKING & NIGHTLIFE

★ SnowDome Coffee Bar
COFFEE

(Map p160; www.607patricia.com; 607 Patricia St; ☺ 7:45am-8pm) The best coffee in Jasper, the Rockies, possibly even Alberta, is – no word of a lie – served out of a launderette! But, Patricia St's coin-op laundry is no ordinary washing place. As well as being surgically clean, it's also an art gallery, shower facility, internet cafe and all-round community resource.

★ Jasper Brewing Co
BREWERY, PUB

(Map p160; ☑ 780-852-4111; www.jasperbrewingco.ca; 624 Connaught Dr; ☺ 11:30am-1am) ✪ Open since 2005, this brewpub, the first of its type in a Canadian national park, uses glacial water to make its fine ales, including the signature Rockhopper IPA or – slightly more adventurous – the Rocket Ridge Raspberry Ale. It's a sit-down affair, with TVs and a good food menu.

Atha-B Nightclub
BAR, CLUB

(Map p160; ☑ 780-852-3386; Athabasca Hotel, 510 Patricia St; ☺ 4pm-2am) Nightclubbing in a national park is about as congruous as wildlife viewing in downtown Toronto. Bear this in mind before you hit the Atha-B, a pub-slash-nightclub off the lobby of the Athabasca Hotel, where mullets are still high fashion and the carpet's probably radioactive.

Downstream Bar
BAR

(Map p160; 620 Connaught Dr; ☺ 4pm-late) A comfy pub that hosts open-mic sessions, jazz, blues or reggae.

Whistle Stop Pub
PUB

(Map p160; cnr Connaught Dr & Miette Ave; ☺ noon-11pm) Shock horror! You may actually meet a local, as opposed to a tourist, in this salt-of-the-earth pub attached to the Whistlers Inn.

⭐ ENTERTAINMENT

Chaba Cinema   CINEMA
(Map p160; 604 Connaught Dr) A cinema is a rarity in a Canadian national park, so make the most of this quaint two-screen affair.

🛍 SHOPPING

Stuffed bears, flimsy trinkets and slogan-bearing T-shirts – shopping in Jasper is invariably of the incidental variety. If you've really got to shop, Canada's largest mall lies four hours east in Edmonton, and SunDog Tour Company (p163) runs daily bus shuttles.

Tangle Creek Gifts   BOOKS, SOUVENIRS
(Map p160; 640 Connaught Dr; ⊙8am-5pm) Sift through the tourist kitsch for books on local history and wildlife.

Totem Ski Shop   OUTDOOR EQUIPMENT
(Map p160; www.totemskishop.com; 408 Connaught Dr; ⊙9am-10pm) An outdoors outfitter selling everything from camping gear to maps; it also rents ski gear and other supplies.

ℹ Information

DANGERS & ANNOYANCES
The biggest dangers are weather, rugged backcountry terrain, wildlife and avalanches. All of these dangers can be minimized with common sense and planning. Always check trail, weather and wildlife conditions before venturing out into the wilderness – even on a day hike – and make sure you are properly equipped.

Rocky Mountain weather can turn on a dime. Prepare for all-seasons weather at any time of year and always carry warm layered clothing. Fickle weather conditions can also create treacherous driving conditions, even during summer.

While crime is low in Jasper, you'd be wise to always keep your car locked when unattended.

MEDICAL SERVICES & EMERGENCY
For emergencies dial ☑911. The 24-hour park warden can be contacted on ☑780-852-6155.

MONEY
CIBC (416 Connaught Dr; ⊙9:30am-5pm Mon-Fri) Bank with ATM.

POST
Post Office (502 Patricia St; ⊙9am-5pm Mon-Fri)

TELEPHONE
All park hotels, lodges and nonprimitive campgrounds have public phones. Courtesy phones (local calls only) are located in Jasper Information Centre. Cell (mobile) phone reception is patchy.

TOURIST INFORMATION
Built in 1913, the attractive **Jasper Information Centre** (☑780-852-6176; www.pc.gc.ca/jasper; 500 Connaught Dr; ⊙9am-7pm May-Oct, 10am-5pm Dec-Apr, closed Nov) has maps, brochures and up-to-date trail information. Parks Canada is represented here and also has a desk at the **Columbia Icefield Centre** (☑780-852-6288; ⊙10am-5pm May-Oct), 103km (64 miles) south of Jasper Town on the Icefields Pkwy.

Also in the Jasper Information Centre, **Jasper Tourism & Commerce** (www.jaspercanadianrockies.com) carries lots of brochures on accommodations and services within the park. **Friends of Jasper** (p155) also has a shop here, with maps and specialist guides to the park. Proceeds from sales are reinvested via grants and volunteer services back into the park.

USEFUL WEBSITES
Head to **Lonely Planet** (www.lonelyplanet.com/canada/alberta/banff-and-jasper-national-parks) for planning advice, author recommendations, traveler reviews and insider tips.

ℹ Getting There & Away

Most people arrive in Jasper by car, utilizing its three main roads that connect the park to Lake Louise (south), Edmonton (east) and British Columbia (west), but there also some good public transport options.

BUS
SunDog Tour Company (www.sundogtours.com; 414 Connaught Dr; ⊙8am-8pm) runs a daily bus between Jasper and Edmonton International Airport (adult/child C$99/59). This service operates year-round. From October to May, SunDog runs another daily shuttle south along the Icefields Pkwy to Calgary airport (adult/child C$115/69). The southbound bus departs Jasper at 7am and arrives at Calgary airport at 1:50pm. The northbound bus leaves Calgary airport at 11:30am and arrives in Jasper at 5:30pm. Buses also stop in Lake Louise and Banff, where passengers must transfer to a Brewster bus for the final leg of the journey (price included in your ticket).

In the summer months (May to October), the entire Jasper–Calgary airport bus route is operated by **Brewster** (www.brewster.ca). This bus can stop at the Columbia Icefield Centre by prior arrangement. Check the website for schedules.

Greyhound (www.greyhound.ca) buses run west to Vancouver (C$145, 12 hours, one daily) and east to Edmonton (C$74, five hours, one daily). Both leave early in the morning.

TRAIN
The luxurious if pricey **VIA** (www.viarail.ca) train connects Jasper with Toronto (C$511, 2½ days) to the east, and Vancouver (C$206, 20 hours) to the west, stopping at numerous stations en

route. There are also trains to Prince Rupert on BC's west coast (C$256, one day). Both trains run three times a week.

❶ Getting Around

Although most people get around the park by private vehicle, with a bit of patience and flexibility, carless travel is possible.

BICYCLE

With numerous bike hire outlets in Jasper, it's easy to rent a bike to get you around the town and its main sights. Alternatively, you can bring your own.

Fortuitously, the park also has one of the most extensive bike-trail networks in Canada. Wide highways with ample shoulders and strict speed limits make road biking easy. The truck-free Icefields Pkwy south to Lake Louise and Banff is a particularly popular ride.

BUS

Brewster (p171) buses stop at the Columbia Icefield Centre daily in summer (May to October) on their Jasper–Banff run. **SunDog Tour Company** (p163) shuttles visit many areas of the park during summer, but to use them

---

AROUND JASPER NATIONAL PARK

Jasper National Park is buffered by additional protected zones to the north and west (Banff National Park borders it to the south). To the west – and in British Columbia – is Mt Robson Provincial Park, home of the Canadian Rockies' highest summit and the headwaters of the mighty Fraser River, along with the roadless Hamber Provincial Park (accessible via the 35km/22-mile Fortress Lake Trail starting on Hwy 93). To the north and lying wholly within Alberta, the Willmore Wilderness Park lures travelers with a penchant for total solitude.

Mt Robson Provincial Park

Bordering Jasper National Park in the west and flanked by the Selwyn Range, the drive through Mt Robson Provincial Park follows a historic pathway of fur traders. Rejected by the Canadian Pacific Railway as a route through the Rockies, it was later adopted by Grand Trunk Pacific and Canadian Northern Pacific Railways and is today a major railway route. The views of snowy mountains and glacial lakes are magnificent.

Bisected by Hwy 16 on its way between Jasper and Prince George, Mt Robson Provincial Park abuts Jasper National Park at the Yellowhead Pass, 24km (15 miles) west of Jasper Town. Covering 2249 sq km (868 sq miles), the park's main hub is an excellent information center (☑ 250-566-4325; www.elp.gov.bc.ca/bcparks; ☉ 8am-5pm Jun & Sep, to 8pm Jul & Aug) near the western border. Here you can pick up trail information, register for hikes with BC Parks staff and take in exhibits on local geography and history – including a short interpretive trail. You'll also find a gas station and cafe situated next door. On clear days the neck-craning views of ice-glazed Mt Robson, glowering like a fiery beacon overhead, are truly amazing.

SIGHTS & ACTIVITIES

The tallest mountain in the Canadian Rockies, Mt Robson, in British Columbia, towers like a misplaced Everest over the surrounding peaks and valleys, dwarfing other rugged giants in its 3954m (12,969ft) shadow. Approaching from the east, no words can prepare you for the sight of its craggy southern face, which rises like a vertical wall over 2439m (8000ft) above Berg Lake. Visible for fewer than 14 days a year, the mountain has left onlookers awestruck for centuries; Aboriginals called it 'Mountain of the Spiral Road' and trappers and explorers revered it as unconquerable. It wasn't until 1913 that the mountain was first officially climbed, and, even today, only approximately 10% of summit attempts are successful.

Hiking is what draws most visitors to the park. The famous 22km (13.7-mile) Berg Lake Trail takes you through the Valley of a Thousand Falls, next to Mt Robson and past the stunning, glacier-fed lake itself, filled with shorn-off chunks of ice. You must register to undertake the hike, which takes two to three days, and while the majority of spaces are filled on a first-come, first-served basis, reservations (☑ 800-689-9025) are accepted for particularly busy periods. Seven backcountry campgrounds are located en route (C$10 per person, per night). Trail information, permits and maps can all be found at the information center.

For those with less time, the first segment of the Berg Lake Trail (bikes allowed) can be taken as far as the Kinney Lake picnic site and viewpoint at 9km (5.6 miles). Look out for mountain goats, black bears, caribou and porcupine. Alternatively, you can heli-hike, ie take a helicopter into the Berg Lake area and hike out. For details enquire with Robson Helimagic Inc (www.robsonhelimagic.com; Hwy 5N, Valemount, British Columbia; per person from C$249).

you'll have to sign up and pay for one of their sightseeing tours. See the website for details. SunDog also run a six-times-a-day shuttle from downtown Jasper to the Jasper Skytram. **Maligne Lake Shuttle** (p278) runs a daily shuttle bus from Jasper Town to Maligne Lake (Maligne Lake/Maligne Canyon C$30/15, May to late September), stopping en route at the Fairmont Jasper Park Lodge, Maligne Canyon, and the Skyline trailhead (north and south). The service runs four times daily in peak season.

CAR & MOTORCYCLE

Speed limits in the park are 90km/h (56mph) on major roads and 60km/h (37mph) on secondary roads. Motorists should regularly scan for wildlife either on or crossing the road. Also beware of other cars stopping or slowing down to view wildlife.

Jasper Town has a number of gas stations. Car rental is available at the VIA railway station with **Thrifty** (607 Connaught Dr; per day from C$49).

Boating is popular within the park, although fishing isn't particularly good. Launch your boat in the green waters of Moose or Yellowhead Lakes. Rearguard Falls, just west of the information center, is known for its salmon viewing (mid-August to early September).

SLEEPING & EATING

Lucerne Campground (☏800-689-9025; Hwy 16, Yellowhead Lake; campsites C$20; ⊙May-Sep) With large, wooded sites, the spacious Lucerne is a great place to set up home for the night. A number of the 36 sites are level and have pull-through for RVs; others are built up for tents. There are two walk-in, lakeside tent sites and a water pump.

Mt Robson Mountain River Lodge (☏250-566-9899; www.mtrobson.com; cnr Hwy 16 & Swift Current Creek Rd; lodge/cabins incl breakfast from C$129/179; ℗ 🛜) On the western border of the park, this friendly lodge commands stunning views of the giant peak – when it's visible. There's a main lodge and a couple of cabins that share a cozy, away-from-it-all atmosphere.

Hamber Provincial Park

Tiny Hamber Provincial Park is cocooned in an alcove on the western border of Jasper National Park. It is the domain of black and grizzly bears, but recent years have seen an influx of backpackers. While there is no road access into the park, an improved 22km (13.7-mile) trail from Sunwapta Falls along the Icefields Pkwy leads to **Fortress Lake**, on the park's eastern border. Fishing for brook trout is popular here, and an air-accessed commercial fishing camp is located on the southern shore.

Along the lake's northeast shore are three basic campgrounds, each with a pit toilet and bear pole. You do not need a permit to camp, but you must register your vehicle with Parks Canada if you plan to leave it at Sunwapta Falls.

For more information about the park and current trail conditions, contact **BC Parks** (www.bcparks.ca).

Willmore Wilderness Park

Spreading across the foothills and mountain ranges north of Jasper National Park, Willmore Wilderness Park has more wildlife passing through it than people. If you really want to get off the beaten track, consider the 750km (466 miles) of trails crossing this park. Access is by foot only from Rock Lake, Big Berland or Grande Cache. At 95km (59 miles), **Mountain Trail** is the longest and most continuous route through the park, from Rock Lake to Grande Cache. The scenic 33km (20.5-mile) **Indian Trail** is popular for hunting and wildlife watching and is in better condition than many of the other trails.

Very little trail maintenance is done here, and while there are designated camping areas, you'll find nothing at them. Water is from lakes and rivers only and must be treated before you consume it. Permits to hike or camp in the park are not required. Be sure to tell someone where you're going and when to expect you back, and be prepared to deal with any emergencies or wildlife you meet on the trail.

For more information on Willmore Wilderness Park, see **Travel Alberta** (www.travelalberta.com). From Jasper Town, the closest source of information is at the **Hinton Visitor Information Centre** (☏780-865-2777; Hwy 16, Hinton; ⊙9am-7pm), 77km (48 miles) north.

174

ALLEN J. SCHABEN / GETTY IMAGES ©

JORDAN SIEMENS / GETTY IMAGES ©

1. Glacier National Park (p176)

A man stands at the edge of a cliff overlooking this magnificent and pristine park.

2. Pyramid Lake (p161)

A lakeside canoe in Jasper National Park, with Pyramid Mountain in the background.

3. Wild Bull Elk

With 69 different mammals, 277 species of bird and 16 amphibians and reptiles, Jasper National Park is ideal for wildlife spotting.

4. Lake McDonald Lodge (p197)

Situated on the northeastern shore of the lake in Glacier National Park, this lodge, built in 1913, is the park's oldest hotel.

MILES ERTMAN / GETTY IMAGES ©

Glacier National Park

Includes ➡

Day Hikes 180
Cycling 189
Other Activities 189
Sights 195
Tours 199
Sleeping 199
Eating 204
Drinking &
Nightlife 205
Entertainment 205

Best Hikes

➡ Highline Trail (p182)

➡ Dawson–Pitamakan Loop (p186)

➡ Iceberg Lake Trail (p187)

➡ Hidden Lake Overlook Trail (p180)

Best Places to Stay

➡ Many Glacier Hotel (p203)

➡ Sperry Chalet (p203)

➡ Granite Park Chalet (p203)

➡ Lake McDonald Lodge (p202)

Why Go?

Few of the world's great natural wonders can compete with the US national-park system, and few national parks are as magnificent and pristine as Glacier. Created in 1910 during the first flowering of the American conservationist movement, Glacier ranks among other national-park classics such as Yellowstone and Yosemite. Perennial highlights include its trio of historic 'parkitecture' lodges, the spectacular Going-to-the-Sun Rd, and a rare, fully intact pre-Columbian ecosystem. This is the only place in the Lower 48 states where grizzly bears still roam in abundance, and smart park management has kept the place accessible yet at the same time authentically wild. Among a slew of other outdoor attractions, the park is particularly noted for its hiking and wildlife spotting, and for its fishing and boating lakes.

Road Distance (KM)

	East Glacier	St Mary	Waterton Townsite	West Glacier
St Mary	30			
Waterton Townsite	85	45		
West Glacier	60	50	100	
Whitefish	80	75	120	30

Note: Distances are approximate

Entrances

Glacier National Park has six official entrance gates. The two busiest are the West Entrance, just north of West Glacier, and the East Entrance, near St Mary at the opposite end of the iconic Going-to-the-Sun Rd. The other entrances are the Camas Creek Entrance and the Polebridge Ranger Station, both off the Outside North Fork Rd on the park's western side; and the Two Medicine Entrance (on Two Medicine Rd, west of Hwy 49) and the Many Glacier Entrance (on Many Glacier Rd, west of US 89) over on the eastern side.

Boards at entrances indicate which park campgrounds are open or full.

DON'T MISS

Glacier's classic 'parkitecture' lodges – Many Glacier Hotel (p203), Lake McDonald Lodge (p202) and Glacier Park Lodge (p211) – are living, breathing, functioning artifacts of another, more leisurely era, when travelers to this wilderness park arrived by train and ventured into the backcountry on horseback. These early-20th-century creations were built with Swiss-chalet features and prototypical Wild West elements. Today they seem to consciously and appealingly conjure up a romantic, almost mythic, vision of rustic luxury – ideal reflections of the beautiful scenery on their doorsteps.

Glacier Park Lodge sits just outside the park's boundaries, in charming East Glacier, while Lake McDonald Lodge and Many Glacier Hotel are both situated within the park on the shores of stunning alpine lakes. The former property is an easy stop while traveling the iconic Going-to-the-Sun Rd, and the latter is ensconced in what long-time visitors consider the heart of the park, with nearby trailheads for several of the park's most stunning day and overnight hikes.

When You Arrive

➡ Glacier National Park is open year-round. Entry per car or RV costs US$25. People arriving on foot, bicycle or motorcycle pay US$12 per person. Both tickets are valid for seven days. Entrance fees are reduced in winter. Fees for Glacier do not include entrance to Waterton Lakes National Park.

➡ Staff at the entrance stations hand out free detailed Glacier & Waterton Lakes National Parks maps; a quarterly newspaper; and the *Glacier Explorer,* a schedule of events and activities, including ranger-led day trips.

PLANNING TIP

Backcountry camping permits (US$5 per adult per night, or US$30 with advance reservation by mail or fax only) can be purchased from the Apgar Backcountry Office (p205).

Fast Facts

➡ **Area** 4099 sq km (1583 sq miles)

➡ **Highest elevation** 3190m (10,466ft)

➡ **Lowest elevation** 980m (3215ft)

Reservations

Glacier National Park operates 13 campgrounds. Sites at Fish Creek and St Mary Campgrounds can be reserved up to six months in advance, and five group sites at Apgar up to a year in advance. Book through Recreation.gov (☎800-365-2267; www.recreation.gov). All other campgrounds are first-come, first-served.

Resources

➡ **Glacier National Park** (www.nps.gov/glac)

➡ **Glacier Park Inc** (www. glacierparkinc.com)

➡ **Glacier National Park Lodges** (www. glaciernationalparklodges. com)

GLACIER NATIONAL PARK

Glacier National Park

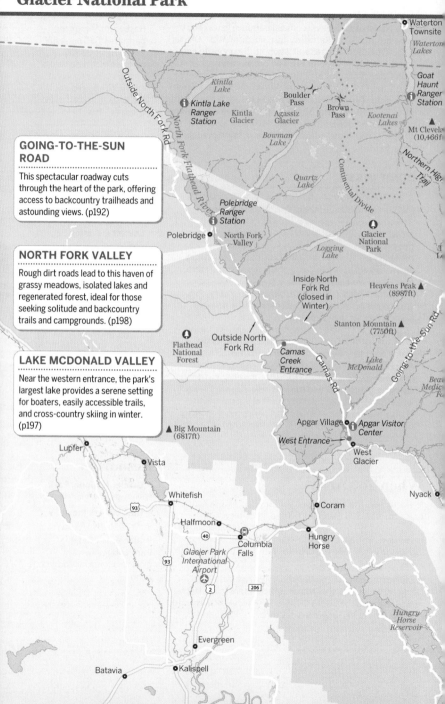

GOING-TO-THE-SUN ROAD

This spectacular roadway cuts through the heart of the park, offering access to backcountry trailheads and astounding views. (p192)

NORTH FORK VALLEY

Rough dirt roads lead to this haven of grassy meadows, isolated lakes and regenerated forest, ideal for those seeking solitude and backcountry trails and campgrounds. (p198)

LAKE MCDONALD VALLEY

Near the western entrance, the park's largest lake provides a serene setting for boaters, easily accessible trails, and cross-country skiing in winter. (p197)

Waterton Townsite

Waterton Lakes

Goat Haunt Ranger Station

Mt Cleveland (10,466ft)

Northern Highline Trail

Kintla Lake

Boulder Pass

Brown Pass

Kootenai Lakes

Kintla Lake Ranger Station

Kintla Glacier

Agassiz Glacier

Bowman Lake

Continental Divide

Quartz Lake

Polebridge Ranger Station

Polebridge

North Fork Valley

Logging Lake

Glacier National Park

Inside North Fork Rd (closed in Winter)

Heavens Peak (8987ft)

Stanton Mountain (7750ft)

Flathead National Forest

Outside North Fork Rd

Camas Creek Entrance

Lake McDonald

Going-to-the-Sun Rd

Big Mountain (6817ft)

Apgar Village

Apgar Visitor Center

West Entrance

West Glacier

Nyack

Lupfer

Vista

Whitefish

93

Halfmoon

40

Columbia Falls

Coram

Hungry Horse

Glacier Park International Airport

93

2

206

Evergreen

Hungry Horse Reservoir

Batavia

Kalispell

N
0   20 km
0   10 miles

ALBERTA

Chief Mountain
Border Crossing

CANADA

Piegan-Carway
Border Crossing

UNITED STATES

MONTANA

Belly River
Ranger Station

Belly River

Ptarmigan
Tunnel

Helen
Lake

Many Glacier
Entrance

Swiftcurrent Lake

Ahern Pass

Many
Glacier
Valley

Iceberg
Lake

Swiftcurrent
Pass

Grinnell
Glacier

Many Glacier
Ranger Station

Lake
Sherburne

Many Glacier Rd

East
Entrance

Babb

Duck
Lake

St Mary River

464

Lower
St Mary
Lake

Blackfeet
Indian
Reservation

MANY GLACIER VALLEY

This region – perhaps the best place
in the park to access the remaining
glaciers, view wildlife and experience
the full mix of the park's scenery – is
anchored by one of Glacier's
signature lodges. (p198)

Logan
Pass

Mt Siyeh
(10,014ft)

St Mary

Going-to-the-Sun Rd

Sperry
Glacier

Virginia
Falls

St Mary
Lake

Red Eagle
Mountain
(8881ft)

Divide
Mountain
(8665ft)

ST MARY VALLEY

With the Great Plains just on the other
side of imposing mountain peaks,
which tower over a strikingly colored
lake, this valley marks the eastern
end of the iconic Going-to-the-Sun
Rd. (p195)

Jackson
Glacier

Blackfoot
Glacier

Kakitos
Mountain
(7779ft)

Cut Bank
Ranger Station

North
Browning

Pumpelly
Glacier

Triple
Divide Peak
(8020ft)

Medicine
Grizzly Peak
(8315ft)

Browning

Harrison
Lake

Mt Stimson
(10,142ft)

Cut Bank
Pass

Pitamakan
Pass

Rising Wolf
Mountain
(9513ft)

Kiowa

Two Medicine
Entrance

Two
Medicine
Lake

LOGAN PASS

Breathtaking panoramic vistas and
two of the park's best hikes leave
from this pass at the pinnacle of the
Going-to-the-Sun Rd atop the
Continental Divide. (p196)

Dawson
Pass

Two Medicine
Valley

49

East Glacier

Middle Fork Flathead River

Great Bear
Wilderness

2

2

TWO MEDICINE VALLEY

No less beautiful, though less visited
than other sections of the park, the
imposing peaks and backcountry
vistas of this valley are closely
intertwined with Native American
legends. (p197)

Marias
Pass

Lewis & Clark
National
Forest

Essex

Walton

Continental Divide

Flathead
National
Forest

🚶 DAY HIKES

You don't have to be an aspiring Everest climber to enjoy the well-tramped trails and scenic byways of Glacier National Park. Indeed, two of the park's most popular hikes are wheelchair accessible, while countless more can be easily tackled by parents with children, vacationing couch potatoes or nervous novices.

Going-to-the-Sun Road

🚶 Sun Point to Virginia Falls

Duration Four hours round-trip

Distance 11.5km (7 miles)

Difficulty Easy

Start/Finish Sun Point shuttle stop

Elevation Change 90m (300ft)

Nearest Town St Mary

Transportation Going-to-the-Sun Rd shuttle, car

Summary Shelter from the famous St Mary Lake winds on this shady but sun-dappled trail that takes you to a trio of waterfalls.

Handily served by the free park shuttle, the myriad trailheads along the eastern side of the Going-to-the-Sun Rd offer plenty of short interlinking hikes, a number of which can be pooled together to make up a decent morning or afternoon ramble.

This particular variation starts at the Sun Point shuttle stop, where you can track down a 400m (0.25-mile) trail to a rocky (and often windy) overlook perched above sparkling St Mary Lake. In the 1910s the Great Northern Railway built some of Glacier's earliest and showiest chalets here in an accommodation chain that stretched from Many Glacier to the Sperry and Granite Park Chalets. Falling into neglect after WWII, the Sun Point chalets were demolished in 1949, though the view remains timeless.

Take the path west through sun-flecked forest along the lake toward shady Baring Falls, at the 1km (0.6-mile) mark, for a respite from the sun and/or wind. After admiring the gushing cascades, cross the river and continue on the opposite bank to link up with the busy St Mary Falls Trail that joins from the right. Undemanding switchbacks lead up through the trees to the valley's most picturesque falls, set amid colorful foliage on St Mary River. Beyond here, the trail branches along Virginia

Creek, past a narrow gorge, to mist-shrouded (and quieter) Virginia Falls at the foot of a hanging valley.

Retrace your steps to Sun Point for the full-length hike or, if your legs start to tire, shortcut to the St Mary Falls or Sunrift Gorge shuttle stops (follow the signs) and hop onto a bus.

🚶 Hidden Lake Overlook Trail

Duration Two hours round-trip

Distance 4.8km (3 miles)

Difficulty Easy-moderate

Start/Finish Logan Pass Visitor Center

Elevation Change 150m (494ft)

Nearest Facilities Logan Pass

Transportation Going-to-the-Sun Rd shuttle, car

Summary An uberpopular hike that's part boardwalk and part path, bisecting lush meadows and melting snowfields before descending to a translucent glacial lake.

For many Glacier visitors this relatively straightforward hike is the one occasion in which they step out of their cars and take a sniff of the sweet-scented alpine air for which the area is famous. Starting at the busy Logan Pass Visitor Center, the hike ascends gradually along a raised boardwalk (with steps) through expansive alpine meadows replete with monkey-flower and pink laurel. Slippery melting snowfields add a challenge for those who decided, misguidedly, to wear flip-flops, but, rain or shine, this trail is a hit with everyone – from adventurous toddlers to spry septuagenarians.

After about 1km (0.6 miles), the boardwalk gives way to a gravelly dirt path. If the snow has melted, the diversity of grasses and wildflowers in the meadows around you is breathtaking. Resident trees include Engelmann spruce, subalpine fir and whitebark pine. Hoary marmots, ground squirrels and mountain goats are not shy along this trail. The elusive ptarmigan, whose brown feathers turn white in winter, also lives nearby. Up-close mountain views include Clements Mountain north of the trail and Reynolds Mountain in the southeast.

About 275m (300yd) before the overlook, you will cross the Continental Divide – probably without realizing it – before your first stunning glimpse of the otherworldly, deep-blue Hidden Lake (and a realization of what all

Going-to-the-Sun Road – Day Hikes

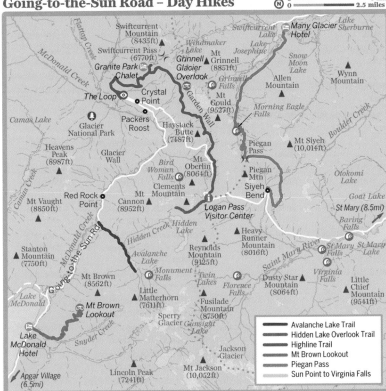

the fuss is about), bordered by mountain peaks and rocky cliffs. Look out for glistening Sperry Glacier visible to the south.

Hearty souls can continue on to Hidden Lake via a 2.4km (1.5-mile) trail from the overlook, steeply descending 233m (765ft).

🚶 Avalanche Lake Trail

Duration 2½ hours round-trip

Distance 6.4km (4 miles)

Difficulty Easy-moderate

Start/Finish Avalanche Creek shuttle stop

Elevation Change 145m (475ft)

Nearest Town Apgar Village

Transportation Going-to-the-Sun Rd shuttle, car

Summary A pleasant, family-friendly stroll through shady forest to the park's most

accessible alpine lake, replete with glacier-strewn boulders and waterfalls.

A handy stop on the shuttle route, the Avalanche Lake Trail provides quick and easy access to one of Glacier National Park's most gorgeous alpine lakes – and you don't have to bust a gut to get there. As a result, the trail is invariably heaving in peak season with everyone from flip-flop-wearing families to stick-wielding seniors making boldly for the treeline. But don't be deceived: while the walk itself might be relatively easy, it's highly recommended you come prepared with bottled water, layered clothing and appropriate footwear.

Starting from the Going-to-the-Sun Rd, the path meanders for 800m (0.5 miles) along the paved Trail of the Cedars to a signposted three-way junction. Bear right here, diverting into thick rainforest, and follow the path along a scenic section of narrow Avalanche Creek. Shaded from the summer sun by

HIKING IN GLACIER NATIONAL PARK

NAME	REGION	DESCRIPTION	DIFFICULTY
Sun Point to Virginia Falls	Going-to-the-Sun Road	Sun-dappled valley trail to a trio of beautiful waterfalls	easy
Hidden Lake Overlook Trail	Going-to-the-Sun Road	Climb steps and scamper across snow fields to a spectacular lookout	easy-moderate
Avalanche Lake Trail	Going-to-the-Sun Road	Very popular forested walk to a stunning lake	easy-moderate
Highline Trail	Going-to-the-Sun Road	Phenomenal alpine scenery all the way to the Granite Park Chalet	moderate
Piegan Pass	Going-to-the-Sun Road	Dense forest, an above-the-tree-line pass, glacier views, lakes and wildflowers	moderate-difficult
Gunsight Pass Trail	Going-to-the-Sun Road	See snowfields, glaciers, lakes and more over two riveting days	moderate-difficult
Northern Highline–Waterton Valley	Going-to-the-Sun Road	Continuation of Highline Trail along the Continental Divide toward the Canadian border	moderate-difficult
Mt Brown Lookout	Going-to-the-Sun Road	Glacier's steepest day hike to a lofty historic viewpoint	difficult
Swiftcurrent Lake Nature Trail	North of Going-to-the-Sun Road	Easy stroll along the shores of several lakes in the heart of the park	easy
Iceberg Lake Trail	North of Going-to-the-Sun Road	Leads to one of the most impressive glacial lakes in the Rockies	easy-moderate
Quartz Lakes Loop	North of Going-to-the-Sun Road	Rare North Fork loop trail in one of Glacier's most remote corners	moderate
Swiftcurrent Pass Trail	North of Going-to-the-Sun Road	Pleasant valley ramble followed by sharp climb to the Continental Divide	moderate-difficult
Dawson–Pitamakan Loop	South of Going-to-the-sun Road	A lengthy but rewarding hike around the true 'Crown of the Continent'	difficult

 Drinking Water   Rest-rooms   Ranger Station Nearby   Great for Families   Waterfall   ▲

mature, old-growth cedar and western hemlock trees, the forest floor is strewn with huge moss-covered boulders, the remnants of a once-powerful glacier.

After hopping over tree roots and fording trickling creeks, you'll emerge, as if by magic, at luminous Avalanche Lake, a circle of water fed by cascading waterfalls and overlooked by the steep, rocky escarpments of Bearhat Mountain. The surrounding scenery is sublime and well worth the moderate 3.2km (2-mile) march to get here. Relax on the lakeshore (there's a pit toilet nearby) with a pair of binoculars, keeping a lookout for birds and other wildlife, including fearless Columbian ground squirrels, before heading back down.

🥾 Highline Trail

Duration 7½ hours one way

Distance 18.7km (11.6 miles)

Difficulty Moderate

Start Logan Pass Visitor Center

Finish The Loop

Elevation Change 255m (830ft)

Nearest Facilities Logan Pass

Transportation Going-to-the-Sun Rd shuttle, car

Summary A vista-laden extravaganza that cuts underneath the Garden Wall ridge

DURATION	DISTANCE	ELEVATION CHANGE	FEATURES	FACILITIES	PAGE
4hr	11.5km (7 miles)	90m (300ft)			p180
2hr	4.8km (3 miles)	150m (494ft)			p180
2½hr	6.4km (4 miles)	145m (475ft)			p181
7½hr	18.7km (11.6 miles)	255m (830ft)			p182
6hr	20.5km (12.8 miles)	509m (1670ft)			p184
2 days	32km (20 miles)	930m (3000ft)			p185
2-3 days	46km (28.8 miles)	1280m (4200ft)			p190
6hr	17.3km (10.8 miles)	1318m (4325ft)			p184
1hr	4km (2.5 miles)	negligible			p187
4½hr	14.5km (9 miles)	370m (1190ft)			p187
7hr	20.5km (12.8 miles)	765m (2470ft)			p188
6hr	11.6km (7.2 miles)	650m (2100ft)			p188
8hr	30km (18.8 miles)	910m (2935ft)			p186

Backcountry Campsite — Wildlife Watching — Restaurant Nearby — Picnic Sites — View — Transport to Trailhead

just below the Continental Divide to the famous Granite Park Chalet.

A Glacier classic, the Highline Trail cuts like an elongated scar across the famous Garden Wall, a sharp, glacier-carved ridge that forms part of the Continental Divide, and the summer slopes of which are covered with an abundance of alpine plants and wildflowers. The stupendous views here are some of the best in the park, and with little elevation gain throughout its course, the treats come with minimal sweat.

Cutting immediately into the side of the mountain (a garden-hose-like rope is tethered to the rockwall for those with vertigo), the trail presents stunning early views of the Going-to-the-Sun Rd and snowcapped Heavens Peak. Look out for the toy-sized red 'Jammer' buses motoring up the valley below you and marvel as the sun catches the white foaming waters of 152m (500ft) Bird Woman Falls opposite.

After its vertiginous start, the trail is flat for 3km (1.8 miles) before gently ascending to a ridge that connects Haystack Butte with Mt Gould at the 5.6km (3.5-mile) mark. From here on it's fairly flat as you bisect the mountainside on your way toward the Granite Park Chalet. After approximately 10.9km (6.8 miles), with the chalet in sight, a spur path (on your right) offers gluttons for punishment the option of climbing up less than

1.6km (1 mile) to the Grinnell Glacier Overlook for a peek over the Continental Divide.

The Granite Park Chalet (p203) appears at around 12km (7.6 miles), providing a welcome haven for parched throats and tired feet (stock up at the chalet on chocolate bars and water).

From here you have three options: you can retrace your steps back to Logan Pass; head for Swiftcurrent Pass and the Many Glacier Valley; or descend 6.7km (4 miles) to the Loop, where you can pick up a shuttle bus to all points on the Going-to-the-Sun Rd.

🥾 Piegan Pass

Duration Six hours

Distance 20.5km (12.8 miles)

Difficulty Moderate-difficult

Start Siyeh Bend shuttle stop

Finish Many Glacier

Elevation Change 509m (1670ft)

Nearest Facilities Many Glacier

Transportation Going-to-the-Sun Rd shuttle, car

Summary A forest, an alpine meadow, a glacier, a pass and a long descent through Glacier's premier wildlife corridor – Piegan Pass isn't lacking in variety.

A popular hike among Glacier stalwarts, this trail starts on the Going-to-the-Sun Rd at a handy shuttle stop on Siyeh Bend east of Logan Pass and deposits you in Glacier's mystic heart, Many Glacier, with transport connections back to St Mary. It also bisects colorful Preston Park, one of the region's prettiest alpine meadows.

The initial climb is through forest from the Siyeh Bend starting point heading directly for the flower-adorned oasis of **Preston Park**. Turn left and head north at the first trail junction at the 1.9km (1.2-mile) mark, and left again at the 4.3km (2.7-mile) mark, where the Siyeh Pass Trail veers off to the right. The trail crosses a creek and begins to traverse more barren terrain along the base of Mt Siyeh and Cataract Mountain. At the 7.2km (4.5-mile) mark you'll reach **Piegan Pass** on a saddle between Piegan Mountain and Mt Pollock. The ruined foundations of a building provide some shelter from the whistling winds. Some people turn around and retrace their steps here, but the savvy descend on the pass's north side to Cataract Creek in the Many Gla-

cier Valley. **Morning Eagle Falls** is reached at the 12.3km (7.7-mile) mark, and at the 14km (8.8-mile) mark you'll enter the Grinnell Lake trail system, popular with boat-hike groups from the Many Glacier Hotel. Stay right at the Grinnell Lake Trail junction and right again at the Lake Josephine link trail and you'll find yourself roaming through classic subalpine scenery with turquoise glimpses of the lakes through the trees. The well-signposted trail will ultimately deposit you in the upper parking lot of the Many Glacier Hotel.

🥾 Mt Brown Lookout

Duration Six hours round-trip

Distance 17.3km (10.8 miles)

Difficulty Difficult

Start/Finish Lake McDonald Lodge

Elevation Change 1318m (4325ft)

Nearest Town Apgar Village

Transportation Going-to-the-Sun Rd shuttle, car

Summary Glacier's steepest day hike involves no technical skills, but a good level of fitness is required to reach a sky-high historic lookout on Mt Brown.

This hike is a means to an end; a steep 8.6km (5.4-mile) grunt up through thick forest to a historic 1929 lookout last manned in 1971 (and refurbished in 1999) on the southwest ridge of 2610m (8563ft) Mt Brown, located about 328m (1076ft) below the summit. The views from here are outstanding, and no mountaineering skills are required – just a strong pair of lungs.

The hike starts on the Going-to-the-Sun Rd opposite the Lake McDonald Lodge on the heavily used Sperry Chalet trail. Pass the horse corral and head up alongside Snyder Creek, which soon drops away to your right. The Mt Brown Lookout trail is the first of three trails to branch off, swinging left after 2.9km (1.8 miles) and starting a climb that makes your ascent so far seem like a Sunday afternoon stroll. The first five switchbacks are the toughest; after that the 20 or so remaining curves are a little more manageable and occasional glimpses through the trees en route offer hints of the splendor to come. As you approach the lookout you'll emerge into meadows swaying with beargrass and wildflowers. The **lookout**, with its distinctive pyramid-shaped roof, is perched at 2282m (7487ft) and is often frequented by mountain

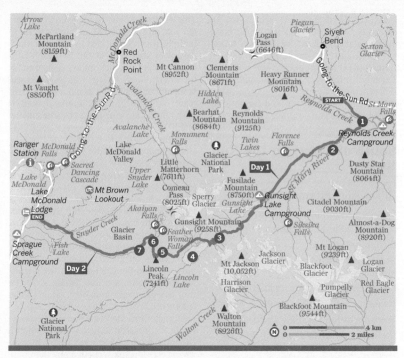

🥾 Overnight Hike
Gunsight Pass Trail

START JACKSON GLACIER OVERLOOK
END LAKE MCDONALD LODGE
LENGTH TWO DAYS / 32KM (20 MILES)

This introduction to Glacier's backcountry offers tremendous views and abundant wildlife, plus the opportunity to stay in the park's historic Sperry Chalet. Truly bionic hikers knock out the trail in one day, but with copious snowfields, glaciers and lakes to marvel at, two days might be more appropriate. The trail is doable in either direction, but most hikers kick off at the Jackson Glacier Overlook (a designated free shuttle stop) and head west. If you're planning to spend a night at the chalet, you'll need to book well in advance.

On the first day follow the trail southeast through fir and spruce forest to Reynolds Creek. The path then follows the creek past ❶ **Deadwood Falls** to a junction with the Gunsight Pass Trail at the 2km (1.3-mile) mark; take the trail on the right. It crosses a bridge past Reynolds Creek Campground and then heads alongside the ❷ **St Mary River**.

Carry on up the valley below Citadel and Fusilade Mountains, taking in views of glaciers clinging to a high ridge to the south. Soon after the Gunsight Lake Campground, a suspension bridge traverses St Mary River and leads up numerous switchbacks to ❸ **Gunsight Pass** (2117m/6946ft) on the Continental Divide. Reaching the pass involves walking over cliff ledges, but the trail is broad.

Steeply descending switchbacks lead to the north shore of ❹ **Lake Ellen Wilson**, a spectacular alpine lake ringed by sheer, glaciated rock walls. The trail continues around the lake's western shore then up the slope to a high shelf overlooking Lincoln Lake. The trail turns gradually to cross ❺ **Lincoln Pass** (2149m/7050ft), then winds its way down past Sperry Campground. Four scenic sites here overlook Lake McDonald far below and the ❻ **Sperry Chalet** (p203) is close by.

On day two the trail leads down into fir and spruce forest past ❼ **Beaver Medicine Falls**. It continues 4km (2.5 miles) down the valley to cross Snyder Creek on a footbridge, then descends through a mossy forest of cedar, hemlock, grand fir, larch and yew to Going-to-the-Sun Rd.

goats. The 270-degree view includes the full spread of Lake McDonald and its surrounding mountains. Look out for the Lake McDonald Lodge and the Granite Park Chalet. The summit of **Mt Brown** blocks views northeast. Though it might look close, mountaineering skills are needed to reach it.

Take care on the steep and (sometimes) slippery trail as you descend.

South of Going-to-the-Sun Road

🏃 Dawson–Pitamakan Loop

Duration Eight hours round-trip

Distance 30km (18.8 miles)

Difficulty Difficult

Start/Finish North Shore trailhead, Two Medicine Lake

Elevation Change 910m (2935ft)

Nearest Facilities Two Medicine Valley

Transportation East Side shuttle, car

Summary Cross the Continental Divide twice on this strenuous but spectacular hike along exposed mountain ridges that provide prime habitat for grizzly bears.

This lengthy hike can be squeezed into a one-day itinerary, if you're fit and up for it. Alternatively, it can be tackled over two or three days with sleepovers at the No Name Lake and Oldman Lake backcountry campgrounds (permit required). Blessed with two spectacular mountain passes and teeming with myriad plant and animal life, this is often touted by park rangers as being one of Glacier's hiking highlights.

As the hike is a loop, departing from the North Shore trailhead on **Two Medicine Lake**, you must first decide which direction you want to go. Progressing clockwise and tackling Dawson Pass first packs the 915m (3000ft) elevation gain into one sharp segment. Head anticlockwise and the same ascent is more drawn out. Walking clockwise, you'll be entering prime grizzly-bear country (rangers have actually used it as a study area), so be on guard and make plenty of noise. Around 8km (5 miles) in you'll reach **No Name Lake**, a prime fishing spot. The trail ascends steeply from here, gaining 366m (1200ft) in 3.2km (2 miles) during a pulse-racing climb to **Dawson Pass**, an exposed saddle notorious for its high winds – 160km/h (100mph) has been recorded. Follow the narrow, sheer-sided path north along the Continental Divide, taking care with your footing amid stunning high-country scenery. You'll

South of Going-to-the-Sun Road – Day Hike

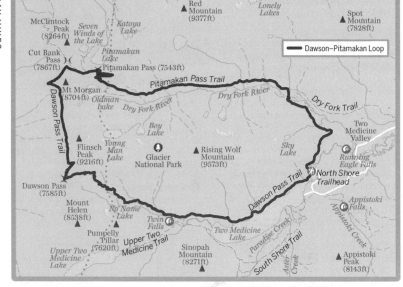

cross the divide again at Cut Bank before descending to Pitamakan Pass and Oldman Lake, a gorgeous blue body of water encased in a cirque and framed by jagged peaks.

From the lake the hike descends into the Dry Fork Drainage, through fields of huckleberries interspersed with clumps of dense forest. Look out for diggings, scat and other evidence of bear activity as you make for Two Medicine Lake and your starting point.

North of Going-to-the-Sun Road

🚶 Swiftcurrent Lake Nature Trail

Duration One hour round-trip

Distance 4km (2.5miles)

Difficulty Easy

Start/Finish Many Glacier Hotel

Elevation Change Negligible

Nearest Facilities Many Glacier

Transportation East Side shuttle, car

Summary From civilization to bear-infested wilderness in less than 60 seconds; natural juxtapositions don't get much more dramatic than this.

Anchoring the trail system that connects Many Glacier's three navigable lakes – Swiftcurrent, Josephine and Grinnell – this easy flat nature trail offers a potent taste of the valley's rugged essence. Take note: despite heavy usage and its proximity to the hotel, the trail often posts bear warnings.

Heading south from the Many Glacier Hotel along the shoreline of shallow Swiftcurrent Lake (9m/30ft at its deepest point), you'll pass an old boathouse and ranger station used as accommodation for summer guides. At a junction for the Grinnell Lake Trail at the southern end of the lake stay right and take a wooden footbridge across the channel between Swiftcurrent Lake and Lake Josephine. Very soon after you'll pass a small dock used by boat-trip groups organized out of the hotel. Continue to the right and finish your lake circumnavigation amid widening mountain views, peeks of the distinctive Salamander Glacier, and possible moose sightings along the willowy shoreline. After skirting close to the Many Glacier campground, the trail turns east and deposits you back in a picnic area adjacent to the handsome hotel.

🚶 Iceberg Lake Trail

Duration 4½ hours round-trip

Distance 14.5km (9 miles)

Difficulty Easy-moderate

Start/Finish Swiftcurrent Motor Inn

Elevation Change 370m (1190ft)

Nearest Facilities Many Glacier

Transportation East Side shuttle, car

Summary A well-trodden, wildlife-studded trail through relatively open terrain to otherworldly Iceberg Lake.

The lake is famed for the bobbing bergs that float like miniature ice cubes in its still waters all summer long, the and Iceberg Lake hike has long been a classic Glacier National Park pilgrimage. The popularity of the hike is understandable. Enclosed in a deep glacial cirque and surrounded on three sides by stunning 914m (3000ft) vertical walls, the lake is one of the most impressive sights anywhere in the Rockies. The ascent to get there is fairly gentle, and the approach is mostly at or above the treeline, affording awesome views. Wildflower fans will love the meadows near the lake.

The trailhead is just past the Swiftcurrent Motor Inn. Bears are often sighted on this trail, so check at the ranger station before setting out and take all of the usual precautions. Starting steeply, the trail packs most of its elevation gain into the first few kilometers. But once you emerge onto the scrubby slopes above Many Glacier the gradient is barely perceptible. After 3.2km (2 miles) the path enters a small section of mature forest and arrives at Ptarmigan Creek, crossed by a footbridge, just upstream from Ptarmigan Falls. Here you climb gently through pine to the Ptarmigan Tunnel Trail junction, which heads right.

Continuing toward Iceberg Lake, you'll come upon the first of several beautiful meadows under Ptarmigan Wall. Descend for a short distance to cross Iceberg Creek via a footbridge, then climb up past Little Iceberg Lake before dropping down to the shores of your hallowed destination, the icy-blue cirque lake.

Iceberg Lake is 45.7m (150ft) deep and about 1.2km (0.75 miles) across. The glacier is now inactive but, as the lake lies in the shadows on the north side of Mt Wilbur, the area remains cool all through summer. After filling your memory card with photos of the lake, retrace your steps to the Swiftcurrent Motor Inn.

North of Going-to-the-Sun Road – Day Hikes

🚶 Quartz Lakes Loop

Duration Seven hours round-trip

Distance 20.5km (12.8 miles)

Difficulty Moderate

Start/Finish Bowman Lake Campground

Elevation Change 765m (2470ft)

Nearest Facilities Polebridge

Transportation Car

Summary Lakes, solitude and scenery are three of the North Fork Valley's primary draws, and all are on display during this multifarious hike.

Remote and hard to get to without a car, the wild North Fork Valley is a solitude seeker's utopia. The Quartz Lakes Loop is one of the area's only loop trails, a hiking staple renowned for its wonderful scenery and close-up views of a forest still regenerating after relatively recent (natural) fires.

From the trailhead, cross Bowman Creek before beginning a gradual ascent along the shores of Bowman Lake. After 1.6km (1 mile) or so you'll start a more precipitous climb up Quartz Ridge, which turns into Cerulean Ridge, with an elevation of 1676m (5500ft), where you'll be afforded fantastic views of a triumvirate of beautiful lakes – Quartz Lake, tiny Middle Quartz Lake and Lower Quartz Lake – shimmering like tinfoil below. The path drops down to the west side of Quartz Lake, passing in and out of forest and providing graphic evidence of the effects of the 1988 Red Bench Fire.

Once in the valley, skirt the edges of all three lakes via a clearly marked path ending up, after 5km (3 miles), in a backcountry campground at the south end of Lower Quartz Lake. From here it's a 2.4km (1.5-mile) ascent to the crest of Quartz Ridge – for the second time – before you drop back down to Bowman Creek.

🚶 Swiftcurrent Pass Trail

Duration Six hours one way

Distance 11.6km (7.2 miles)

Difficulty Moderate-difficult

Start Swiftcurrent Motor Inn

Finish Granite Park Chalet

Elevation Change 650m (2100ft)

Nearest Facilities Many Glacier

Transportation East Side shuttle, car

Summary A pleasant meander through the Many Glacier Valley, followed by a steep climb up to the Continental Divide.

This popular trail departs from the west side of the Swiftcurrent Motor Inn parking lot and can be linked up with the Loop or Highline Trails to make an arduous one-day, or slightly less arduous two-day, hike.

Easing in slowly, the first 6.4km (4 miles) of the trail are relatively gentle, bisecting low lodgepole forest sprinkled with aspen, the result of dynamic regrowth following the 1936 Heavens Peak Fire. Looking around, you'll see the highest visible summit, Mt Wilbur, to the northwest, jagged Grinnell Mountain to the south, and Swiftcurrent Mountain, which this path eventually ascends, to the southwest.

Hiking through the potentially hot open terrain, you will soon find relief amid the foliage, including Engelmann spruce, subalpine fir, fireweed, maple and the shade-giving quaking aspen. Wildflower spotters will enjoy colorful landscapes dotted with forget-me-nots, paintbrush, harebell, yellow columbine and Siberian chive. Watch for stinging nettles along the way and make plenty of noise to ward off Many Glacier's many bears.

Less than 2.4km (1.5 miles) into the trail, the path brushes the northern tip of Red Rock Lake, and the waterfalls become visible in the distance. Beavers are active along streams in this valley; look out for beaver lodges on the other side of the lake. At the 5.3km (3.3-mile) mark you'll hit Bullhead Lake and from here you'll begin a 4.8km (3-mile) climb up to Swiftcurrent Pass, with an elevation of 2064m (6770ft), gaining 610m (2000ft) in the process. The switchbacks on the ascent are numerous, and the path, which cuts sharply into the mountainside, becomes ever more vertiginous as you climb (if you suffer badly from vertigo, this route a miss). The Continental Divide at Swiftcurrent Pass is marked by an unruly pile of rocks surrounded by dwarf trees. For those still with energy, the optional spur trail up a further set of switchbacks to the Swiftcurrent Lookout offers one of the park's most tower-topping views. Returning to the pass, head the final 1.5km (0.9 miles) down to the Granite Park Chalet for a welcome rest (remember to book ahead if you wish to stay overnight) or to link up with other trails.

⚙ CYCLING

Glacier National Park diverges from Banff, Waterton Lakes and Jasper in that none of its trails are open to cyclists. An alternative for two-wheeled travelers is to make use of the park's only allocated bike path (a flat 4km/ 2.5-mile ramble from West Glacier to Apgar Village), or to ply the limited road network – essentially the Going-to-the-Sun Rd – which has further restrictions on when you can and can't use it.

Despite the limitations, committed cyclists can be spied daily throughout summer attempting the 85km (53-mile) Going-to-the-Sun Rd, where the spectacular vistas and copious twists and turns are befitting of a challenging Tour de France stage. For safety

and congestion reasons, the upper stretches of the road are officially shut to cyclists between 11am and 4pm daily (mid-June to Labor Day), so you'll need to be flexible with your schedule. If you do decide to take the plunge (and it's a memorable ride), start early, pack plenty of water and take extreme care on the long and potentially precarious descents. From a physical point of view, it's easier to start your ride in St Mary and tackle the climb east–west.

On full-moon nights during summer months, the Going-to-the-Sun Rd between the Loop and Logan Pass is closed off for cyclists making the memorable run; wear proper gear, including headlamps.

The closest thing to a mountain-biking venture in the park is the Inside North Fork Rd (Glacier Rte 7) to Kintla Lake. Cyclists craving trail rides should consider Waterton Lakes, which has five trails.

You'll encounter plenty of colorfully clad cyclists just outside the park's eastern boundary, plying Hwys 49 and 89, on the edge of the Blackfeet Indian Reservation. Inclines here are gentler, although the stiff winds off the adjacent prairies can be punishing.

Hiker-biker campgrounds are available at Apgar, Avalanche Creek, Fish Creek, Many Glacier, Rising Sun, Sprague Creek, St Mary and Two Medicine campgrounds. You can find cruiser and tandem bikes at Go Glacier Outfitters (☑406-219-7466; www.goglacierout fitters.com; 184 Apgar Loop Rd, Apgar Village; ⊙9am–5pm) and Eddie's Cafe (www.eddiescafegifts. com; Apgar Village; bikes per half-/full day $25/40; ⊙7am-9pm late May–mid-Sep) on the west side of the park, and a stash of basic machines in the St Mary KOA Campground (106 West Shore Rd, St Mary; bikes per hour/day US$2.50/20) on the east side. Better bicycles are available at Glacier Cyclery (p214) in Whitefish, 72km (45 miles) southwest.

⚘ OTHER ACTIVITIES

Boating

McDonald, Bowman, Swiftcurrent, Two Medicine and St Mary Lakes have launching ramps available for boats. Sailors might find St Mary Lake's winds to their liking. Stand-up paddleboarding is popular on Lake McDonald – Eddie's Cafe and Go Glacier Outfitters in Apgar Village rent boards for around US$20 for two hours – and also on Bowman Lake in the North Country.

White-Water Rafting & Float Trips

The loaded-up school buses ferrying groups from outfitters in and around West Glacier and US 2 give you an idea of rafting's popularity. All tours take place on or outside the park's boundaries, primarily on the North and Middle Forks of the Flathead River. The best water flow is from May to September, with the rapids ranking an unterrifying class I to III. All of the operators can customize highly recommended overnight adventures on the North Fork from near the Canadian border (tents and sleeping gear are provided). Or you can float down McDonald Creek on your own inner tubes.

Glacier Raft Co   RAFTING
(📞 800-235-6781; www.glacierraftco.com; rafting trips $45-120; ⏲ Jun-Aug) Arguably the most reputable raft company in the area, with offices in the Glacier Outdoor Center on US 2, as well as behind the Alberta Visitor Center in West Glacier Village.

Wild River Adventures   RAFTING
(📞 406-387-9453; www.riverwild.com; 11900 Hwy 2, West Glacier; half-day rafting trip adult/child $55/45) Under new and accommodating ownership, Wild River offers four launch times for half-day trips. For those who need more autonomy and maybe more of a rush, it also rents inflatable kayaks (you can join up with the rafting tours).

Great Northern Whitewater Raft   RAFTING
(📞 800-735-7897; www.greatnorthernraft.com; 12127 Hwy 2, West Glacier) Based out of a resort of the same name (with a railroad-car cafe on-site), this company offers a wide variety of guided rafting and fly-fishing trips.

Fishing

The fishing season in streams and rivers is late May to late November, though lakes are open for fishing year-round. While anglers explore easily accessible waters such as Lake McDonald and St Mary Lake, it is some of the hike-in destinations that can prove the most tranquil getaways; try Hidden Lake, Oldman Lake or Red Eagle Lake.

Most of Glacier's fish were introduced to provide 'sport' for visitors up until the 1960s. Species include cutthroat trout, northern pike, whitefish, burbot, kokanee salmon, brook trout, rainbow trout, mackinaw and grayling.

Overnight Hike
Northern Highline– Waterton Valley

START THE LOOP, GOING-TO-THE-SUN ROAD
END GOAT HAUNT RANGER STATION
LENGTH TWO TO THREE DAYS / 46KM (28.8 MILES)

This moderately difficult hike follows the splendid Highline Trail beyond the Granite Park Chalet to Waterton, Canada. An extension of the popular 'Garden Wall' section of the Highline Trail (p182), this route, often known as the Northern Highline, forges deeper into the backcountry across open subalpine terrain toward the Goat Haunt region and the US–Canada border. It is also the end point of the 5000km (3100-mile) Continental Divide Trail (CDT) that runs from Mexico up to Canada, of which Glacier National Park guards the final 176km (110 miles). As you hike, keep an eye out for moose, as well as for short-eared owls, American kestrels, mountain bluebirds and pine siskins.

Start this hike from the Loop, a tightly angled switchback on the Going-to-the-Sun Rd, 12.8km (8 miles) northwest of Logan Pass, that also serves as a free shuttle stop. An alternative starting point is the trailhead for the Highline Trail at Logan Pass, an option that will add a scenic 5.8km (3.6 miles) to your overall trip.

From the Loop, the climb begins almost immediately through landscape scarred by the 2003 Trapper Fire. Burnt tree trunks characterize a mountainside slowly coming back to life after the inferno. The views are superb. After 1km (0.6 miles), the Packers Roost trail joins in from the left. Continue walking uphill gaining 701m (2300ft) of elevation within 6.4km (4 miles) to reach the historic ❶ **Granite Park Chalet**, built in 1915 as the last link in a chain of backcountry chalets constructed by the Great Northern Railway (only two remain). The chalet offers hostel accommodation (reserve ahead), a campground, drinks and snacks. There is no running water.

You may want to spend the night at the chalet and incorporate a short side trip up to Swiftcurrent Pass and Lookout. If you're pressing on, get moving quickly, as it's still

18.5km (11.6 miles) to the next campground at Fifty Mountain.

Take the trail to Swiftcurrent Pass and fork almost immediately left to follow the far less crowded Northern Highline Trail as it parallels the Continental Divide through high subalpine terrain with tremendous vistas of peaks, meadows and safe-from-a-distance wildlife (grizzlies, moose and wolves have all been spotted here). After about 8km (5 miles) an overlook trail to ❷ **Ahern Pass** and a view of Helen Lake forks off to the right; another nearby short spur, just to the north of the one for Helen Lake, leads to the Sue Lake Overlook. If you're not up for either detour, continue straight ahead climbing up toward the Continental Divide, which you will cross after a short sharp climb 17km (10.5 miles) from the Granite Park Chalet.

The ❸ **Fifty Mountain Campground** is just over the other side, situated in an alpine bowl below a meadow. It is named for the number of mountains you can see from its stunning viewpoint (count them!) and is arguably the finest backcountry campsite in the park – a grand place to rest your feet after eight or nine hours on the trail.

Wake up amid the moody magnificence of Fifty Mountain and try to tear yourself away from the view and the braver-than-usual deer. Day two (or three, depending on your schedule) involves a 732m (2400ft) descent to the Waterton Valley and Goat Haunt on Upper Waterton Lake – a hike of around five to six hours. Most of the descending is in the first 8km (5 miles), as you drop from the Fifty Mountain plateau to the intersection with the Stoney Indian Trail at the 4.2km (2.7-mile) mark – you will pass many avalanche chutes, which open up the scenery for great views. Soon after, you'll come across the Pass Creek ranger hut and footbridge. Back below the timberline is the epiphanic sight of ❹ **Kootenai Lakes** (reached via a short trail on the left), often frequented by day-hikers from Goat Haunt. The lake is renowned for its moose sightings.

Continue along the valley for a further 4km (2.5 miles) to the Goat Haunt ranger station where you will need to show your passport in order to board a boat – or alternatively hike the 11.2km (7 miles) – to Waterton Townsite in Canada.

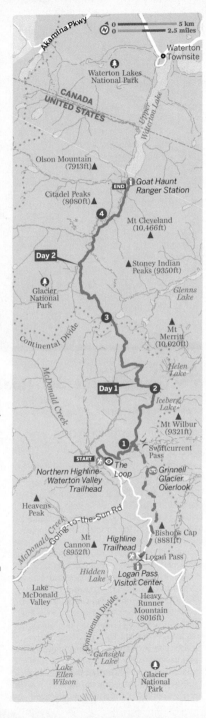

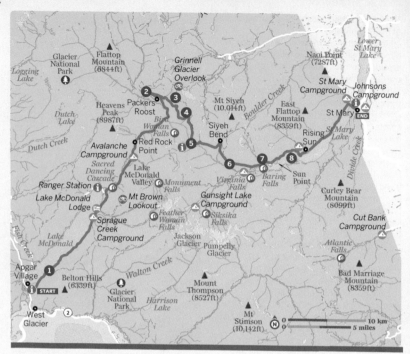

Driving Tour
Going-to-the-Sun Road

START WEST ENTRANCE, NEAR APGAR VILLAGE
END ST MARY VISITOR CENTER
LENGTH THREE HOURS (WITH STOPS) / 85KM (53 MILES)

This is, quite literally, one of the most spectacular drives in the US. The Going-to-the-Sun Rd starts at the park's western entrance before tracking northeast along ❶**Lake McDonald**. Characterized by the famous Lake McDonald Lodge, the valley here is lush and verdant, though a quick glance through the trees will highlight the graphic evidence of the 2003 Robert Fire on the opposite side of the water.

After following McDonald Creek for about 16km (10 miles), the road begins its long, slow ascent to Logan Pass with a sharp turn to the southeast at the ❷**Loop**, a famous hiking trailhead and the start of an increasingly precipitous climb toward the summit. Views here are unfailingly sublime as the road cuts precariously into the ❸**Garden Wall**, a 2743m (8999ft) granite ridge that delineates the west and east regions of the park along the Continental Divide. Look out for Bird Woman Falls, stunning even from a distance, and the more in-your-face ❹**Weeping Wall**, as the gaping chasm to your right grows ever deeper.

Stop at lofty ❺**Logan Pass** to browse the visitor center or to stretch those legs amid alpine meadows on the popular Hidden Lake Overlook Trail. Be forewarned: the Logan Pass parking lot gets very busy in July and August.

Descending eastwards, keep an eye out for majestic Going-to-the-Sun Mountain, omnipresent to the north. At the 58km (36-mile) mark, you can pull over to spy one of only 25 remaining park glaciers at the ❻**Jackson Glacier Overlook**, while a few clicks further on, you can sample narrow ❼**Sunrift Gorge** near the shores of St Mary Lake. ❽**Wild Goose Island**, a photogenic stub of land, is situated in the center of the lake.

The St Mary Visitor Center on the lake's eastern shore is journey's end. The plains on this side of the park stretch east from St Mary to Minneapolis.

No vehicles over 6m (21ft) are allowed from east of Sun Point to Avalanche Creek.

A Montana state fishing license is not required within Glacier National Park, though anglers should familiarize themselves with the general park regulations available at any visitor center. Anglers are generally limited to possession of five fish daily, with caps varying by species. Some waters, including Hidden Lake and the North and Middle Forks of the Flathead River, are purely catch-and-release zones. Read the park's *Fishing Regulations* pamphlet. Portions of the North Fork and Middle Fork of the Flathead River outside the park are subject to Montana state fishing regulations. Part of Lower Two Medicine Lake is on reservation land and subject to Blackfeet Indian Reservation regulations.

Glacier Guides Inc   FISHING, RAFTING
(☑ 800-521-7238; www.glacierguides.com; fishing trips half-/full-day US$375/475) This company runs fishing trips to the Middle and North Forks of the Flathead River, plus beginners can sign up for full-day lessons (US$475; part classroom, part practical). It also runs rafting trips and guided hikes in the park.

Glacier Outdoor Center   FISHING
(☑ 800-235-6781; www.glacierraftco.com; 12400 Hwy 2, West Glacier; fishing trips half-/full-day US$375/475) You can organize fly-fishing trips, as well as up to week-long customized adventures (US$400 per person per day for three or more), with the Glacier Raft Co; its fishing operation is run out of the Glacier Outdoor Center, the best shop for gear in West Glacier.

Horseback Riding

Glacier may be stingy toward cyclists, but there are far fewer restrictions toward horseback riders – this, after all, is Cowboy-land Montana. Equestrian lovers looking for longer multiday trips in similar wilderness scenery should consider the Bob Marshall Wilderness area, not far south of Glacier.

Swan Mountain Outfitters   HORSEBACK RIDING
(☑ 877-888-5557; www.swanmountainoutfitters. com; ☉ early May–early Sep) The park's only horseback-riding guides, Swan Mountain Outfitters offers a variety of trips lasting from a one-hour circumnavigation of Lake Josephine (US$40) to an all-day foray to Cracker Lake (US$160). Its three corrals are maintained at Lake McDonald, Many Glacier Corral and Apgar Village. All trips are led by experienced wranglers who'll furnish you with plenty of entertaining tales.

Back in the 'old' days, before the Going-to-the-Sun Rd was built, getting around by horse between the various tourist chalets was the primary means of transport, and horses still run a regular supply line up to the Sperry Chalet, a route that can be incorporated into an excellent day ride.

Rock Climbing

While Glacier's sharp ridges and steeply stacked cliff faces might look like a rock-climber's paradise, the opposite is often the case. Due to the nature of the Rocky Mountains' loose sedimentary rock – much of it metamorphosed mudstone and limestone – technical climbing in the park is not the sport of choice. Climbers and adrenaline junkies can find solace in the tough but nontechnical ascent of the park's highest peak, 3190m (10,466ft) Mt Cleveland. Interested parties should enquire at visitor centers and ranger stations, and sign a register before setting out.

Golf

Two golf courses lie just outside the park limits.

Glacier Park Lodge Golf Course   GOLF
(☑ 406-892-2525; www.glacierparkinc.com; 9/18 holes US$20/29, club rental US$14/21) Located in East Glacier, this is the oldest golf course in Montana, and the most picturesque.

Glacier View Golf Club   GOLF
(☑ 406-888-5471; www.glacierviewgolf.com; 9/18 holes US$20/32, club rental US$10/14) Overlooking the Middle Fork of the Flathead River, this golf club in West Glacier offers great mountain views. The entrance road to the pro shop, lined with cookie-cutter suburban-style houses, is decidedly ordinary.

Skiing & Snowshoeing

Jasper and Banff this is not. From October to May, when the Going-to-the-Sun Rd is snowed under, most services in Glacier close, leaving the park to wildlife and intrepid, self-sufficient cross-country skiers and snowshoers, most of whom base themselves out of Whitefish or Kalispell.

The one exception is the Izaak Walton Inn (p211) in Essex, a handy Amtrak train stop on the park's southern boundary that maintains its own small network of groomed

Glacier National Park Region

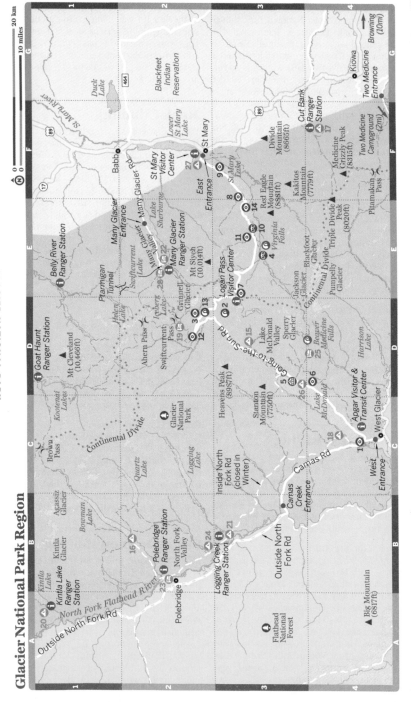

Glacier National Park Region

⊙ Sights
1 Apgar Village C4
2 Bird Woman Falls D3
3 Garden Wall D2
4 Jackson Glacier Overlook E3
5 Lake McDonald Lodge D3
6 Lake McDonald Valley D4
7 Logan Pass E3
8 Rising Sun F3
9 St Mary Lake F3
10 Sun Point E3
11 Sunrift Gorge E3
12 The Loop D2
13 Weeping Wall D2
14 Wild Goose Island E3

⊜ Sleeping
Apgar Campground .... (see 1)
Apgar Village Lodge .... (see 1)
15 Avalanche Creek Campground D3
16 Bowman Lake Campground B2
17 Cut Bank Campground F4
18 Fish Creek Campground C4
19 Granite Park Chalet D2
20 Kintla Lake Campground A1

Lake McDonald Lodge .... (see 5)
21 Logging Creek Campground B3
Many Glacier Campground .... (see 28)
22 Many Glacier Hotel E2
23 North Fork Hostel & Square Peg
   Ranch B2
24 Quartz Creek Campground B2
Rising Sun Campground .... (see 8)
Rising Sun Motor Inn .... (see 8)
25 Sperry Chalet D4
26 Sprague Creek Campground D3
27 St Mary Campground F2
28 Swiftcurrent Motor Inn E2
Village Inn at Apgar .... (see 1)

⊗ Eating
Eddie's Cafe .... (see 1)
Jammer Joe's Grill &
   Pizzeria .... (see 5)
Polebridge Mercantile .... (see 23)
Ptarmigan Dining Room .... (see 22)
Russells Fireside Dining
   Room .... (see 5)
Swiftcurrent Restaurant .... (see 28)
Two Dog Flats Grill .... (see 8)

and partly floodlit cross-country skiing and snowshoeing trails – 33km (20.5 miles) worth – from November to April. Instructors based here can organize private ski lessons (US$50) or take you on customized backcountry skiing or snowshoeing trips (US$125 per person for two to eight people) into the almost-deserted winter park. The inn rents out snowshoes/skis for US$15/30 per day.

Self-sufficient cross-country skiers can choose from a number of popular marked but ungroomed trails in the park itself, the bulk of them emanating from Apgar Village and Lake McDonald. A well-used favorite is to ski along an unplowed section of the Going-to-the-Sun Rd from the (closed) Lake McDonald Lodge to Avalanche Creek. The road is always plowed as far as the lodge, allowing easy access by car. Another regularly tackled trail is the 18.5km (11.5-mile) McGee Meadow Loop heading up the unplowed Camas Rd and back down the Inside Fork Rd to Apgar Village. Far more difficult is the steep 8.3km (5.2-mile) ascent to the Apgar Lookout.

Other lesser-used park penetration points are St Mary for the Red Eagle Lake Trail, Polebridge for the Bowman Lake Trail, and Two Medicine for the unplowed Two Medicine Rd as far as Running Eagle Falls.

Although all hotels and restaurants stay closed, and the park registers only a handful of visitors, Glacier's mountains and valleys remain gloriously open all winter to those intrepid enough to breach them. For ultimate safety, organize a guided backcountry ski tour with Glacier Adventure Guides (☑877-735-9514; www.glacieradventureguides.com; 729 Nucleus Ave, Columbia Falls), which operates out of Columbia Falls, MT. Day rates hover at around US$180 per person.

⊙ SIGHTS

⊙ Going-to-the-Sun Road

If it were possible to mathematically measure 'magnificence,' the Going-to-the-Sun Rd would surely hit the top end of the scale. Chiseled out of raw mountainside and punctuated by some of the most vertiginous drop-offs in the US, this vista-laden artery of asphalt that bisects the park west to east is an engineering marvel without equal. It is hardly surprising that it's considered by many motorists to be the best drive in the country.

St Mary Lake   LAKE
Located on the park's dryer eastern side, where the mountains melt imperceptibly into the Great Plains, St Mary Lake lies in a deep, glacier-carved valley famous for its astounding

GLACIER'S GLACIERS

Today's visitors could be some of the last to actually see a glacier in the park. Current figures suggest that, if current warming trends continue, the park could be glacier-free by as soon as 2020. Thanks to a Glacier Research Monitoring program carried out by the US Geological Survey, the Montana park's icy monoliths have been more studied than any of their counterparts. The estimates are based on research undertaken on the Sperry, Agassiz, Jackson and Grinnell Glaciers, all of which have lost approximately 35% of their volume since the mid-1960s. Many are surprised to learn that the park's current number of glaciers – 25 – is significantly less than other American national parks, including the North Cascades (with over 300) and Mt Rainier (with 25 on one mountain).

However, whatever scenario ultimately transpires, the park – contrary to popular opinion – will not have to change its name. The 'glacier' label refers as much to the dramatic ice-sculpted scenery as it does to its fast-melting rivers of ice, and these remarkable geographical features ought to be dropping jaws for a good few millennia to come.

views and ferocious winds. Overlooked by the tall, chiseled peaks of the Rockies and still dramatically scarred by the landscape-altering effects of the 2006 Red Eagle Fire, the valley is spectacularly traversed by the Going-to-the-Sun Rd and punctuated by numerous trailheads and viewpoints.

St Mary's gorgeous turquoise sheen, easily the most striking color of any of Glacier's major bodies of water, is due to the suspension of tiny particles of glacial rock in the lake's water that absorb and reflect light.

Wild Goose Island   ISLAND

Ths tiny stub of an island with a handful of lopsided trees perches precariously in the middle of St Mary Lake, providing a perfect photo op for incurable camera-clickers.

Rising Sun   LANDMARK

You'll welcome this handy pit stop on the Going-to-the-Sun Rd, with useful tourist facilities including a motel, restaurant, showers, small grocery and boat launch. At the peculiarly named Two Dog Flats nearby, thick trees give way to grassy meadows making it much easier to spot bears, coyotes and elk.

Sun Point   VIEWPOINT

This rocky, often windy promontory overlooks St Mary Lake and was the site of some of the park's earliest and most luxurious chalets (now demolished). Trails link to Baring Falls and St Mary Falls.

Sunrift Gorge   CANYON

Just off the Going-to-the-Sun Rd and adjacent to a shuttle stop lies this narrow canyon carved over millennia by the gushing glacial meltwaters of Baring Creek. Look out for picturesque Baring Bridge, a classic example

of rustic Going-to-the-Sun Rd architecture, and follow a short, tree-covered trail down to misty Baring Falls.

Jackson Glacier Overlook   VIEWPOINT

This popular pull-over, located a short walk from the Gunsight Pass trailhead, offers telescopic views of the park's fifth-largest glacier, which sits close to its eponymous 3064m (10,052ft) peak – one of the park's highest.

★ Logan Pass   LANDMARK

Perched above the treeline, atop the wind-lashed Continental Divide, and blocked by snow for most of the year, 2026m (6646ft) Logan Pass – named for William R Logan, Glacier's first superintendent – is the park's highest navigable point by road. Two trails, Hidden Lake Overlook (which continues on to Hidden Lake itself) and Highline, lead out from here. Views are stupendous; the parking situation, however, is not – you might spend a lot of time searching for a spot when it's busy.

Garden Wall   LANDMARK

The sharp steep-sided ridge that parallels the Going-to-the-Sun Rd as it ascends to Logan Pass from the west was carved by powerful glaciers millions of years ago. Its western slopes, bisected by the emblematic Highline Trail, are covered by a classic Glacier Park feature: steep velvety meadows embellished by an abundance of summer wildflowers.

Weeping Wall   WATERFALL

Located 610m (2000ft) below the iconic Garden Wall, the glistening Weeping Wall creates a seasonal waterfall that was formed when Going-to-the-Sun Rd construction workers drilled their way across a network of mountain springs. The water has subsequently been diverted over the lip of a 9m (30ft) artificial cliff, and frequently gives unwary cars and motorbikes a good soaking.

Bird Woman Falls   WATERFALL
Standing at the artificially created Weeping Wall, look across the valley to this distant natural watery spectacle; the spectacular Bird Woman Falls drops 152m (500ft) from one of Glacier's many hanging valleys.

The Loop   LANDMARK
This sharp hairpin bend acts as a popular trailhead for hikers descending from the Granite Park Chalet and the Highline Trail. Consequently, it's normally chock-a-block with cars. The slopes nearby were badly scarred by the 2003 Trapper Fire, but nature and small shrubs are beginning to reappear.

Lake McDonald Valley   LAKE, FOREST
Greener and wetter than the St Mary Valley, the Lake McDonald Valley harbors the park's largest lake and some of its densest and oldest temperate rainforest. Crisscrossed by a number of popular trails, including the wheelchair-accessible, 1.3km (0.8-mile) Trail of the Cedars, the area is popular with drive-in campers, who frequent the Sprague Creek and Avalanche Creek campgrounds, as well as winter cross-country skiers who use McDonald Creek and the Going-to-the-Sun Rd as seasonal skiing trails.

Lake McDonald Lodge   HISTORIC BUILDING
On the northeastern shore of the lake, this rustic lodge, first built in 1895 as the Glacier Hotel, is the park's oldest hotel. It was replaced by a newer Swiss-style structure in 1913, before any roads had penetrated the region; the current lodge's imposing entrance was built facing the lake, meaning modern-day road travelers must enter via the back door.

Apgar Village   VILLAGE
Supporting little more than a couple of lodges, a gift shop or two and a restaurant, this collection of tourist facilities sits quietly on the southern shores of Lake McDonald. Dimon Apgar, for whom the settlement is named, built the first road from Belton to the lake in 1895, allowing a handful of early homesteaders to establish themselves on Salish and Kootenai tribal territory.

A fire destroyed much of the early settlement in 1930, but it spared the original schoolhouse, dating from 1915, which is now a gift shop. Nearby, the tiny Discovery Cabin (1929) acts as an activity center for children.

Junior ranger programs start here at 9am and 1pm in July and August.

◎ South of Going-to-the-Sun Road
With no hotels, no restaurants and only one dead-end road, the Two Medicine Valley is a favorite haunt for ambitious hikers intent on reaching one of a trio of high-altitude passes that guard the gusty Continental Divide. The more intrepid forge further west, beyond Cut Bank Pass, where faintly marked trails descend into the barely visited Nyack Creek Wilderness, a rough mélange of fordable rivers and primitive campsites that surrounds the isolated hulk of Mt Stimson, the park's second-highest peak at 3091m (10,142ft).

Two Medicine Valley
Before the building of the Going-to-the-Sun Rd in the 1930s, the Two Medicine Valley was one of the park's most accessible hubs, situated a mere 19.2km (12 miles) by horseback from the Great Northern Railway and the newly inaugurated Glacier Park Lodge. Famous for its healthy bear population and deeply imbued with Native American legends, the region is less visited these days, though it has lost none of its haunting beauty. Hikers can grab a picnic at the historic Two Medicine Campstore (p204), once the dining hall for the now defunct Two Medicine Chalets and the venue for one of President FD Roosevelt's famous 'fireside chats.' Towering authoritatively over sublime Two Medicine Lake is the distinctive hulk of Rising Wolf Mountain, named for Canadian-turned–Piegan Native American, Hugh Monroe, who was the first white person to explore the region in the mid-19th century.

Located 5km (3.1 miles) to the northwest, 2444m (8020ft) Triple Divide Peak marks the hydrologic apex of the North American continent. Empty a bucket of water on its summit and it will run into three separate oceans: the Pacific, the Atlantic and the Arctic.

◎ North of Going-to-the-Sun Road
You can penetrate the park's rugged north from both east and west sides. The northeast is accessible through the popular Many Glacier nexus and is crowned by a historic

GLACIER NATIONAL PARK SIGHTS

DON'T MISS

RIDING THE RAILS

Glacier National Park owes its existence to the Great Northern Railway constructed by Canadian-born entrepreneur James J Hill in the 1890s and later used to carry the park's first pioneering visitors into some of America's most uncompromising backcountry. Still running daily between West Glacier and East Glacier Park train stations, the line remains one of the best ways to view the park's impressive southern perimeter, demarcated by the Middle Fork of the Flathead River and guarded by the rampart-like mountains of the Lewis Range. On the south side of the line lies the even wilder **Great Bear Wilderness Area**, a roadless landscape, uninhabited bar for its bears, beavers et al.

The journey of one hour and 40 minutes between the two stations costs US$15 for reclining business-class seats and access to an onboard cafe and observation car on the legendary *Empire Builder*; board the train in West Glacier, 1km (0.6 miles) from the park's western entrance, and let the geographical drama unfold. The Flathead River is your constant companion as the train labors its way up to Marias Pass, the mythical mountain crossing that once eluded Lewis and Clark. On the way you'll pass **Essex Station**, the only 'flagstop' (request stop) on the *Empire Builder* route between Seattle and Chicago. Clearly visible from the train is the **Izaak Walton Inn** (p211), built by the Great Northern in 1939 and now a favored stopover for train buffs who stay in old cabooses restored as luxury accommodation.

Soon after Essex the train reaches the 1590m (5213ft) **Marias Pass**, the country's lowest pass over the Continental Divide. An obelisk stands next to an imposing statue of the green-before-his-time US president, Theodore Roosevelt, darling of the early US conservationist movement.

The vegetation quickly thins out as you approach East Glacier Park train depot, a historic station that marks the sudden, almost incongruous, meeting of mountains and prairie. Disembark here and walk 365m (400yd) across manicured lawns to the classic 'parkitecture' East Glacier Lodge, an apt end to a magnificent journey.

lodge. The northwest is more remote and requires a good car, self-sufficiency and an adventurous spirit.

Many Glacier Valley

Dubbed the 'heart and soul' of Glacier by park purists, Many Glacier Valley is a magical mélange of lush meadows and shimmering lakes, where the pièce de résistance is the strategically positioned Many Glacier Hotel (p203), constructed by the Great Northern Railway in 1915. Known traditionally for its 'rivers of ice' – though there aren't quite so many of them these days – the valley nurtures some of the park's most accessible glaciers, including the rapidly shrinking **Grinnell Glacier**, spotted by conservationist and naturalist George Bird Grinnell in 1885, and the **Salamander Glacier** that sits tucked beneath the saw-toothed Ptarmigan Ridge, so-named for its distinctive amphibian-like shape. Other 'unmissables' include **Iceberg Lake**, where turquoise waters are fed from a surrounding snowfield, and the **Ptarmigan Tunnel**, a 56m (183ft) corridor through the rock, blasted out of the mountain in the 1930s to cut some

distance off the hike to Belly River Valley (an environmental anomaly that would win few backers today).

Many Glacier is probably the best place in the park to spot wildlife. Avalanche chutes around the lakes attract bears, and mountain goats are easy to pick out on the steep scree slopes above Swiftcurrent Lake.

North Fork Valley

Glacier's most isolated nook is a riot of grassy meadows and regenerated forest that protects the park's only pack of wolves and hides some of its best backcountry trails and campgrounds. North and east of Polebridge, bone-rattling roads lead to a couple of secluded lakes. **Bowman Lake** is Lake McDonald without the tourists, an ideal spot to enjoy a picnic, launch a canoe or scan the horizon for wildlife. Meanwhile, 22.5km (14 miles) further north, **Kintla Lake** is a secret haven for solitude-seeking fishermen. Stalwart hikers venture out from here along the backcountry Boulder Pass Trail.

☞ TOURS

Red Jammer Buses   BUS TOUR

(www.glaciernationalparklodges.com; adult/child from US$40/20) Glacier's stylish red 'Jammer' buses (a legacy of when drivers had to 'jam' hard on the gears) are synonymous with the park. Jammers transport visitors along a dozen memorable routes, from the Western Alpine Tour, a 3½-hour trip between Lake McDonald Lodge and Logan Pass, to the Big Sky Circle Tour, an 8½-hour journey that circles the park via US 2. Book online.

The buses, a nostalgic reminder of the pioneering days of early motorized transportation, were introduced on the Going-to-the-Sun Rd between 1936 and 1939. They have thus been serving the park loyally for nearly 80 years, save for a two-year sabbatical in 1999 when the fleet was briefly taken out of service to be reconfigured by the Ford Motor Company. After an extensive makeover, they are safer, sturdier and 93% more environmentally friendly (now running off propane gas).

In 2015, the company introduced a Jammer outfitted to serve passengers with disabilities.

Glacier Park Boat Co   BOAT TOUR

(406-257-2426; www.glacierparkboats.com; St Mary Lake cruise adult/child $25.50/12.50) Six historic boats – some dating back to the 1920s – ply five of Glacier's attractive mountain lakes, and some of them have the added bonus of combining the watery ride with a short guided hike led by interpretive, often witty, guides.

One of the best excursions leaves from the Many Glacier Hotel twice daily (July to September), chugging across Swiftcurrent Lake. Groups disembark on the southern shore and stroll to Lake Josephine where another boat whisks you to another landing; from here your guide leads you a further 2.4km (1.5 miles) overland to Grinnell Lake for wondrous glacial views.

A similar boat-hike combo can be undertaken on Two Medicine Lake, which marries a 45-minute cruise with a 3.2km (2-mile) walk to double-flumed Twin Falls. On St Mary Lake, boats departing from Rising Sun incorporate a 1½-hour cruise with a longer 4.8km (3-mile) hike to St Mary Falls.

Sun Tours   BUS TOUR

(406-226-9220; www.glaciersuntours.com; adult/child US$40/20) Blackfeet tribal members lead these interpretive tours of the Going-to-the-Sun Rd. Air-conditioned buses leave from various points in East Glacier, St Mary and Browning; tours last for approximately four hours.

Kruger Helicop-Tours   SCENIC FLIGHTS

(800-220-6565; www.krugerhelicopters.com; 30min/1hr tour from US$125/245) To get a view from above the eagles' nests, consider a helicopter tour run by this outfit, which has offices on US 2, 1.6km (1 mile) west of West Glacier.

Glacier Guides Inc   HIKING

(800-521-7238; www.glacierguides.com) Leads guided day hikes and backpacking trips from mid-May through September.

☞ SLEEPING

In the early 1910s, James Hill's Great Northern Railway built a series of grand hotels to lure rich tourists to Glacier National Park. Two of these so-called 'parkitecture' structures, Many Glacier Hotel and Lake McDonald Lodge, still stand within the park boundaries, conjuring up nostalgic memories of times gone by.

In keeping with the park's back-to-nature ethos, the lodges have been kept religiously 'rustic,' so they are bereft of distracting modern appliances such as TVs, room phones and wi-fi. All are also nonsmoking and offer at least one wheelchair-accessible room. Operated by two companies, Glacier National Park Lodges (855-733-4522; www.glaciernationalparklodges.com) and Glacier Park, Inc (406-892-2525; www.glacierparkinc.com), accommodations can be booked through their respective central reservations systems.

For comprehensive information about camping in the park, see www.nps.gov/glac/planyourvisit/camping.htm.

☞ Going-to-the-Sun Road

Camping

All of the Going-to-the-Sun Rd campgrounds act as bus stops on the free summer shuttle route, making link-ups with trailheads and visitor centers refreshingly easy. Two campgrounds – St Mary and Apgar – are open in winter.

Rising Sun Campground   CAMPGROUND $

(tent & RV sites US$20; ☺ mid-Jun–mid-Sep) Situated on Glacier's more unprotected eastern side, 8km (5 miles) west of St Mary entrance station, sites here vary, with lush and diverse vegetation providing some shade. A host of

GLACIER NATIONAL PARK CAMPGROUNDS

CAMPGROUND	LOCATION	DESCRIPTION	NO OF SITES
Apgar	Going-to-the-Sun Road	The park's largest campground is near trails, a lake and Apgar Village	196
Avalanche Creek	Going-to-the-Sun Road	In old-growth forest and close to hikes; also has an outdoor amphitheater for evening programs	87
Rising Sun	Going-to-the-Sun Road	Part-open, part-covered sites close to camp store, restaurant and boat launch	83
Sprague Creek	Going-to-the-Sun Road	No RVs allowed, but tranquil lake views are hindered by proximity to Going-to-the-Sun Rd	25
St Mary	Going-to-the-Sun Road	Large and fairly open, with cracking views; visitor center nearby	148
Bowman Lake	North of Going-to-the-Sun Road	Remote and basic, but great for tent campers; pit toilets available; bring mosquito repellent	48
Fish Creek	North of Going-to-the-Sun Road	Large, wooded campground that offers plenty of privacy	180
Kintla Lake	North of Going-to-the-Sun Road	The park's most remote campground; listen to the howls of wolves at night	13
Logging Creek	North of Going-to-the-Sun Road	Small and primitive with no services, although there are pit toilets	8
Many Glacier	North of Going-to-the-Sun Road	One of the park's most popular campgrounds, set in a beautiful valley with facilities nearby	110
Quartz Creek	North of Going-to-the-Sun Road	Smallest campground in the park, this place is primitive; RVs not recommended	7
Cut Bank	South of Going-to-the-Sun Road	Small, quiet and secluded campground; access to several trailheads; no RVs	14
Two Medicine	South of Going-to-the-Sun Road	Secluded campground with space for larger RVs, and an evening ranger program	99

 Drinking Water   Flush Toilets   Ranger Station Nearby   Great for Families

facilities, including the Rising Sun Motor Inn, an excellent store, shower facilities (only one stall each for men and women), a restaurant and a boat launch, are nearby.

A handful of sites, including 35, 37 and 39 especially, offer outstanding views of Red Eagle Mountain.

Sprague Creek Campground   CAMPGROUND $

(tent sites US$20; ☉ May–mid-Sep) Off Going-to-the-Sun Rd on the upper shores of Lake McDonald, the park's smallest campground draws mostly tents – no vehicles over 6.4m (21ft) are allowed – and feels more intimate than many of the park's other options, at least at night when the passing traffic goes to bed. Arrive early to claim a site overlooking the lake.

Avalanche Creek Campground   CAMPGROUND $

(tent & RV sites US$20; ☉ mid-Jun–mid-Sep) This lush campground abutting the park's old-growth cedar forest gets more rainfall than most. Some sites are overshadowed by old stands of hemlock, cedar and Douglas fir,

ELEVATION	OPEN	RESERVATIONS REQUIRED?	DAILY FEE	FACILITIES	PAGE
960m (3153ft)	May-Oct & Nov-Mar	no	US$15-20		p201
1067m (3500ft)	Jun-Sep	no	US$20		p200
1463m (4800ft)	Jun-Sep	no	US$20		p199
1067m (3500ft)	May-Sep	no	US$20		p200
1372m (4500ft)	year-round	available	US$23		p201
1372m (4500ft)	year-round	no	US$15		p202
1067m (3500ft)	Jun-Sep	available	US$23		p203
1372m (4500ft)	year-round	no	US$15		p203
1372m (4500ft)	Jul-Sep	no	US$10		p203
1372m (4500ft)	May-Sep	no	US$20		p202
884m (2900ft)	Jul-Oct	no	US$10		p203
1562m (5125ft)	May-Sep	no	US$10		p202
1585m (5200ft)	Apr-Oct	no	US$20		p202

 Wheelchair Accessible

 Grocery Store Nearby

 Summertime Campfire Program

 RV Dump Station

but you're close to Lake McDonald and right in the path of a couple of very popular trailheads.

Apgar Campground CAMPGROUND $
(📞 406-888-7800; www.recreation.gov; tent & RV sites $15-20; ⊙ May-Oct & Nov-late Mar) This large wooded campground is a good choice for its proximity to the conveniences of Apgar Village and West Glacier, as well as for being only a short stroll to Lake McDonald. It feels, however, far from the wilderness.

St Mary Campground CAMPGROUND $
(📞 406-732-7708; www.recreation.gov; tent & RV sites $23; ⊙ year-round) Cottonwood and aspen trees predominate in the most shaded sites at this large, mostly flat campground just west of St Mary entrance station, though sites in general are less protected than elsewhere. Showers for registered campers. There's a 0.8km (0.5 mile) walking path to the St Mary Visitor Center.

Lodging

★ Lake McDonald Lodge   HISTORIC HOTEL **$$**

(☑855-733-4522; www.glaciernationalparklodges. com; r US$85-190, cabins US$140-205, ste US$329; ☺mid-May–Sep; 🕾) 🏄 Fronting luminous Lake McDonald and built in classic US 'parki-tecture' style, the lodge welcomes its guests through a more mundane backdoor setting – they originally disembarked from a boat on the lakeside. Once inside the main building, a huge fireplace, Native American–themed paintings and taxidermied animal heads ensure you know you're out West. Small, old-fashioned rooms are complemented by cottages and a 1950s motel.

Built on the site of an earlier lodge commissioned by park pioneer George Snyder in the 1890s, the present building was constructed in 1913 and rooms remain sans air-con and TV – it's worth requesting one of the more than two dozen rooms and cabins renovated for the 2016 season. Two restaurants are on-site and evening ranger programs are held nightly in the summer. The lakefront location is fairly ideal and close to trailheads on the Going-to-the-Sun Rd.

Village Inn at Apgar   MOTEL **$$**

(☑855-733-4522; www.glaciernationalparklodges. com; Apgar Village; r US$150, ste US$205; ☺Jun–mid-Sep) When you lean out on your sunrise-facing balcony at this motel, occupying a serene setting at the southern end of Lake McDonald in Apgar Village, you are quite literally within spitting distance of the park's largest and most tranquil lake. The rooms, rustic and gadget-free, were undergoing a top-to-bottom renovation at the time of writing, including new carpeting and bedding.

Rising Sun Motor Inn   MOTEL **$$**

(☑855-733-4522; www.glaciernationalparklodges. com; r US$135, cabin US$140; ☺Jun–mid-Sep; 🕾) One of two classic 1940s-era motor inns in the park, the Rising Sun is getting a make-over. The rustic motel and cabin rooms that lie in the back of the compound across the road from the upper north shore of St Mary Lake are being gutted and upgraded. Expect the same general cozy feel, only with more up-to-date furnishings.

The motel is part of a small complex that includes an excellent general store, campground and boat launch. The lobby and check-in is in the same building as the friendly restaurant and gift shop.

Apgar Village Lodge   MOTEL, CABINS **$$**

(☑406-888-5484; www.glacierparkinc.com; r US$115, cabins US$130-300; ☺mid-May–Sep) This lodge (one of two in Apgar Village) offers well-maintained motel-style rooms and cabins. The cabins are spacious and most come with kitchenettes, while the smaller rooms are more rustic.

🛏 South of Going-to-the-Sun Road

Two Medicine Campground   CAMPGROUND **$**

(Two Medicine Valley; tent & RV sites US$20; ☺mid-Apr–Oct) This campground below Rising Wolf Mountain, 4.8km (3 miles) southwest of Two Medicine entrance station, is your only accommodation in the park's relatively ignored southwest corner. It's a picturesque area with nicely wooded sites and easy lake and creek access; a campstore with prepared foods is close by.

Cut Bank Campground   CAMPGROUND **$**

(tent sites US$10; ☺May-Sep) Strangely enough, considering its appealing out-of-the-way feel, park rangers at Glacier's visitor centers sometimes forget about this small, peaceful site. It's accessed via an 8km (5-mile) gravel road off US 89 halfway between St Mary and the junction for Two Medicine; several recommended hikes, including the much-favored Medicine Grizzly Lake, leave from here.

🛏 North of Going-to-the-Sun Road

Camping

All campgrounds are first-come, first-served, except Fish Creek.

Many Glacier Campground   CAMPGROUND **$**

(tent & RV sites US$20; ☺mid-May–Sep) With access to phenomenal trails, this heavily wooded campground is one of the park's most popular. It lies within strolling distance of the Swiftcurrent Motor Inn complex, which includes a restaurant, hot showers, a laundry and camp store. The Many Glacier Hotel and its facilities are a short drive away.

Bowman Lake Campground   CAMPGROUND **$**

(North Fork; tent & RV sites US$15; ☺year-round) Rarely full, this campground 9.7km (6 miles) up Inside North Fork Rd from Polebridge offers very spacious sites in forested grounds,

BACKCOUNTRY ACCOMMODATIONS

Sperry Chalet (☎888-345-2649; www.sperrychalet.com; Lake McDonald Valley; s/d incl full board $135/332; ◔Jul–early Sep) Built by the Great Northern Railway in 1914, this 17-room historic Swiss-style chalet is a good three-hour hike from the nearest road. Guests must either walk or horseback ride here via an ascending 10.5km (6.5-mile) trail that begins at Lake McDonald Lodge. With no lights, heat or water, staying at Sperry rates alongside a night in the African bush.

Part of an old accommodations network that once spanned the park before the construction of the Going-to-the-Sun Rd, Sperry offers phenomenal views. Be sure to bring a flashlight for midnight trips to the outdoor toilets. Rooms are private; walls, however, are paper-thin. Rates include three excellent meals (box lunches are available) and mules can be hired to carry gear.

Granite Park Chalet (☎406-387-5555; www.graniteparkchalet.com; 1st person US$107, extra person US$85; ◔Jul–mid-Sep) A popular stopping point for hikers on the Swiftcurrent Pass and Highline trails, this very basic chalet (pit toilets) dates back to the park's early- 20th-century heyday. A rustic kitchen is available for use (with propane-powered stoves), though you must bring and prepare your own food. Snacks and freeze-dried meals are available for purchase. Twelve guest rooms sleep two to six people.

Bedding costs US$20 extra per person. Book in advance as it gets busy, and remember to bring as much of your own water as possible (bottled water and sodas are also available to buy).

and beautiful Bowman Lake is only steps away. It has a visitors information tent with reference books and local hiking information. The road from Polebridge can be especially rough after heavy rain. Also open in winter.

Fish Creek Campground   CAMPGROUND $
(☎406-888-7800; www.recreation.gov; tent & RV sites US$23; ◔Jun–early Sep) Cocooned inside a dense cedar-hemlock forest along Lake McDonald and only 4km (2.5 miles) from Apgar Village, this large campground with showers for registered campers offers sites that are tucked among the trees. Some offer quick access to the lake and views.

Kintla Lake Campground   CAMPGROUND $
(North Fork; tent sites US$15; ◔year-round) If you've come to Glacier to dip your nose into *Ulysses* and *War and Peace,* you'll find little to disturb you at this primitive campground, at the top of Inside North Fork Rd around 24km (15 miles) north of Polebridge.

Logging Creek Campground   CAMPGROUND $
(North Fork; tent sites US$10; ◔Jul–mid-Sep) It takes some determination to reach this primitive campground, on Inside North Fork Rd 27.4km (17 miles) north of Fish Creek Campground, but it is worth it if you're looking for tranquility amid the trees. The atmosphere is very still here, except for the sound of a flowing creek.

Quartz Creek Campground   CAMPGROUND $
(North Fork; tent sites US$10; ◔Jul-Oct) The campground here, on Inside North Fork Rd, is tranquil, and the sites, surrounded by thick vegetation, feel private.

Lodging

★**Many Glacier Hotel**   HISTORIC HOTEL $$
(☎855-733-4522; www.glaciernationalparklodges.com; r US$165-225, ste US$330; ◔mid-Jun–mid-Sep; ☎) Enjoying the most wondrous setting in the park, this fine old parkitecture-style lodge sits pretty on the northeastern shore of Swiftcurrent Lake. Built in the style of a huge Swiss chalet by the Great Northern Railway in 1915, the hotel sprawls over five floors with an imposing open-plan lobby. Despite the majesty of the location, expect comfortable, if rustic rooms.

Shimmering snow and glacier-capped peaks are within view, and some of the park's most iconic hikes leave from nearby. A complete renovation is scheduled to be completed by the 2017 season, however the medieval-heavy decor will likely stick around. Several restaurants are part of the complex.

Swiftcurrent Motor Inn   MOTEL, CABIN $$
(☎855-733-4522; www.glaciernationalparklodges.com; cabin with/without bath US$105/90, r US$145; ◔mid-Jun–mid-Sep; ☎) A relic from the early days of the motorcar, the Swiftcurrent,

conveniently located next to numerous Many Glacier trailheads, purposefully replicates the austerity of the 1940s with basic, but cozy, facilities. A mixture of cabins and motel-style rooms come with or without showers and are bereft of modern luxuries such as TV and air-con.

Directly outside the front door is a handy store, a restaurant and a laundry facility, all of which are also heavily frequented by guests at the campground across the street. If you book far in advance, ask for one of the recently renovated cabins.

✕ EATING

✕ Going-to-the-Sun Road

Jammer Joe's Grill &
Pizzeria   PIZZA, AMERICAN **$**
(Lake McDonald Lodge; sandwiches & pizza US$11; ⊘ 11am-9pm late May–early Sep; 🖐) Only steps away, but light-years from Lake McDonald Lodge's decor and vibe, Jammer Joe's looks like a pizzeria from a Midwestern suburban strip mall circa 1970. In Glacier, it's something of a pleasant apparition for exhausted hikers and kids enamored by the simple no-frills menu, which, in addition to whole-grain pizzas, includes burgers, pasta and salads.

The pizza, pasta and salad lunch buffet (adult/child US$13/10) is an especially good deal.

Two Dog Flats Grill   AMERICAN, TEX-MEX **$$**
(Rising Sun Motor Inn; mains US$15-20; ⊘ 6:30am-10pm mid-Jun–mid-Sep) With a clientele made up primarily of famished hikers and tour-bus passengers happy just to stretch their legs, Two Dog doesn't have to try too hard to satisfy. However, with a new emphasis on organic, vegetarian and locally sourced ingredients, its typical Montana fare with a Tex-Mex twist certainly rises above average and the staff are especially friendly.

Eddie's Cafe   AMERICAN, ICE CREAM **$$**
(Apgar Village; mains US$12-22; ⊘ 7am-9pm late May–mid-Sep; 🖐) Summer jobbers man the diner-style tables inside Apgar Village's only eating joint, serving up meatloaf, fish and chips and buffalo burgers from a kitchen where quantity rules over quality. There's usually a line at the side window, which dishes out quality ice cream, lemonade, tea and coffee drinks.

Russells Fireside Dining
Room   INTERNATIONAL **$$$**
(Lake McDonald Lodge; mains US$12-30; ⊘ 6:30am-9:30pm late May–mid-Sep; 🖉) 🖐 Lake views and stuffed animal heads characterize the interior of this handsome restaurant at the Lake McDonald Lodge, where you can enjoy hash browns for breakfast, substantial sandwiches for lunch, and crab cakes and Caesar salad for dinner.

✕ South of Going-to-the-Sun Road

Two Medicine
Campstore   SANDWICHES, GROCERY **$**
(📞 406-892-2525; Two Medicine Valley; ⊘ 7am-9pm mid-Apr–Sep) While the Two Medicine Valley has no standard restaurants, you can forgo alfresco campground cooking and chow down on excellent chili, soups and sandwiches, as well as grab coffee, ice cream and ingredients to make up a decent picnic at this historic building-cum-grocery-store that once served as a dining hall for the erstwhile Two Medicine Chalets.

President FD Roosevelt, accompanied by John D Rockefeller Jr, chose to give one of his famous 'fireside chats' here in the 1930s.

✕ North of Going-to-the-Sun Road

Swiftcurrent Restaurant   PIZZA **$$**
(Italian Garden Ristorante; Swiftcurrent Motor Inn; mains US$12-24; ⊘ 6:30am-10pm mid-Jun–mid-Sep) The Italian moniker aside, there's little European influence here, unless you count the continental summer waitstaff. No doubt, the quality of the pizzas and sandwiches is heightened by the fact that it's mostly famished hikers and campers eating here. Breakfasts of pancakes and eggs are satisfying, and the restaurant can prepare food to carry on hikes.

Ptarmigan Dining Room   INTERNATIONAL **$$$**
(Many Glacier Hotel; mains US$15-35; ⊘ 6:30am-9:30pm mid-Jun–mid-Sep) With magnificent lakeside views, this spacious and handsomely designed restaurant with vaulted ceilings is the most refined of the park's lodges. Enjoy steak, seafood, pasta, wine and microbrews, as bears munch on berries in the bushes outside.

🍷 DRINKING & NIGHTLIFE

Both the Many Glacier Hotel and Lake Mc-Donald Lodge have cozy bars, good for a post-hike alcoholic beverage. The Many Glacier Hotel also has a pianist and occasional live music in its lobby.

☆ ENTERTAINMENT

The park visitor centers give out a free newspaper listing evening programs, including ranger talks, educational slide shows, exhibits on the park's geography and geology, and Native American Speaks. Summer events kick off nightly between 7:30pm and 8:30pm, rotating between the Lake McDonald Lodge, St Mary Visitor Center, and the Apgar, Many Glacier and Two Medicine Campgrounds. The Glacier Institute (p274) offers workshops, youth camps and courses year-round.

ℹ Information

DANGERS & ANNOYANCES

Glacier is prime grizzly bear country and, although you're more likely to be involved in a car accident than be maimed by a bear, attacks have happened. Bear spray costs US$45 and is available in all outdoor stores in and around the park; a few stores rent spray by the day.

The Going-to-the-Sun Rd is crowded and vertiginous with a steep drop-off. As it is a historic monument there are no modern guardrails. Drive with care.

INTERNET ACCESS

Mobile wi-fi signals generally don't extend far past park entrances. The visitor center in Apgar provides free service, and the park lodges make their wi-fi available to guests only. There are also internet points in St Mary and West Glacier.

LAUNDRY & SHOWERS

St Mary and Fish Creek have showers for registered campers. The camp stores at Rising Sun and Many Glacier have **showers** (per 8min US$2.50; ☺6:30am-10pm) open to the public. The latter also has laundry facilities.

MEDICAL SERVICES

Basic first aid is available at visitor centers and ranger stations in the park. A **clinic** (p209) in West Glacier is the closest facility for minor injuries.

MONEY

Canadian currency is not widely accepted in Glacier. The nearest banks are in Columbia Falls and Browning. Many Glacier Hotel and Lake McDonald Lodge have 24-hour ATMs. There's also an ATM at the camp store at Eddie's Cafe in Apgar Village.

TELEPHONE

All park lodges and nonprimitive campgrounds have public phones. Cell (mobile) phone service in the park is unreliable, however most networks have sporadic reception near the entrances, and Verizon even further into the park.

TOURIST INFORMATION

The park has three informative visitor centers and three fully staffed ranger stations scattered within its midst. All are overseen by knowledgeable and helpful rangers during peak season. Visitor centers usually offer other amenities such as restrooms, drinking water, bookstores, maps and interpretive displays.

Infrequently staffed ranger stations are also situated at Goat Haunt, Cut Bank, Walton, Belly River, Logging Creek and Kintla Lake.

Apgar Backcountry Office (Apgar Village; ☺7am-5pm May–late Oct) The place to go for information on backcountry camping all over Glacier. Check out the binder with detailed information and photos of every route and site. It sells bear spray and highly recommended topographic maps.

Apgar Visitor Center (☎406-888-7939; ☺7am-4:30pm Jun-Sep; 🛜) Opened in 2014, this new, LEED–certified center with a large parking lot and free wi-fi signal lies about 2.4km (1.5 miles) north of the West Glacier entrance to the park. Opening hours vary outside summer months.

Logan Pass Visitor Center (☎406-888-7800; Going-to-the-Sun Rd, Logan Pass; ☺9am-7pm Jun–mid-Oct) Certainly the most magnificent setting of all the park's visitor centers; the building also has a good gift shop. The Hidden Lakes Overlook and Highline trails begin from here.

Many Glacier Ranger Station (☎406-732-7740; ☺7am-5pm late May–mid-Sep) Call here for local hiking information and details of recent bear activity.

Polebridge Ranger Station (☎406-888-7842; ☺9am-5pm late May–mid-Sep) A small historic station with North Fork information. One of the rangers is the owner of the nearby North Fork Hostel (p209).

St Mary Visitor Center (☎406-732-7750; ☺8am-6pm May–mid-Oct) Houses interesting exhibits on wildlife, geology and Native American culture and history, as well as an auditorium featuring slide shows, ranger talks and Native American Speaks. There's a walking path to St Mary Campground from here.

Two Medicine Ranger Station (☎406-226-4484; ☺7am-5pm late May–mid-Sep) A good source for Two Medicine area hikes.

ℹ Getting There & Around

AIR

Glacier Park International Airport (www.iflyglacier.com), located between Whitefish and Kalispell, has direct flights to and from Seattle, the Twin Cities, Las Vegas, Salt Lake City and Denver. **Flathead-Glacier Transportation** (☏ 406-892-3390) runs taxi shuttles to Whitefish (US$25) and West Glacier (US$50); reserve ahead.

BICYCLE

Getting around by bike is feasible on the Going-to-the-Sun Rd at certain times of day (see p189) – although the ride is tough. With all trails out of bounds, cyclists are confined to plying the park's scant road network. A 4km (2.5-mile) paved bike path runs between Apgar Village and West Glacier.

BUS

Free park shuttle buses ferry visitors between spots on the Going-to-the-Sun Rd, which means all of the park's major trailheads (bar those in the remote North Fork area) are well served by public transportation from July 1 to mid-September. Service in 23-seater buses between the Apgar Visitor Center (via Apgar Village) for all westside stops leave every 30 minutes from 9am to 5:45pm. For nonstop service to Logan Pass, several smaller buses leave in the morning between 7am and 7:30am. To continue on down to the St Mary Visitor Center you have to transfer to another bus. The buses have air-conditioning, are wheelchair accessible and run on biodiesel. Most of the shuttles have bike racks. Clear route maps are provided at every shuttle stop or can be viewed on the park website at www.nps.gov/glac.

On the park's eastern side, **Glacier Park Inc** (www.glacierparkinc.com) runs the East Side Shuttle between Glacier Park Lodge, Two Medicine, St Mary Lodge, Many Glacier Hotel/ Swiftcurrent Motor Inn, and Prince of Wales Hotel in Waterton (Canada), from early June to mid- to late September. Journeys cost US$15 per trip segment and reservations are required.

CAR & MOTORCYCLE

The only paved road to completely bisect the park is the 85km (53-mile) Going-to-the-Sun Rd. The partly unpaved Inside North Fork Rd links Apgar with Polebridge. To connect with any other roads, vehicles must briefly leave the park and re-enter via another entrance.

A decades-long upgrade of Going-to-the-Sun Rd means construction and minor delays aren't uncommon. Also, because of forest fires or other natural events, unexpected road closures do happen.

Hertz (www.hertz.com) has vehicles available for pickup at the West Glacier and East Glacier train stations. Other outlets can be found at Glacier Park International Airport and in the nearby town of Whitefish.

TRAIN

Largely responsible for opening up the region in the 1890s, the train has been a popular method of transport to Glacier since the park's inception in 1910. Amtrak's *Empire Builder* continues to ply the Great Northern Railway's historic east–west route from Chicago to Seattle once daily (in either direction) stopping in both East Glacier (6:45pm westbound, 9:54am eastbound) and West Glacier (8:23pm westbound, 8:16am eastbound). The same train also connects with Whitefish and (by request only) Essex.

Around Glacier National Park

Includes ➡

West Glacier 208
St Mary 209
East Glacier........210
Blackfeet Indian
Reservation........212
Whitefish 212

Best Places to Stay

➡ Belton Chalet (p208)

➡ Garden Wall (p214)

➡ Izaak Walton Inn (p211)

➡ Glacier Park Lodge (p211)

Best Places to Eat

➡ Belton Chalet Grill Dining Room & Taproom (p208)

➡ Serrano's Mexican Restaurant (p211)

➡ Montana Coffee Traders (p215)

Why Go?

Although Glacier National Park's tourist numbers are relatively high (two million a year), almost all visit between June and September. Choose your moment and splendid isolation is yours for the taking. The park remains open year-round; however, most services are open only from mid-May to September.

Glacier's 1562 sq miles are divided into five regions, each centered on a ranger station: Polebridge (northwest); Lake McDonald (southwest), including the West Entrance and Apgar Village; Two Medicine (southeast); St Mary (east); and Many Glacier (northeast).

When to Go

Glacier National Park

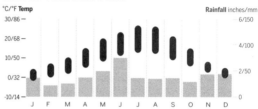

May–Jun The thaw begins and lower-altitude destinations attract the intrepid and hardy.

Jul–Aug Peak summer when most trails and all park facilities are open.

Sep Fewer crowds, quieter campgrounds and a reliable weather window before the first snows.

West Glacier

Lying less than 1km (0.6 miles) from the park's busiest entrance gate and equipped with an Amtrak train station, West Glacier is the park's most pleasant gateway town, with an attractive cluster of serviceable facilities. Known as Belton until 1949, the settlement was the site of the park's oldest hotel, the Belton Chalet, built in 1910 and still hosting guests.

🛏 Sleeping

Glacier Campground   CAMPGROUND **$**
(🖉 406-387-5689;   www.glaciercampground.com; tent/RV sites US$25/30, cabins US$40-60; 🛜) This well-run and friendly campground, located 1.6km (1 mile) west of West Glacier and off US 2, sits on 16 hectares (40 acres) of densely wooded grounds. Sites (all have electrical outlets) come in a variety of sizes and configurations, so it's best to check out several before committing. It also offers basic wooden cabins

Hearty grub, such as gumbo and catfish po'boys, is served from 5pm to 10pm in the **Hungry Sasquatch** restaurant (mains US$10), an outdoor pavilion open to nonguests as well.

Glacier Highland Resort Motel   MOTEL **$**
(🖉 406-888-5427;   www.glacierhighland.com;   US 2; r US$70-100; 🛜) The majority of the rooms at this popular place are in a low-slung motel-style building just up the hill from the West Glacier train station. It has a faux log-cabin exterior, whereas the blandly furnished, carpeted rooms offer little suggestion you're out West; they do have flat-screen TVs.

★ Belton Chalet   HISTORIC HOTEL **$$**
(🖉 406-888-5000; www.beltonchalet.com; 12575 US 2; r US$160-185) 🅿 Built and opened the same year as the national park (1910), this Swiss chalet overlooking the railroad tracks in West Glacier was Glacier's first tourist hotel. Other incarnations, including time as a pizza parlor, followed, and it lay rotting until a late-1990s refurb, which dusted off 25 traditional yet elegant rooms, arts-and-crafts-style furnishings, a spa and a celebrated taproom.

Glacier Guides Lodge   B&B **$$**
(🖉 406-387-5555; www.glacierguides.com; Highline Blvd; r US$171; �ⓢ🛜) 🅿 One of West Glacier's nicest properties, Glacier Guides Lodge is set in a quiet pocket just off US 2, opposite the West Glacier train station. It's an attractive wooden B&B–style lodge (built to LEED standards) with a stylish, rustic authenticity that doesn't forsake creature comforts such as wi-fi, air-con and TV.

Vista Motel   MOTEL **$$**
(🖉 406-888-5311; www.glaciervistamotel.com; US 2; r from US$135; 🛜🏊) The no-nonsense Vista does at least have a vista, along with comfortable beds, powerful showers and a spatially challenged swimming pool. Located a 0.8km (0.5-mile) hike along US 2 (there's a wide shoulder) from the West Glacier train station, it's a viable crash pad if you're arriving by train and plying the park by public transport.

West Glacier Motel
& Cabins   MOTEL, CABINS **$$**
(🖉 406-888-5662;   www.glacierparkinc.com;   d/ cabins US$105/200) A bed and a Bible are the only two guarantees at the closest motel to the park entrance, located on the north side of the railroad tracks in West Glacier Village. Motel-style rooms are situated in the village, while cabins are perched on a bluff overlooking Flathead River. No TVs, fridges, coffee machines or wi-fi.

🍴 Eating & Drinking

Oso   CAFE **$**
(12127 US 2 East; sandwiches US$8; ⊘8am-5pm) Housed in a bright red Great Northern Railway train caboose, with a kitchen the size of a food truck's, this little cafe serves up excellent breakfast burritos and pressed chicken and pork sandwiches and tacos. It's attached to the Great Northern Rafting company office and has a large outdoor patio.

West Glacier Restaurant   AMERICAN **$**
(🖉 406-888-5359; 200 Going-to-the-Sun Rd; mains US$6-18; ⊘7am-10pm mid-May–Oct; 🖑) Basic diner fare in a classic if drab diner setting, but it's conveniently located close to the park's western entrance. Kids, with their parents' cash in hand, stop in for excellent ice cream.

★ Belton Chalet Grill Dining
Room & Taproom   INTERNATIONAL **$$$**
(www.beltonchalet.com; 12575 US 2; mains US$21-34; ⊘3-10pm) 🅿 For a step up from unadorned meatloaf, hit West Glacier's historic chalet for some equally historic food. The sit-down restaurant sports tablecloths, wine glasses and menu items such as coffee-dusted duck breast and Montana beef fillet cured in bourbon. The adjoining taproom is a more casual, economical affair that offers an

POLEBRIDGE

Glacier's most isolated outpost is populated with more wildlife than people (although if you plan your journey around Polebridge's raucous July 4th celebration, the opposite may be true). Sandwiched between the towering Livingstone and Whitefish mountain ranges, the 'town' is a low-key place really consisting of two hubs: the **Northern Lights Saloon** (✆ 406-888-9963; Polebridge Loop Rd; mains US$10-22; ⊙ 4pm-midnight May-Sep) – offering ales, tall tales and a standard pub-grub menu – and the historic **Polebridge Mercantile** (Map p194; ✆ 406-888-5105; www.polebridgemerc.com; Polebridge Loop Rd, North Fork Valley; pastries from US$4; ⊙ 8am-6pm mid-May–Nov; ☎), a combination store, post office, gas station and local gathering spot.

Camping is free along the North Fork of the Flathead River or you can stop by Glacier's quirkiest lodgings – the **North Fork Hostel & Square Peg Ranch** (Map p194; ✆ 406-888-5241; www.nfhostel.com; 80 Beaver Dr; tent sites/dm/teepees/cabins US$14/20/45/50; ☎) ✐; expect no electricity, few facilities and even fewer worries.

Polebridge is located on the Outside North Fork Rd, 42km (26 miles) northwest of the park's western entrance. The Polebridge Ranger Station (p205) lies 1.6km (1 mile) to the east, next to the park entrance. Driving a car is the only reliable way of getting to Polebridge, although you'll need good snow tires in the winter. The North Fork Hostel sometimes runs a shuttle service from West Glacier.

excellent antipasto plate and some inventive sandwiches and microbrews.

Packer's Roost BAR
(✆ 406-387-9922; 9640 US 2, Coram; ⊙ 11am-2am) One local summed up the experience at this classic Western roadside bar as 'it looks like crazy bikers are going to stab you, but they are in fact really nice.' Count on cheap beer, burgers and a frisson of fish-out-of-water feel.

Shopping

Glacier Outdoor Center OUTDOOR EQUIPMENT
(✆ 406-888-5454; www.glacierraftco.com; 11957 US 2; ⊙ 7:30am-9pm) Just outside the park, about 800m (0.5 miles) from the train station on US 2, this is the best one-stop shop for outdoor gear. It rents and sells everything you could need for rafting, fishing, mountain biking, camping and backpacking.

ⓘ Information

Most basic facilities can be found here, including a gas station, a grocery store, a post office and an ATM. There's also a coin-operated laundry in the back of the parking lot where the Alberta Information Centre is located.

Alberta Information Centre (✆ 406-888-5743; off US 2; ⊙ 8am-7pm; ☎) A large and comprehensive visitor centre for wilderness junkies keen on heading north to Waterton Lakes, Banff and Jasper National Parks, as well as other destinations in Alberta and British Columbia.

Glacier National Park Headquarters (✆ 406-888-7800; www.nps.gov/glac; West Glacier; ⊙ 8am-4:30pm Mon-Fri) Inhabits a small complex just south of the park's West Entrance. No longer the focus for visitor information, but might be worth checking out in winter months.

West Glacier Clinic (✆ 406-888-9924; 100 Rea Rd, West Glacier Fire Hall; ⊙ 9am-4pm) The most convenient place to head to for medical attention for minor injuries such as sprains and infections when on the western side of the park. Staffed by nurse practitioners and physician assistants and affiliated with the North Valley Hospital in Whitefish.

ⓘ Getting There & Around

A 4km (2.5-mile) paved cycle path links West Glacier with Apgar Village and transit center inside the park, from where you can catch free Going-to-the-Sun Rd shuttles. Amtrak's *Empire Builder* stops at the West Glacier train station once a day traveling in either direction.

Hertz (www.hertz.com) has cars available for rent parked at the train station.

St Mary

Sitting on the Blackfeet Indian Reservation just outside the park's east entrance, St Mary makes a handy base for exploring Glacier's dryer eastern side. Though it's less salubrious than its western counterpart, West Glacier, the views of the mountains are better here, and it's a shorter walk (1km/0.6 miles) to the first free shuttle stop on the Going-to-the-Sun Rd (outside the St Mary visitor and transit center). A cluster of handy services not found inside the park crowd around the junction of Hwy

89 and the Going-to-the-Sun Rd, including campgrounds, a motel, a supermarket, a gas station and the region's swankiest modern hotel. The East Side Shuttle provides easy access to East Glacier, Two Medicine, Many Glacier and Waterton.

🍴 Sleeping & Eating

Johnson's of St Mary
CAMPGROUND, CABINS $

(☑ 406-732-4207; www.johnsonsofstmary.com; off US 89; tent/RV sites US$25/35, cabins US$149; ☺ May-Sep; ☎) Set on a knoll overlooking St Mary, RV sites here get gorgeous views of St Mary Lake with the crenellated peaks of the Continental Divide glimmering in the background. Tent sites, well suited to large groups, are shaded peacefully by alder trees. This long-running family operation also includes cabins, a cottage and Johnson's World Famous Historic Restaurant (mains US$10 to US$24).

St Mary KOA Campground
CAMPGROUND, CABINS $

(☑ 406-732-4122; www.koa.com/campgrounds/st-mary; 106 West Shore Rd; tent/RV sites US$45/72; ☺ mid-May–Sep; ☎) Set in an open meadow 1.6km (1 mile) down a paved road, beside St Mary's eponymous river, this unshaded campground can accommodate tents and RVs and also offers some cottages and cabins. A plethora of other services includes bike rental (US$2.50/20 per hour/day), canoe rental (US$10 per hour), a grocery store, coffee counter, laundry, hot tub, playground and the A-OK Grille.

Red Eagle Motel
MOTEL $

(☑ 406-732-4453; www.redeaglemotelrvpark.com; US 89; r US$95; ☺ mid-Apr–Nov; ☻) Perched on a small hill above St Mary Village, this basic motel is a crash pad for visitors intending to spend most of their waking time outdoors. Enjoy tranquillity away from the gadgetry of TVs, microwaves or fridges (although there's internet access at reception). Various restaurants are a short stroll down the hill, and the views of the park from the front balcony are to die for.

St Mary Lodge & Resort
HOTEL $$

(☑ 406-732-4431; www.glacierparkinc.com; cnr Hwy 89 & Going-to-the-Sun Rd; r US$139-345; ☺ mid-May–Sep; ✸☎) Despite mountains looming in the background and the park entrance a half-mile away, this hotel's location at the junction of Hwy 89 and the eastern terminus of the Going-to-the-Sun Rd is surprisingly mundane. It's part of a large, paved lot with a gas station, gift shop and grocery store. However, in terms of modern comforts it outdoes the rustic park lodges.

Myriad facilities include a coffee bar, the Snowgoose Grille and a grand stash of rooms, from motel-style to luxury teepees to plush rooms in the main Great Bear Lodge.

Rising Sun Pizza
PIZZA $$

(☑ 406-732-9995; Hwy 89; pizza from US$16; ☺ 4-11pm; ☎) Small-town locals generally greet any new joint with curiosity and excitement, but this pizzeria's positive reviews have outlived the initial honeymoon period. The menu, only whole pies produced with homemade sauce and dough, and salads, is as basic as the completely unadorned dining room.

Park Café
AMERICAN $$

(☑ 406-732-9979; www.parkcafe.us; US 89; mains US$12-25; ☺ 7:30am-9pm Jun-Sep) With its long-time celebrated pie-maker gone, along with its previous owner, the Park no longer enjoys the vaunted reputation among locals it once did. Hearty breakfasts, burgers and fairly high-priced mains such as bratwurst and ahi tuna, not to mention homemade pies, remain. So does the dilapidated diner decor.

Two Sisters Cafe
AMERICAN $$

(☑ 406-732-5535; www.twosistersofmontana.com; US 89; mains US$10-23; ☺ 11am-10pm Jun-Sep) 'Aliens welcome', blasts the colorful sign on the roof, whereas inside it's all honky-tonk Americana at this casual joint situated halfway between Babb and St Mary. It's run by two sisters of the Blackfeet tribe who insure that the quality of dishes such as chicken-fried steak and bison burgers remains above average.

Snowgoose Grille
STEAK $$$

(US 89; mains lunch US$5-9, dinner US$12-28; ☺ 6:30am-9:30pm mid-May–Sep) If you're craving an opportunity to break away from the hikers' breakfast/picnic-lunch monotony, try this wheelchair-accessible restaurant in the St Mary Lodge & Resort, where the steaks are succulent and the footwear is more heels than hiking boots.

East Glacier

A summer-only stop on Amtrak's *Empire Builder* route, East Glacier grew up around the train station (which splits the small, slightly scruffy settlement in half) and the adjacent Glacier Park Lodge. While its eating and sleeping options offer more variety than West Glacier, its location away from the Going-to-the-Sun Rd makes quick forays into the park less convenient.

Other facilities include a post office (15 Blackfoot Ave; ⊙9am-noon & 2-5pm Mon-Fri), ATMs and a couple of gas stations.

🛏 Sleeping & Eating

Brownie's   HOSTEL $
(☑406-226-4426; www.brownieshostel.com; 1020 Hwy 49; dm US$20, s/d US$30/40; ⊙mid-May–Sep; ⟨?⟩) Above Brownie's Deli & Bakery, this casual HI hostel is packed with travelers staying in the eight-person single-sex dorms or small, rustic private doubles. It has a common room, kitchen and balcony with a hodgepodge of secondhand furniture. Linen is provided free of charge. Those who want a decent night's sleep should bring earplugs.

Circle R Motel   MOTEL $$
(☑406-226-9331; www.circlermotel.net; 402 US 2; r/ste $100/190; ⊙year-round; ⟨?⟩) On East Glacier's little mall strip just east of the train station, old-school Circle R has added a two-story extension for the 2015 season. A modest 'workout room' and kitchenette is available for guests, alongside basically furnished rooms with TVs and good-sized bathrooms. Winter rates are, of course, better value.

★Glacier Park Lodge   HISTORIC HOTEL $$
(☑406-226-5600; www.glacierparkinc.com; r $169-256; ⊙Jun-Sep; ⟨?⟩ ⟨≋⟩) 🏊 Set in attractive, perfectly manicured, flower-filled grounds overlooking Montana's oldest golf course, this historic 1914 lodge was built in the classic national-park tradition with a splendid open-plan lobby supported by lofty 900-year-old Douglas fir timbers (imported from Washington State). Eye-catching Native American artwork adorns the communal areas, and a full-sized teepee is wedged incongruously onto a 2nd-floor balcony.

In keeping with national-park tradition, the rooms here are 'rustic' with no TVs, telephones or air-con; bathrooms and showers, especially, are small. Rocking chairs are dispersed inside, and out on the shaded porch; the pool out back has little shade. Wi-fi available in the lobby.

★Serrano's Mexican
Restaurant   MEXICAN $
(☑406-226-9392; www.serranosmexican.com; 29 Dawson Ave; mains US$11-16; ⊙5-10pm May-Sep) Just across the road from the train station, this is East Glacier's most buzzed-about

WORTH A TRIP

IZAAK WALTON INN

Izaak Walton Inn (☑406-888-5700; www.izaakwaltoninn.com; 290 Izaak Walton Inn Rd; r US$117-168, cabooses US$230; ⟨?⟩) Situated like a misplaced fragment of Shakespearean England within snowball-throwing distance of Glacier National Park's southern boundary, this mock-Tudor inn was originally built in 1939 to accommodate local railway personnel. It remains a daily flag-stop (request stop) on Amtrak's *Empire Builder* train route. Caboose cottages with kitchenettes are available, along with a historic GN441 locomotive refurbished as a luxury four-person suite (US$299).

Located close to the Park Creek area, the lodge became something of an incongruity after WWII, when a plan to build a new southern park entrance in the vicinity never materialized. Dubbed the 'Inn between' in the years since, the Izaak has enjoyed a modern renaissance with cozy rooms, a sauna and easy access to skiing trails.

restaurant. Renowned for its excellent iced margaritas, it also serves economical burritos, enchiladas and quesadillas in the vintage Dawson house log cabin, originally built in 1909. In back there's a deck for dining, and three tiny cabins (dorm/room US$18/45) in the adjoining garden.

Luna's Restuarant   AMERICAN $
(☑406-226-4433; www.lunasrestaurant.com; 1112 Hwy 49; mains US$8-18; ⊙4-9pm May-Sep; ⟨?⟩) Big burgers and even larger desserts, plus good salads such as a spinach walnut salad with huckleberry vinaigrette dressing.

Whistle Stop   AMERICAN $
(☑406-226-9292; 1024 3rd St; mains US$9-15; ⊙6:30am-9pm May-Sep) This casual place with a pleasant outdoor patio is a good spot to chow down on ribs; the barbecue sandwiches and burgers are only average.

Brownie's Deli & Bakery   CAFE, DELI $
(www.brownieshostel.com; 1020 Hwy 49; sandwiches US$5-8; ⊙7am-10pm mid-May–Sep; ⟨?⟩) Brownie's is an enterprising culinary one-man-band selling pastries, strong coffee, sandwiches, internet time and even the odd brownie or three.

Great Northern
Dining Room INTERNATIONAL $$
(Glacier Park Lodge; mains US$17-24; ⊙6:30am-9:30pm Jun-Sep) This big restaurant in the Glacier Park Lodge serves both upscale classics such as surf and turf and porterhouse steaks, as well as more ordinary burgers and fish and chips. If you want to mix things up, there are also a few Thai-inspired dishes on the menu.

🛈 Getting There & Around

The three-times-daily East Side Shuttle links East Glacier with Two Medicine (US$10), Cut Throat Creek (US$20), St Mary (US$30), Many Glacier (US$40) and Waterton (US$50). The Amtrak (www.amtrak.com) *Empire Builder* stops at the train station once daily traveling in either direction.

Dollar Rent A Car (☑ 406-226-4432; www. dollar.com) has an office in East Glacier.

Blackfeet Indian Reservation

The short-grass prairie east of Glacier is home to the Blackfeet Nation, which includes the Northern Piegan (Blackfeet), Southern Piegan and Blood tribes that came south from the Alberta area in the 1700s. Originally an agrarian people, the Blackfeet took quickly to horses and guns, eventually developing a reputation as the fiercest warriors in the West. Today approximately 10,000 tribal members reside on or around the reservation (www.blackfeetcountry.com), where unemployment is high and the struggling economy is primarily driven by ranching, farming and the sale of oil, natural gas, lumber and other mineral rights. Tribal members are rightfully proud of the Chief Mountain Hotshots, an elite fire-fighting crew of Blackfeet sent to the front lines of wilderness blazes throughout the West.

Browning, an ordinary, if rundown town 29km (18 miles) east of Glacier National Park, is where most of the reservation's amenities lie. Attractions are scarce, so it's worth mentioning the new skate park sponsored by Jeff Ament, one of the founders of Pearl Jam. The winter months can be fairly brutal, when strong, cold winds blow unimpeded across the plains and the town's two casinos begin looking like welcome refuges.

Every second weekend of July there's a pow-wow, a celebration of tribal arts, culture and food, held on the grounds to the north of the newly built Holiday Inn Express. **Heart Butte**, 45 km (28 miles) to the south, holds its annual pow-wow on the second weekend of August.

Browning is worth a detour if for no other reason than the excellent **Museum of the Plains Indians** (cnr Hwys 2 & 89, Browning; adult/child US$4/1; ⊙9am-4:30pm), which honors the culture of the Crow, Cree, Sioux, Cheyenne and, above all, the Blackfeet. Housed in a bland building that looks like a 1970s-era suburban elementary school, the museum provides extensive descriptions for exhibits of costumes, art and craftwork. Ernie Heavy Runner sits at the desk in front and can act as a guide if you choose. You can also chat with local artisans working in an attached gallery.

As far as overnighting in Browning, it's a no-brainer. Bed down in one of the teepees set rather majestically onto the plains at the **Lodgepole Gallery & Tipi Village** (☑406-338-2787; www.blackfeetculturecamp.com; US 89; 1-/2-/3-person teepees US$60/75/90), a large property 3.2km (2 miles) west of Browning. The owners, Darrell, a Blackfeet member, and his friendly and knowledgeable wife, Angelika, are both talented artists and show their works in the attached gallery. They can help arrange horseback-riding trips in the area.

Browning is a seasonal stop on Amtrak's *Empire Builder* from April to October with daily trains to Seattle and Chicago.

Whitefish

To be both 'rustic' and 'hip' within the same square kilometer is a hard act to pull off, but tiny Whitefish (population 8000) makes a good stab at it. Once sold as the main gateway to Glacier National Park, this charismatic New West town has earned enough kudos to merit a long-distance trip in its own right. Aside from grandiose Glacier (which is within an easy day's cycling distance), Whitefish is home to an attractive stash of restaurants, a historic train station and an underrated ski resort.

◎ Sights & Activities

City Beach Park BEACH, PARK
Glued to the southern shore of Whitefish Lake, this is where the whole town comes to date and debate in the summer months. The swimming area is roped off. Parking is free.

Whitefish Mountain Resort RESORT
(☑406-862-2900; www.bigmtn.com; adult/child US$71/37) Whitefish Mountain Resort, known as Big Mountain until 2008, guards 3000

NATIVE AMERICANS: LIVELIHOODS ON THE LAND

Where the grassy plains of the prairies meet the saw-toothed mountains of Glacier National Park, three legendary Native American tribes once intermingled – and the results weren't always peaceful.

One of the most populous tribes in the Montana region was the Blackfeet (Niitsítapi), a westward-dwelling subset of the Algonquian-speaking Plains Native Americans, a linguistic group that included the Crow, Cheyenne and Sioux. Warlike and highly mobile, the Blackfeet acquired horses in the 1730s from the Shoshoni people, and they used their new bounty to hunt buffalo and assert territorial rights over the mountains east of the Continental Divide where numerous sacred sites (including Two Medicine and Chief Mountain) were integral to the tribe's creation story.

Glacier's western slopes (this includes the present-day site of Apgar Village), meanwhile, were the domain of the more peaceful Plateau Native Americans, most notably the Flathead and Kootenai tribes. The former were Salish people, related through language to a much larger family of tribes that spread west as far as the Pacific coast. The latter were a cultural anomaly whose anthropological roots remain sketchy, and whose language is a linguistic isotope unrelated to any other Native American tongue.

The Salish and Kootenai were skilled fishermen and canoeists who subsisted on a diet of salmon plucked from the region's teeming rivers, but who sometimes crossed the Rockies to hunt buffalo. It was on these eastern forays that they came into contact and – inevitably – conflict with the more numerous Blackfeet. Though the Flatheads, over time, adopted some Plains Native American characteristics (horses and teepees for instance), the superior firepower of the Blackfeet meant that they slowly pushed the Plateau tribes back west.

In 1805–06, all three tribes had their first contact with white settlers when the Lewis and Clark Expedition passed through the region on an abortive attempt to find a northern route over the Rockies. Relations were initially cordial, particularly among the Salish and Kootenai, with whom the explorers traded horses, but events took a turn for the worse on the expedition's return leg when a small party led by Lewis got into a skirmish with a group of Blackfeet and two very young braves were killed. Tellingly, they were the only fatalities of the group's two-year adventure.

All three tribes suffered during the westward expansion of white settlers in the early 19th century and the near extinction of the buffalo that ensued. Relying increasingly on government money, Native Americans had little choice but to agree to one-sided treaties in 1855. The Salish and Kootenai were signatories to the ambiguous Hellgate Treaty, which merged them into the Confederated Salish and Kootenai tribes of the Flathead Nation (no Native American identifies as 'Flathead') on the Flathead Indian Reservation in northwest Montana. The Blackfeet, meanwhile, signed the Lame Bull Treaty the same year, creating a sprawling reservation a little larger than Delaware. The reservation originally included all of the Glacier National Park region east of the Continental Divide; however, in 1896, due to continuing economic difficulties, the Blackfeet sold a further 3200 sq km (2000 sq miles) of this land for US$1.5 million to the US government, which was intent on prospecting for copper and gold. When no minerals were found, the government, recognizing the area's potential as a tourist destination, formed Glacier National Park in 1910.

Today, approximately 10,000 Blackfeet live on a 6100-sq-km (3812-sq-mile) reservation immediately to the east of the park that includes important park access points such as St Mary and East Glacier (another 5000 or so live elsewhere, including many who have relocated to Seattle); Browning is the largest town and commercial hub. Unlike many Native American reservations, this is the Blackfeet's traditional territory. Despite their dispossession, the land in and around the east side of Glacier holds significant ceremonial and cultural significance. A battle that began in the early 1980s to prevent oil and natural gas drilling in the area continues to this day. You can learn more about the issue at www.badger-twomedicine.org.

To the southwest, approximately 6800 Flathead and Kootenai Native Americans inhabit a 5000-sq-km (1938-sq-mile) reservation between Kalispell and Missoula.

AROUND GLACIER NATIONAL PARK

Skiers descend from the summit at Whitefish Mountain Resort (p212)

acres of varied ski terrain and offers night skiing on weekends. In the summer there's lift-assisted mountain biking and zip-lines.

Glacier Cyclery   BICYCLE RENTAL
(☑ 406-862-6446; www.glaciercyclery.com; 326 2nd St E; bikes per day/week from US$35/160; ☺ 9am-6pm) A super-friendly and knowledgeable bike store (with rentals available) located in the center of Whitefish that extols the virtues and benefits of cycling in and around Whitefish and Glacier.

🛏 Sleeping

A string of chain motels lines US 93 south of Whitefish, but the savvy dock in town.

Whitefish Lake State Park Campground   CAMPGROUND $
(☑ 406-862-3991; State Park Rd; campsites US$20; ☺ late May–early Oct) On the southwest edge of Whitefish Lake, shady forested grounds hold 25 first-come, first-served sites, including one that is wheelchair-friendly.

Note that trains frequently rumble past all day and night; earplugs are recommended for light sleepers.

★ **Garden Wall**   B&B $$
(☑ 406-862-3440; www.gardenwallinn.com; 504 Spokane Ave; r US$155-215, ste US$275; ☎) Shoehorned into a shady spot, this elegant home is an efficiently run B&B. Guests enjoy art-deco rooms, log fires blazing in the living room on cold days, and gourmet breakfasts prepared by a chef (preceded by a wake-up coffee tray delivered to your room). The suite sleeps up to four.

Downtowner Inn   MOTEL $$
(☑ 406-862-2535; www.downtownermotel.cc; 224 Spokane Ave; r from US$130; ✸@☎) Cozier than the chain motels that line US 93 south of Whitefish, the cheerful Downtowner has spacious rooms, friendly staff and a morning bagel bar. (There's no longer a Jacuzzi and fitness center, though, despite the signs.)

🍴 Eating & Drinking

Buffalo Café   CAFE $
(www.buffalocafewhitefish.com; 514 3rd St E; breakfast mains US$8-10; ☺ 7am-2pm & 5-9pm Mon-Sat, from 8am Sun) Hopping with neighborly locals, the Buffalo serves hearty meals a step above standard cafe fare. Try the 'Buffalo pie,' a

mountain of poached eggs and various add-ins (cheese, veggies, bacon) piled atop a wedge of hash browns. You won't leave hungry.

Jersey Boy's Pizzeria   PIZZA $

(www.jerseyboyspizzeria.net; 550 E 1st St; mains US$10; ☺noon-9pm) Jersey attitude is in short supply in the service-with-a-smile at this popular pizza joint, although you might wish for a little more hustle in the kitchen when orders pile up on warm summer nights. Calzones and strombolis are obscenely huge, salads are excellent, and the pies (also sold by the slice) are the best in town.

Wasabi Sushi Bar &
the Ginger Grill   JAPANESE $$

(☑406-863-9283; www.wasabimt.com; 419 2nd St E; meals US$12-21; ☺5-11pm Tue-Sat) Yes, you're in Montana and, yes, this is exceptionally good sushi. Confirming Whitefish's cosmopolitan credentials, this place delivers the fish in both traditional and fusion styles. For those who don't crave it raw, you can choose from an array of cooked pan-Asian main dishes. Reservations are recommended.

★Montana Coffee Traders   CAFE

(www.coffeetraders.com; 845 Wisconsin Ave; ☺7am-6pm Mon-Sat, 9am-5pm Sun; 🛜) Whitefish's home-grown microroasters run this always-busy cafe, cum gift shop, cum computer-geek hangout, situated in the old Skyles building in the center of town. The organic, fair-trade beans are roasted in an old farmhouse on Hwy 93; the formidable paninis are prepared in-house.

Great Northern Bar & Grille   BAR

(www.greatnorthernbar.com; 27 Central Ave; ☺11am-2am) The look and vibe of this bar, not to be confused with the brewery of the same name, is a cross between biker saloon, classic dive and sports bar. It all works. Live music is performed in the vine-covered backyard patio, and there's ping-pong and billiards inside.

Casey's   BAR

(www.caseyswhitefish.com; 101 Central Ave; ☺11am-2am) Each of Casey's three floors has a different identity. The first is a restaurant with an upscale menu; the second is a large performance space with live music and bar; and, the pièce de résistance, the third is a rooftop lounge and bar with fantastic views and a good selection of craft beers, as well as an eclectic menu.

Great Northern Brewing Co   BREWPUB

(☑406-863-1000; www.greatnorthernbrewing.com; 2 Central Ave; ☺tours 1pm & 3pm Mon-Thu) Stop in to this high-ceilinged brewpub and tasting room for a pint or sampler anytime, or join a tour to up your beer-nerd game.

ℹ Information

Whitefish Visitor Center (www.whitefishvisit.com; 307 Spokane Ave; ☺9am-5pm Mon-Fri) Check with the Whitefish Visitor Center for info on activities.

ℹ Getting There & Away

S.N.O.W. Bus (www.bigmtncommercial.org; adult/child round-trip US$10/5; ☺Jul–early Sep) Daily summertime shuttle service between Whitefish (the most convenient stop is the Whitefish Library) and the Apgar Visitor Center in Glacier National Park. Tickets can be purchased online in advance, or at several commercial outlets in Whitefish, including Montana Coffee Traders.

Waterton Lakes National Park

Includes ➜

Day Hikes. 217
Driving 220
Cycling 222
Other Activities. 223
Sights 225
Tours. 227
Sleeping 227
Eating 230
Drinking &
Entertainment. 230
Shopping 230

Best Local Haunts

➡ Mexican Restaurant (p230)

➡ Grizz Cafe & Steakhouse (p230)

➡ Thirsty Bear Saloon (p230)

➡ Wieners of Waterton (p230)

Best Views

➡ Prince of Wales Hotel (p229)

➡ Cameron Lake (p225)

➡ Carthew-Alderson Trail (p219)

➡ Lineham Ridge (p224)

Why Go?

Small and obscure, at least compared to its neighbors to the north and south, Waterton is unrivaled in North America for offering almost instant access to rugged stretches of high alpine terrain well above the treeline. The equal of any of the parks in terms of flora and fauna, Waterton is a sanctuary for numerous iconic animals – including grizzlies, elk and cougar – along with 800-odd wildflower species.

Inaugurated in 1895 and part of a Unesco World Heritage site, Unesco Biosphere Reserve and International Peace Park, 505-sq-km (195-sq-mile) Waterton is geographically almost identical to Glacier, with which it shares a unique frontier border. The eponymous town, compact and quaint with modern hotels, sits prettily on the west side of Upper Waterton Lake, which is essentially the centerpiece of the park, with boat tours and shuttles to distant shoreline trailheads.

Road Distance (KM)

	Banff	Chief Mountain Border	Jasper	St Mary
Chief Mountain Border	385			
Jasper	290	670		
St Mary	410	45	700	
Waterton Townsite	370	35	660	75

Note: Distances are approximate

🚶 DAY HIKES

There are around 200km (125 miles) of trails in Waterton, and a number of them are multi-purpose routes, accommodating hikers, horseback riders, cross-country skiers and cyclists. Short, easy hikes lie in the vicinity of the townsite, while further afield, day hikes such as the much-lauded Carthew-Alderson Trail can rival anything in Glacier or Banff National Parks for variety of scenery.

🚶 Rowe Lakes

Duration Three hours round-trip (Lower Lake), five hours (Upper Lake), four hours (Rowe Meadow)

Distance 8km/5 miles round-trip (Lower Lake), 12.6km/7.9 miles (Upper Lake), 10.4km/6.5 miles (Rowe Meadow)

Difficulty Easy-moderate

Start/Finish Akamina Parkway

Elevation Change 250m (820ft)

Nearest Town Waterton Townsite

Transportation Tamarack hiker shuttle, car

Summary A tempting foray to the cusp of Waterton's easily accessible backcountry that may have you coming back for more.

This hike starts innocuously enough on the Akamina Pkwy approximately halfway between Waterton Townsite and Cameron Lake. The first section to Lower Rowe Lake is moderately easy. Beyond this, you can hike further up to Rowe Meadow and Upper Rowe Lake. For backcountry hikers this is the start and end point of the multiday Tamarack Trail (p224).

From the Akamina Pkwy, follow a sinuous but well-defined trail through a mix of larch and evergreen trees alongside Rowe Creek. The path can be muddy after rain, but with only 250m (820ft) of elevation gain spread over the first 4km (2.5 miles) to Lower Rowe Lake, the ascent is only gradual.

After 3.8km (2.4 miles) a trail branches off to the left. Follow this side trail 200m (220yd) to reach Lower Rowe Lake, a small, beautifully clear body of water laid out in a natural amphitheater. A 150m (492ft) waterfall links it with Upper Rowe Lake, which sits in a hanging valley above.

Back at the main trail you have a choice. Turn right and retrace your steps to the parkway or turn left toward Rowe Meadow, a wonderful array of wildflowers situated on the edge of the timberline. After crossing a creek at the far end of the meadow, you'll encounter another junction. The Tamarack Trail goes right here up to Lineham Ridge. A left turn offers a last steep climb to Upper Rowe Lake, actually two alpine lakes backed by the

Waterton Lakes – Day Hikes

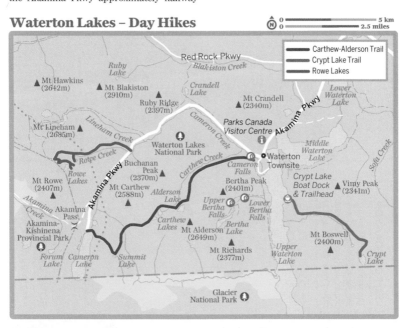

Waterton Lakes National Park

RED ROCK CANYON

This small canyon of striking colors and age-old geological formations boasts short hikes and beautiful mountain landscapes. (p221)

WATERTON TOWNSITE

Bucolic, well-manicured hamlet on Upper Waterton Lake offering modern luxuries – especially welcome for those returning from nearby backcountry adventures. (p225)

CARTHEW-ALDERSON TRAIL

Memorable hike that offers beautiful scenery and sweeping views. (p219)

CAMERON LAKE

Backed by the slopes of Mt Custer and tucked beneath the Continental Divide, this placid lake is popular with boaters and hikers looking to spot wildflowers and wildlife. (p225)

ROWE LAKES TRAIL

A foray to the cusp of Waterton's backcountry will leave you yearning to return. (p217)

Pincher Creek (35km);
Calgary (252km)

Cardston (26km)

Mountain View

ALBERTA

CANADA

Blood Timber Reserve

Birdseye Butte

Crooked Creek

Muskinonge Lake

Lower Waterton Lake

Entrance Station

Waterton River

Galwey Brook

Cottonwood Creek

Lakeview Ridge

Bellevue Hill (2078m)

Mt Galwey (2310m)

Waterton Lakes National Park

Mt Dungarvan (2525m)

Yarrow Creek

Dungarvan Creek

Mt Glendowan (2611m)

Goat Creek

Sage Pass

Avion Ridge

Twin Lakes

Mt Bauerman (2370m)

Kishinena (2228m)

South Kootenay Pass

Lost Mountain (2509m)

Lone Mountain (2381m)

Festubert Mountain (2520m)

Mt Hawkins (2642m)

Mt Blakiston (2910m)

Anderson Peak (2698m)

Snowshoe Trail Trailhead

Red Rock Canyon

Bauerman Creek

Blakiston Creek

Ruby Lake

Ruby Ridge (2397m)

Crandell Lake

Crandell Lake Trail

Mt Crandell (2340m)

Parks Canada Visitor Centre

Cameron Falls

Waterton Townsite

Red Rock Pkwy

Tamarack Trail

Lineham Lakes

Mt Lineham (2680m)

Lineham Trail

Buchanan Peak (2370m)

Carthew-Alderson Trail

Akamina Pkwy

Rowe Lakes Trail

Lower Rowe Lake

Mt Rowe (2407m)

Akamina Creek

Akamina Pass

Wall Lake

Forum Lake, Cameron Lake

Akamina-Kishinena Provincial Park

BRITISH COLUMBIA

Mt Carthew (2588m)

Summit Lake

Akamina Lake

Cameron Lake

Carthew Lakes

Mt Alderson (2649m)

Alderson Lake

Upper Bertha Falls

Bertha Lake

Lower Bertha Falls

Mt Richards (2377m)

Upper Waterton Lake

Middle Waterton Lake

Sofa Creek

Sofa Mountain (2475m)

Crypt Lake Boat Dock & Trailhead

Crypt Lake Trail

Mt Boswell (2400m)

Crypt Lake

Glacier National Park

North Belly River

Border Crossing

MONTANA (USA)

ALBERTA

BRITISH COLUMBIA

5 miles
10 km

N

vertiginous cliffs of the Continental Divide. Look out for marmots and bighorn sheep along the way.

Retrace your steps to the parkway. Strong, speedy hikers might want to climb a further 3.4km (2.1 miles) from the trail junction below Upper Rowe Lake to Lineham Ridge, one of the highest paths in the park, with views stretching for 50km (31 miles).

🥾 Carthew-Alderson Trail

Duration Six hours one way

Distance 20km (12.5 miles)

Difficulty Moderate

Start Cameron Lake

Finish Cameron Falls

Elevation Change 610m (1968ft)

Nearest Town Waterton Townsite

Transportation Tamarack hiker shuttle

Summary A panoramic parade through myriad forests, lush meadows and rough scree, showcasing the best of Waterton Lakes National Park.

Long considered one of North America's best mountain day hikes, so it comes as no surprise to find that many seasoned hikers make this scenic sojourn the subject of many repeat visits. As a result, the trail is well trafficked, though this takes nothing away from its beauty and incredible sweeping views.

Most hikers embark from Cameron Lake in the west (at the end of Akamina Pkwy) and tramp east back to Waterton Townsite (thus incorporating a gentler elevation gain). This scenario is made possible courtesy of the Tamarack hiker shuttle that runs from Waterton to Cameron Lake daily at 8:15am (9:15am in September) in summer (trail conditions permitting).

The trail heads southeast from the Cameron Lake boat ramp and enters a pine-encased slope alongside the lake's eastern shore, before ascending through a series of switchbacks to the smaller Summit Lake. This pool, surrounded by meadow and pine, incorporates the bulk of the hike's elevation gain.

Turn left (northeast) here for the Carthew Lakes Trail, a more gradual ascent through scrub, grass and then just open mountainside, with stupendous views over Montana, British Columbia and Alberta, while the distinctive form of Mt Cleveland frames the backdrop. The ascent culminates in several switchbacks

followed by a sharp scramble up loose scree to the ridgeline, where you'll get an expansive panorama including northern Glacier National Park summits to the south and Carthew Lakes to the north.

After the climbing is done, the trail descends from the ridge and weaves between the two starkly located Carthew Lakes, where snow can linger all summer. A steep cliff is negotiated at the exit of the Carthew basin before Alderson Lake becomes visible below. The trail reenters the trees shortly before the lake; a detour of 0.5km (0.3 miles) leads to the water itself.

From here the path follows the Carthew Valley, descending gradually through the forest to Waterton Townsite. A fitting end to the day is the impressive Cameron Falls (p225).

🥾 Crypt Lake Trail

Duration Six hours round-trip

Distance 17.2km (10.6 miles)

Difficulty Difficult

Start/Finish Crypt Lake Boat Dock & Trailhead

Elevation Change 710m (2329ft)

Nearest Town Waterton Townsite

Transportation Water taxi

Summary A veritable obstacle course that incorporates a ride in a water taxi, a climb up a ladder and a crawl through a narrow rocky tunnel to gorgeous Crypt Lake.

Crypt Lake or Carthew-Alderson? The choice is a toss up. Indeed, both hikes have gained kudos from leading outdoor writers for their interesting nooks and delightful scenery. No doubt the rating of Crypt Lake by *National Geographic* as one of the world's top 20 hikes in the 'Thrilling Trails' category in 2014 has only added to its popularity.

Once an overnight jaunt, Crypt Lake Trail is now tackled in a single day thanks to a water taxi service that transports hikers to the trailhead from the townsite marina twice daily, at 9am and 10am. The return taxi is in the afternoon, allowing hikers time for a relaxed lunch break at Crypt Lake.

From the trailhead, the ascent begins quickly, forging through thick green vegetation and copious clumps of wildflowers. Make plenty of noise here, as this trail has been known to attract the odd bear. Once in more open terrain, you'll take in up-close views of waterfalls, mountains and an unnamed lake below.

HIKING IN WATERTON LAKES NATIONAL PARK

REGION	NAME	DESCRIPTION	DIFFICULTY
Cameron Lake	Carthew-Alderson Trail	Memorable hike that offers beautiful scenery and sweeping views	moderate
Waterton Townsite	Rowe Lakes	Quick access to forested trails and shimmering alpine lakes	easy-moderate
Waterton Townsite	Tamarack Trail	Waterton's big backcountry adventure through glacial moraines and kaleido-scopic wildflower displays	moderate-difficult
Waterton Townsite	Crypt Lake Trail	Involves tunnel crawling and a cable-assisted walk along sheer cliffs	difficult

 Drinking Water   Restrooms   Ranger Station Nearby   Public Transport to Trailhead

The hike now turns into something of an obstacle course. First, you must climb up a narrow ladder to a small tunnel that will take you – via a combination of crawling or crouching – to a glacial cirque (the tunnel, though natural, was enlarged in the 1960s). On the other side you'll encounter a sheer rock face that must be negotiated with the assistance of a cable. It's not as terrifying as it sounds, but take extra care when it's raining. The cirque encloses gorgeous Crypt Lake, nestled in an amphitheater-like setting close to the international boundary (which crosses the lake's southern shore). Plenty of other hikers will, no doubt, be enjoying lunch in the exquisite natural surroundings. Choose your spot and soak up the beauty.

Ensure that you allow enough time for your return trip down, as the boats to the townsite are the only easy way back!

🚗 DRIVING

With only three paved roads, none of which measures more than 24km (15 miles) in length, opportunities for lengthy road trips in Waterton are limited. If you arrive by car, you'll probably end up plying at least one of either Akamina Pkwy or Red Rock Pkwy.

🚗 Akamina Parkway

Duration 20 minutes one way

Distance 16km (10 miles)

Speed Limit 50km/h (30mph)

Start Waterton Townsite

Finish Cameron Lake

Nearest Town Waterton Townsite

Summary Winter cross-country skiing trail and summer wildlife corridor, the Akamina makes for a dreamy afternoon motoring trip.

The road begins 500m (0.3 miles) from the townsite center. After you've climbed the first 500m (0.3 miles), you'll get a sideways glance at the town and lake below. Rocky cliff faces on the right and tree-packed slopes on the left predominate during the first few kilometers (2 miles), and soon you'll glimpse Cameron Creek.

The curious structure at the 7.6km (4.7-mile) mark is the Lineham Discovery Well National Historic Site, the first oil well in western Canada. It was struck in 1902, along with premature optimism that led to dubbing the area 'Oil City.' After two years the flow was poor, and the well dripped her last in 1936.

The parkway ends at the stellar Cameron Lake (p225).

🚗 Red Rock Parkway

Duration 20 minutes one way

Distance 15km (9 miles)

Speed Limit 50km/h (30mph)

Start Waterton Townsite

Finish Red Rock Canyon

Nearest Town Waterton Townsite

Summary A short but sweet sojourn to Red Rock Canyon, driving past over 500 million years of geological history.

DURATION	DISTANCE	ELEVATION CHANGE	FEATURES	FACILITIES	PAGE
6hr	20km (12.5 miles)	610m (1968ft)			p219
3hr	8km (5 miles)	250m (820ft)			p217
2 days	31.6km (19.6 miles)	1460m (4700ft)			p224
6hr	17.2km (10.6 miles)	710m (2329ft)			p219

View   Wildlife Watching   Backcountry Campsite   Fishing

Red Rock Pkwy originates at a junction with Hwy 5, about 8km (5 miles) southwest of the park entrance. This road, running alongside Blakiston Creek for much of its route, is full of wildflower-speckled prairie spilling onto incredible mountains. South of the parkway, the awe-inspiring Mt Blakiston is Waterton's tallest peak at 2910m (9547ft). A few picnic spots are dotted along the way, and at the 4.9km (3-mile) mark, Bison Jump – a small native history exhibit – is worth a stop.

Most visitors persevere to the end of the road, 15km (9 miles) in, where Red Rock Canyon sits colorfully aglow. A 700m (0.4-mile) self-guided loop trail circuits the edge of the canyon. Consisting of ancient Grinnell argillite, the canyon is a fantastic introduction to one of the geologically wondrous aspects of Waterton.

Akamina Parkway

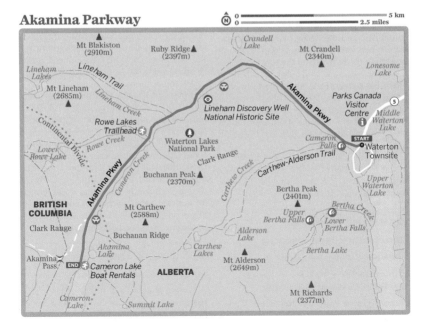

Red Rock Parkway

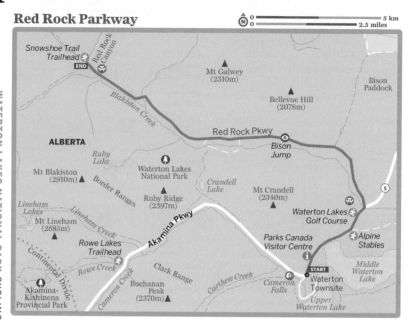

🚴 CYCLING

In contrast to Glacier, Waterton has five trails open for cycling. On top of the two we've described, you'll also find the **Akamina Pass Trail**, which is 1.3km (0.8 miles) one way; the **Wishbone Trail**, which is 21km (33.8 miles) round-trip; and the 6.9km (4.3-mile) **Kootenai Brown Trail**, which parallels the entrance road from the park gate to the townsite.

Cyclists on park trails should adhere to a few basic rules. Ride single file to prevent trail damage or erosion; alert hikers ahead of you when passing; and when encountering a horse, get off your bike and stand aside until it passes. Always stay on the trail and be careful not to surprise wildlife.

Mountain bikes can be rented in Waterton at **Pat's** (Map p226; ☎ 403-859-2266; www.patswaterton.com; 224 Mount View Rd; bikes per hour/day C$15/50). Helmets are included.

🚴 Crandell Lake Loop

Duration Three hours round-trip

Distance 20.6km (12.8 miles)

Difficulty Moderate

Start/Finish Waterton Townsite

Nearest Town Waterton Townsite

Summary Mix road biking with singletrack on a multifarious romp around Waterton's classic parkways.

Incorporating the hikeable Crandell Lake Trail with the paved Akamina and Red Rock Pkwys, this popular loop can be tackled from one of three starting points: Waterton Townsite; the Crandell Mountain Campground (off the Red Rock Pkwy); or a trailhead 6.4km (4 miles) along the Akamina Pkwy.

All three approaches make for a varied and pleasant half-day ride that mixes 6.4km (4 miles) of rocky off-road with 10km (6.2 miles) of smooth asphalt. The only technicalities come with the ascent to the lake (less steep if you travel anticlockwise), which involves a 100m (328ft) elevation gain from the respective parkways. The clear **Crandell Lake**, with Mt Crandell visible to its southeast, is a serene setting with sandy areas and rocks perfect for a picnic perch. Cyclists should beware of hikers on the Crandell Lake Trail and wildlife (including bears) on both parkways.

🚴 Snowshoe Trail

Duration 1½ hours round-trip

Distance 16.4km (10.2 miles)

Difficulty Moderate

Start/Finish Red Rock Canyon parking lot

Nearest Town Waterton Townsite

Summary Tackle part of the Tamarack Trail on this short but steep sojourn into Waterton's northwestern corner.

This fine Waterton cycle follows Bauerman Creek on an abandoned fire road from the Red Rock Canyon parking lot. The turnaround point is a Snowshoe Warden Cabin, 8.2km (5.1 miles) further on.

Don't be deceived by the initial wideness of the track; the gradient gets noticeably steeper beyond the Goat Lake turnoff, and there are also a couple of rocky streams that will need to be forded in late spring and early summer.

Wedged into the park's northwestern corner, mountain views are excellent throughout this ride, and vibrant wildflowers add color during summer. Although bikes aren't allowed on any of the connecting trails (including Castle Divide and Twin Lakes), the ride makes for a popular bike-hike excursion, with cyclists locking their bikes close to the trail junctions, before continuing along spur paths to destinations such as Goat Lake and Avion Ridge.

⚡ OTHER ACTIVITIES

Waterton offers all the activities available in Glacier, with a couple of hidden extras thrown in for good measure. Golf is possible inside the park perimeter or you can take to the trails on horseback. Even scuba diving is possible – committed divers brave the frigid waters of Upper Waterton Lake at Emerald Bay, where *Gertrude,* a 1900 paddle wheeler, sits 20m (66ft) below the surface.

Because its sedimentary rock is soft and crumbly, Waterton is not hugely popular for rock climbing, but the upper and lower bands of Bear's Hump offer 10 approaches ranging from grades 5.4 to 5.8, while aficionados rave about the park's ice-climbing potential.

Waterton Lakes Golf Course   GOLF
(Map p228; ☑ 403-859-2114; www.golfwaterton.com; green fees 9/18 holes C$35/47) Sterling scenery is part of the game at this 18-hole course.

Alpine Stables   HORSEBACK RIDING
(Map p228; ☑ 403-859-2462; www.alpinestables. com; guided rides per hour from C$40) Visitors interested in horseback riding should hook up with Alpine Stables, off Hwy 5 and across the road from the golf course. It has handsome horses suited for all levels, from never-ridden-before to advanced.

Awesome Adventures   DIVING
(☑ 403-328-5041; www.awesomeadventure.ca; 314 11th St S, Lethbridge) With no in-park dive specialists, your closest equipment rental and guide service is with this company located in Lethbridge.

Fishing & Boating

Fishing is popular in Waterton Lakes National Park, with the waters hosting 24 species of fish, including northern pike, whitefish and various types of trout.

A Parks Canada permit is required to fish in Waterton. Permits cost C$9.80 for the day or C$34.30 for the season and can be purchased at the visitor center, park headquarters or at campground entry booths. Not all lakes are open to fishing and there are some seasonal regulations; check first. There has

---

INTERNATIONAL PEACE PARK HIKE

A unique opportunity to visit two parks – and two different countries – in one day, the International Peace Park Hike leads participants on a free guided 13.7km (8.5-mile) walk alongside twinkling Upper Waterton Lake, from Waterton Townsite in Canada to Goat Haunt in Glacier National Park in the US. Led by a duo of rangers from both nations, hikers follow an undulating path (with some moderately difficult uphill sections) south through sun-dappled forest and scenic shoreline, to the unguarded border. Arriving at Goat Haunt late afternoon, you are first required to show your passport to special customs rangers. After that you are free to soak up the impressive mountainscape and examine exhibits in a small 'peace pavilion' at the boat dock. When making your reservation you will have assured passage on the 5:25pm boat back to Waterton (adult/child C$24/12).

The International Peace Park Hike departs from the Bertha Trailhead in Waterton at 10am every Saturday from early June to late August. Places are available for up to 30 people, but reserve beforehand at the Parks Canada Visitor Centre (p231) as the hike is perennially popular.

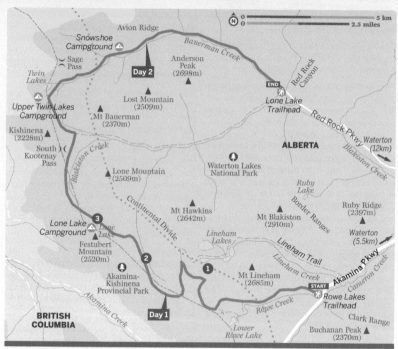

Overnight Hike
Tamarack Trail

START ROWE LAKES TRAILHEAD
END LONE LAKE TRAILHEAD
LENGTH TWO DAYS; 31.6KM (19.6 MILES)

Waterton's only real backcountry adventure is this moderately difficult hiking trail with an overall elevation change of 1460m (4700ft) – usually tackled over two days. Glacial moraines and wildflower meadows, lakes and larch, and perhaps even an animal or two, are viewed along the way. Tricky descents over scree, extreme winds at high altitude and long stretches without treatable water sources are potential difficulties that must be considered before heading out.

Choose between two starting points: the Rowe Lakes Trail off Akamina Pkwy for a clockwise loop, or the Lone Lake Trail from Red Rock Canyon for a counterclockwise alternative. Early autumn is the best time to make this journey, when the namesake tamarack tree or alpine larch (a deciduous conifer) sheds its needles in a riot of rustic yellows. The reservation-only Tamarack hiker shuttle can deliver you to your chosen trailhead.

From the Rowe Lakes trailhead, the hike junctions with the main Tamarack Trail at the 5.1km (3.2-mile) mark, before ascending ❶ **Lineham Ridge**. Offering breathtaking panoramic views, this ridge is a huge highlight. The trail soon leaves the ridge and traverses open slopes, then descends to the west bank of ❷ **Blakiston Creek**. From here, it's mostly a steep ascent to a saddle with Festubert Mountain in the background before descending to Lone Lake Campground, on the north side of ❸ **Lone Lake**. You can overnight here or carry on another 7.3km (4.5 miles) to Upper Twin Lakes Campground, beautifully situated just under Kishinena Peak. Lone Lake to Twin Lakes involves an easy descent past the South Kootenay Pass and Blakiston Creek trail junctions, the fording of a creek, a moderate climb to a saddle west of Mt Bauerman, and then a hike down scree. A third campground – Snowshoe – is only another 4.6km (2.9 miles) from here, and the striking colors of Red Rock Canyon are an easy 8.2 km (5.1 miles) from there along Bauerman Creek.

been a general move toward more catch-and-release fishing among anglers in recent years.

Popular hike-in destinations for anglers include Bertha Lake and Carthew Lakes.

Motorboats and water skis are permissible only on Upper and Middle Waterton Lakes. Wear a wetsuit as the water is cold. Waterton Shoreline Cruises (p227) manages the docking facilities at the townsite's marina.

Blakiston & Co Adventure Rentals
BOATING

(Map p226; ☑800-955-2552; Crandell Mountain Lodge; ☺Jun-Aug) Offers stand-up paddleboard (SUP) and kayaking rentals for Emerald Bay, the mostly calm patch of water across the street from the Crandell Mountain Lodge where this shop operates.

Cameron Lake Boat Rentals
KAYAKING, CANOEING

(Map p228; www.cameronlakeboatrentals.com; kayak per hour C$35; ☺8am-6:30pm Jul & Aug, reduced hours Jun & Sep) Rents boats for kayaking, canoeing or rowing on the exquisite Cameron Lake.

Winter Activities

In winter, Akamina Pkwy is the most popular access point for cross-country skiing, while the Cameron Lake area is a favorite for snowshoeing.

Waterton, along with Kootenay, Jasper and Banff, is considered to be one of the world's premier waterfall ice-climbing destinations. Since the sport comes loaded with a number of inherent risks, aspiring climbers are encouraged to check avalanche bulletins (☑250-837-2141; www.avalanche.ca). *Waterfall Ice: Climbs in the Canadian Rockies* by Joe Josephson is the definitive text on the topic.

◎ SIGHTS

◎ Waterton Townsite

The diminutive town of Waterton is a manicured and peaceful little place. Of course, it wouldn't warrant a visit if not for the gorgeous alpine scenery and outdoor adventures on its doorstep. It's low-key and walkable – really nothing more than a few streets – and its wintertime population shrinks to the size of an extended family (only around 35 residents). A number of short walking trails make the most of lakeside vistas. A 3.2km (2-mile) loop trail along Upper Waterton Lake and around the townsite provides a good introduction to the area. There's also the shorter 2km (1.2-mile) Emerald Bay Loop.

Cameron Falls
WATERFALL

(Map p226) Located at the west end of Cameron Falls Dr, a short hop from the central townsite, is this dramatically poised torrent of foaming water, notable among geologists for harboring the oldest exposed Precambrian rocks in the Canadian Rockies. Estimates suggest they are 1.5 billion years old, give or take the odd millennium. The lookout here is paved for wheelchair access and the falls are rather fetchingly lit up at night.

Upper Waterton Lake
LAKE

Visible all over town, this is the deepest lake in the Canadian Rockies, sinking to a murky 120m (394ft). One of the best vantage points is from the Prince of Wales Hotel, where a classic view is framed by an ethereal collection of Gothic mountains, including Mt Cleveland, Glacier National Park's highest rampart. A more placid spot is Emerald Bay, around by the marina, famous for its turquoise waters and ever popular with scuba divers.

◎ Cameron Lake

Backed by the sheer-sided slopes of Mt Custer, placid Cameron Lake, with an elevation of 1660m (5445ft), is tucked tantalizingly beneath the Continental Divide at the three-way meeting point of Montana, Alberta and British Columbia. The climax of the 16km (10-mile) Akamina Pkwy, the lake is a popular destination with day-trippers who come here to picnic, hike and rent boats. From foam flowers to fireweed, copious wildflower species thrive here, while grizzly bears are known to frequent the lake's isolated southern shores.

There are some interesting interpretive displays outlining the area's flora and fauna under a shelter adjacent to the parking lot, along with restrooms and a hut that sells snacks and sodas. A number of trails start from here, including the short Cameron Lakeshore and the ever-popular Carthew-Alderson.

Waterton Townsite

N 0 —————— 200 m
0 —————— 0.1 miles

Parks Canada Visitor Centre (500m);
Prince of Wales Hotel (850m);
Alpine Stables (1.8km);
Waterton Lakes Golf Course (1.8km);
Red Rock Pkwy (2.6km);
Park Entrance (7.1km)

Cameron Lake
(14km)

Emerald
Bay

WATERTON LAKES NATIONAL PARK

Waterton Townsite

◎ Sights
1 Cameron Falls A3

✦ Activities, Courses & Tours
Blakiston & Co
Adventure Rentals ....(see 7)
2 Pat's D2
3 Waterton Shoreline
Cruises D2

🛏 Sleeping
4 Aspen Village Inn C2
5 Bayshore Inn D2
6 Bear Mountain Motel C2
7 Crandell Mountain
Lodge B1
8 Northland Lodge A3
9 Waterton Glacier Suites C2
10 Waterton Lakes Resort C3
11 Waterton Townsite
Campground C4

✕ Eating
12 49° North Pizza C3
13 Grizz Cafe & Steakhouse D3
Mexican Restaurant ....(see 19)
14 Pearl's C3
15 Welch's Chocolates, Ice Cream &
Desserts C3
16 Wieners of Waterton C2
17 Zum's Eatery D3

◖ Drinking & Nightlife
18 Thirsty Bear Saloon D3

✪ Entertainment
19 Waterton Lakes Opera House C3

⌂ Shopping
20 Akamina Gifts & Book Nook D2
21 Tamarack Outdoor Outfitters C2
22 Waterton Heritage Centre D3

THE LONELIEST BORDER CROSSING IN THE US

Welcome to what must be the most low-key and pleasant border crossing in the US – and with not a car in sight! **Goat Haunt** is a rare foot-traffic-only land border between the US and Canada located at the southern end of Upper Waterton Lake, 9.6km (6 miles) below the 49th parallel international boundary. The nearest US road to this lonely outpost is the Going-to-the-Sun Rd, 46km (28.8 miles) to the south via a steep but visually stunning trail. Consequently most people arrive here from Canada on the MV *International,* a historic boat that sails south from Waterton Townsite four times daily (summer only). The boat has a 30-minute scheduled stopover that allows visitors to check out the 'haunt's' very basic facilities: a boat dock, restrooms, a hikers' shelter, drinking water, the peace pavilion interpretive exhibit (chronicling the history of the park and exploring the meaning of the word 'peace' worldwide) and a tiny **ranger station** (Goat Haunt; ⊙11am-5pm) that doubles up as one of North America's smallest border posts. Anyone staying longer than the 30-minute stop must clear customs, show valid photo ID and – should they be non-Canadian/American – have their passport stamped with a unique print of a goat!

Short- and long-term hiking options abound. You can walk 11.2km (7 miles) back to Waterton along the lakeshore, undertake a wild backcountry adventure up Waterton Valley beneath the shadow of 3190m (10,466ft) Mt Cleveland (the highest peak in the peace park), or indulge in one of half-a-dozen shorter hikes before catching a later boat back to Waterton.

☞ TOURS

Waterton Shoreline Cruises　　BOAT TOUR
(☎403-859-2362;　www.watertoncruise.com; adult/child C$45/22;　⊙May-Oct) Waterton Shoreline Cruises runs boats on Upper Waterton Lake. The service operates from early May to early October and leaves four times daily (10am, 1pm, 4pm and 7pm) during July and August. The 2¼-hour cruises with running commentary from knowledgeable and amusing guides are conducted on the vintage MV *International* boat, built in 1927, and stop at Goat Haunt, MT, for 30 minutes. Round-trip boat passengers to Goat Haunt do not have to go through customs before heading toward the Canadian sector again.

If you take the boat one way, hiking to or from Goat Haunt, you'll need your passport. The company also provides a 'shuttle' (C$22) to the trailhead for the Crypt Lake hike with two departures in the morning (9am and 10am) and two returns in the afternoon. This family-owned business has been around for several generations.

⌶ SLEEPING

For such a small town, Waterton is loaded with accommodations options offering TVs, wi-fi and air-con. July and August are insanely busy; book ahead.

Camping

In high season Waterton Townsite Campground can fill by late morning. If staying at Crandell Mountain or Belly River Campgrounds, you can use the showers at Waterton Townsite Campground free of charge.

★**Crandell Mountain Campground**　　CAMPGROUND $
(Map p228; ☎403-859-5133; Red Rock Pkwy; tent & RV sites C$22; ⊙mid-May–early Sep; ℗) For a rustic accommodations alternative, head out to this secluded camping spot a few minutes' drive from the park gates. Some of the loops, especially H and L, offer beautiful mountain views and direct access to Blakiston Brook. Evening ranger talks are held in an amphitheater.

Belly River Campground　　CAMPGROUND $
(Chief Mountain Hwy; tent sites C$16; ⊙May-Sep) Outside of the pay area of the park, this primitive campground sits in parkland terrain with aspen trees and far-off views of the mountains. Availability is first-come, first-served.

Waterton Townsite Campground　　CAMPGROUND $
(Map p226; ☎877-737-3783; www.reservation.pc.gc.ca; Vimy Ave; tent/RV sites C$28/39; ⊙May-Oct; ℗) Dominating the southern end of Waterton village, the town campground isn't ideal, but it's a means to an end. Consisting mainly of an enormous gopher-hole-covered field

Waterton Lakes National Park Region

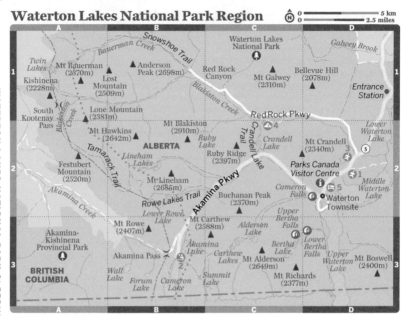

Waterton Lakes National Park Region

⊙ Activities, Courses & Tours
1 Alpine Stables D2
2 Cameron Lake Boat Rentals B3
3 Waterton Lakes Golf Course D2

⊜ Sleeping
4 Crandell Mountain Campground C2
5 Prince of Wales Hotel D2

aimed at RV campers, it has all the charm of camping in a grassy parking lot at a music festival. There are some treed sites near the edges, but by midsummer you'll be lucky to get anything. Book ahead for this one.

Lodging

There's a moratorium on development in the park, including in and around the townsite where all of the lodging is located, so it's unlikely there will be any expansion in alternatives anytime soon. Three lodges stay open year-round.

Bayshore Inn   HOTEL $$
(Map p226; ☑ 403-859-2211; www.bayshoreinn.com; 111 Waterton Ave; r C$174-225; ☺ Apr–Oct; P @ ☎) A large, spread-out place with rooms with balconies facing the lakefront, the Bayshore offers amenities such as satellite TV, heart-shaped bath tubs, coffee machines and honeymoon suites. There are also four on-site eating and drinking options, from the upscale Lake-

side Chophouse to the Starbucks-like Glacier Bistro (which serves Starbucks and has wi-fi).

Aspen Village Inn   HOTEL $$
(Map p226; ☑ 403-859-2255; www.aspenvillageinn. com; 111 Windflower Ave; r $114-210; ☺ May–mid-Oct; P ☎) Consisting of two main buildings and several cottage units, the Aspen is a family favorite with a kids' playground and resident deer finding shade in the grounds. Barbecues and picnic tables invite a warm-summer-night ambience, while satellite TV can take the chill out of a damp autumn evening.

Northland Lodge   B&B $$
(Map p226; ☑ 403-859-2353; www.northlandlodge canada.com; 408 Evergreen Ave; r C$130-215; ☺ mid-May–mid-Oct; ☎) None other than Louis Hill, the railroad magnate and genius behind most of the peace park's venerable lodges, built this Swiss-style B&B in 1927. This one, however, Hill built for *himself.* Take a tour before booking a room, as they vary in quality and some share a bath. All are furnished in a froufrou fashion.

Crandell Mountain Lodge   HOTEL **$$**
(Map p226; ☑ 403-859-2288; www.crandellmountain lodge.com; 102 Mount View Rd; r C$140-220; ☎) Doing a good impersonation of a Tudor cottage plucked from a quiet English village, the Crandell has old-fashioned rooms with a front deck facing Emerald Bay across the street.

Bear Mountain Motel   MOTEL **$$**
(Map p226; ☑ 403-859-2366; www.bearmountain motel.com; 208 Mount View Rd; r from C$119; ☉ mid-May–Sep; ℗) Upfront about its offerings, Bear Mountain is a standard retro-style motel (in other words, it could use an update) with small but serviceable rooms at an affordable rate.

★ **Prince of Wales Hotel**   HISTORIC HOTEL **$$$**
(Map p228; ☑ 403-859-2231; www.princeofwales waterton.com; Prince of Wales Rd; r from C$239; ☉ May-Sep; ℗ ☎) With a Hogwarts-like setting on a bluff overlooking Upper Waterton Lake, the grand Prince of Wales blends Swiss-style architecture with the atmosphere of a Scottish castle. The hotel is definitely Old Empire, exhibiting such inherent British-isms as waitresses in kilts and high tea in the main lounge. Not far outside the large lake-facing windows, a rawer wilderness awaits.

This regal hotel built by the US–owned Great Northern Railway is the only Canadian link in its chain of historic accommodations.

Waterton Lakes Resort   RESORT **$$$**
(Map p226; ☑ 403-859-2150; www.waterton lakeslodge.com; 101 Clematis Ave; lodge C$200-245, ste C$234-300; ℗ ☎ ☒) A family-oriented sprawler with the kind of ample facilities that will make you feel a million miles from the trailhead, this place has a gym, indoor pool, hot tub, and snazzy on-site lounge and grill (Vimy's). Large lodge rooms (up to four people) come in standard or deluxe – the latter have fireplaces and Jacuzzis. Suites have kitchenettes.

Waterton Glacier Suites   HOTEL **$$$**
(Map p226; ☑ 403-859-2004; www.waterton suites.com; 107 Windflower Ave; ste from C$239; ℗ @ ☎ ☒) This polished year-round lodge counts 26 rooms, all fully equipped with whirlpool bath, satellite TV, gas fireplace, fridge, microwave and air-con. If it's the wilderness you're after, stick to the backcountry campgrounds. If you prefer a little frontcountry luxury, this could be your bag.

WATERTON LAKES NATIONAL PARK SLEEPING

FROM EXPLORATION TO CONSERVATION

Englishman Peter Fidler, of the Hudson Bay Company, is thought to be the first European to have explored this southern portion of the Canadian Rockies, setting out in 1792. Explorer Thomas Blakiston first came upon Waterton Lakes in 1858, naming them after famous British naturalist Charles Waterton.

The seed to designate the area a reserve was sown by Fredrick William Godsal, a rancher and conservationist in southern Alberta who had the prescience to see that, if the beautiful lakes region was not hastily set aside as protected land, private interests would soon take hold. In 1893 he wrote a letter to William Pearce, the superintendent of mines who, in turn, urged government officials in Ottawa to consider the issue and, in 1895, what is now known as Waterton Lakes was given protective status by the Canadian federal government as a forest park.

In the days before the 1930 National Parks Act, Cameron Valley had a brief stint as an 'Oil City,' beginning in 1902, when copious barrels of the liquid gold poured out from western Canada's first oil well. The oil discovery also led to the foundation of a townsite, whose first structures included a cookhouse, stable and blacksmith's shop. In 1910, 150 town lots were offered for leasehold at C$15 per annum and the settlement opened up its first hotel, but, when the oil dried up prematurely a few years later, local businesses quickly turned their attention to tourism.

Fortunately, the changes occurred just as Louis W Hill, son of Great Northern Railway magnate and 'Empire Builder' James J Hill, was formulating a plan to link Waterton to his great chain of railway-inspired hotels as a means of circumventing Prohibition in the US. A Swiss-style hotel, occupying a prime perch overlooking windy Upper Waterton Lake, opened in 1927 and was named for the then Prince of Wales (later Edward VIII).

Linked with Glacier in the world's first International Peace Park in 1932, Waterton had the distinction of becoming the first Canadian national park to be designated a Unesco Biosphere Reserve in 1979. In 1995 it was declared a Unesco World Heritage site.

✕ EATING

Wieners of Waterton
HOT DOGS $

(www.wienersofwaterton.com; 301 Windflower Ave; hot dogs C$10; ⊙11am-11pm; ✍) Not all wieners are junk and those served here approach the gourmet level, including much-sought-after vegetarian varieties. Rightfully popular – lines out the door are common in the summer.

49° North Pizza
PIZZA $

(Map p226; ☑403-859-3000; www.49degreesnorth pizza.com; 303 Windflower Ave; small/medium/large pizza C$10/15/20; ⊙noon-10pm May-Sep) Superior pizzas – the 'gourmet' option with bison and Saskatoon berries is recommended – to its next-door competition, plus a nice outdoor patio.

Mexican Restaurant
MEXICAN $

(Map p226; ☑403-859-2466; www.watertonlakes operahouse.wordpress.com; Windflower Ave, Waterton Lakes Opera House; mains US$9-22; ⊙10am-10pm Wed-Sun mid-May–Oct) Other than a paper menu taped to the seemingly defunct ticket booth there's little signage indicating there's a restaurant inside the town's 'opera house.' It's a funky place set up in front of the stage serving good tacos, burritos, burgers and sandwiches.

Welch's Chocolates, Ice Cream & Desserts
DESSERTS $

(Map p226; cnr Windflower Ave & Cameron Falls Dr; ⊙9am-10pm May-Oct) The front of this rambling shop, a family-run Waterton institution in business for over 50 years, is filled with a Willy Wonka's worth of homemade chocolates in fudge and candy form. There's an equally kaleidoscopic choice of ice cream, pies and pastries, and you can munch on your goodies and down coffee out on the wraparound porch.

Pearl's
CAFE $

(Map p226; www.pearlscafe.ca; 305 Windflower Ave; mains C$13; ⊙7am-11pm mid-May–Sep; 🛜) This casual place doubles as a cafe and pizzeria, with an especially inviting sunny front patio. Several hearty, innovative variations on French toast are highly recommended for hikers looking to calorie- and carbo-load in the morning. Sandwiches, salads and specialty pizzas are available the rest of the day.

Zum's Eatery
CANADIAN $

(Map p226; ☑403-859-2388; 116b Waterton Ave; mains C$13-18; ⊙8am-9:30pm May–mid-Oct) Good homestyle cooking of the burger, pizza and fried-chicken variety is brought to you by hard-up students working their summer breaks. The lack of sophisticated flavors is made up for by the character of the decor: several hundred North American license plates embellish almost every centimeter of wall.

★ Grizz Cafe & Steakhouse
STEAK $$

(Map p226; ☑403-859-2676; 110 Waterton Ave; mains C$15-44; ⊙5pm-midnight Tue, 11am-9pm Wed-Mon mid-May–mid-Sep) Opened by a couple of local boys who grew up working around town, Grizz has added a dash of contemporary cool to the summer dining scene. It's embraced as much as a place to down early-evening drinks on the outdoor patio as for its use of local ingredients and its excellent steaks and burgers.

The burger and duck sandwiches are topped by homemade blackberry jam and the 16oz porterhouse and wild boar chops are as good as you'll find in the big city.

☆ DRINKING & ENTERTAINMENT

Hang around the lakefront of an evening and chances are somebody will be tuning up a guitar or cracking open a few beers.

Thirsty Bear Saloon
PUB

(Map p226; ☑403-859-2211; 111 Waterton Ave; ⊙4pm-2am Mon-Sat mid-May–Sep) Wild nights in the wilderness happen in this pub/performance space aided by live music, karaoke and good beer.

Waterton Lakes Opera House
LIVE PERFORMANCE

(Map p226; ☑403-859-2466; www.watertonopera house.ca; cnr Cameron Falls Dr & Windflower Ave; tickets C$10) Waterton has its own live-performance space (which also doubles as a Mexican restaurant), with shows starting at 8pm. Check the website for an up-to-date schedule of events.

🛍 SHOPPING

Akamina Gifts & Book Nook
SOUVENIRS, BOOKS

(Map p226; ☑403-859-2361; 108 Waterton Ave; ⊙mid-May–Sep) This souvenir shop can satisfy any desires for maple syrup, kitschy gifts and replacement T-shirts, along with park-related literature.

Tamarack Outdoor Outfitters
OUTDOOR EQUIPMENT

(Map p226; ☑ 403-859-2378; www.hikewaterton.com; Mount View Rd; ☺ 8am-8pm May-Sep) Waterton's most comprehensive equipment store, which stocks everything from backpacks to bear spray. Also runs shuttles for hikers and exchanges US currency.

Waterton Heritage Centre
BOOKS

(Map p226; ☑ 403-859-2267; 117 Waterton Ave; ☺ 9am-9pm mid-May–late Sep) Basically a gift shop, bookstore and information desk for the Blackfeet Nation, run by the nonprofit Waterton Natural History Association. Inside you'll find a large mural of homesteader and oil prospector John 'Kootenai' Brown's arrival in Waterton in the 1870s by Albertan artist Donald Frache.

ℹ Information

Waterton is essentially a three-lane town: lodgings, restaurants and other services line Mount View Rd, Waterton Ave and Windflower Ave.

The closest town with full services is Pincher Creek (population 3665), 55km (34 miles) north via Hwy 6. To the east, Cardston (population 3475) is 56km (36 miles) from the park on Hwy 5. En route to Cardston, the small hamlet of Mountain View, 20km (12.6 miles) from the park, has limited amenities.

INTERNET
The town itself provides free, if generally weak, wi-fi. Many of the restaurants and cafes also have their own.

MEDICAL SERVICES & EMERGENCY
Police, Fire & Ambulance (☑ 403-859-2636)
Royal Canadian Mounted Police (☑ 403-859-2244; 202 Waterton Ave; ☺ May-Oct)

MONEY
Most businesses in Waterton Townsite will accept US dollars. The caveat, however, is that they won't calculate the conversion rate, which means you lose out; debit and credit cards are good options. Pat's, Prince of Wales Hotel, Caribou Clothes, Bayshore Inn and Tamarack Outdoor Outfitters have ATMs; the latter is also one of the only places in town to exchange US for Canadian dollars.

POST
Post Office (102a Windflower Ave; ☺ 8:30am-4:30pm Mon-Fri)

SHOWERS & LAUNDRY
The **Waterton Health Club & Recreation Centre** (101 Clematis Ave) has public showers (C$3) and a laundry; you can use the whole facility (pool,

ℹ WHEN YOU ARRIVE

➡ The park is open 24 hours a day, 365 days a year, although many amenities and a couple of park roads close in winter.

➡ Entry costs C$7.80/3.90 per adult/child aged six and up per day. An annual Waterton pass costs C$39.20. Free park admission is the norm on Canada Day (July 1) and Parks Day (third Saturday in July).

➡ Passes, to be displayed on your vehicle's windshield, are valid until 4pm on the date of expiration. If you enter the park when the booth is shut, get a pass early the next morning at the Parks Canada Visitor Centre or the Parks Canada Administration office.

➡ Upon entering, you'll receive a map of Waterton Lakes and Glacier National Parks, and the quarterly information-packed newspaper *Waterton-Glacier Guide*.

spa, sauna and gym) for C$6 per day. It's part of the Waterton Lakes Resort complex. Showers at the Waterton Townsite Campground are available to campers there and at Crandell Mountain.

Laundromat (Windflower Ave; ☺ 7am-9pm) Only accepts Canadian currency – be sure you have at least four dollar coins, and a bunch of 25¢ coins for the dryer.

TOURIST INFORMATION
The **Parks Canada Visitor Centre** (☑ 403-859-2378; www.pc.gc.ca/waterton; ☺ 8am-7pm May-Sep), across the road from the Prince of Wales Hotel, has a wealth of front- and backcountry information. The park has no separate ranger stations, though staff at Waterton Townsite and Crandell Mountain Campgrounds can provide area information.

From early October to early May, **Parks Canada Administration** (☑ 403-859-5133; Mount View Rd; ☺ 8am-4pm Mon-Fri) serves as the visitor center.

ℹ Getting There & Away

Waterton Lakes National Park lies in Alberta's southwestern corner. The closest airport, though with limited service, is in **Lethbridge** (p275), 130km (78 miles) to the northeast. **Calgary International Airport** (YYC; www.calgaryairport.com) is 264km (159 miles) north.

The one road entrance into the park is in its northeast corner along Hwy 5. Most visitors coming from Glacier and the USA reach the

ℹ WILDERNESS PERMITS & REGULATIONS

Permits are not required for day hikes, but overnight trips do require them. Up to 24 hours before the start of your journey, make arrangements at the visitor center. The nightly fee is C$9.80 per adult. Kids 16 years and under get free permits. All of the backcountry sites are reservable, and advance **reservations** (☑ 406-859-5133) can be made up to 90 days ahead; an extra fee of C$11.70 is charged.

junction with Hwy 5 via Hwy 6 (Chief Mountain International Hwy) from the southeast. From Calgary and Pincher Creek to the north, Hwy 6 shoots south toward Hwy 5 into the park. From the east, Hwy 5 through Cardston heads west and then south into the park.

Waterton is a weak link in Alberta's already scant public transportation network. From the north the nearest public transport that will get you to the park is from the town of Pincher Creek on a daily Greyhound (www.greyhound.ca) bus from Calgary. From here you'll need to book a taxi with Pincher Creek Taxi (p276) to travel the last 45km (30 miles; C$65, 45 minutes) to Waterton Townsite.

At the time of writing, it looked as though the East Side Glacier shuttle would end its service to the Prince of Wales Hotel by the 2016 season. It will still drop passengers off at the **Chief Mountain Border Crossing** (⊙ 7am-10pm Jun-Labour Day, 9am-6pm mid-May-late May & Labour Day-Sep 30), where you can connect to the Tamarack Outdoor Outfitter's shuttle to town (C$20); reservations for both are necessary.

ℹ Getting Around

BICYCLE

In marked contrast to Glacier, biking in Waterton is both popular and encouraged. Indeed, you can rent out everything from mountain bikes to large two-person rickshaws from Pat's (p222) in the townsite. The multipurpose Kootenai Brown Trail links the park gate with the townsite and there are four further designated trails open to bicycles.

CAR & MOTORCYCLE

The speed limit in the townsite is 30km/h (19mph) unless otherwise posted; campgrounds post 20km/h (12mph) limits. Akamina Pkwy has a limit of 50km/h (31mph) unless otherwise posted.

The town's two gas stations are at Pat's and Tamarack Outdoor Outfitters, both on Mount View Rd and open May to October; to fuel up in winter, head to Mountain View. Parking is simple around town; there are no meters or any unusual restrictions, and the town has a few free parking lots (no parking between 11pm and 6am).

PUBLIC TRANSPORTATION

Boat

Waterton Shoreline Cruises (p227) operates a water-shuttle service to the east shore of Upper Waterton Lake for the Crypt Lake trailhead. The boat leaves Waterton marina at 9am and 10am and picks up returns at 4pm and 5:30pm during July and August. Throughout May, June and September the service is reduced to one boat daily (10am departure and 5:30pm pickup). The round-trip fare is C$15/7.50 per adult/child.

Bus

Tamarack Outdoor Outfitters (p231) runs hiker shuttles that depart daily from the store in season. The Cameron Express (C$13.50) to Cameron Lake – handy for Carthew-Alderson Trail hikers – leaves daily at 8:15am or 9:15am (depending on the date); reserve your seat in advance in person or by phone. Staff can also arrange customized service throughout the park.

Understand Banff, Jasper & Glacier

THE PARKS TODAY **234**

Discover how the national parks are facing up to the challenges of conservation and climate change, and how First Nations people are addressing their future.

HISTORY **236**

The story of how the parks came to be involves pioneering explorers, intrepid mountaineers, enterprising railroad magnates and enduring Native American tribal nations.

GEOLOGY **243**

The views are never less than spectacular, but you'll have a better appreciation of the scenery if you understand how it was formed and how it's changing.

WILDLIFE **246**

From native berries that fill the bellies of bears to charismatic megafauna, the Rocky Mountains are home to all sorts of wonderful wildlife.

CONSERVATION **254**

Protecting the precious natural environment of the national parks is perhaps more vital now than ever, so it's important to understand the issues and what you can do to help.

The Parks Today

Fire and ice and natural cycles of destruction and regeneration have shaped the ecosystems and landscapes of these parks for millennia. However, the quickening pace of climate change, especially warming, means that today's visitors, whose impact must be managed, will likely be the last to experience the parks as generations before have done. Meanwhile, Native American people on both sides of the international border continue to actively assert their relationship to the lands and the traditions that have sustained them.

Best on Film

Brokeback Mountain (2005) An unorthodox cowboy tale partly filmed in Kananaskis Country.

The Shining (1980) The opening scene tracks a car plying its way along the Going-to-the-Sun Rd in Glacier National Park.

River of No Return (1954) The peroxide beauty of Marilyn Monroe is pitted against the natural beauty of Banff and Jasper.

Days of Heaven (1978) Terrence Malick's magnum opus utilized Waterton and Banff for its stunning cinematography.

Inception (2010) Fortress Mountain in Kananaskis Country served as the setting for this film's ski-chase scene.

Best in Print

The Melting World (Christopher White; 2013) What the warming climate is doing to Glacier's glaciers.

People Before the Park (Sally Thompson, Kootenai Cultural Committee & Pikunni Traditional Association; 2015) Tribal histories of Glacier before it was a park.

Old Indian Trails of the Canadian Rockies (Mary Schäffer; 1911) Early-20th-century account of Schäffer's wilderness adventures.

Night of the Grizzlies (Jack Olsen; 1969) The story of two deadly bear attacks on the same night.

First Nations

Formalized in a treaty (the first since the 1880s), there's now an ongoing First Nations effort to reintroduce buffalo into the northern tier of Glacier National Park, as well as neighboring tribal areas in Alberta, Canada. The endeavor is spearheaded by the InterTribal Buffalo Council, whose president, Ervin Carlson, is a member of the Blackfeet tribe. The long-term goal is the restoration of the buffalo's ceremonial and cultural standing, not fully realized since the late 19th century. In order to accomplish this, the traditional roaming patterns of the buffalo, which include crossing the international border (sans passports), need to be restored. Not surprisingly, northern Rockies ranchers are not on board. In the meantime, the Blackfeet also see potential in tourism: plans call for the building of an interpretive center on US 2 dedicated to the history of the buffalo, as well as overnight buffalo drives where tourists can sleep in teepees along the way.

In another significant milestone, Energy Keepers – a corporation formed by the Salish and Kootenai confederation – took over ownership of the Kerr Dam on the Flathead River near Polson, MT, in September 2015, renaming it the Salish Kootenai Dam. Opposition to the dam was strong among tribal leaders when it was originally proposed in 1930 – understandably so, as it was built on an important religious site without consultation. Now, however, it will be the first Native American–owned hydroelectric facility in the US and, equally important, it will be a return to the historical management of the river and lake as natural resources by local tribespeople.

The Heat is On

South of the 49th parallel, Glacier National Park juggles issues of both the hot (forest fires) and cold (melting glaciers) variety. Ongoing studies by the US Geological Survey on Glacier's 'rivers of ice' have revealed that many of these frozen behemoths have shrunk by more than a third since the 1960s – evidence enough, suggest some scientists, of potentially damaging climate change. And even more dramatically, the consensus from the scientific community is that not a single Glacier National Park glacier will survive past 2030 (some say as soon as 2020). North of the border, the easily accessible Athabasca Glacier in Jasper National Park is melting at an alarming rate of approximately 5m (5.5yd) a year.

The parks have always faced an annual battle with summer fires, Glacier especially, but the frequency and intensity of the blazes have increased. Over 10% of Glacier National Park's total tree cover burned in 2003, the hottest summer on record. The heat was turned up again in 2006 when over 137 sq km (53 sq miles) was razed in the Red Eagle Fire on the south side of St Mary Lake. The Reynolds Creek Fire in August 2015 shut down the east side of Going-to-the-Sun Rd, while in Jasper the Excelsior Fire resulted in the temporary evacuation of the Maligne Lake area after an exceptionally dry spring and summer. Acknowledged as an important natural process, the fires become problematic when human-ignited and/or when they threaten property and livelihoods. Also, importantly, they burn a large hole in the area's economy.

Beyond Borders

Despite the fact that the pristine wilderness areas of Banff, Jasper and Glacier are protected, the areas just outside the park boundaries are continually threatened by encroaching development. Oil and natural gas exploration either exists or is in the proposal stage throughout the region. And, in part because of the impact of warming, wildlife seeking more suitable habitats – and seemingly oblivious to signage marking park borders – roam elsewhere. Conservationists recognize the growing importance of not only safeguarding the status of the parks, but equally important, of expanding protections beyond park borders.

In collaboration with a handful of ranching families, tens of thousands of acres of private lands adjoining Waterton Lakes National Park in Canada have been preserved. Beginning in 1997, it's considered one of the country's largest conservation projects. Not far south of the border, the passage of the Rocky Mountain Front Heritage Act in December 2014 meant an additional 270 sq km (105 sq miles) was added to the deservedly well-loved Bob Marshall Wilderness Area just to the south of Glacier. Another several hundred thousand acres of Bureau of Land Management areas, national forest and conservation management areas were also earmarked for additional protections.

BANFF AREA: 6641 SQ KM (2564 SQ MILES)

JASPER AREA: 11,228 SQ KM (4335 SQ MILES)

GLACIER AREA: 4099 SQ KM (1583 SQ MILES)

WATERTON LAKES AREA: 505 SQ KM (195 SQ MILES)

ecoregions of Banff
(% of national park)

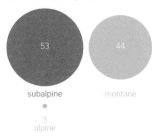

53 — subalpine

44 — montane

3 — alpine

if 100 people come to Banff

44 visit in Summer
21 visit in Spring
20 visit in Autumn
15 visit in Winter

population per sq mile

BANFF   JASPER   CANADA

≈ 1 people

History

First Nations people lived for millennia in scattered nomadic tribes in the areas that later became Jasper, Banff, Glacier and Waterton Lakes. In the late 18th century European expeditions edged unstoppably west. Exploration quickly led to exploitation, and some of the pristine land was mined for minerals, while other parts were earmarked by cross-continental railroad companies. All four parks were inaugurated between 1885 and 1910 through an unconventional alliance between foresighted conservationists and railway entrepreneurs eager to market the region as America's very own Swiss Alps.

Banff National Park

The history of Banff National Park begins in 1875 with the selection of Kicking Horse Pass, just west of the present-day park, over the more northerly Yellowhead Pass (in present-day Jasper), as the route for the nascent Canadian Pacific Railway (CPR). It was during the building of this railway in 1882 that three railroad laborers, William and Tom McCardell and Frank McCabe, stumbled upon the Cave and Basin hot springs at the base of Sulphur Mountain.

While Stoney Aboriginals had known about the springs and their supposed healing powers for centuries, it took the entrepreneurship of the trio to bring the waters to national attention. But, caught up in an acrimonious battle over ownership rights, the workers' tentative proposal to develop the springs as a lucrative tourist destination was rudely quashed by a Canadian government that had already, surreptitiously, made similar plans of its own.

In 1885, as the last spike was driven into the transcontinental railway at Craigellachie in British Columbia, a 26-sq-km (10-sq-mile) federal reserve was established around Banff Springs by the Conservative government of John A MacDonald. Sensing a tourist bonanza, not just from the recuperative springs, but from the astounding mountainscapes that surrounded them, the fledgling CPR was quick to jump on the bandwagon. 'If we can't export the scenery, we'll import the tourists,' announced CPR president William Van Horne portentously in 1886. His idea was to build a luxurious chain of grand hotels across the railway network that would

For a comprehensive history of the Rocky Mountain parks go to the website of Parks Canada (www.pc.gc.ca) or the US National Park Service (www.nps.gov).

TIMELINE	10,000 BC	1750	1793
	First Nations tribes begin to settle and hunt throughout the Rockies. Groupings include the Kootenay and Stoney from the high plateaus and the bison-hunting Piegan (North Blackfeet) from the plains.	European explorers and traders arrive in the area via the fur trade. The introduction of modern weapons, European diseases and horses filters down to First Nations tribes, causing disruption.	British explorer Alexander Mackenzie becomes the first European to cross the Rocky Mountains via the Peace and Fraser River systems on his journey to the Pacific coast in British Columbia.

lure wealthy tourists and repay the railway's outstanding loans. The plan clearly worked. Opened in 1888 as the grandest and most expansive hotel in the chain, the chateau-style Banff Springs Hotel was a runaway success and quickly established itself as an icon of Canadian architecture.

By 1888, over 5000 tourists had been ferried into the embryonic park to be rejuvenated in the magic spring water, and Banff Town listed 300 permanent residents, as well as churches, hotels, saloons and shops. The national park, which had been Canada's first – and the world's third – when it was created in 1885, was expanded in 1892 to include the area surrounding Lake Louise and, before long, Banff had spawned another of Van Horne's fairy-tale hotels, the beguiling Chateau Lake Louise.

> In 1885 Banff became the world's third national park (and the first in Canada), after Yellowstone in the US, inaugurated in 1872, and Royal National Park in Australia, founded in 1879.

Welcoming the Masses

A coach road was opened to Banff in 1911, and the following year public traffic was allowed into the park. Suddenly the wilderness was accessible to all kinds of visitors, rather than just wealthy Victorians, and the opportunities for outdoor recreation multiplied. Campsites were set up on Tunnel Mountain and at Two Jacks Lake, and affordable lodging began to appear in the Bow Valley. Pursuits diversified: skiing, the arts and short-lived sports like ice boating all drew participants and spectators. A road was built to Norquay ski slopes, and Lake Louise soon began to welcome skiers as well. The year 1917 saw the initiation of the Banff Winter Carnival, a week of everything from dances to dogsled races.

Throughout WWI, immigrants from enemy countries were detained in camps below Castle Mountain and near Cave and Basin hot springs. Forced to labor, they established much of the infrastructure throughout the park, including making horse trails friendly to cars. In the 1930s similar work was taken up by relief workers during the Depression, when the Icefields Pkwy was first initiated. Relief workers also built gardens in Banff Town and an airfield for private planes.

The National Parks Act, passed in 1930, established the boundaries of the park much as they are today, along with many of the conservation laws that are still in place. While the number of tourists to the park diminished during WWII, Banff became a popular honeymoon destination in the 1940s and '50s, attracting returning war veterans and their brides. By 1962, when the Trans-Canada Hwy officially opened, the park had begun to market itself as an international holiday destination.

> Banff unsuccessfully bid for the Winter Olympics three times: in 1964, 1968 and 1972. The controversial 1972 bid was ultimately withdrawn when environmental groups lobbied the government.

Balancing Act

Banff gained further global recognition as a summer and winter resort with the 1988 Winter Olympics in nearby Calgary. Although events were actually held at Nakiska ski resort in Kananaskis Country and the Nordic Centre in neighboring Canmore, the Olympics drew tourists and

1800s	1805–06	1811	1862
Dislocated First Nations tribes begin to settle in their hunting grounds along the Athabasca Valley using the area's various passes and valleys as migratory routes.	The Lewis and Clark Expedition passes close to the Glacier area, but misses Marias Pass. On their return journey Lewis gets into a skirmish with the Blackfeet tribe and two young braves are killed.	· Heading west from a post near present-day Jasper Town, David Thompson becomes the first European to cross the Athabasca Pass on his way to the Columbia River and the Pacific.	The pioneering 'Overlanders' pass through on their epic trek west from Ontario to British Columbia in search of gold. Short on supplies, they barely survive their journey through Yellowhead Pass.

publicity to the park. Banff Town's economy boomed, further strengthening the tourism infrastructure. In 1990, after more than a century of being governed federally, Banff Town was granted the right to become a self-governing community. That year, the CPR train service, which had played such an important role in the town's late-19th-century take-off, was discontinued. Tourism in Banff has continued to grow over recent years, but greater numbers of visitors have led to worries about ecological imbalance. As a result, the public zeitgeist has changed and the park today energetically promotes environmental as well as economic concerns.

Jasper National Park

First Nations peoples traditionally used the land that is now Jasper National Park as seasonal hunting and gathering grounds. It wasn't until the 1800s, when fur traders began to push west across the continent, dislocating various indigenous groups, that some First Nations tribes began utilizing the Athabasca Valley as a more permanent base.

Soon after, a dispute with Piegan people, over access to Howse Pass near present-day Banff, led British-Canadian explorer David Thompson to look for a new route across the Rockies to link up with lucrative trading centers on the west coast. Veering north during the winter of 1810, he trudged with his party through deep snow to the top of Athabasca Pass, crossing the Continental Divide in January 1811.

Before departing for Athabasca Pass, Thompson left fellow explorer William Henry in the Athabasca Valley, where he established Henry House, the region's first staging post, situated close to Old Fort Point, near present-day Jasper Town. In 1813 the Northwest Company established a more permanent post, 40km (25 miles) to the east, at Jasper House on Brûlé Lake, which remained in operation until 1884.

In an effort to build good trade relations, the traders were encouraged to take Aboriginal wives. In doing so, a distinct Métis (French for 'mixed blood') culture was formed, and the unique language of Michif arose. Descendents of the Métis continued to farm in the Athabasca Valley well into the 20th century, greatly influencing the area's development. In 1910, they were given compensation payments and forced to leave their land, which by then had become a federal reserve.

Adventurers & Mountaineers

In the early 1860s, around 200 pioneers set out from Ontario with their sights on the gold rush in British Columbia. The Overlanders, as they would come to be known, passed through Jasper and struggled over Yellowhead Pass, the park's present-day boundary with Mt Robson Provincial Park. The planned two-month journey turned into six months of near starvation. Poorly equipped and inexperienced, a number of men

---

Named After...

Banff *Banffshire in Scotland*

Jasper *Jasper Hawse, Northwest Company clerk*

Waterton *Charles Waterton, English naturalist*

Yoho *Cree word for 'awe'*

Kootenay *Kootenay River*

Historic Sites

Old Fort Point (Jasper)

Many Glacier Hotel (Glacier)

Prince of Wales Hotel (Waterton)

Cave & Basin National Historic Site (Banff)

1882	1885	1885	1892
Three railway workers, Tom and William McCardell and Frank McCabe, discover the Cave and Basin hot springs near present-day Banff and unwittingly usher in the age of tourism.	The Trans-Canada Railway is completed, and a federal reserve is established around Cave and Basin hot springs in response to a dispute about who has the right to develop them commercially.	Naturalist George Bird Grinnell visits the Glacier area and discovers the Grinnell Glacier in the Many Glacier Valley. He coins the term 'Crown of the Continent' and lobbies for protective status.	The Banff reserve, which originally measured only 26 sq km (10 sq miles), is enlarged to include Lake Louise as alpinists brought over from Europe begin scaling the area's peaks.

MARY SCHÄFFER

Breaking the mold in an era when most women didn't even have the right to vote, Mary Schäffer was a rather unlikely park pioneer who, according to some, was Jasper's and the Rocky Mountains' first real tourist. A spirited Philadelphia widow, Schäffer first ventured to Jasper in the early 20th century to – in her own words – 'turn the unthumbed pages of an unread book.' Her quest was an elusive mountain lake known to the Stoney people as Chaba Imne. Guided by a map sketched from memory by Stoney Aboriginal Sampson Beaver 14 years earlier, she became the first non-Aboriginal to set eyes on Maligne Lake in July 1908. Her subsequent book about her brave and sometimes turbulent adventures, *Old Indian Trails of the Canadian Rockies,* was republished on its 100th anniversary in 2011 and still resounds with poignant, poetic aphorisms.

died en route, some swept away by turbulent rivers, others succumbing to hypothermia. The only woman to accompany the group managed to survive, giving birth upon reaching Kamloops.

With the fur trade in decline and a new national park in Banff prospering to the south, mountaineers and adventurers began heading into Jasper's rugged wilderness in search of unnamed peaks and fabled glacial lakes. In 1906, Irish-born mountaineer and surveyor AO Wheeler founded the Alpine Club of Canada and began organizing periodic assaults on Mt Robson. Three years later he was instrumental in helping two colorful local characters, Reverend Kinney and Donald 'Curly' Phillips, in their brave but ultimately abortive attempt on the summit. The mountain was eventually conquered by Austrian Conrad Kain in 1913.

The Emergence of a Park

Jasper's founding, rather like Banff's, is closely entwined with the development of the railway. Passed over in the 1880s by the CPR in favor of Kicking Horse Pass in Banff, Jasper got its revenge in 1903 when Wilfred Laurier's government gave the go-ahead for the Grand Trunk Pacific Company to build a line from the west coast through Yellowhead Pass. All too aware of how the railway had significantly boosted the fortunes of Banff, the Ministry of the Interior opportunistically created Jasper Forest Park in 1907, the Rocky Mountains' fifth – and Canada's sixth – national park.

Built between 1910 and 1913, construction of the railway reached the tiny settlement of Fitzhugh at mile marker 113 in 1911, bringing an immediate influx of adventurers, mountaineers and railway workers. Almost overnight the burgeoning town jumped from a population of 125 to around 800 and was promptly renamed Jasper after Jasper Hawse, a fur-trading manager who had been based at the Jasper House trading post in the 1820s.

The term 'parkitecture' was used to describe the type of rustic architecture used in national parks in the early 20th century. Employing local materials in order to blend in with the forests from whence they sprang, the buildings took root in numerous national parks including Glacier and Waterton Lakes.

1895	1896	1907	1908
Upon the urging of rancher and conservationist Frederick William Godsal, Waterton Lakes is given protective status by the Canadian federal government.	The Blackfeet reluctantly accept the US government's offer to purchase all of the land east of the Continental Divide in what is now Glacier National Park for US$1.5 million.	Jasper Forest Park is established as Canada's sixth national park, although it doesn't acquire its present-day boundaries until the passing of the National Parks Act in 1930.	Mary Schäffer discovers Maligne Lake with her Stoney Aboriginal guide and opens up what is to become one of Jasper's most alluring sights and tourist attractions.

DAVID THOMPSON

The history of Jasper National Park will always be synonymous with indefatigable British-Canadian explorer David Thompson, born in London in 1770, but resident in Canada from 1784, where he was nicknamed 'Stargazer' by First Nations people and 'the greatest map-maker who ever lived' by those who had the good fortune to follow in his footsteps.

Thompson developed his prodigious navigational skills working as a fur trader, first for the Hudson Bay Company and later for its bitter rivals the Northwest Company, with whom he was mandated the task of establishing fur-trading posts along the hotly contested US–Canada border. In 1806, in response to the American-sponsored Lewis and Clark Expedition, Thompson was sent west to establish new Northwest Company posts closer to the Pacific, a journey that soon turned into a race over which group would reach the mouth of the Columbia River first. The explorer's biggest challenge was crossing the Rocky Mountains through precipitous terrain still largely controlled by Native American tribes. Thompson found his preferred southern route over Howse Pass near Banff blocked by the hostile Piegan tribe, forcing him to tack north toward the uncharted lands of what is now Jasper National Park. Enlisting the help of a local Aboriginal, Thomas the Iroquois, Thompson forged a route across Athabasca Pass in January 1811, becoming the first white person to cross the Rockies via a northerly route. For the next 50 years, until the advent of the railway era, Athabasca Pass became the preferred route of fur traders making for the Pacific.

Before the passage of the National Parks Act in 1930, the park faced far fewer limitations on its industrial and commercial development. Consequently, in the 1910s, local outfitters and guides, eyeing a potential business bonanza, sprang up all over the Athabasca Valley intent on bringing the wilderness to the masses. Plans for an enlarged town were laid out, a school was built, and clearing began for roads and climbing trails. The first grocery store opened in 1914, meaning that residents no longer had to wait for a month's supply by train from Edmonton. The following year, 10 crudely constructed tents were set up for visitors on the shores of Lac Beauvert, an encampment that would soon metamorphose into the Jasper Park Lodge.

In 1910, a coal mine was established at Pocahontas, near the eastern boundary of the park. A small mining town grew up in the vicinity, but was short-lived. The coal that was mined from the area burned at a high heat and was virtually smokeless, making it useful for warships during WWI. But, with the war over by 1918, and competition heating up with larger operations in the industrial east, the mine was shut down and the town dismantled by 1921.

1910	1911	1912	1914–18
US President Taft signs a bill creating Glacier as the nation's 10th national park. William Logan is named as the park's first superintendent.	Grand Trunk Pacific's railway reaches the shantytown of Fitzhugh, which is renamed Jasper two years later. Almost simultaneously the Canadian Northern Railway builds a second line through the park.	The Great Northern Railway begins building grand hotels and chalets within Glacier National Park (and, later, Waterton Lakes) to promote its railway line and open up the region to tourism.	Prisoners of war – most notably from Germany, Austria and Ukraine – are detained in camps within Banff National Park; their labor is used to improve the park's infrastructure.

Sharing the Limelight

The road from Jasper to Edmonton was opened in 1928, and by the onset of WWII legions of Depression-era workers had completed the legendary Icefields Pkwy linking Jasper to Lake Louise. In 1930 the National Parks Act was passed, fully protecting Jasper as the largest park in the nation, and tourists began visiting in droves; famous guests included King George VI, Marilyn Monroe and Bing Crosby. By 1948 the Athabasca Glacier had become a major sight, and the Banff-based Brewster brothers manufactured a ski-equipped Model A Ford truck to cart tourists out over the ice.

Since the 1950s, Jasper's tourism infrastructure has been gradually strengthened. Major highways into the park have been paved and roads to sights like Maligne Lake and Miette Hot Springs have been cleared or upgraded. In 1961 the Marmot Basin ski area got its first rope tow while, three years later, the Jasper Tramway took its first trip to the top of Whistlers Mountain.

Since 2001 Jasper Town has been governed jointly by the Specialized Municipality of Jasper and Parks Canada. These days there are strict development laws in place (eg no second homes are allowed) and, in 2010, the two bodies drafted the town's first Community Sustainability Plan.

> Winter sports were first ignited in the Rockies at the Banff Winter Carnival in 1917. Skiing began at Mt Norquay in the 1920s and at Sunshine Village in the 1930s. Norquay installed Canada's first chairlift in 1948 and, in 1961, Jasper added its own ski resort, Marmot Basin.

Glacier National Park

The ancestors of Montana's present-day Native Americans have inhabited the Glacier region for over 10,000 years. At the time of the first European contact, two main indigenous groups occupied the Rocky Mountains region. The valleys in the west were the hunting grounds of the Salish and Kootenai people, while the prairies in the east were controlled by the Blackfeet, a fiercely independent warrior tribe whose territory straddled the border with Canada. Linked spiritually to the land, the Blackfeet knew Glacier as the 'Backbone of the World', and within the area of the park, many sites – including the oddly shaped Chief Mountain – were considered sacred to the people.

In the mid-18th century, when trappers and explorers began to arrive out west, the Blackfeet controlled most of the northern plains and adjacent mountain passes. Although they resisted the European invaders at first, a catastrophic smallpox epidemic in 1837 dealt them a deadly blow, wiping out 6000 of their 30,000 population. Eventually both the Blackfeet, and Salish and Kootenai, were forced into one-sided treaties that sequestered them to reservation lands.

A romantic wanderer, James Willard Shultz spent many years living among the Blackfeet people, whom he considered his relatives and closest

> **History & Culture Museums**
> ....
> *Whyte Museum of the Canadian Rockies (Banff, AB)*
> ....
> *Museum of the Plains Indians (Browning, MT)*
> ....
> *Jasper-Yellowhead Museum & Archives (Jasper, AB)*
> ....
> *Waterton Heritage Centre (Waterton Townsite, AB)*

1920s	1932	1940	1984
Automobile organizations lobby for a road through Jasper, and in 1922 the first car breaches the Yellowhead Pass. The road to Edmonton opens in 1928 and the Yellowhead Hwy in 1970.	The Going-to-the-Sun Rd is completed east–west across Glacier National Park. Two new motels are constructed at Rising Sun and Swiftcurrent Lake to cater for the new influx of auto traffic.	The Icefields Pkwy opens linking Lake Louise with Jasper Town to the north; a remarkable feat of engineering, it is named for the copious icy behemoths visible from the roadside.	Banff, along with Jasper, Yoho and Kootenay, is declared a Unesco World Heritage site, adding an extra layer of protection, but invoking more environmental commitments.

Historic Lodges & Hotels
....
Chateau Lake Louise, 1913
....
Lake McDonald Lodge, 1913
....
Banff Springs Hotel, 1914
....
Many Glacier Hotel, 1915
....
Prince of Wales Hotel, 1927

Founded in 1906 by Irish-born surveyor and mountaineer AO Wheeler, the Alpine Club of Canada still stands at the sharp end of mountaineering in the Canadian Rockies. Check out its excellent website, www.alpineclubof canada.ca.

friends. As a result, he became one of the first European American men to lay eyes on much of Glacier's interior. In the 1880s he introduced the area to Dr George Bird Grinnell, a leading conservationist who lobbied Congress vociferously for a decade until, in 1910, President Taft signed the bill that created Glacier National Park.

From Gilded-Age Railroads to Modern Age Cars

Visitors began coming regularly to the park around 1912, when James J Hill of the Great Northern Railway instigated an intense building program to promote his newly inaugurated line. Railway employees built grand hotels and a network of tent camps and mountain chalets, each a day's horseback ride from the next. Visitors would come for several weeks at a time, touring by horse or foot and staying in these elegant but rustic accommodations.

But the halcyon days of trains and horse travel weren't to last. In response to the growing popularity of motorized transportation, federal funds were appropriated in 1921 to connect the east and west sides of Glacier National Park by a new road. Over a decade in the making, the legendary Going-to-the-Sun Rd was finally opened in 1932, crossing the Continental Divide at 2026m (6646ft) Logan Pass and opening up the park to millions.

That same year, thanks to efforts from Rotary International members in Alberta and Montana, Glacier joined with Waterton Lakes in the world's first International Peace Park, a lasting symbol of peace and friendship between the USA and Canada.

WWII forced the closure of almost all hotel services in the park, and many of Glacier's rustic chalets fell into disrepair and had to be demolished. Fortunately, nine of the original 13 'parkitecture' structures survived and – complemented by two wood-paneled motor inns that were added in the 1940s – they form the basis of the park's accommodations today.

Over the years, the Going-to-the-Sun Rd has been the primary travel artery in the national park and, for many, its scenic highlight. Still sporting its original stone guardrail and embellished with myriad tunnels, bridges and arches, the road has been designated a national historic landmark. In the 1930s a fleet of bright red 'Jammer' buses was introduced onto the road to enable tourists to gain easy access to the park's jaw-dropping scenery; the same buses (although now environmentally upgraded to run on propane gas) still operate today.

1990	2013	2014	2015
Banff Town becomes self-governing, though it is still subject to national-park planning and development laws. The Canadian Pacific Railway passenger service is discontinued after 105 years.	Dozens of campgrounds, over 150km (93 miles) of trails and numerous bridges, not to mention the Kananaskis Country golf course, are damaged in massive June floods.	Native American tribes in Alberta and Montana sign a treaty to reestablish the bison's migratory patterns across the Canada–US border.	Much of the east side of Glacier, including the Going-to-the-Sun Rd from St Mary to Logan Pass, is shut down in August due to the Reynolds Creek Fire.

Geology

Majestic, indomitable and bursting with life, the Canadian Rockies are environmentally unique. Formed over 170 million years ago when a massive collision in the earth's crust caused a giant lateral displacement known as the Lewis Overthrust, the mountains today are the product of several million years of glaciation. Anointed rather regally with the title 'Crown of the Continent,' the parks are home to a plethora of glaciers, dwindling in number and size, relics of a colder and mightier age.

The Land

The Canadian Rockies are a rock-lover's paradise, a striking mix of towering mountain chains and multicolored terrain that is considered to be one of the most important fossil localities in the world. Everywhere you look you'll see graphic evidence of 1.5 billion years of the earth's history laid out like hieroglyphics in well-preserved sedimentary strata. Even more dramatic are the region's crenellated peaks and U-shaped valleys, a lasting testimony to the formidable power of ancient glaciers and ice fields.

The Rocky Mountain Trench is a large valley up to 25km (15.6 miles) wide that runs from Montana up to the Yukon/BC border, separating the Rocky Mountains from the Columbia/ Cassiar Mountains to the west. Although partially glaciated, it was caused primarily by faulting.

The First Supercontinent

In the beginning there was nothing much at all. And then, approximately 1.5 billion years ago, sediments began to be laid down in an inland sea within a hypothesized supercontinent known as Rodinia (a combination of landmasses that later broke apart into the continents we recognize today). Consisting of sands, silts and cobbles, these ancient sedimentary layers are now so deeply buried that they appear on the earth's surface in only a few places, two of which are Waterton Lakes and Glacier National Parks.

On the west side of the parks, the oldest layer is known as the Pritchard Formation and preserves evidence of a deep sea visible in thin layers of fine green rock along MacDonald Creek. Other strata such as the Altyn, Appekunny and Snowslip Formations are also evident in places such as St Mary Lake and Logan Pass. Perhaps the most eye-catching and easy-to-recognize layer of rock is the brick-red coloration of the Grinnell Formation, which is exposed in Red Rock Canyon in Waterton Lakes National Park.

The Big Breakup

About 750 million years ago, the supercontinent Rodinia began to break up along a giant rift, creating a new shoreline where North America split off from the future continents of Australia and Antarctica. Various sediments accumulated in an ancient sea during this epoch and, over time, these deposits hardened to form limestone, mudstone and sandstone.

A significant transition occurred around 570 million years ago, with the onset of the Cambrian period, a transitional era that sparked an incredible proliferation of complex new fauna in what became known as the 'Cambrian explosion.' Embedded in the region's rock, many well-preserved fossils of multicellular organisms remain from this period, and have taught scientists much about evolution and the development of species diversity worldwide. Some of the planet's best Cambrian fossils were uncovered at the Burgess Shale site in Yoho National Park in 1909.

Situated on the western side of the Continental Divide, Yoho National Park receives over 884mm (35in) of rain annually; meanwhile, dryer Banff National Park on the eastern side gets 472mm (19in).

The Cambrian era was followed by a long period of relative stability as desert landmasses eroded and sedimentary layers accumulated along the continental coastline. For a period of over 350 million years the dozens of different rock layers that comprise the bulk of the peaks in today's Canadian Rockies were laid down in contrasting bands, documenting an encyclopedia of geological history, a record that shows how seas advanced and retreated numerous times across the region.

Collision Course

This period of stability came to a close around 200 million years ago when the continental plate began a steady march westward, pushing against the part of the earth's crust that lies under the Pacific Ocean. Like a slow-motion collision, the leading edge of the continental plate buckled against the impact. At first, the buckled edge may have simply created folds in the earth's crust, but over time these folds became steeper and started to fracture under the stress.

Extending progressively eastward, the fractures reached the region of the Canadian Rockies about 100 million years ago where dynamic tectonic movement pushed up a huge wedge of rock and displaced it over 80km (50 miles) to the east, forming the basis of the mountains we see today.

The main period of compression reached its apex 60 to 80 million years ago, then subsided slowly, leaving behind layers of deep old Paleozoic rock wedged up on top of younger Mesozoic rock. This compressing process is known as thrust faulting and it geologically sets the northern Rockies apart from their smoother southern cousins, which were formed by broader tectonic uplifting.

Highest Peaks

Jasper: Mt Columbia 3782m (12,408ft)

Banff: Mt Forbes 3612m (11,850ft)

Yoho: Mt Goodsir 3567m (11,703ft)

Kootenay: Delta-form Mountain 3424m (11,234ft)

Glacier: Mt Cleveland 3190m (10,466ft)

Waterton Lakes: Mt Blakiston 2910m (9547ft)

Glaciers

For the past 60 million years, the primary force in the Canadian Rockies has been erosion, not deposition. The most dramatic erosive process has been that of glaciation, precipitated by the great glaciers and ice fields of the Ice Age that have sculpted rugged peaks and gouged out deep valleys from Pocahontas to Marias Pass. Two million years ago, huge sheets of ice covered much of the Canadian Rockies. These giant sheets produced incredible amounts of weight and pressure, and as tongues of ice crept across the landscape they tore apart rocks and transformed narrow V-shaped ravines into broad open valleys. Trillions of tons of debris were left behind when the ice finally retreated 10,000 years ago, much of it forming distinctive ridges called moraines, such as the one that the chateau at Lake Louise is perched on.

ROCKY MOUNTAINS GLACIERS UP CLOSE

Four of the park's glaciers are easily accessible to day hikers:

Victoria Glacier (Banff) The crystal crown of Banff is visible from Chateau Lake Louise at the far end of the eponymous lake, or in close-up on the Plain of Six Glaciers trail.

Sperry Glacier (Glacier) Perched above the backcountry Sperry Chalet on Gunsight Mountain, this dwindling glacier is accessible by a steep but rewarding hike across high-alpine terrain.

Grinnell Glacier (Glacier) Named for the famous US naturalist, this river of ice is Glacier National Park's most photographed and precarious. An 8.8km (5.5-mile) trail leads out from the Many Glacier Hotel.

Athabasca Glacier (Jasper) The Rockies' most famous glacier dips its toe close to the Icefields Pkwy from where you can arrange excursions to walk or drive (yes, drive!) on it with a Snocoach tour.

THE GLACIAL LANDSCAPE OF THE ROCKIES

The Rocky Mountains national parks provide a perfect outdoor classroom for wannabe students trying to digest the geomorphological (surface) features created by glacial erosion. Here are some of the best examples, although there are plenty more:

FEATURE	DEFINITION	BEST EXAMPLE
Arête	A thin sharp ridge that forms between two parallel glaciers	Garden Wall (Glacier)
Glacial cirque	A bowl-shaped amphitheater formed at the head of a valley glacier	Iceberg Cirque (Glacier)
Glacial horn	A pyramidal peak formed when three glacial cirques form together	Mt Assiniboine (Mt Assiniboine Provincial Park)
Glacial lake	A lake left behind when glaciers retreat	Lake Louise (Banff)
Hanging valley	Small side valleys left 'hanging' above a deeper U-shaped glacier-carved valley	Maligne Valley (Jasper)
Moraine	An accumulation of glacial rock and soil	Moraine Lake (Banff)
Rouche moutonnée	Tear-shaped hills formed when a glacier erodes down to the bedrock	Old Fort Point (Jasper)
U-shaped Valley	A steep-sided, flat-bottomed valley formed by a glacier moving downhill	St Mary Valley (Glacier)

Nearly every feature seen in the Canadian Rockies today is a legacy of the Ice Age. Peaks that were simultaneously carved on multiple sides left behind sharp spires called horns, as can be seen at Mt Assiniboine. Mountains that had glaciers cutting along two sides ended up as sharp ridges known as arêtes. Side streams flowing into valleys that were deepened by glaciers were often left hanging in midair, creating hanging valleys, with the streams pouring out as waterfalls down over sheer cliffs.

Glaciers Today

Even though the Ice Age ended 10,000 years ago, the story of ice and glaciers in the Canadian Rockies is far from over. Mini ice ages have regularly altered the climate in the years since, the most recent of which peaked in the 1840s when the frozen tip of the Athabasca Glacier reached as far as the present-day Icefield Centre – it has retreated 1.6km (1 mile) since 1844. Even today, along the spine of the Continental Divide, smaller ice fields continue to craft and shape the landscape and the relatively larger ice fields in Banff and Jasper are probably safe for a good couple of centuries, whatever the warming effects from climate change.

However, intensifying concerns and research suggest that the glaciers in Glacier National Park (which now number only 25) will be all but extinct by 2030 (Waterton Lakes National Park is already a glacier-free zone). These grand and seeming indomitable monuments formed over millennia are now vanishing before our eyes. In 1850, northwest Montana was home to nearly 150 glaciers, and when Sperry Glacier was first photographed in 1887 surely the photographer never imagined it would some day vanish. Harrison is now the largest and Weasel Collar is predicted to be the last surviving – south-facing glaciers with more sun exposure are the most vulnerable. Research scientists studying the park's glaciers are part of a global network sharing data with the World Glacier Monitoring Service (WGMS; www.wgms.ch), which is tracking global trends. Of course, the melting glaciers aren't simply an aesthetic concern. The downstream impact on water systems, surrounding ecosystems and the survival of various species of wildlife are all threatened.

A common feature of a hanging valley is a waterfall caused when a river drops from the higher side valley down to the U-shaped valley below. Visible from Glacier National Park's Going-to-the-Sun Rd, 152m (500ft) Bird Woman Falls near Mt Oberlin is a classic example.

A coyote in winter, Spray Lakes Reservoir (p123), Canmore

Wildlife

Rising like snow-coated sentinels above the plains and prairies of Alberta and Montana, the Rockies protect a narrow, wildlife-rich corridor that stretches down the continent from northern Canada to Mexico. With the adjacent lowlands taken over by roads, farms and cities, the mountains have provided a final refuge for wolves, mountain lions, bears, elk, deer and many other large mammals. While populations of these animals are only a fraction of their former numbers, they are still impressive enough to lure wildlife enthusiasts to the region by the truckload.

Animals

While the prospect of seeing 'charismatic megafauna' is one the region's biggest draws, the Canadian Rockies support nearly 70 species of mammals, including eight species of ungulate (hoofed mammal). In the fall and winter, many large mammals move down into valleys for protection against the weather; high concentrations can be seen along the Icefields Pkwy during these seasons.

Bears

The black bear roams montane and subalpine forests throughout the Canadian Rockies in search of its favorite foods: grasses, roots, berries and the occasional meal of carrion. They can frequently be seen along roadsides feeding on dandelions. While most black bears are black in color, they can also be light reddish brown (cinnamon). Black bears are somewhat smaller than grizzlies and have more tapered muzzles, larger ears and smaller claws. These claws help them climb trees to avoid their main predator, grizzly bears, which are known to drag black bears out of their dens to kill them. Although they are generally more tolerant of humans and less aggressive than grizzlies, black bears should always be treated as dangerous.

Grizzly bears once roamed widely in North America, but most were killed by European settlers who feared this mighty carnivore. Thanks to conservation efforts, their numbers have increased since they were listed as endangered in 1975. Today, an ongoing and complicated legal battle wends its way through the courts as to whether to 'delist' them or classify them as threatened. Even with rebounding populations, they aren't particularly easy to see or count, in part because males roam 3885 sq km (1500 sq miles) in their lifetimes. Male grizzlies reach up to 2.4m (8ft) in length (from nose to tail) and 1.05m (3.5ft) high at the shoulder (when on all fours) and can weigh more than 315kg (700lb) at maturity. Although some grizzlies are almost black, their coats are typically pale brown to cinnamon, with 'grizzled,' white-tipped guard hairs (the long, coarse hairs that protect the shorter, fine underfur). They can be distinguished from black bears by their concave (dish-shaped) facial profile, smaller and more rounded ears, prominent shoulder hump and long, nonretractable claws.

Both bears are omnivorous opportunists and notorious berry eaters, with an amazing sense of smell that's acute enough to detect food miles away. Their choice of meal varies seasonally, ranging from roots and winter-killed carrion in early spring to berries and salmon in the fall. Before hibernation, bears become voracious. Black bears will eat for 20 hours straight and gain an incredible 1.8kg (4lb) each day before retiring to their dens, and grizzly bears are known to eat 200,000 buffalo berries a day.

Sometime in October, bears wander upslope to where snows will be deep and provide a thick insulating layer over their winter dens. There the bears scrape out a simple shelter among shrubs, against a bank or under a log and sink into deep sleep (not true hibernation, as their body temperatures remain high and they are easily roused). Winters are particularly hard, since bears live entirely off their fat and lose up to 40% of their body weight. Females who have been able to gain enough weight give birth to several cubs during the depths of winter, rearing the cubs on milk while she sleeps.

There have been 10 human fatalities from bear attacks in Glacier National Park's 106-year history. By remarkable coincidence two of them occurred on the same night – 13 August 1967 – 16.1km (10 miles) apart in separate attacks by different bears. Both victims were 19-year-old females.

Figures in 2014 for grizzly bear numbers in Alberta Province, Canada (including Jasper, Banff and Waterton National Parks) are cited as approximately 690, while up to 16,000 are in British Columbia.

Coyotes & Wolves

The cagey coyote is actually a small opportunistic wolf that devours anything from carrion to berries and insects. Its slender, reddish-gray form is frequently seen in open meadows, along roads and around towns and campgrounds. Coyotes form small packs to hunt larger prey such as elk calves or adults mired in deep snow. Frequently mistaken for a wolf, the coyote is much smaller – 11.3kg to 15.8kg (25lb to 35lb), versus 20.3kg to 65.3kg (45 to 145lb) for a wolf – and runs with its tail carried down (a wolf carries its tail straight out).

The gray wolf, once the Rocky Mountains' main predator, was nearly exterminated in the 1930s, then again in the 1950s. It took until the mid-1980s for them to reestablish themselves in Banff, and today they are common only from Jasper National Park north; in Glacier National Park, wolves can be found in North Fork Valley. Wolves look rather like large, blackish German shepherd dogs. Colors range from white to black, with gray-brown being the most common hue. They roam in close-knit packs of five to eight animals ruled by a dominant (alpha) pair. The alpha pair are the only members of a pack to breed, though the entire pack cares for the pups. Four to six pups are born in April or May, and they remain around the den until August. Packs of wolves are a formidable presence, and they aren't afraid of using their group strength to harass grizzly bears or kill coyotes, but more often they keep themselves busy chasing down deer, elk or moose.

Bighorn Sheep & Mountain Goats

Living on high slopes near rocky ridges and cliffs, bighorn sheep are generally shy creatures of remote areas. Unlike other parts of their range, however, bighorn sheep in the Canadian Rockies come down to roadsides in search of salts, invariably causing traffic jams of excited visitors. Males, with their flamboyant curled horns, spend summer in bachelor flocks waiting for the fall rut, when they face off and duel by ramming into each other at 96km/h (60mph). Their horns and foreheads are specially modified for this brutal but necessary task. When not hanging around roadsides looking for salt and handouts (strictly forbidden), bighorn sheep use their extraordinary vision and smell to detect humans up to 300m (1000ft) away and keep their distance, making them extremely difficult to approach.

Occupying even steeper cliffs and hillsides, pure white mountain goats are a favorite with visitors. Finding one is another matter altogether, as goats live high on remote cliffs and are seldom observed close-up. These cliffs provide excellent protection from predators, and both adults and kids are amazingly nimble on impossibly sheer faces. Occasionally they descend to salt licks near roads. In Jasper they occur in high densities on Mt Kerkeslin; around Banff try scanning the slopes of Cascade Mountain; and in Glacier National Park you might see goats at Logan Pass.

Estimated Species Numbers in Jasper

Bighorn sheep: 1200

Grizzly bears: 114

Moose: 180

Woodland caribou: 125

Estimated Species Numbers in Glacier

Bighorn sheep: 800

Black bears: 800

Grizzly bears: 300

Wolves: 60

Woodland caribou: 6

BEST PLACES TO SEE WILDLIFE

What	Where	When
Bighorn sheep	Lake Minnewanka (Banff), Highline Trail (Glacier)	Nov–Apr
Black bear	Bow Valley Pkwy (Banff), Maligne Lake Rd (Jasper)	May–Oct
Caribou	Tonquin Valley (Jasper)	Nov–May
Elk	Vermilion Lakes (Banff), Maligne Lake Rd (Jasper)	Mar–May
Grizzly bear	Many Glacier (Glacier), Carthew-Alderson Trail (Waterton)	May–Oct
Marmot	Skyline Trail (Jasper), Highline Trail (Glacier)	May–Sep
Moose	Moose Lake (Jasper), Kootenai Lake (Glacier)	May–Aug
Mountain goat	Logan Pass (Glacier)	year-round
Wolf	North Fork Valley (Glacier), Lake Minnewanka (Banff)	Nov–Apr

White-tailed deer, Banff National Park

Deer

Two species of deer are common in valleys and around human dwellings throughout the region. More common by far are the mule deer of dry, open areas. Smaller, and with a large, prominent white tail, are the white-tailed deer of heavily forested valley bottoms. Both species graze extensively on grasses in summer and on twigs in winter. Delicate, white-spotted fawns are born in June and are soon observed following their mothers. Adult males develop magnificent racks of antlers in time for their mating season in early December.

Elk & Moose

Weighing up to 450kg (1000lb) and bearing gigantic racks of antlers, male elk are the largest mammals that most visitors will encounter in these parks. Come September, valleys resound with the hoarse bugling of battle-ready elk, a sound that is both exciting and terrifying, as hormone-crazed elk are one of the area's most dangerous animals. Battles between males, harem gathering and mating are best observed from a safe distance or from your car. While numbers increase dramatically in winter, quite a few elk now spend their entire year around towns like Banff and Jasper, where they can be dependably observed grazing in yards and on golf courses.

At 495kg (1100lb), the ungainly moose is the largest North American deer. Visitors eagerly seek this odd-looking animal with lanky legs and periscope ears, but they are uncommon and not easily found. Moose spend their summers foraging on aquatic vegetation in marshy meadows and shallow lakes, where they readily swim and dive up to 6m (20ft). Visitors can look for moose in the Miette Valley of Jasper, around Upper Waterfowl Lake of Banff, in the McDonald Valley of Glacier and in similar areas. The male's broadly tined antlers and flappy throat dewlap are unique, but

The Canadian Rockies are home to the only fully protected caribou herds in North America. Two herds with six members each roam Glacier and Mount Revelstoke, whereas Jasper has four herds, a northern one and three southern ones totaling around 125 head.

like their close relative the elk, moose can be extremely dangerous when provoked. Moose are no longer as common as they were in the days when they freely wandered the streets of Banff; numbers have been reduced due to vehicle traffic (roadkills), a liver parasite and the suppression of the wildfires that rejuvenate their favorite foods.

Pikas, Marmots & Beavers

Hikers into the realm of rock and open meadow will quickly become familiar with two abundant mammals. When you encounter a pika, you are likely to hear its loud bleating call long before you spot the tiny, guinea-pig-like creature staring back at you with dark beady eyes. Pikas live among jumbles of rocks and boulders, where they are safe from predators, but they still have to dart out into nearby meadows to harvest grasses that they dry in the sun to make hay for their winter food supply.

Another rock dweller is even more of a tempting morsel for predators. Hoary marmots are plump and tasty, but they have a system for protecting themselves. First, they stay near their burrows and dart in quickly when alarmed. Second, all the marmots on a hillside cooperate in watching out for predators and giving shrill cries whenever danger approaches. Marmots may shriek fiercely when humans come near, warning everyone in the neighborhood about the approach of two-legged primates. Whistlers, a mountain outside Jasper, is named after these common rodents.

The aquatic beaver has a long history of relations with humans. Reviled for its relentless efforts to block creeks and praised for its valuable fur, the Canadian Rockies' largest rodent is now widely recognized as a 'keystone species' – an animal whose activities have a tremendous influence on the lives of many other species. Beavers' shallow-water dams create vibrant wetlands, mini-ecosystems that promote biodiversity, and dozens of animals, including ducks, frogs, fish, moose and mink, depend on beavers for their livelihood. Although their numbers have declined as much as 90% in recent decades, beavers are still fairly common around marshes and

Three members of the cat family are found in the parks: the mountain lion (cougar), the Canadian lynx and the bobcat. All are elusive and rarely seen by humans, moving mainly at night. The Canadian lynx has been listed as threatened since 2000. Lynx hunt hares, while mountain lions prefer deer.

FISH TALES

That dreamy image of a philosophical fisher sitting with rod and line beside a high-country lake might seem like a typical Rocky Mountains idyll, but the reality is a little less pure. In truth, high mountain lakes do not naturally support native fish. Instead, countless non-native species were introduced to the national parks over a period of 50 years in a bid by wildlife and park agencies to 'improve' the visitor experience and attract more fishing tourists. Today Banff counts at least 119 lakes stocked with non-native fish (when only 26 contained fish historically). As a consequence, native fish populations and aquatic ecosystems in lower lakes have suffered, while several species of non-native fish have thrived. Though the fish-stocking policies have been phased out (in 1971 in Glacier and 1988 in Banff and Jasper), millions of non-native fish remain.

Surviving native fish include the threatened bull trout, the dwindling populations of which are protected by law. Once the most widespread native fish in the Canadian Rockies, bull trout are now seen at only a few sites. Your best bet is Peter Lougheed Provincial Park, south of Canmore, where they migrate up creeks out of Lower Kananaskis Lake from late August to mid-October. They are distinguished from other trout by their lack of black lines or spots. Return them to the water if you accidentally catch one.

Representative of the nine non-native fish that have become most common, brook trout are found in most low-elevation streams and lakes. Brook trout can be recognized by their olive-green color, reddish belly and yellow squiggly lines along their back.

Aquatic habitats in the Canadian Rockies support many more kinds of fish than just trout – 40 species in all. One of the healthiest populations is mountain whitefish, a bottom-feeder that preys on small invertebrates in the major watercourses and lakes.

ponds in valley bottoms. Here, each beaver cuts down as many as 200 aspens and willows per year, feeding on the sweet inner bark and using the trunks and branches to construct dams.

Birds

Although more than 300 species have been found in the Canadian Rockies, birds are readily overshadowed by the presence of so many eye-catching large mammals. However, casual observers will notice some of the more conspicuous species without even trying.

You'd be hard-pressed to find a campsite or picnic table where you aren't quickly approached by gray jays hoping for a handout. They stash most of their food away in small caches for winter. The stash master, however, is the larger Clark's nutcracker. Each nutcracker buries up to 98,000 seeds in thousands of small caches across miles of landscape then returns to dig them up over the course of several years – an unbelievable test of memory.

Two large raptors (birds of prey) are frequently encountered. Working their way along rivers and lakes are white and brown fish hawks, better known as ospreys. Fairly common from May to September, when the ice has melted, ospreys specialize in diving into water to catch fish. Plunging feet first into the water, ospreys grab fish up to 90cm (3ft) deep, then fly off to eat their scaly meal on a high perch. Osprey nests are enormous mounds of sticks piled on top of dead trees or artificial towers.

In recent years the Canadian Rockies have gained some fame for the spectacular golden eagle migration. Each year 6000 to 8000 golden eagles migrate both north and south along a narrow corridor on the east side of the main mountain divide (the official count site is near Mt Lorette, in Kananaskis Country, just east of Banff). Spring migration peaks at the end of March, and fall migration peaks in October. While migrating, golden eagles do little feeding, though some pairs stay for the summer and nest on high, remote cliffs.

Of the region's eight species of owl, only the great horned owl is familiar to most visitors. Fearless around humans, highly vocal and sometimes active in the daytime, these large birds are a perennial sight around towns and campgrounds at lower elevations.

Plants

The Canadian Rockies are home to over 1000 species of plants, comprising a fairly diverse mix for such a relatively cold, northern climate. One of the main reasons for this mix is that the Continental Divide not only creates a strong elevational gradient, but also splits the region into westside and eastside habitats. With a wet, ocean-influenced climate on the west side and a dry, interior climate on the east side, this geographic split is a very significant division. Adding to the region's botanical diversity are alpine plants from the Arctic, grassland plants of the eastern prairies, and forest plants from the Pacific Northwest.

The mountain pine beetle is an insect that attacks and kills mature trees (turning their needles a distinctive red color). Rather like wildfires, this process is a natural part of the Rocky Mountain ecosystem and park management bodies have tried to let it continue with minimal interference.

Trees

Except for areas of rock, ice or water, landscapes of the Canadian Rockies are mostly covered with coniferous forest. Only a handful of species are present, and these are easy to identify – recognizing these species makes it easier to understand the layout of life zones and to predict where you might find specific animals.

Montane and subalpine forests are dominated by two spruces – white and Engelmann. White spruce occurs mainly on valley bottoms, and Engelmann spruce takes over on higher slopes, but the two frequently overlap and hybridize. Many animals feed on spruce seeds or rely on spruce forests for their livelihood in some way.

Wildflowers in bloom, Glacier National Park

Sharing the higher slopes with the Engelmann spruce is the subalpine fir, the namesake tree of the subalpine zone in the Canadian Rockies. Recognized by their flattened, blunt-tipped needles, subalpine firs have narrow, conical profiles. This shape allows the trees to shed heavy winter snows so their branches don't break off under the weight.

At the uppermost edges of the subalpine forest, mainly growing by themselves on high, windswept slopes, are whitebark pines. Intense wind and cold at these elevations can cause these trees to grow in low, stunted mats. Their squat, egg-shaped cones produce highly nutritious seeds favored by Clark's nutcrackers and grizzly bears, but an introduced disease is threatening this important tree and the animals that depend on it.

Synonymous with the expansive evergreen forests of Alberta and British Columbia, the Douglas fir tree is named after Scottish botanist David Douglas (1799–1834), who first visited Jasper in 1827, when he wrongly declared Mt Brown and Mt Hooker to be the highest peaks in North America.

One of the oddest trees of the Canadian Rockies is the subalpine larch, a rare tree found most easily in Larch Valley, just south of Lake Louise. Although it's a conifer, this remarkable tree has needles that turn golden in September then drop off for the winter in October. This makes places like Larch Valley a photographers' paradise during the peak display.

After fires or other disturbances, lodgepole pines quickly spring up and form dense 'doghair' thickets. In some areas, lodgepoles cover many square kilometers so thickly that the forests are nearly impossible to walk through. These conditions eventually promote hot fires that create seedbeds for more lodgepoles; in fact, lodgepole cones are sealed in resin that only melts and releases seeds after a fire.

A beautiful tree of dry, open areas, the quaking aspen has radiant, silver-white bark and rounded leaves that quiver in mountain breezes. Aspen foliage turns a striking orange-gold for just a few weeks in fall.

Shrubs

Half a dozen species of blueberry occur in the Canadian Rockies, with common names like huckleberry, grouseberry, bilberry and cranberry.

Often these plants grow in patches large enough that berries for a batch of pancakes or muffins can be harvested within minutes.

Closely related and similar in appearance to blueberry plants is the kinnikinnik, also known as bearberry. This ground-hugging shrub has thick glossy leaves and reddish woody stems. Its leaves were once mixed with tobacco to make a smoking mixture, and the berries have been a staple food for many First Nations peoples.

It's something of a surprise to encounter wild roses growing deep in the woods, but at least five types grow here. All look like slender, somewhat scraggly versions of what you'd see in a domestic garden.

Wildflowers

The flowering season in the Canadian Rockies begins as soon as the snows start to melt. Though delicate in structure, the early rising glacier lily pushes up so eagerly that the stems often unfurl right through the snow crust. Abundant in montane and subalpine forests or meadows, each lily produces several yellow flowers, with six upward-curled petals. Wherever lilies occur in great numbers, grizzlies paw eagerly through the soil in search of the edible bulbs.

Within days of snowmelt, pretty purple pasqueflowers (aka prairie crocuses) cover montane slopes. Growing close to the ground on short, fuzzy stems, these brilliant flowers stand out because of their yellow centers. Later in the summer, 'shaggy mane' seed heads replace the flowers. All parts of this plant are poisonous and may raise blisters if handled.

One of the most photographed flowers of Glacier National Park is the striking bear grass. From tufts of grasslike leaves, the plant sends up 1.5m-high (5ft) stalks of white, star-shaped flowers that may fill entire subalpine meadows. Grizzlies favor the tender spring leaves, hence the plant's common name.

Hike almost anywhere in these mountains and you're bound to encounter the easy-to-recognize bluebell, with its large, bell-like flowers held up on a long, skinny stem. After flowering, seeds are produced in capsules that close in wet weather then open in dry winds to scatter the seeds far and wide.

Many visitors know the familiar Indian paintbrush for its tightly packed red flowers, but fewer know that the plant is a semiparasite that taps into neighbors' roots for nourishment. By stealing some energy from other plants, paintbrushes are able to grow luxuriantly in desolate places like roadsides or dry meadows, where they are often the most conspicuous wildflower. Paintbrush patches are also one of the best sites for finding hummingbirds.

The big, showy cow parsnip can grow to an impressive height of 1.8m (6ft). Its huge, celery-like stalks and umbrella-shaped flower clusters are familiar sights along streams and in moist aspen groves throughout the region. The stems are eaten by many animals and favored by grizzlies (avoid tasting yourself because of their similar appearance to other deadly species), so caution is urged when approaching a large patch.

More localized in its distribution, but sometimes confused with cow parsnip because it has the same large leaves, is the devil's club. This stout, 2.7m-high (9ft) plant practically bristles with armor. Completely covered in poisonous spikes (even the leaves are ribbed with rows of spines) that break off in the skin when contacted and cause infections, this plant further announces itself with its strong odor and large clusters of brilliant red berries. Despite these features, devil's club has a rich and important history of medicinal use among First Nations tribes of the area.

WILDLIFE PLANTS

The Rockies feature three different life zones: the montane (warm, dry tree-filled valley bottoms), the subalpine (wetter forests of smaller stunted trees) and alpine (high windy slopes of flower meadows and barren rock).

Conservation

Despite their remoteness and relatively late colonization, the Rocky Mountains parks were conceived in the infancy of the evolution of wilderness protection. And as the public perception of wilderness changed, so too have the parks. Banff was Canada's first – and the world's third – national park when it was inaugurated in 1885, while Jasper, Waterton and Glacier (all given protective status by 1910) were three more early beneficiaries of the nascent North American conservation movement.

The Early Conservationists

The American environmental movement was born during the progressive era in the late 19th and early 20th centuries at a time when early eco-thinkers were separating into two philosophical camps: the conservationists led by US president Theodore Roosevelt and his chief environmental advisor Gifford Pinchot; and the more radical preservationists epitomized by John Muir, founder of the Sierra Club. The former proposed federal intervention in order to manage and conserve natural resources; the latter considered nature to be sacred and tourism sustainable only under strict limits.

When Lewis and Clark traversed America in the early 1800s, there were approximately 100,000 grizzly bears roaming the Lower 48 states of the US. Now there are around 1800 occupying an area that is less than 2% of their traditional range.

While Muir remains an icon to modern environmentalists, it was the conservationists who had the biggest impact on the public zeitgeist during the early flowering of the North American national-park network in the 1890s. In the Rocky Mountains, their chief exponent was George Bird Grinnell, an anthropologist and naturalist from New York City who was more at home mingling with the Blackfeet Native Americans and leading sorties into the mountains of northwest Montana than he was tramping the streets of Manhattan. It was Grinnell who christened the Glacier/Waterton region 'the Crown of the Continent' and, using his influential position as editor of *Field and Stream* magazine, he badgered the US Congress relentlessly for protective status. His entreaties were rewarded in 1910 when Glacier became the nation's 10th national park. In 1911 the Canadian government formed the Dominion Parks Branch (an early incarnation of Parks Canada) as the world's first national-park coordinating body, and in 1930 the National Parks Act laid down the first firm set of ground rules for conservation and preservation. The huge debt owed to Grinnell and his contemporaries by our current generation is immeasurable.

But, with conflicting commercial interests and an inordinate influence wielded by the all-powerful cross-continental railway companies, early park rules were sketchy and haphazard. Waterton once supported an oil well, Jasper and Banff flirted briefly with coal mining, and all three Canadian parks developed – and still retain – significant and relatively prosperous townsites. While the parks today still promote recreation and education as a crucial part of the overall wilderness experience, the concept of ecological integrity has taken center stage with a shift toward a more populist strand of environmentalism in the 1980s.

Environmental Issues

Tourism Boom

Fatefully, the work of Grinnell et al was just the beginning of a protracted process. Tourism and the ongoing impact of millions of visitors trampling through important wildlife corridors is one of the parks' most ticklish issues in modern times and nowhere is this problem more apparent than in Banff. Hosting an incorporated town with a permanent population of 8400 or so people, along with main roads, a ski resort and over three million annual visitors, Banff's environmental credentials have long been a subject for hot debate. Comparisons with Glacier (governed by the US parks system) further south are particularly telling.

In 1996 a two-year investigation by the Banff–Bow Valley study group provided a crucial turning point in Banff's modern evolution. Putting forward 500 urgent recommendations – a list that included everything from population capping to quotas on hiking trails – the study prompted the implementation of a 15-year development plan designed to redress the park's ecological balance and save its priceless wilderness from almost-certain long-term damage. Two decades later, progress has certainly been made, though growing concerns and awareness about climate change give the issue even more urgency.

Long lauded as one of the continent's most pristine parks, Banff's smaller American cousin is a veritable wilderness, with no population center, no fast-food franchises and no water-sapping golf courses. Furthermore, Glacier bans bikes from all park trails, runs an environmentally friendly free shuttle service to minimize car pollution, and has barred its historic lodges from installing supposed modern 'luxuries' such as TVs and room phones. Not surprisingly, the park's unique ecosystem is frequently acclaimed for its rich biodiversity, and its grizzly bear population is said to be one of the healthiest in the whole of North America.

Jasper sits somewhere between the two extremes. While it is closer to Banff in infrastructure and park policies (it hosts a townsite, golf course, pubs and restaurants), its superior size and smaller annual visitor count (less than half of Banff's) means environmental pressures are less corrosive. Its most symbolic conservation issue is the preservation of the woodland caribou, a species no longer present in Banff, but still surviving precariously further north. Jasper Town was made a Specialized Municipality in 2001 and began drafting a similarly comprehensive Community Sustainability Plan in the late 2000s.

Despite the very developed nature of little Waterton Townsite, tourism in Waterton Lakes, the smallest of the parks, will be limited as long as the moratorium on new accommodations and buildings remains in effect.

The Human Hand

Climate change and its attendant cascade of environmental impacts, which even in a best-case scenario point to a staggering number of potential losses, is one of the most important ways human behavior is threatening these wilderness areas. However, it's far from the only one. Often, the direst threat to an individual species' sustainability, whether flora or fauna, is disguised, at least to the untrained eye, as natural and endemic. But whether it's a fungus that arrived in the early 20th century or a fish stocked in lakes by park authorities in the 1960s, invasive species can potentially alter ecosystems, lead to hybridization and decimate habitats for true endemics.

Just one example in Waterton-Glacier is the whitebark pine population, ravaged by a combination of forces, including a foreign fungus, decreased mortality of native pine beetles that feed on the trees' bark, and the many decades previous when best forestry practice called for fire suppression (whitebark pines need the sunlight created by canopy-destroying wildfires).

Of all the Rocky Mountains parks, Waterton-Glacier is the best protected, listing four different layers: National Park (1895 Waterton, 1910 Glacier), International Peace Park (1932), Unesco Biosphere Reserve (1979) and Unesco World Heritage site (1995).

Unhindered by human-created forces, wildfires are perfectly natural events that open up new habitats, promote the growth of fresh seedlings and replenish soil nutrients with decomposed organic matter. Understanding this, park authorities today carefully monitor annual blazes and let them run their natural course, unless they have been human-ignited or are directly threatening property and livelihoods.

SUSTAINABILITY TIPS

The behavior of individual visitors in the parks can play a vital role in ensuring their long-term health and sustainability. Here are a few green recommendations:

➡ Glacier National Park runs a free shuttle bus designed to ease congestion on the increasingly traffic-choked Going-to-the-Sun Rd. The Canadian parks have a number of paying shuttles.

➡ Stay on friendly terms with bears by using bear-proof containers and recycling bins, making noise on the trails, and giving bears a wide and respectful berth.

➡ Look into local volunteer organizations. Many people work tirelessly to protect fragile park wildernesses from degradation and neglect, and it's easy to join them.

➡ By staying in a Glacier National Park–run hotel you are lodging with a profoundly 'green' organization, whose policies include large-scale garbage recycling, use of low-energy light fixtures and donation of old furniture to charity.

➡ Jasper and Glacier National Parks can still be reached by using the train. The VIA/Amtrak services are economical, scenic, 'green' and comfortable.

➡ Glacier's red 'Jammer' buses run on propane and emit 93% less pollutants than their gas-powered equivalents.

➡ Stay on the trail – wandering 'off-piste' or bushwhacking your own path damages flora and causes erosion.

➡ You can gain more in-park knowledge by talking to rangers, reading the local literature and swapping ideas with other hikers on the trail.

The risk is not simply that attractive trees are being killed, but that healthy whitebark pines are integral to the health of their particular ecosystem.

But it is the rapid pace of warming that complicates all other conservation issues. Fires are becoming more frequent and more intense. High alpine meadows are being colonized by seedlings that formerly couldn't have survived dense snowpacks. Pika, cute rodent-like mammals, are running out of alpine tundra and room to construct their burrows to escape the life-threatening summer temperatures. Wolverines lose habitat to roam. Earlier snowmelt leads to less runoff in summer, which means streams warm and fish that depend on cold water adapt or die. Avalanche patterns are disrupted and so on and on. Research scientists worry that their surveys and studies cumulatively point to the impending loss of biodiversity. While this is a concern the world over, these national parks are both laboratories to witness and document the change, as well as ideal environments to experiment with localized interventions.

Solutions

There's no magic solution, obviously, and each park faces its own particular challenges. And no matter the prospect for small successes, what happens outside the park boundaries matters just as much. However, each national-park system continues to address how to limit the carbon footprint of its visitors, improve energy efficiency and increase alternative energy use. As habitats change and shift and animals roam looking for more suitable climes, conservation authorities have looked to maintain and create suitable corridors outside the park boundaries. Large landowners have been enlisted and efforts to limit mining and oil and natural gas exploration have intensified. Volunteers are planting thousands of whitebark pine seedlings grown disease-free in greenhouses in order to restore the population of this important linchpin tree species. Fishing and boating regulations are strictly enforced to stop the spread of invasive aquatic species. And tourism-dependent businesses do their best to educate the public. After all, their survival also depends on that of the wilderness around them.

Survival Guide

HEALTH & SAFETY . . 258

BEFORE YOU GO 258

IN THE PARKS 259

SAFE HIKING 262

SAFE CYCLING 263

CLOTHING & EQUIPMENT 264

Clothing 264

Equipment 264

Buying & Renting Locally 266

DIRECTORY A–Z 267

Accommodations 267

Climate 269

Customs Regulations . . . 269

Electricity 270

Food 270

Insurance 270

Internet Access 270

Legal Matters 271

Maps 271

Money 272

Opening Hours 272

Post 272

Public Holidays 272

Telephone 272

Time 273

Toilets 273

Tourist Information 273

Travelers with Disabilities 273

Volunteering 274

Women Travelers 274

TRANSPORTATION . . 275

GETTING THERE & AWAY 275

Air .275

Bus 275

Car & Motorcycle 276

Train 277

GETTING AROUND 277

Bicycle 278

Bus 278

Car & Motorcycle 278

Hitchhiking 279

Health & Safety

If you have an emergency while staying in the national parks dial ☑911. Major centers like Banff, Jasper and Waterton have medical facilities. If you're traveling out of your home country, be sure to purchase medical insurance before you leave. It is also important to read the policy's small print and ascertain exactly what you are covered for. Medical services in Canada and the US are not reciprocal.

BEFORE YOU GO

If you require medications bring them in their original, labeled containers. A signed and dated letter from your physician describing your medical conditions and medications, including generic names, is a good idea. If carrying syringes or needles, be sure to have a physician's letter documenting their necessity.

Some of the walks in this book are physically demanding and most require a reasonable level of fitness. Even if you're tackling the easy or easy-moderate walks, it pays to be relatively fit, rather than launch straight into them after months of fairly sedentary living. If you're aiming for the demanding walks, fitness is essential.

If you have any medical problems, or are concerned about your health in any way, it's a good idea to have a full checkup before you start walking.

Medical Checklist

➡ acetaminophen (paracetamol) or aspirin

➡ adhesive or paper tape

➡ antibacterial ointment for cuts and abrasions

➡ antibiotics

➡ antidiarrheal drugs (eg loperamide)

➡ antihistamines (for hay fever and allergic reactions)

➡ anti-inflammatory drugs (eg ibuprofen)

➡ bandages, gauze swabs, gauze rolls

➡ DEET–containing insect repellent for the skin

➡ elasticized support bandage

➡ iodine tablets or water filter (for water purification)

➡ nonadhesive dressing

➡ oral rehydration salts

➡ paper stitches

➡ permethrin-containing insect spray for clothing, tents and bed nets

➡ pocket knife

➡ scissors, safety pins, tweezers

➡ sterile alcohol wipes

➡ steroid cream or cortisone (for allergic rashes)

➡ sticking plasters (Band-Aids, blister plasters)

➡ sunblock

➡ sutures

➡ syringes and needles – ask your doctor for a note explaining why you have them

➡ thermometer

Further Reading

➡ *International Travel Health Guide* (Stuart Rose MD; Travel Medicine Inc) The only traveler's health book that is updated annually.

➡ *Medicine for Mountaineering & Other Wilderness Activities* (James Wilkerson) An outstanding reference book for the layperson; describes many of the medical problems typically encountered while trekking.

➡ *Hypothermia, Frostbite and Other Cold Injuries* (James Wilkerson) Good background reading on the subject of cold and high-altitude problems.

➡ *Backcountry Bear Basics: The Definitive Guide to Avoiding Unpleasant Encounters* (Dave Smith) Good on the basics of bear behavior and biology.

➡ *Mountaineering: The Freedom of the Hills* (eds Don Graydon and Kurt Hanson) Discusses outdoor fundamentals from beginner to advanced.

IN THE PARKS

Visiting city dwellers will need to keep their wits about them in order to minimize the chances of suffering an avoidable accident or tragedy. Dress appropriately, tell people where you are going, don't bite off more than you can chew and, above all, *respect* the wilderness and the inherent dangers that it conceals.

Crime is far more common in big cities than in sparsely populated national parks. Nevertheless, use common sense: lock valuables in the trunk of your vehicle, especially if you're parking it at a trailhead overnight, and never leave anything worth stealing in your tent.

Medical Assistance

➡ **Banff National Park**
For medical emergencies, head to the modern **Mineral Springs Hospital** (☎403-762-2222; 305 Lynx St, Banff Town; ◷24hr).

➡ **Jasper National Park**
The two local hospitals are **Seton General Hospital** (☎780-852-3344; 518 Robson St) and **Cottage Medical Clinic** (☎780-852-4885; 505 Turret St).

➡ **Glacier National Park**
Basic first aid is available at visitor centers and ranger stations in the park. The closest hospitals to the west side are **Kalispell Regional Medical Center** (☎406-752-5111; 310 Sunnyview Lane, Kalispell) and **North Valley Hospital** (☎406-863-3500; www.nvhosp.com; 1600 Hospital Way, Whitefish) in Whitefish; the **West Glacier Clinic** (☎406-888-9924; 100 Rea Rd, West Glacier Fire Hall; ◷9am-4pm) can provide treatment for minor injuries. If you're in the northeast, you may find that **Cardston Municipal Hospital** (☎403-653-4411; 144 2nd St W, Cardston), in Alberta, Canada, is the closest bet,

though customs could consume time en route.

➡ **Waterton Lakes National Park** The summer-only number for ambulance service and other medical emergencies in Waterton is ☎403-859-2636. Full medical help is available at **Cardston Municipal Hospital** (☎403-653-4411; 144 2nd St W, Cardston) and **Pincher Creek Municipal Hospital** (☎403-627-1234).

Infectious Diseases

Giardiasis

While water running through the mountains may look crystal-clear, much of it carries *Giardia lamblia*, a microscopic parasite that causes intestinal disorders. To avoid getting sick, boil all water for at least 10 minutes, treat it with water tablets or filter at 0.5 microns or smaller. Note that iodine in cold water doesn't destroy giardiasis.

Symptoms include stomach cramps, nausea, a bloated stomach, watery, foul-smelling diarrhea and frequent gas. Giardiasis can appear several weeks after you have been exposed to the parasite. The symptoms may disappear for a few days and then return; this can go on for several weeks.

Seek medical advice if you think you have giardiasis, but where this is not possible, tinidazole or metronidazole are the recommended drugs. Treatment is a 2g single dose of tinidazole, or 250mg of metronidazole three times daily for five to 10 days.

Environmental Hazards

Altitude

Altitude sickness can strike anyone heading up into the mountains. Thinner air means less oxygen is reaching your muscles and brain,

EMERGENCY NUMBERS

The following are the emergency 24-hour park warden numbers for each park:

Banff (☎403-762-1470)

Glacier (☎406-888-7800)

Jasper (☎780-852-6155)

Waterton Lakes (☎403-859-2636)

requiring the heart and lungs to work harder. Many trailheads begin at high elevations, meaning that you don't have to go very far before feeling the effects.

Symptoms of acute mountain sickness (AMS) include headache, lethargy, dizziness, difficulty sleeping and loss of appetite. AMS may become more severe without warning and can be fatal. Severe symptoms include breathlessness, a dry, irritating cough (which may progress to the production of pink, frothy sputum), severe headache, lack of coordination and balance, confusion, irrational behavior, vomiting, drowsiness and unconsciousness. There is no hard-and-fast rule as to what is too high – AMS has been fatal at 3000m (9843ft) – although 3500m to 4500m (11,483ft to 14,764ft) is the usual range.

Treat mild symptoms by resting at the same altitude until recovery, usually a day or two. Paracetamol or aspirin can be taken for headaches. If symptoms persist or become worse, however, *immediate descent* is necessary; even 500m (1640ft) can help. Drug treatments should never be used to avoid descent or to enable further ascent.

The drugs acetazolamide and dexamethasone are recommended by some

WATER PURIFICATION

To ensure you are getting safe, clean drinking water in the backcountry you have three basic options:

Boiling

Water is considered safe to drink if it has been boiled at 100°C (212°F) for at least a minute. This is best done when you set up your camp and stove in the evening.

Chemical Purification

There are two types of chemical additives that will purify water: chlorine or iodine. You can choose from various products on the market. Read the instructions carefully first, be aware of expiration dates and check you are not allergic to either chemical.

Filtration

Mobile devices can pump water through microscopic filters and take out potentially harmful organisms. If carrying a filter, take care it doesn't get damaged in transit, read the instructions carefully and always filter the cleanest water you can find.

doctors for the prevention of AMS; however, their use is controversial. They can reduce the symptoms, but they may also mask warning signs; severe and fatal AMS has occurred in people taking these drugs. In general we do not recommend them for travelers.

To prevent acute mountain sickness:

➡ Ascend slowly – have frequent rest days, spending two to three nights at each rise of 1000m (3281ft). If you reach a high altitude by trekking, acclimatization takes place gradually and you are less likely to be affected than if you fly directly to high altitude.

➡ It is always wise to sleep at a lower altitude than the greatest height reached during the day, if possible. Also, once above 3000m (9843ft), care should be taken not to increase the sleeping altitude by more than 300m (984ft) per day.

➡ Drink extra fluids. The mountain air is dry and cold and moisture is lost as you breathe; evaporation of sweat may occur unnoticed and result in dehydration.

➡ Eat light, high-carbohydrate meals for more energy.

➡ Avoid alcohol and sedatives.

Bites & Stings
MOSQUITOES

Mosquitoes can be rampant in all parks, particularly on summer evenings. In Banff and Jasper, you'll notice them around lakes and on wooded hikes; they are particularly prevalent along parts of the remote North Boundary Trail. In Glacier and Waterton Lakes, mosquitoes tend to be more annoying on the west side of the park than in the windier east. Use repellent, wear light-colored clothing and cover yourself in the evening.

TICKS

Ticks are most active from spring to autumn, especially where there are plenty of sheep or deer. They usually lurk in overhanging vegetation, so avoid pushing through tall bushes.

If a tick is found attached to the skin, press down around its head with tweezers. grab the head and gently pull upward. Avoid pulling the rear of the body as this may squeeze the tick's gut contents through its mouth into your skin, increasing the risk of infection and disease. Smearing chemicals on the tick will not make it let go and is not recommended.

Lyme's disease is a tick-borne illness that manifests itself in skin lesions and, later on, intermittent or persistent arthritis. To avoid contracting it, use all normal mosquito preventative measures, including wearing long-sleeved shirts and trousers, checking clothing for ticks after outdoor activity, and using an effective brand of DEET or insect repellent.

Rocky Mountain spotted fever is another tick-borne disease that is potentially lethal, but usually curable if diagnosed early. Symptoms include fever and muscle pain followed by the development of a rash. Treatment is with antibiotics, but to prevent it take the usual anti-tick measures especially when walking in areas of tall grass or brush.

Cold
HYPOTHERMIA

This occurs when the body loses heat faster than it can produce it and the core temperature of the body falls.

It is frighteningly easy to progress from very cold to dangerously cold due to a combination of wind, wet clothing, fatigue and hunger, even if the air temperature is above freezing. If the weather deteriorates, put on extra layers of warm clothing; a wind and/or waterproof jacket, plus wool or fleece hat and gloves are all essential. Have something energy-giving to eat and ensure that everyone in your group is fit, feeling well and alert.

Symptoms of hypothermia are exhaustion, numb skin (particularly toes and fingers), shivering, slurred speech, irrational or violent behavior, lethargy, stumbling, dizzy spells, muscle cramps and violent bursts of energy.

Irrationality may take the form of sufferers claiming they are warm and trying to take off their clothes.

To treat mild hypothermia, first get the person out of the wind and/or rain, remove their clothing if it's wet and replace it with dry, warm clothing. Give them hot liquids – not alcohol – and some high-energy, easily digestible food. Do not rub victims: instead, allow them to slowly warm themselves.

FROSTBITE

This refers to the freezing of extremities, including fingers, toes and nose. Signs and symptoms of frostbite include a whitish or waxy cast to the skin, or even crystals on the surface, plus itching, numbness and pain. Warm the affected areas by immersion in warm (not hot) water, or with blankets or clothes, only until the skin becomes flushed. Frostbitten parts should not be rubbed. Pain and swelling are inevitable. Blisters should not be broken. Get medical attention right away.

Heat
DEHYDRATION & HEAT EXHAUSTION

Dehydration is a potentially dangerous and generally preventable condition caused by excessive fluid loss. Sweating combined with inadequate fluid intake is one of the common causes in trekkers, but other causes are diarrhea, vomiting and high fever.

The first symptoms are weakness, thirst and passing small amounts of very concentrated urine. This may lead to drowsiness, dizziness or fainting on standing up, and finally, coma.

It's easy to forget how much fluid you are losing via perspiration while you are trekking, particularly if a strong breeze is drying your skin quickly. You should always maintain a good fluid intake – a minimum of 3L a day is recommended.

Dehydration and salt deficiency can cause heat exhaustion. Salt deficiency is characterized by fatigue, lethargy, headaches, giddiness and muscle cramps. Salt tablets are overkill; just adding extra salt to your food is probably sufficient.

HEATSTROKE

This is a serious, occasionally fatal condition that occurs if the body's heat-regulating mechanism breaks down and the body temperature rises to dangerous levels. Long, continuous periods of exposure to high temperatures and insufficient fluids can leave you vulnerable to heatstroke.

The symptoms are feeling unwell, not sweating very much (or at all) and a high body temperature of around 39°C to 41°C (102°F to 106°F). Where sweating has ceased, the skin becomes flushed and red. Severe, throbbing headaches and lack of coordination will also occur, and the sufferer may be confused or aggressive. Eventually the victim will become delirious or convulse. Hospitalization is essential but, in the interim, get victims out of the sun, remove their clothing, cover them with a wet sheet or towel, and then fan continually. Give fluids if they are conscious.

Snow Blindness

This is a temporary, painful condition resulting from sunburn of the surface of the eye (cornea). It usually occurs when someone walks on snow or in bright sunshine without sunglasses. Treatment is to relieve the pain – cold cloths on closed eyelids may help. Antibiotic and anesthetic eye drops are not necessary. The condition usually resolves itself within a few days and there are no long-term consequences.

Sun

Protection against the sun should always be taken seriously. Particularly in the rarefied air and deceptive coolness of the mountains, sunburn occurs rapidly. Slap on the sunscreen and a barrier cream for your nose and lips, wear a broad-brimmed hat and protect your eyes with good-quality sunglasses with UV lenses, particularly when walking near water, sand or snow. If, despite these precautions, you get burnt, calamine lotion, aloe vera or other commercial sunburn-relief preparations will soothe.

WALK SAFETY – BASIC RULES

➡ Allow plenty of time to accomplish a walk before dark, particularly when daylight hours are shorter.

➡ Study the route carefully before setting out, noting the possible escape routes and the point of no return (where it's quicker to continue than to turn back). Monitor your progress during the day against the time estimated for the walk, and keep an eye on the weather.

➡ It's wise not to walk alone. Always leave details of your intended route, number of people in your group and expected return time with someone responsible before you set off, and let that person know when you return.

➡ Before setting off, make sure you have a relevant map, compass and whistle, and that you know the weather forecast for the area for the next 24 hours. In the Rockies always carry extra warm, dry layers of clothing and plenty of emergency high-energy food.

BEAR ISSUES

Although people have an inordinate fear of being hurt by bears, the Canadian Rockies are a far more dangerous place for the bears themselves. In Banff National Park alone, 90% of known grizzly bear deaths have occurred within 400m (0.25 miles) of roads and buildings, with most bears either being killed by cars or by wardens when bears and people got mixed up. Cross-continental trains traveling through the parks have also killed many of these magnificent beasts.

Bears are intelligent opportunists that quickly learn that humans come with food and tasty garbage. Unfortunately, once this association is learned, a bear nearly always has to be shot. Remember: 'A fed bear is a dead bear,' so never feed a bear, never improperly store food or garbage, and always clean up after yourself.

Bears are also dangerous creatures that can sprint the length of a football field in six seconds. Although such encounters are rare, bears will readily attack if their cubs are around, if they're defending food or if they feel surprised and threatened. Your best defenses against surprising a bear are to remain alert, avoid hiking at night (when bears feed) and be careful when traveling upwind near streams or where visibility is obscured.

To avoid an encounter altogether, hike in groups (bears almost never attack hiking groups of more than four people) and make noise on the trail, preferably by talking or singing. Jangling bear bells aren't really loud enough to be effective.

If you do encounter a bear, there are several defensive strategies to employ, but no guarantees. If the bear doesn't see you, move a safe distance downwind and make noise to alert it to your presence. If the bear sees you, slowly back out of its path, avoid eye contact, speak softly and wave your hands above your head slowly. Never turn your back to the bear and never kneel down.

Sows with cubs are particularly dangerous, and you should make every effort to avoid coming between a sow and her cubs. A sow may clack her jaws, lower her head and shake it as a warning before she charges.

If a bear does charge, do not run and do not scream (which may frighten the bear and make it more aggressive), because the bear may only be charging as a bluff. Drop to the ground, crouch face down in a ball, and play dead, covering the back of your neck with your hands and your chest and stomach with your knees. Do not resist the bear's inquisitive pawing – it may get bored and go away.

If the bear continues to attack you, it may be a (rare) predatory bear, in which case you should fight back aggressively. Park authorities recommend hikers carry bear spray, which can be used as a last resort. It has proved to be effective if aimed into the face of a charging bear from a range of about 10m (33ft). For more bear advice, check www.nps.gov/subjects/bears/safety.htm.

SAFE HIKING

Avalanches

Avalanches are a threat during and following storms, in high winds and during temperature changes, particularly when it warms in spring. Educate yourself about the dangers of avalanches before setting out into the backcountry. Signs of avalanche activity include felled trees and slides. For up-to-date information on avalanche hazards in Banff, Kootenay and Yoho, contact ☑403-762-1470 and for Jasper ☑780-852-6155. For other areas, contact the **Canadian Avalanche Association** (☑800-667-1105) or local park information centers.

Before adventuring in Waterton, check with the **park warden** (☑403-859-5140) for avalanche updates, as winter trails are not maintained. In Glacier, call ☑406-257-8402 or ☑800-526-5329 for information. Local radio stations broadcast reports on area avalanche conditions studied by the Northwest Montana Avalanche Warning System.

If you are caught in an avalanche, your chance of survival depends on your ability to keep yourself above the flowing snow and your companions' ability to rescue you. The probability of survival decreases rapidly after half an hour, so the party must be self-equipped, with each member carrying an avalanche beacon, a sectional probe and a collapsible shovel.

Crossing Streams

Sudden downpours are common in the mountains and can speedily turn a gentle stream into a raging torrent. If you're in any doubt about the safety of a crossing, look for a safer passage upstream or wait. If the rain is short-lived, it should subside quickly.

If you decide it's essential to cross (late in the day, for example), look for a wide, relatively shallow stretch of the stream rather than a bend. Take off your trousers and socks, but keep your boots on to prevent injury. Put dry, warm clothes and a towel in a plastic bag near the top of your pack. Use a walking pole, grasped in both hands, on the upstream side as a third leg, or go arm in arm with a companion, clasping at the wrist, and cross-side-on to the flow, taking short steps.

Lightning

If a storm brews, avoid exposed areas. Lightning has a penchant for crests, lone trees, small depressions, gullies, caves and cabin entrances, as well as wet ground. If you are caught out in the open, try to curl up as tightly as possible with your feet together and keep a layer of insulation between you and the ground. Place metal objects such as metal-frame backpacks and walking poles away from you.

Rescue & Evacuation

If someone in your group is injured or falls ill and can't move, leave somebody with them while another one or more goes for help. They should take clear written details of the location and condition of the victim, and of helicopter landing conditions. If there are only two of you, leave the injured person with as much warm clothing, food and water as it's sensible to spare, plus the whistle and torch. Mark the position with something conspicuous – an orange bivvy bag, or perhaps a large stone cross on the ground.

SAFE CYCLING

One of the most common problems cyclists will encounter is unobservant motorists busy gawping at the scenery and wildlife. The arterial Going-to-the-Sun Rd in Glacier, built in the early days of the motorcar, is notoriously precipitous and narrow, with no shoulders for cyclists. Jammed with dawdling people-carriers and oversized SUVs, the highway is a cycling obstacle course and, as a result, cyclists are prevented from using it between 11am and 4pm (June to September), largely for their own safety.

Wildlife is another problem, particularly for off-roaders who run the risk of surprising large animals such as moose or bears when progressing rapidly along twisting forested trails. To avoid potentially dangerous encounters with foraging megafauna, cyclists are encouraged to take heed of posted trail warnings and make plenty of noise on concealed corners and rises (remember, a bear can easily outsprint a cyclist).

Helmets are mandatory in all North American national parks. Off-roaders may also want to invest in elbow and knee pads.

Clothing & Equipment

Visitors to the Rockies should prepare themselves for fickle weather, whatever the season. Double down on this if you're planning on backcountry camping. Take the time to get properly kitted out and you're guaranteed to have a safer and more comfortable trip. This, of course, means good boots and layering, but you may also want to consider strapping on a canister of pepper spray to use as a last resort against aggressive wild animals, especially bears.

Clothing
Layering
A secret of comfortable walking is to wear several layers of light clothing, which you can easily take off or put on as you warm up or cool down. Most walkers use three main layers: a base layer next to the skin; an insulating layer; and an outer-shell layer for protection from wind, rain and snow.

For the upper body, the base layer is typically a shirt of synthetic material that wicks moisture away from the body and reduces chilling. The insulating layer retains heat next to your body, and is usually a (windproof) fleece jacket or sweater. The outer shell consists of a waterproof jacket that also protects against cold wind.

For the lower body, the layers generally consist of either shorts or loose-fitting trousers, thermal underwear ('long johns') and waterproof overtrousers.

When purchasing outdoor clothing, one of the most practical fabrics is merino wool. Though a little pricier than other materials, natural wool absorbs sweat, retains heat even when wet, and is soft and comfortable to wear. Even better, it doesn't store odors like other sports garments, so you can wear it for several days in a row without inflicting antisocial smells on your tent-mates.

Waterproof Shells
Jackets should be made of a breathable, waterproof fabric, with a hood that is roomy enough to cover headwear, but that still allows peripheral vision. Other handy accessories include a large map pocket and a heavy-gauge zip protected by a storm flap.

Waterproof pants are best with slits for pocket access and long leg zips so that you can pull them on and off over your boots.

Footwear, Socks & Gaiters
Running shoes are OK for walks that are graded easy or moderate. However, you'll probably appreciate, if not need, the support and protection provided by hiking boots for more demanding walks. Nonslip soles (such as Vibram) provide the best grip.

Buy boots in warm conditions or go for a walk before trying them on, so that your feet can expand slightly, as they would on a hike. It's also a good idea to carry a pair of sandals to wear at night for getting in and out of tents easily or at rest stops. Sandals are also useful when fording waterways.

Gaiters help to keep your feet dry in wet weather and on boggy ground; they can also deflect small stones or sand and maintain leg warmth. The best are made of strong fabric, with a robust zip protected by a flap, and secure easily around the foot.

Walking socks should be free of ridged seams in the toes and heels.

Equipment
Backpack & Daypacks
For day walks, a daypack (30L to 40L) will usually suffice, but for multiday walks you will need a backpack of between 45L and 90L capacity. Even if the manufacturer claims your pack is waterproof, use heavy-duty liners.

Navigation Equipment
MAPS & COMPASS
You should always carry a good map of the area in which you are walking, and know how to read it. Before setting off on your walk,

ROUTE FINDING

While accurate, our maps are not perfect. Natural features such as river confluences and mountain peaks are in their true position, but sometimes the location of towns and trails is not always so. This may be because a village is spread over a hillside, or the size of the map does not allow for detail of the trail's twists and turns. However, by using several basic route-finding techniques, you will have few problems following our descriptions:

➡ Be aware of whether the trail should be climbing or descending.

➡ Check the north-point arrow on the map and determine the general direction of the trail.

➡ Time your progress over a known distance and calculate the speed at which you travel in the given terrain. From then on, you can determine with reasonable accuracy how far you have traveled.

➡ Watch the path – look for boot prints and other signs of previous passage.

ensure that you are aware of the contour interval, the map symbols, the magnetic declination (difference between true and grid north), plus the main ridge and river systems in the area and the general direction in which you are heading. On the trail, try to identify major landforms such as mountain ranges and valleys, and locate them on your map to familiarize yourself with the geography.

Buy a compass and learn how to use it. The attraction of magnetic north varies in different parts of the world, so compasses need to be balanced accordingly. Compass manufacturers have divided the world into five zones. Make sure your compass is balanced for your destination zone. There are also 'universal' compasses on the market that can be used anywhere in the world.

GLOBAL POSITIONING SYSTEM

Originally developed by the US Department of Defense, the Global Positioning System (GPS) is a network of more than 20 earth-orbiting satellites that continually beam encoded signals back to earth. Small, computer-driven devices (GPS receivers) can decode these signals to give users an extremely accurate reading of their location – to within 30m, anywhere on the planet, at any time of day, in almost any weather. The cheapest handheld GPS receivers now cost less than US$40 (although these may not have a built-in averaging system that minimises signal errors). Other important factors to consider when buying a GPS receiver are its weight and battery life.

Remember that a GPS receiver is of little use unless used with an accurate topographical map. The receiver simply gives your position, which you must then locate on the local map. GPS receivers will only work properly in the open. The signals from a crucial satellite may be blocked (or bounce off rock or water) directly below high cliffs, near large bodies of water or in dense tree cover and give inaccurate readings. GPS receivers are more vulnerable to breakdowns (including dead batteries) than the humble magnetic compass – a low-tech device that has served navigators faithfully for centuries – so don't rely on them entirely.

Bear Spray

Most of the hikes/activities in the parks are also in bear country. As a last resort, bear spray (pepper spray) has been used effectively to deter aggressive bears, and park authorities often recommend that you equip yourself with a canister when venturing into backcountry. Be sure to familiarize yourself with the manufacturer's instructions before use, and only use as a last resort (ie on a charging bear approximately 9m to 15m/30ft to 50ft away from you). Most shops in or around the parks stock bear spray, which sells for approximately US$45; some rent it by the day. It is best kept close at hand on a belt around your waist.

Tent

A three-season tent will fulfill most walkers' requirements. The floor and the outer shell, or fly, should have taped or sealed seams and covered zips to stop leaks. The weight can be as low as 1kg for a stripped-down, low-profile tent, and up to 3kg for a roomy, four-season model.

Dome- and tunnel-shaped tents handle windy conditions better than flat-sided tents.

Sleeping Bag & Mat

Down fillings are warmer than synthetic for the same weight and bulk but, unlike synthetic fillings, do not retain warmth when wet. Mummy-shaped bags are best for weight and warmth. The given figure (-5°C/23°F, for instance) is the coldest temperature at which a person should feel comfortable in the bag (although the ratings are notoriously unreliable).

An inner sheet helps keep your sleeping bag clean, as well as adding an insulating layer; silk 'inners' are lightest, but they also come in cotton or synthetic fabric.

Self-inflating sleeping mats work like a thin air cushion between you and the ground; they also insulate from the cold. Foam mats are

CLOTHING & EQUIPMENT CHECKLIST

This list is a general guide to the things you might take on a walk. Your list will vary depending on the kind of walking you want to do, whether you're camping or planning to stay in hostels or B&Bs, and on the terrain, weather conditions and time of year.

Clothing

- ☐ boots and spare laces
- ☐ gaiters
- ☐ warm hat, scarf and gloves
- ☐ waterproof pants
- ☐ rain jacket
- ☐ athletic or trail shoes and sandals
- ☐ shorts and trousers
- ☐ socks and underwear
- ☐ sunhat
- ☐ sweater or fleece jacket
- ☐ thermal underwear
- ☐ T-shirt and long-sleeved shirt with collar

Equipment

- ☐ backpack with waterproof liner
- ☐ bear spray
- ☐ first-aid kit
- ☐ flashlight (torch) or headlamp, spare batteries and bulb (globe)
- ☐ food and snacks (high energy) and one day's emergency supplies
- ☐ insect repellent
- ☐ map, compass and guidebook
- ☐ map case or clip-seal plastic bags
- ☐ plastic bags (for carrying rubbish)
- ☐ pocket knife
- ☐ sunglasses
- ☐ sunscreen and lip balm
- ☐ survival bag or blanket
- ☐ toilet paper and trowel
- ☐ water container
- ☐ whistle

Overnight Walks

- ☐ cooking, eating and drinking utensils
- ☐ dishwashing items
- ☐ matches and lighter
- ☐ sewing/repair kit
- ☐ sleeping bag and bag liner/inner sheet
- ☐ sleeping mat
- ☐ spare cord
- ☐ stove and fuel
- ☐ tent, pegs, poles and guy ropes
- ☐ toiletries
- ☐ towel
- ☐ water purification tablets, iodine or filter

Optional Items

- ☐ backpack cover (waterproof, slip-on)
- ☐ binoculars
- ☐ camera, film and batteries
- ☐ candle
- ☐ cell (mobile) phone
- ☐ emergency distress beacon
- ☐ GPS receiver
- ☐ groundsheet
- ☐ mosquito net
- ☐ swimsuit
- ☐ walking poles

---

a low-cost, but less comfortable, alternative.

Stoves & Fuel

The easiest type of fuel to use is butane gas in disposable containers; true, it doesn't win many environmental points, but it's much easier to come by than liquid fuels. The most widely used brands are Coleman and Camping Gaz, available from outdoor gear shops and, in some remote areas, from small supermarkets.

Liquid fuel includes Coleman fuel, methylated spirits and paraffin. Again, outdoor gear shops, possibly hardware stores or even small supermarkets are the best places to look for it. You may be able to obtain small quantities of unleaded petrol from service stations.

Airlines prohibit the carriage of any flammable materials and may well reject empty liquid-fuel bottles or even the stoves themselves.

Buying & Renting Locally

More specialized gear such as bikes, snowshoes, hiking poles and climbing harnesses can usually be rented either in the parks or in one of the surrounding settlements.

Kayaks, canoes and increasingly popular stand-up paddleboards (SUP), including inflatable options of all three, are available for rental in many locations throughout the parks.

Directory A–Z

Accommodations

There is an enormous choice of accommodations both inside and around the national parks, ranging from campgrounds and hostels through to B&Bs, country cabins and top-end hotels. Rates are a lot more expensive compared to many other areas of Canada and the US, however, and it can be extremely hard to find a room if you leave things to the last minute.

➡ Prices increase considerably during the peak summer months of July and August, and during the main ski season from December to March. Book well ahead if you want to stay during either period.

➡ In Banff and Jasper, most of the accommodations are concentrated around the main townsites.

➡ Staying beyond the park boundaries can be a good way to find cheaper hotel rates. For example, consider staying in Canmore for visiting Banff; Field for Lake Louise; or St Mary, Babb or Polebridge for East and West Glacier. The downside, of course, is that instead of being surrounded by pristine wilderness you might be situated along an ordinary commercial strip.

➡ Skiing as part of an organized package (including lift passes and accommodations) is usually much cheaper than booking both separately, but not always. Many hotels offer good deals during ski season to compete with package tours.

B&Bs & Guesthouses

Staying with locals can be a great way to immerse yourself in the park and get some insiders' tips on the best things to see and do during your stay. Many residents offer B&B rooms in their own homes to travelers, but standards vary widely. Some places are fairly basic, while others will give many top-end hotels a run for their money. B&Bs are less common in Glacier than the Canadian parks.

➡ Breakfast is nearly always included in room rates, but if you have special requirements (eg vegetarian, vegan, gluten-free), let the owners know in advance.

➡ Not all B&B rooms have private bathrooms, so check before booking if that's important to you.

➡ Remember to check the B&B's policies on pets, kids and credit cards. Some will accept all three, while others won't accept any.

Camping

FRONTCOUNTRY CAMPING

Camping is a wonderful (and popular) way of experiencing the national parks. All of the Canadian and US parks offer a good range of frontcountry campgrounds that are accessible from the main roads.

Facilities vary widely: large campgrounds might have flush toilets, drinking water, public phones, fire pits and RV hookups, while others might only have pit toilets and a standpipe for drinking water. In general, the more popular campgrounds (especially those close to tourist centers) are better equipped than those further afield.

➡ In the Canadian parks, the only campgrounds that currently accept reservations are Tunnel Mountain, Two Jack, Johnston Canyon and Lake Louise (in Banff); Pocahontas, Whistlers, Wapiti and Wabasso (Jasper); and the townsite campground in Waterton. Two Jack (Banff) and Whistlers (Jasper) now offer oTENTiks, small A-frame tents with hot water and electricity (C$120).

BOOK YOUR STAY ONLINE

For more accommodations reviews by Lonely Planet authors, check out http://lonelyplanet.com/hotels/. You'll find independent reviews, as well as recommendations on the best places to stay. Best of all, you can book online.

Contact the **Parks Canada Reservation Service** (☎877-737-3783; www. reservation.parkscanada. gc.ca). Reservations can be made up to three months in advance for a C$11.70 fee.

➜ In Glacier National Park, reservations are available up to six months in advance at Fish Creek and St Mary campgrounds through the **National Park Reservation Service** (☎800-365-2267; www.recreation.gov).

➜ All other sites operate on a first-come, first-served basis. Arrive before checkout time at 11am for the best chance of securing a site. Campground availability bulletins are published regularly and are available at visitor centers and on park radio.

➜ Most campgrounds are suitable for tents, campervans and RVs, although not all have pull-throughs or paved sites.

➜ At more remote campgrounds, facilities are generally limited to pit toilets and drinking water, although some also have recycling bins and bear-proof storage lockers.

➜ Some campgrounds operate on a self-registration basis. Find an available site first, then fill in your details (name, site number, length of stay, registration number) on the payment envelope and drop it in the box near the entrance. Credit cards are accepted.

➜ The maximum stay at any campground is usually 14 days.

➜ Fires are usually allowed in designated fire pits (provided no fire restrictions are currently in force), although in Canada you'll need to buy a fire permit (C$10). The permit includes a bundle of wood.

BACKCOUNTRY CAMPING

Backcountry campgrounds are mainly geared for hikers exploring the trails, so facilities are extremely rudimentary. Most only offer cleared tent pads and a pit privy; some also have food-storage cables where you should suspend toiletries, garbage and food items to avoid attracting bears to the campground.

➜ Overnight backcountry stays require a special permit, known in Canadian parks as a wilderness pass (C$9.80 per night) and in US parks as a backcountry permit (US$5 per night). Popular spots fill up quickly in peak months so reservations (for a fee) are recommended. At present, the application process, for Glacier at least, is low-tech and slow. Read the National Park Service Glacier Backcountry Guide (search for 'backcountry camping' at www.nps.gov) carefully before planning your trip.

➜ Visitor numbers on backcountry trails are limited, so you'll usually need to specify your campgrounds when you purchase your wilderness pass. The

maximum stay at any one campground is generally three nights.

➜ In some very remote areas of the parks, wild camping is allowed – choose a site at least 50m (55yd) from the trail, 70m (77yd) from water sources and 5km (3 miles) or more from the trailhead.

➜ See the useful Leave No Trace website (www. leavenotrace.ca) for tips on how to travel responsibly in the backcountry.

Hostels

Another cheap way of visiting the parks is to stay in a hostel. They're not just for backpackers and hikers these days: most are happy to rent out whole dorms and private rooms, making them ideal for families or couples on a budget. The best hostels in Banff and Jasper are run by Hostelling International (HI; www.hihostels.ca), which has flagship hostels in Banff Town, Lake Louise and Jasper Town. Dorm rooms cost between C$25 and C$40 depending on the season. The hostel closest to Glacier is in East Glacier.

➜ Accommodations are usually in dorms with four to 10 beds, with a communal kitchen and lounge. Some also have cafes, games rooms and TV rooms.

➜ Dorms are often (but not always) organized along gender lines. Bathrooms and showers are shared. Some hostels have en suite bathrooms for each dorm, while others have communal bathrooms in the corridor.

➜ HI members qualify for discounts on nightly rates. Annual membership costs C$35 and is free for people under the age of 17.

➜ The HI also runs several basic wilderness hostels (such as Mosquito Creek and Rampart Creek), which are essentially wood cabins with a kitchen, dining area and communal lounge (often with a cozy wood-burning stove).

ACCOMMODATIONS PRICE RANGES

The following price ranges are based on a double room with private bathroom in high season; cheaper rates may be available in shoulder and low seasons. Prices are based on Canadian dollars (C$) in Canada and US dollars (US$) in the United States.

$ less than $100

$$ $100–$250

$$$ more than $250

→ The **Alpine Club of Canada** (☏403-678-3200; www.alpineclubofcanada.ca) operates simple hut hostels in the backcountry, mostly used by climbers and hikers. Reservations are essential.

Hotels

There's no shortage of hotels in Banff, Jasper and Glacier, but they're generally not cheap. Room rates, especially in Banff, are notoriously expensive, and always shoot upward in the peak season between May and September. Things are a bit more affordable in Jasper, as well as in the neighboring provincial parks.

Except at the top end of the price ladder, the standard of accommodations is often pretty mediocre for the price you'll pay.

→ Nearly all hotel rooms come with en suite bathroom, telephone and cable TV, and most places offer free wi-fi for guests. Breakfast is often charged as an extra.

→ Some hotels (such as all of Glacier's historic 'parkitecture' lodges and motor inns, Num-Ti-Jah Lodge on Peyto Lake, and Jasper's heritage hotels) make a deliberate point of not providing TVs and telephones.

→ Room rates are nearly always quoted per room, but without sales tax.

→ There's usually a string of cheap motels on the edge of the larger towns.

Condos & Vacation Apartments

Local by-laws prohibit the rental of vacation homes or apartments in Banff, Lake Louise and Jasper, but many hotels offer suites or chalets that are specifically intended for families, often including a full kitchen, bathroom and two or three bedrooms.

Vacation apartments and condos are available outside the park borders (eg in Canmore, Kootenay or Whitefish),

Climate

Banff National Park

Glacier National Park

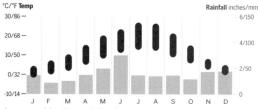

Jasper National Park

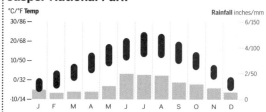

but only certain properties are licensed to be used for the purpose. Make sure you use a legitimate operator, avoid arranging anything directly with the owner or paying anything up-front, and always check the terms and conditions carefully before booking. Whitefish properties available on popular booking sites are especially sought-after by skiers in winter months (a resort tax might be applied to rentals).

Some useful websites:

Canmore Holiday Accommodation (www.canmoreholiday accommodation.com) Canmore condos and apartments.

Field (www.field.ca/accommo dations) Options for Field.

Rentals in the Rockies (www. rentalsintherockies.com) Agency based in Canmore.

Tourism Golden (www.tourism golden.com/accommodations/ vacation-homes) Listings of self-catering apartments around Golden.

Customs Regulations

→ Visitors entering either Canada or the US can bring 200 cigarettes (one carton), 50 cigars and 7 ounces of tobacco; 1.5L or 53 fl oz of liquor or wine, or 24 cans of beer; and gifts up to the value of C$60 (US$100) per item.

→ There are strict restrictions on the import of plants, seeds and animal products to prevent the spread of pests and diseases. This also applies to firewood, which can't be transported across the border.

➜ Importing firearms, explosives and other weapons is illegal unless you're carrying an appropriate permit.

➜ You can bring bear spray across the border as long as the specific intended usage is clearly indicated.

Electricity

Canada and the US both use plugs with either two or three pins. Adaptors to convert power plugs are easily available from electrical outlets and travel shops.

In order to charge phones and other electrical devices, nonguests at the various park's accommodations can request to use outlets in lobbies and restaurants. Obviously, don't go overboard. There are also a handful of outlets in the visitor centers, however use is encouraged only for emergencies. If you are driving, a universal car charger might come in handy.

120V/60Hz

120V/60Hz

Food

Restaurants, diners and cafes are plentiful around the park townsites, but choice is a lot more limited once you get out into the rest of the national parks. If you're eating out, remember that service is usually not added to your bill – a tip of 15% to 20% is the expected norm.

The following price indicators are based on the cost of a main meal. Prices are based on Canadian dollars (C$) in Canada and US dollars (US$) in the United States.

$ less than $15

$$ $15–$25

$$$ more than $25

Insurance

Travel insurance is always a worthwhile investment if you're visiting another country. Worldwide travel insurance is available at www. lonelyplanet.com/travel-insurance. You can buy, extend and claim online any time – even if you're already on the road.

➜ Choose your policy carefully, especially for coverage against flight delays, 'acts of God' or force majeure events, and baggage loss, and check the excess to be paid in the event of a claim.

➜ If you're undertaking outdoor activities such as hiking, cycling, climbing or water sports, and especially if you're skiing or snowboarding, make sure your travel insurance policy covers you against medical treatment and emergency repatriation, as hospital bills are cripplingly expensive.

➜ Most standard US health plans aren't valid for treatment in Canada, so you'll need to ensure you're covered under a separate travel insurance policy.

➜ Auto insurance purchased in Canada and the US is usually applicable to either country, but confirm this with your provider before you leave home.

➜ Many auto insurance policies extend to rental cars, and some credit-card providers grant coverage if you pay for the rental with your card.

Internet Access

Access is widespread around Banff and Jasper, and around Waterton townsite, but it's patchy around Glacier.

➜ Most hotels including the historic 'parkitecture' lodging in Glacier offer free wireless access to customers with their own laptops, and wi-fi hot spots are common in cafes and restaurants.

➜ In reviews, the wi-fi icon (🛜) denotes wireless access is available.

➜ The internet icon (@) denotes that there is a computer available for public use.

➜ Most public libraries offer internet access, usually for a small fee.

INTERNATIONAL VISITORS

Entering the US & Canada by Air

➡ Visitors from many countries, including the US, most European Union nations, the UK, Australia and New Zealand, do not require a visa to enter Canada. You are usually permitted to remain in the country for six months, after which you will have to apply for an extension to your stay.

➡ If you're arriving in the US from one of these countries, you should qualify for entry under the Visa Waiver Program. This will qualify you to remain in the US for a stay of up to 90 days. Citizens of the 38 countries in the US Visa Waiver Program need to register with the government online (www.cbp.gov/travel/international-visitors/esta); apply at least 72 hours in advance (notification is usually immediate and registration is valid for two years).

➡ Citizens of other countries will need to apply for a visitor's visa from either the **Citizenship and Immigration Service Canada** (☏888-576-8502; www.cic.gc.ca) or the **US Citizenship and Immigration Services** (☏800-375-5283; www.uscis.gov), or apply directly to the embassy or consulate in their own country.

➡ There's a comprehensive list of Canadian consular offices at www.cic.gc.ca/english/information/offices/apply-where.asp, and of US embassies at www.usembassy.state.gov.

Entering the US & Canada via the Land Border

Most US-based visitors heading for Canada cross via the land border, either by train, bus or, more likely, car. With thousands of people crossing the border on a daily basis it's one of the busiest land borders in the world and, unsurprisingly, the wait times can be horrendously long. You can get the heads-up on the likely delays at specific checkpoints via the Canada Border Services Agency website (www.cbsa-asfc.gc.ca).

At the checkpoint, you'll need to present your passport, plus driver's license, insurance and registration if you're arriving by car. Note that if you're bringing a rental car across the border, you might have to have this cleared with the rental company beforehand, and you might have to present your rental agreement to border officials for inspection. If you're on public transportation, you may have to disembark and carry your own luggage across the border.

Be prepared to answer standard questions from border guards about the purpose of your visit, length of stay and any items you're intending to bring across the border. Unless you fancy prolonging the experience, answer sensibly and politely; this is definitely not a time for wisecracking. Evasiveness only tends to lead to more detailed queries and prolonged questioning.

Legal Matters

➡ It's illegal to remove any flora or fauna from the national parks, including rocks, minerals and fossils, as well as bird eggs, plants and wildflowers.

➡ Tree bark and pine cones harbor destructive parasites such as pine beetle, so don't collect them.

➡ Hunting and firearms are not permitted in the national parks.

Maps

The best topographical maps are produced by Gem Trek Publishing (www.gemtrek.com), which has several excellent 1:100,000 maps covering Banff, Jasper and Waterton Lakes, as well as Lake Louise and Yoho, Bow Lake and the Crossing, Columbia Icefield, Canmore, Kananaskis and several other areas.

All major trails and points of interest are clearly marked on the maps, which are supposedly waterproof and tear-proof (although in practice they'll only take so much punishment). They're available everywhere, including from retail stores, bookstores, grocery stores and many gas stations.

National Geographic's *Trails Illustrated* series offers topographical, waterproof, tear-proof maps of Glacier and Waterton Lakes (the smaller maps within this series that only cover a region such as Two Medicine Valley are recommended because they include water hazards), while the United States Geological Survey (USGS) publishes a 1:100,000 topographical map for Glacier National Park.

Map Art Publishing (www.mapart.com) produces a range of road maps covering the Canadian Rockies.

Note that our maps aren't intended for serious backcountry hikes; we highly recommend you purchase one of the options above.

Money
Canada

Banks and ATMs are fairly widespread in the main townsites, and you'll find branches of at least one major bank (CIBC, ATB, Scotiabank or Bank of Montreal) in Jasper, Banff and Canmore as well as in several other gateway towns. Many gas stations, supermarkets and malls also have ATMs, and there are handy ATMs at Samson Mall in Lake Louise Village and Saskatchewan Crossing on the Icefields Pkwy. For exchange services in Waterton, head to **Tamarack Outdoor Outfitters** (☑403-859-2378; Mount View Rd; ☺8am-8pm). The closest banks are in Cardston and Pincher Creek.

➡ Banks generally offer better exchange rates than currency bureaus.

➡ If your bank is a member of the Cirrus or Maestro networks, you should be able to withdraw cash from ATMs featuring these logos, but fees for using the facility can be high.

➡ Visa, MasterCard and American Express are accepted practically everywhere.

➡ Prices for almost everything in Canada are quoted without GST.

USA

In Glacier, the nearest banks are in Columbia Falls and Browning. The lodges at Lake McDonald, Glacier Park and Many Glacier have ATMs, as does Eddie's Camp Store in Apgar and the St Mary Lodge and St Mary supermarket. There are also several ATMs in West Glacier.

➡ Credit cards are widely accepted.

➡ There's no sales tax in Montana.

➡ For Glacier visitors crossing over to Waterton, keep in mind that most businesses accept US currency, but don't bother to calculate the exchange rate, which means you lose out.

Opening Hours

➡ Opening hours noted in reviews are for high season. Low-season hours may be reduced, or businesses may close altogether.

➡ Standard opening hours for retailers and services are from 9am to 5:30pm, although grocery and convenience stores, tourist services, gift shops, cafes and chain stores often open later.

➡ Banks open 9am to 5:30pm Monday to Friday.

➡ Standard restaurant hours are from around 7am to 10:30am for breakfast, 11am to 3pm for lunch and 5pm to 10pm for dinner.

➡ Bars open any time from 4pm onwards to around midnight or later.

Post

Mail services are much the same in the national parks as in the rest of the US and Canada, although it can take longer for letters to arrive in winter, when heavy snow sometimes causes delays. Banff, Jasper, Waterton and Glacier all have large, efficient post offices, while you'll find smaller branches in most gateway towns.

Public Holidays

Both Canada and the US observe a number of national holidays, when most shops, visitor attractions and services shut or operate on limited hours, and banks, schools and post offices are all closed. Accommodations, transportation and main highways are usually very busy around major holidays, especially Easter, Labor Day, Thanksgiving and Christmas.

Canada

New Year's Day January 1

Good Friday March/April

Easter Monday First Monday after Good Friday

Victoria Day Monday preceding May 25

Canada Day July 1

Labour Day First Monday of September

Thanksgiving Day Second Monday of October

Remembrance Day November 11

Christmas Day December 25

Boxing Day December 26

USA

New Year's Day January 1

Martin Luther King Day Third Monday in January

President's Day Third Monday in February

Memorial Day Last Monday in May

Independence Day July 4

Labor Day First Monday in September

Columbus Day Second Monday in October

Veterans' Day November 11

Thanksgiving Day Fourth Thursday in November

Christmas Day December 25

Telephone
Cell Phones

Cell-phone coverage outside the main towns can be extremely erratic, especially in the backcountry.

PRACTICALITIES

Newspapers The most widely read daily newspapers in Alberta are the *Calgary Herald* (www.calgaryherald.com) and *Edmonton Journal* (www.edmontonjournal.com), plus the *Calgary Sun* (www.calgarysun.com) and *Edmonton Sun* (www.edmontonsun.com) tabloids. There are many regional newspapers; look out for the historic *Crag & Canyon* (www.thecragandcanyon.com) and the *Rocky Mountain Outlook* (www.rmoutlook.com). In Montana pick up the *Whitefish Pilot* (www.whitefishpilot.com) and *Daily Inter Lake* (www.dailyinterlake.com).

Radio The nationwide Canadian Broadcasting Company (CBC) is the main radio service in Canada, although reception is patchy across the parks; try 96.3FM for CBC Radio One in Banff and 98.1FM in Jasper. The volunteer-run Banff Park Radio is on 101.1FM. In Montana KJJR (880AM) has news and talk.

Taxes A goods and services tax (GST) of 5% is added to most goods in Alberta and British Columbia. Montana has no sales tax.

Weights & Measures Distances in Canada are quoted in kilometers, with elevations in meters. In the US it's miles and feet. Both countries quote weights in imperial pounds.

➡ It's always worth taking a cell with you if you're on a wilderness trip, but don't automatically assume you'll have reception.

➡ Canadian and US cell-phone networks are generally compatible. If you're bringing a phone from abroad, check that it works with the cell-phone systems in the US and Canada.

➡ A temporary pay-as-you-go SIM card is a good way to avoid expensive roaming charges.

➡ Most networks provide sporadic coverage in and around the entrances to Glacier National Park; Verizon offers the best service there and in Waterton.

Payphones

You'll find plenty of payphones in the main towns, as well as at major campgrounds and visitor attractions. In general, it costs 50¢ to make a call from a payphone.

Phone Codes

Area codes are denoted by the first three digits of phone numbers (eg ☎403 or ☎780 in Alberta, ☎406 in Montana). If you're outside the area code, you'll need to dial it along with the relevant phone number.

Other commonly used dialing codes:

☎1 international prefix, used for calling the US and Canada from abroad

☎1-800/1-888 toll-free

Time

Alberta and Montana are both in the 'Mountain Time-zone,' one hour ahead of Pacific Time (used by the US west coast and western parts of British Columbia), one hour behind Central Time, two hours behind Eastern Time (the US east coast) and seven hours behind Greenwich Mean Time (London).

Like most Canadian provinces, Alberta observes daylight-saving time between the second Sunday in March and the first Sunday in November. The clocks are put forward one hour during this period so nightfall is later.

Toilets

Public toilets are common in the major townsites as well as visitor attractions and visitor centers at the park entrances. If you're out and about in the national parks, you'll find pit-toilet cabins at most of the trailheads (and

in backcountry campsites in Glacier).

Tourist Information

For general information on the national parks, your first port of call should be the comprehensive websites for either Parks Canada (www.pc.gc.ca) or the US National Park Service (www.nps.gov). The chamber of commerce website for Waterton Lakes (www.mywaterton.ca) is another handy resource.

For more specific information, the staff at the main park visitor centers are hugely knowledgeable and very helpful, and can provide leaflets, brochures and guide booklets on practically every imaginable activity in the park. All the provincial parks have their own visitor centers.

Travelers with Disabilities

Visiting Banff, Jasper and Glacier still presents quite a challenge for people with auditory, visual or physical disabilities and for people with restricted mobility.

Your best bet is to contact park visitor centers directly

with questions on specific activities or refer to the Disabled Traveler's Companion website (www.tdtcompanion.com). Glacier also publishes an informational brochure available on the park's website.

➡ Most hotels have at least some wheelchair-accessible rooms.

➡ The larger campgrounds at Tunnel Mountain, Johnston Canyon and Lake Louise (plus Waterfowl Lakes) in Banff, as well as Whistlers, Wabasso and Wapiti in Jasper, have limited facilities for disabled users, including wheelchair-friendly campsites and washrooms.

Banff

Most of the main sights in Banff, including Lake Louise, Banff's museums, Upper Hot Springs Pool and Peyto Lake along the Icefields Pkwy are all wheelchair-accessible, as is the main visitor center. Most restaurants in Banff are on the ground floor, so should be accessible to wheelchair users.

➡ Paved trails ideal for wheelchair users include the lower section of Johnston Canyon, the paved section of the Lake Minnewanka Shoreline Trail, the Lake Louise Shoreline Trail and the mixed-use Sundance Trail in Banff.

➡ In Kananaskis Country, William Watson Lodge has been designed specifically to give people with disabilities access to the area, with 22 fully accessible cottages and over 18km (11.2 miles) of accessible trails.

Glacier & Waterton Lakes

➡ In Glacier, two short, scenic trails are paved for wheelchair use: Trail of the Cedars, off the Going-to-the-Sun Rd; and the Running Eagle Falls Trail in Two Medicine. The cycling path between Apgar Village and the visitor center is also accessible.

➡ Hearing-impaired visitors can get information at ☑406-888-7806.

➡ Park visitor centers have audio guides for visually impaired visitors.

➡ At least one or two ground-floor, wheelchair-friendly rooms are available at all in-park lodges.

➡ All shuttles in Glacier are ADA accessible, as is a new specially designed 'Jammer' bus.

➡ The Waterton Townsite campground has wheelchair-accessible bathroom facilities, as do a few of the lodges in the townsite.

➡ Waterton's Linnet Lake Trail, Waterton Townsite Trail and Cameron Lake Day area are wheelchair accessible.

Jasper

Jasper's museum, Miette Hot Springs, Maligne Lake, Medicine Lake, Jasper Tramway and the visitor center are all wheelchair accessible, as is Athabasca Falls and the Icefield Centre along the Icefields Pkwy.

➡ Several trails are good for wheelchair users, including the initial paved section of the Mary Schäffer Loop, Maligne Lake, the Clifford E Lee Trail at Lake Annette, and Pyramid Isle in Pyramid Lake.

➡ Few accommodations in Jasper have dedicated rooms for wheelchair users, although most have elevators, and there are usually ground-floor rooms that can accommodate disabled visitors.

➡ Many of Jasper's restaurants are on ground floors and have accessible toilets.

Volunteering

There are many organizations that volunteer their efforts for free to ensure the continuing welfare of the parks.

Among the best known are the 'Friends' organizations:

Friends of Banff (www.friendsofbanff.com), Friends of Jasper (www.friendsofjasper.com) and Friends of Kootenay (www.friendsofkootenay.com). These organizations undertake everything from administrative work and fundraising to trail maintenance, and are often looking for volunteers to help with current programs.

Banff Volunteer Program (www.pc.gc.ca/eng/pn-np/ab/banff/edu/benevole-volunteer.aspx) Park-wide volunteer opportunities, ranging from trail ambassadors to citizen scientists. There are regular 'drop-in' days if you have limited time.

Alberta Institute for Wildlife Conservation (☑403-946-2361; www.aiwc.ca) Wildlife charity that helps protect native species through animal rehabilitation, habitat protection and volunteer training.

American Hiking Society (☑800-972-8608; www.americanhiking.org) A national advocacy organization that arranges volunteering 'vacations' to maintain hiking trails.

Glacier National Park Associates (www.glaciernationalparkassociates.org) Volunteer group that tackles projects such as trail maintenance, building preservation and habitat regeneration.

Glacier Institute (☑406-755-1211; www.glacierinstitute.org; Apgar Village) The Glacier Institute, founded in 1983, offers one- to three-day workshops, youth camps and courses year-round from US$65 to US$375.

Women Travelers

The national parks don't present many unusual dangers for women traveling alone. Both the parks and the main townsites are generally friendly and safe places to visit, although obviously it pays to take the usual precautions – avoid unlit or unpopulated areas after dark, join up with other people if you're walking home late at night, and don't hitchhike.

Transportation

GETTING THERE & AWAY

Air

Airports & Airlines

BANFF & JASPER NATIONAL PARKS

➡ Calgary (www.calgaryairport.com) and Edmonton (www.flyeia.com) are the closest international airports to Banff and Jasper, respectively.

➡ It's feasible to fly into Vancouver (www.yvr.ca), but you'll have a long drive – it's 845km (523 miles) to Banff and 795km (492 miles) to Jasper.

➡ Air Canada and WestJet cover the majority of Canadian routes, and connect through Montreal and Toronto to many European destinations.

➡ US-based airlines, including United and Delta, connect through major American cities.

➡ British Airways mainly serves London Heathrow.

GLACIER NATIONAL PARK

Glacier Park International Airport (FCA; ☑406-257-5994; www.iflyglacier.com) Glacier's most convenient airport is between Kalispell and Whitefish, MT, and approximately 41km (26 miles) from the park's West Entrance. It's currently served by Alaska Airlines/Horizon Air, Allegiant, Delta and United with non-stop year-round flights to Denver, Las Vegas, Minneapolis, Salt Lake City and Seattle. Additional seasonal flights to Atlanta, Chicago, LA, Portland and San Francisco.

Great Falls International Airport (GTF; www.gtfairport.com) Located 249km (155 miles) from Glacier.

Missoula International Airport (MSO; www.flymissoula.com; 5225 Hwy 10 W) Missoula International Airport is 8km (5 miles) west of Missoula on US 10 W (which becomes W Broadway in town).

WATERTON LAKES NATIONAL PARK

The closest airport to Waterton Lakes, 129km (80 miles) to the northeast, is **Lethbridge County** (YQL; ☑403-329-4466; www.lethbridgeairport.ca). It's served by Air Canada and Integra Air, but the limited flight schedule usually means it's more convenient (and cheaper) to fly into Calgary, 266km (165 miles) north of Waterton.

Bus

Banff & Jasper National Parks

AIRPORT SHUTTLES

There are a number of shuttle services from Calgary to Jasper and Banff.

Airporter Shuttle Express (☑403-509-1570; www.airportshuttleexpress.com) Close to hourly buses (adult/child C$62/31) between Calgary and Banff from 10am to 10:30pm. Charter services available to Jasper. Also has

CLIMATE CHANGE & TRAVEL

Every form of transport that relies on carbon-based fuel generates CO_2, the main cause of human-induced climate change. Modern travel is dependent on aeroplanes, which might use less fuel per kilometer per person than most cars but travel much greater distances. The altitude at which aircraft emit gases (including CO_2) and particles also contributes to their climate change impact. Many websites offer 'carbon calculators' that allow people to estimate the carbon emissions generated by their journey and, for those who wish to do so, to offset the impact of the greenhouse gases emitted with contributions to portfolios of climate-friendly initiatives throughout the world. Lonely Planet offsets the carbon footprint of all staff and author travel.

shuttles to downtown Calgary (C$15).

Banff Airport Taxi (☏403-678-2776; www.banffairporttaxi.com) Private shuttle bus to Banff hotels plus Lake Louise on request. Ski shuttle service available in season. Monitors incoming flights, so if you're delayed it'll adjust pickup time accordingly. One to three passengers is C$225 one way, C$425 return.

Banff Airporter (☏403-762-3330; www.banffairporter.com) Runs nine times daily from Calgary airport to Banff (adult/child C$59/29.50).

Brewster (Map p87; ☏866-606-6700; www.explorerockies.com/airport-shuttles) Calgary airport to Banff (adult/child C$57/27.50).

SunDog Tour Company (☏780-852-4056; www.sundogtours.com) One daily bus between Jasper and Edmonton airport for adult/child C$99/59. Services from Calgary airport to Banff are run by Brewster, but can be booked through SunDog.

PUBLIC BUSES

Greyhound (www.greyhound.ca) runs five daily buses that run north–south along Hwy 1, stopping at Calgary, Canmore (one way C$23.60, 1¼ hours) and Banff (C$27.30, 1¾ hours). Note that this bus does not currently stop at Calgary airport, so you'll either have to catch a taxi into the city (C$30 to C$45) or take the half-hourly shuttle bus provided by Airporter Shuttle Express, then take the Greyhound from there.

There are also four daily Greyhounds between Jasper and Edmonton International Airport (one way/return C$64.70/129.40), and four daily from Vancouver to Golden, Field, Lake Louise and Banff.

Brewster and SunDog Tour Company run daily buses between Banff and Jasper, and Roam (www.roamtransit.com) buses run hourly between Canmore and Banff (C$6, 25 minutes).

Sample fares and fastest journey times from Vancouver:

TO	ONE WAY (C$)	TIME (HOURS)
Banff	110	13½
Golden	132	11
Lake Louise	138	12¾

➡ Cheaper advance fares are available by booking online, but these are nonrefundable and you won't be able to change your dates without incurring a fee.

➡ Greyhound depots for both Banff and Jasper are inside the townsite train stations.

Glacier & Waterton Lakes National Parks

AIRPORT SHUTTLES

Public transport from Glacier airport is limited. The only shuttle bus is provided by **Flathead-Glacier Transportation** (☏406-892-3390; www.glaciertransportation.com); it also provides regular taxi service from the airport.

If you're flying into Calgary, you can charter a passenger minivan (seating eight) to Glacier and Waterton with **Airport Shuttle Express** (☏403-509-1570; www.airportshuttleexpress.com) for C$630.

PUBLIC BUSES

Greyhound (www.greyhound.ca) stops in Pincher Creek, 53km (33 miles) from the Waterton Townsite; contact **Pincher Creek Taxi** (☏403-632-9738; www.pinchercreektaxi.com) for transport between Pincher Creek and Waterton (C$65 for up to four people).

Car & Motorcycle

Major Routes

BANFF & JASPER NATIONAL PARKS

There are various road routes into the parks.

➡ Trans-Canada Hwy (Hwy 1) runs from Calgary to Canmore, Banff and Lake Louise, before continuing into Yoho National Park.

➡ Hwy 93 (aka the Icefields Pkwy) travels from Jasper to Lake Louise and Castle Junction, then south into Kootenay National Park and Radium Hot Springs.

➡ Hwy 11 heads west from Red Deer and enters Banff on the Icefields Pkwy, just south of the border with Jasper.

➡ To reach Jasper from Edmonton, take Hwy 16 west.

GLACIER & WATERTON LAKES NATIONAL PARKS

The west side of Glacier is most easily reached from Whitefish, Kalispell and Flathead Lake; the east side is closer to Great Falls and Helena. West Glacier and East Glacier are connected by US 2, below the southern boundary of the park.

If you're traveling north into Waterton Lakes, you'll have to cross the border on the eastern side of Glacier (the crossing north of Polebridge in the northwest has been closed for decades), passing through customs en route. You'll need two forms of ID (driver's license and passport are standard).

Port of Piegan/Carway (☏in Canada 403-653-3009, in US 406-732-5572; ⏲7am-11pm) On Trans-Canada Hwy 2 (US Hwy 89); open year-round.

Port of Chief Mountain (☏in Canada 403-653-3535, in US 406-732-5572; ⏲7am-10pm Jun-Aug, 9am-6pm mid-May–end May & Sep) On US 17; closed in winter.

Car Rentals

The vast majority of people visiting the parks rent a car. It's the most convenient way to travel, allowing you to explore at your own pace and visit even the most remote sights, though you have to factor in fuel costs, traffic and breakdown.

All the major car-rental agencies have branches at the main airports and townsites. Airport branches generally stay open from around 6am to midnight; town branches keep regular business hours.

→ Booking online will get the best rates, but check carefully for hidden extras such as high excess, mileage caps, limits on interstate travel and GST. Most deals these days include unlimited mileage.

→ One-way rentals will incur a 'drop fee,' the price of which varies depending on the vehicle and how far you're taking it.

→ Airport rentals charge a different tax rate, so it's worth checking equivalent rates with town branches (such as in Banff and Canmore); it can work out cheaper for long rentals, even with the one-way drop fee.

→ Think about whether you need Collision Damage Waiver (CDW); you may be covered by your own auto or travel insurance, or by your credit-card company if you use the card to pay for the rental.

→ If considering doing any off-roading or merely getting off the major arteries, a 4WD or at least a vehicle with high clearance is recommended.

Recreational Vehicles & Campervan Rentals

Cruising the parks in a recreational vehicle (RV) has many advantages – you won't incur hotel bills, you can cook your own meals, and you can experience a taste of the outdoors without having to rough it too much.

There are drawbacks, though: they're big, unwieldy, heavy on fuel, and slow, and can be difficult to maneuver if you're not used to driving a large vehicle.

→ Make sure you get a full rundown on the vehicle before you leave the rental agency.

→ Check that the campground you're staying at has spaces suitable for RVs.

→ Rates spike in peak season. Deals are often available at other times.

→ Popular van sizes are often booked out in summer, so reserve well ahead.

→ Mileage is nearly always extra to the quoted rental rates.

CanaDream (☎888-480-9726; www.canadream.com) Rents truck campers, campervans and motor homes from locations in Calgary, Edmonton and various other places. Prices start from around C$140 per day for a midsized motor home.

Cruise Canada (☎800-671-8042; www.cruisecanada.com) Rents three sizes of RV from locations in Calgary and Vancouver. Rates start at around C$650 to C$750 per week plus mileage. Three-night minimum rental.

Cruise America (☎480-464-7300; www.cruiseamerica.com) Rents RVs in the US, with pick ups in Billings, Bozeman and Missoula. The latter is closest to Glacier.

Train

Banff National Park

The only passenger trains that stop in Banff run solely as tour operations.

Rocky Mountaineer Rail Tours (☎877-460-3200; www.rockymountaineer.com) Scenic train trips through the Rockies, Banff and Jasper. Most of the travel is done during daylight hours, and prices include park passes, hotel accommodations and day trips. Cheapest packages start from around C$900.

Royal Canadian Pacific (☎877-665-3044; www.royalcanadianpacific.com) Luxury train trips through the Rockies in a heritage train carriage with full silver service. Book at least a year ahead.

Jasper National Park

Jasper is served by mainline intercity trains provided by **VIA Rail** (☎1-888-842-7245; www.viarail.com), which stop in Jasper on their route between Vancouver and Edmonton at least three times per week. You can connect onto this route from most other US and Canadian cities. Sample fares from Jasper:

TO	ONE WAY (C$)	TIME (HOURS)
Edmonton	113	5½
Saskatoon	151	14½
Vancouver	239	20
Winnipeg	231	26¼

Glacier & Waterton Lakes National Parks

Amtrak (www.amtrak.com) operates the cross-country *Empire Builder* line from Seattle all the way to Chicago, serving stations in East Glacier, West Glacier and Whitefish.

Eastbound trains run in the early morning; westbound trains travel through in the early evening. There are ticket offices at East Glacier and Whitefish, but you'll have to pre-book or buy on board from West Glacier. Sample one-way fares include Whitefish to West Glacier (US$7 to US$16, 30 minutes), Whitefish to East Glacier (US$15 to US$33, two hours, eight minutes) and West Glacier to East Glacier (US$15, one hour, 38 minutes).

GETTING AROUND

All the parks are accessible on good roads. Most visitors arrive in their own vehicle and drive.

→ Getting around the parks without a car can be challenging, but not impossible, with a small selection of expensive shuttles. Glacier has an excellent free park shuttle linking most of the trailheads (summer only). Public transportation within Waterton Lakes is limited.

➡ VIA trains serve Jasper. Amtrak serves Glacier with its trans-continental *Empire Builder* service.

Bicycle

Cycling is a popular and ecofriendly way of getting around the parks, but the distances between sights are long, so bikes are mainly useful for commuting around the townsites.

➡ Bikes are readily available for rent in Banff, Jasper, Glacier and Waterton. Expect to pay C$12 to C$15 (US$9 to US$11) per hour or C$35 to C$45 (US$26 to US$34) per day.

➡ Bikes are banned on all trails (but not roads) in Glacier.

➡ Relatively few trailheads have bike racks.

Bus

Getting around by bus in the parks is just about possible, but takes some planning.

Banff to Jasper

Officially, there's no public bus service between Banff and Jasper, but you can easily hop on board one of the scheduled services offered by Greyhound, Brewster or SunDog Tour Company, as long as there's space.

Banff National Park

Banff's public buses are known as **Roam** (☑403-762-1215; www.roamtransit.com). All routes travel via Banff Ave, and serve destinations including the Banff Gondola, Tunnel Mountain campgrounds, the Banff Centre and Sulphur Mountain, as well as running between Canmore and Banff.

A summer shuttle bus run by **White Mountain Adventures** (☑403-760-4403; www.whitemountainadventures. com; 120 Eagle Crescent, Banff Town; ☺8am-5pm Mon-Fri) runs from Banff townsite to Sunshine Meadows.

To get to other trailheads, you'll have to drive or organize your own transport with one of the private hike-and-bike shuttles (p73).

Jasper National Park

Jasper's bus system is fairly limited, but there are a couple of useful services to some of the most popular sights:

Jasper Tramway Shuttle (☑780-852-4056; C$35) Runs from the train station and includes a tramway ticket.

Maligne Lake Shuttle Service (Map p160; www.malignelake. com; 616 Patricia St) Travels from Jasper townsite to Maligne Lake (adult/child C$30/15) and Maligne Canyon (C$20/10, four daily).

Glacier National Park

Glacier is the easiest park to get around by bus thanks to the free biodiesel shuttle buses along the Going-to-the-Sun Rd, which run frequently throughout the summer. All are wheelchair-accessible, and most can carry bikes. And, of course, Glacier's signature red 'Jammer' buses (www.glaciernationalpark lodges.com) ferry passengers to points throughout the heart of the park on the Going-to-the-Sun Rd.

The East Side Shuttle Bus (www.glacierparkinc.com/shuttle_information.php) travels between the Glacier Park Lodge in East Glacier and the Prince of Wales Hotel in Waterton (Canada), calling at Two Medicine, St Mary, Many Glacier and Chief Mountain. Journeys cost US$15 per trip segment and run from the beginning of June to late September.

Car & Motorcycle

Automobile Associations

The **Alberta Motor Association** (☑in Calgary 403-240-5300; www.ama.ab.ca) is the province's main motoring organization and is affiliated with the Canadian Automobile Association (CAA). It can help with queries on driving in Alberta, as well as arrange breakdown cover and insurance for members; members also sometimes qualify for special rates on hotels and other services.

The **American Automobile Association** (☑406-758-6980; www.aaa.com; 135 Hutton Ranch Rd, Ste 106, Kalispell) is the US equivalent, and offers a similar range of services. There are other branches in Missoula, Great Falls and Bozeman.

Driver's License

➡ Foreign driver's licenses can be used in Alberta for up to three months. International driver's licenses can be used for up to 12 months.

➡ It's required that you carry your license and vehicle registration at all times.

Fuel & Spare Parts

➡ Gas is readily available in the main townsites, but make sure you fill your tank before setting out on a driving tour.

➡ There are gas stations at Castle Mountain and Saskatchewan Crossing in Banff, but prices are much more expensive here.

➡ There are no gas stations within Glacier National Park itself.

➡ Most car-rental companies provide breakdown cover as part of the rental package.

➡ If you're driving your own vehicle, it is probably worth joining one of the major breakdown agencies to avoid getting stranded.

Road Conditions

Most of the main roads are well maintained, although minor roads to trailheads and mountains are often steep, narrow and winding, making them nasty driving for RVs.

➡ Some roads (such as the Smith-Dorrien/Spray Trail Rd from Canmore into Kananaskis) are unsealed, so take extra care when driving on them.

➡ Ice and snow are frequent hazards in winter, so be prepared if you're driving during the colder months.

➡ Accidents involving trains and automobiles are one of the major causes of animal fatalities in the mountain parks. Wildlife can appear suddenly, and bolt across the road when scared, so slow down and be alert.

➡ Some road passes (such as the Highwood Pass in Kananaskis and Logan Pass on the Going-to-the-Sun Rd in Glacier) are closed in winter due to snow.

➡ For up-to-date Glacier road conditions and closure information check out http://home.nps. gov/applications/glac/ roadstatus/roadstatus.cfm.

Driving in Winter

Driving around in winter in any of the parks can be dangerous, but especially so in the Canadian parks, which are blanketed by snow and ice for well over six months of the year. Whiteouts are not uncommon and several roads (including the Icefields Pkwy) are closed during mid-winter or periods of heavy snow – check ahead with the park offices and keep abreast of local news and traffic bulletins. The iconic Going-to-the-Sun Rd in Glacier is plowed in winter only between the West Glacier entrance at Apgar and Lake McDonald Lodge.

In Banff and Jasper, it's legally required that you carry snow tires or chains on all roads in winter except the main Trans-Canada Hwy 1 (obviously it's also worth knowing how to fit them). Car-rental agencies should provide these if you're renting from them in winter, although you might be charged extra.

It's also worth carrying a small emergency supply kit, including antifreeze, blankets, water, flashlight, snow shovel, matches and emergency food supplies. A cell phone will also come in handy in case you need to phone for an emergency tow. Top up antifreeze, transmission, brake and windshield-washer fluids.

Be especially careful of invisible patches of ice on the road, especially once the temperature drops at night. Slow down, take extra care and use your gears rather than your brakes to slow down (look for the 'L' or 'Low' gear if you're driving an automatic). Slamming on your brakes will only increase your chances of skidding.

Road Rules

In Canada and the US, driving is on the right. You are legally required to wear a seatbelt at all times, and headlights must be turned on when visibility is restricted to 150m (500ft) or less. Motorcyclists are required to wear helmets and drive with headlights on.

One rule that often confuses overseas drivers is that it's legal to turn right on a stoplight (as long as there is no traffic coming from the left). At four-way stop junctions, drivers should pause and allow the first vehicle that stopped to pull away first.

Hitchhiking

Hitching is never entirely safe in any country, and we don't recommend it. Travelers who decide to hitch should understand that they are taking a small but potentially serious risk. That said, thumbing a lift is an option in the mountain parks, although you might find you're waiting on the highway for quite a while before anyone stops.

As always, take the usual precautions: hitch in groups, avoid hitching in remote areas and after dark, and make sure you keep an eye on your pack.

On the trail you can often hook up with hikers who have their own transport by hanging around at the trailhead. Many people will give you a lift if you smile sweetly and they've got space in the car.

Behind the Scenes

SEND US YOUR FEEDBACK

We love to hear from travelers – your comments keep us on our toes and help make our books better. Our well-traveled team reads every word on what you loved or loathed about this book. Although we cannot reply individually to postal submissions, we always guarantee that your feedback goes straight to the appropriate authors, in time for the next edition. Each person who sends us information is thanked in the next edition – the most useful submissions are rewarded with a selection of digital PDF chapters.

Visit **lonelyplanet.com/contact** to submit your updates and suggestions or to ask for help. Our award-winning website also features inspirational travel stories, news and discussions.

Note: We may edit, reproduce and incorporate your comments in Lonely Planet products such as guidebooks, websites and digital products, so let us know if you don't want your comments reproduced or your name acknowledged. For a copy of our privacy policy visit lonelyplanet.com/privacy.

OUR READERS

Many thanks to the travelers who used the last edition and wrote to us with helpful hints, useful advice and interesting anecdotes: Lynne Farrell, David Freese, Anna Harrison, Dorothy Hearst, Richard Hill, Bill Holland, Phil Houlden, Lucretia McCulley, Annette Montgomery, Ignace Van den Broeck, Kevin Vangrunderbeeck

AUTHOR THANKS

Brendan Sainsbury

Thanks to all the untold bus drivers, tourist info volunteers, burger-flippers, Parks Canada staff and backcountry hikers who helped me during my research. Special thanks to my wife, Liz, and nine-year-old son, Kieran, for their company on the road.

Michael Grosberg

Of course, thanks primarily go to my wife, Carly, who, seven months pregnant at the time, joined me on the trails and in the tent for part of my research trip. Our gratitude to the American and Australian travelers who allowed us to sleep in their teepee for the night; to all of the dedicated park rangers who answered my many questions; and to Ivana and friends for a nice night by the fire in Waterton.

ACKNOWLEDGMENTS

Climate map data adapted from Peel MC, Finlayson BL & McMahon TA (2007) 'Updated World Map of the Köppen-Geiger Climate Classification', *Hydrology and Earth System Sciences*, 11, 163344.

Cover photograph: Moraine Lake, Banff National Park, Canada; Pietro Canali/4Corners.

THIS BOOK

This 4th edition of Lonely Planet's *Banff, Jasper & Glacier National Parks* guidebook was written and researched by Brendan Sainsbury and Michael Grosberg. The previous edition was written and researched by Brendan Sainsbury and Oliver Berry. This guidebook was produced by the following:

Destination Editor Alexander Howard

Product Editors Martine Power, Jenna Myers

Regional Senior Cartographer Alison Lyall

Cartographers Corey Hutchison, David Kemp

Book Designer Virginia Moreno

Assisting Editors Carolyn Bain, Sally O'Brien, Saralinda Turner

Cover Researcher Marika Mercer

Thanks to Bruce Evans, Ryan Evans, Andi Jones, Bella Li, Karyn Noble, Susan Paterson, Kirsten Rawlings, Diana Saengkham, Luna Soo, Angela Tinson, Lauren Wellicome, Dora Whitaker, Clifton Wilkinson

Index

A

accommodations 41, 116, 207, 267-9, *see also individual locations*, camping, historic hotels, lodges
Alpine Club of Canada Huts 102, 127, 269
apartments 269
B&Bs 267
backcountry 168, 203, 268
campervan rentals 277
chalets 23
children, travel with 41
condos 269
guesthouses 267
hostels 268-9
hotels 269
huts 168
pets, travel with 43-44
reservations 47, 98, 135, 163, 172, 177, 232
activities 21, 24-5, 30-37, *see also individual activities, individual locations*, winter activities
air travel 275
Akamina Parkway 220, **221**
animals 247-51, *see also individual animals*, wildlife watching
Apgar Village 20, 197
area codes 19, 273
Athabasca Falls 159
Athabasca Glacier 16, 157, **16**
Athabasca River Valley Loop 149-50, **149**
Avalanche Lake Trail 181-2, **181**
avalanches 262

B

backcountry 162

Map Pages **000**
Photo Pages **000**

accommodations 168, 203, 268
dangers 171
kayaking 154
skiing 156
backpacking 31-3
Bald Hills Loop 140-1, 145, **144**
Banff Avenue 86
Banff Gondola 88
Banff National Park 46-113, **48-9**, **94-5**, **46**, **116**
accommodations 98-107
activities 50-85
boating 46
camping 98, 99, 100-1, 102, 103-6
canoeing 78-9
cycling 72-6, **74**, **75**, **76**
drinking 110
driving 46, 76-7, 78-9, 80-1, 84, **77**, **79**, **81**
entertainment 110
fishing 82
food 107-9
golf 83
highlights 48-9
hiking 46, 50-72, **51**, **61**, **65**, **69**, **70**, **71**
history 90, 93, 97, 236-8
horseback riding 83-4
ice-climbing 85
ice-skating 85
information 111-12
internet resources 47
kayaking 78, 80
medical services 112
planning 46-7
road distances 46
rock climbing 82-3
safety 105, 111-12
shopping 110-11, **111**
sights 86-97
skiing 84-5
snowboarding 36-7
tourist information 112

tours 78, 97-8
travel to/from 112-13
travel within 113
white-water rafting 80, 82
Banff Park Museum 23, 86
Banff Summer Arts Festival 24-5
Banff Town 86-91, **87**, **88**, **111**
Banff Upper Hot Springs 88
bathrooms 273
bear spray 265
bears 16, 247, **16**
Beaver, Summit & Jacques Lakes 140-1, 144-5, **144**
beavers 250-1
Beehives, the 52-3, 62-3, **61**
Berg Lake 162
bicycle travel 278, *see also* cycling, mountain biking
Big Head 117
Big Three 36, 40
bighorn sheep 248
Bird Woman Falls 197
birds 251
Blackfeet Indian Reservation 212
boating 153-4, 189, *see also* canoeing, kayaking, white-water rafting
books 234, 258
border crossings 227
Bow Falls 86
Bow Falls & the Hoodoos 50, 52-3, **51**
Bow Glacier Falls 52-3, 65-6, **65**
Bow Valley Parkway 78-9, 93, **79**
Bowman Lake 188, 198
breweries 108, 110, 120-121, 170
Brewster Tours 97-8
budgeting 19
Buffalo Nations Luxton Museum 90
Burgess Shale 124-5, **114**

bus travel 275-6, 278

C

cable cars
Banff Gondola 88
Jasper Skytram 13, 143, 160-1, **13**
Lake Louise Gondola 21, 96, **114**
Cameron Falls 225
Cameron Lake 225
campervan rentals 277
camping 267-8, **34**
Banff National Park 98, 99, 100-1, 102, 103-6
Canmore 119
East Glacier 211
Glacier National Park 199-201, 202-3
Golden 132
Jasper National Park 164, 165, 166-7, 168-9
Kananaskis Country 122
Kootenay National Park 130
Lake O'Hara 127
Mt Assiniboine Provincial Park 128
Radium Hot Springs 130
St Mary 210
Waterton Lakes National Park 227-8
West Glacier 208
Whitefish 214
Canmore 117-21, **118**
Canmore Highland Games 24-5
Canmore Museum & Geoscience Centre 117
Canmore Nordic Centre 12, 117, **12**
canoeing 35
Banff National Park 78-9
children, travel with 39
Waterton Lakes National Park 225

canyons
Marble Canyon 129
Maligne Canyon 151, 162
Mistaya Canyon 64-5, 81
Johnston Canyon 58, 78, 93
Stewart Canyon 56-7, 91
Sundance Canyon 54
Sunrift Gorge 198
Red Rock Canyon 221, **218**
car rentals 276-7
car travel 18, 41, 46, 276-7, 278-9
Carthew-Alderson Trail 17, 219, 220-1, **217**, **17**
Cascade Amphitheatre 52-3, 57, **51**
Cascade Mountain 57, **30**
Cave & Basin National Historic Site 89
caving 21
cell phones 18, 272-3
chalets 23
children, travel with 38-41
C-Level Cirque 52-3, 56, **51**
climate 18, 116, 207, 269
climate change 234-5, 275
climbing 154, see also rock climbing, ice-climbing
clothing 264-6
Columbia Icefield 156
Columbia Icefield Centre 157
condos 269
conservation 235, 254-6
conservationists 254
Consolation Lakes Trail 52-3, 60, **61**
Cory Pass Loop 52-3, 57-8, **51**
costs 19
coyotes 247-8, **246**
Crandell Lake Loop 222
cross-country skiing 37, 128, 156, see also skiing
Crypt Lake Trail 219-20, 220-1, **217**
culture 234-5
customs regulations 269-70
cycling 33-4, 149-50, 189, 222, 263, see also mountain biking
Athabasca River Valley Loop 149-50, **149**

D
Dark Sky Festival 157
Dawson Pass 186
Dawson–Pitamakan Loop 182-3, 186-7, **186**
day hikes 31-2, see also hiking, overnight hikes
Avalanche Lake Trail 181-2, **181**
Bald Hills Loop 140-1, 145, **144**
Banff National Park 50-68, **51**, **61**, **65**
Beaver, Summit & Jacques Lakes 140-1, 144-5, **144**
Bow Falls & the Hoodoos 50, 52-3, **51**
Bow Glacier Falls 52-3, 65-6, **65**
Carthew-Alderson Trail 17, 219, 220-1, **217**
Cascade Amphitheatre 52-3, 57, **51**
C-Level Cirque 52-3, 56, **51**
Consolation Lakes Trail 52-3, 60, **61**
Cory Pass Loop 52-3, 57-8, **51**
Crypt Lake Trail 219-20, 220-1, **217**
Dawson–Pitamakan Loop 182-3, 186-7, **186**
Fenland Trail & Vermilion Lakes 50-1, 52-3, **51**
Garden Path Trail & Twin Cairns Meadow 54-5, 58-9, **51**
Geraldine Lakes 139-40, 140-1, **138**

Banff National Park 72-6, **74**, **75**, **76**
Crandell Lake Loop 222
Glacier National Park 189
Goat Creek Trail 74-5, **75**
Jasper National Park 135, 149-50, 152
Legacy Trail 73-4, **74**
Moraine Lake via Tramline 75-6, **76**
rentals 73, 149
Saturday Night Lake Loop 150
Snowshoe Trail 222-32
Valley of the Five Lakes 150, 152
Waterton Lakes National Park 222-3

Glacier National Park 180-4, 186-9
Healy Pass & Simpson Pass 54-5, 59-60, **51**
Helen Lake 52-3, 67, **65**
Hidden Lake Overlook Trail 180, **181**
Highline Trail 182-4, **181**
Iceberg Lake Trail 182-3, 187, **188**
International Peace Park Hike 223
Jasper National Park 138-46
Johnson Lake 52-3, 54-5, **51**
Johnston Canyon & the Inkpots 52-3, 58, **51**
Lake Agnes & the Beehives 52-3, 62-3, **61**
Larch Valley & Sentinel Pass 54-5, 62, **61**
Mina & Riley Lakes Loop 140-1, **142**
Mistaya Canyon 52-3, 64-5, **65**
Moose Lake Loop 140-1, 143-4, **144**
Mt Brown Lookout 182-3, 184, 186, **181**
Old Fort Point Loop 140-1, 143, **142**
Paradise Valley & the Giant's Steps 52-3, 64, **61**
Parker Ridge 52-3, 66, **65**
Path of the Glacier & Cavell Meadows Trails 138-9, 140-1, **138**
Peyto Lake & Bow Summit Lookout 52-3, 66-7, **65**
Piegan Pass 182-3, 184, **181**
Plain of Six Glaciers 52-3, 60-2, **61**
Quartz Lakes Loop 182-3, 188, **188**
Rowe Lakes 217, 219, 220-1, **217**
Saddleback & Fairview 52-3, 63-4, **61**
Stewart Canyon 52-3, 56-7, **51**
Sulphur Mountain 52-3, 55-6, **51**
Sulphur Skyline 140-1, 145-6, **146**
Sundance Canyon 52-3, 54, **51**

Sun Point to Virginia Falls 180, 182-3, **181**
Sunset Lookout 52-3, 67-8, **65**
Swiftcurrent Lake Nature Trail 182-3, 187, **188**
Swiftcurrent Pass Trail 182-3, 188-9, **188**
Waterton Lakes National Park 217-20, **217**
Whistlers Summit 140-1, 143, **142**
deer 249, **22**, **249**
dehydration 261
disabilities, travelers with 273-4
Discover Banff Tours 98
Discovery Trail 161
dogsledding 119, **22**
Dolomite Pass 67
drinking
Banff National Park 110
Glacier National Park 205
Jasper National Park 170
Waterton Lakes National Park 230
driver's license 278
driving 152-3, see also car travel
Akamina Parkway 220, **221**
Banff National Park 46, 76-7, 78-9, 80-1, 84, **77**, **79**, **81**
Bow Valley Parkway 78-9, 93, **79**
Glacier National Park 192, **192**
Going-to-the-Sun Road 192, **192**
Icefields Parkway 9, 152-3, **153**, **9**
Into the Icefields 80-1, **81**
Jasper National Park 151, 152, **151**
Maligne Lake Road 151, **151**
Minnewanka Loop 76-7, **77**
Red Rock Parkway 220-1, **222**
safety 84, 279
Smith-Dorrien/Spray Trail Road 123
Waterton Lakes National Park 216, 220-1, **221**, **222**
driving in winter 279

E

East Glacier 210-12
ecology 254-6
economy 234-5
Egypt Lake & Gibbon Pass 54-5, 68, 70-1, **70**
electricty 270
elk 249-50, **174**
Emerald Lake 124
entertainment
  Banff National Park 110
  Glacier National Park 205
  Jasper National Park 171
  Waterton Lakes National Park 230
entrances, *see* park entrances
entrance fees 18
environmental hazards 234-5, 259-60, 275
  altitude 259-60
  bites & stings 260
  cold 260-1
  heat 261
  snow blindness 261
  sun 261
  winter driving 279
environmental issues 255-6
equestrian facilities 44
equipment 264-6
  buying & renting 266
  checklist 266
events 24-5
exchange rates 19

F

Fairmont Banff Springs 91
Fairmont Banff Springs hotel 102
Fairview 21, 63-4
Fenland Trail & Vermilion Lakes 50-1, 52-3, **51**
festivals 24-5
films 234
Fireweed Trail 129
First Nations 234
fish 250
fishing 34, 82, 154, 190, 193, 223
  rules & regulations 34
  seasons 34
float trips 35, 152-3, 190
food 116, 207, 270
  Banff National Park 107-9
  Glacier National Park 204
  Jasper National Park 169-70, 173

Waterton Lakes National Park 216, 230
frostbite 261
fuel 278

G

Garden Path Trail & Twin Cairns Meadow 54-5, 58-9, **51**
Garden Wall 196
geology 243-5
Geraldine Lakes 139-40, 140-1, **138**
giardiasis 259
Glacier National Park 176-206, **176**, **178-9**, **194-5**, **207**, **174-5**
  accommodations 176, 199-204
  boating 189
  camping 199-201, 202-3
  cycling 189
  driving 192, **192**
  entertainment 205
  fishing 190, 193
  float trips 190
  food 204
  glaciers 196
  golf 193
  highlights 178-9
  hiking 176, 180-9
  history 241-2
  horseback riding 193
  information 205
  internet access 205
  internet resources 177
  medical services 205
  nightlife 205
  planning 176-7
  road distances 176
  rock climbing 193
  sights 195-8
  skiing 193, 195
  snowshoeing 193, 195
  tourist information 205
  tours 199
  travel to/from 206
  travel within 206
  white-water rafting 190
glaciers 21, 196, 244-5
  Athabasca Glacier 16, 157, **16**
  Crowfoot Glacier 80
  Grinnell Glacier 196, 198
  Jackson Glacier 185, 196
  Saskatchewan Glacier 66
  Stanley Glacier 129
Glacier Skywalk 20-1, 159
glamping 20

Goat Creek Trail 74-5, **75**
Goat Haunt 227
Going-to-the-Sun Road 10, 192, **192**, **10**
Golden 131-3
golf 83, 155, 193, 223
Grassi Lakes Trail 118
Great Bear Wilderness Area 198
Great Northern Railway 198, 203, 206, 240, 242
Gunsight Pass Trail 182-3, 185, **185**

H

Hamber Provincial Park 173
Hamilton Falls 124
health 258-63
  books 258
  infectious diseases 259
  medical assistance 259
  medical checklist 258
Healy Pass 54-5, 59-60, **51**
heat exhaustion 261
heatstroke 261
Helen Lake 52-3, 67, **65**
heritage 23
Hidden Cove 20, 154
Hidden Lake Overlook Trail 180-1, 182-3, **181**
Highline Trail 182-4, **181**
hiking 22-3, 31-3, *see also* day hikes, overnight hikes
  backcountry hikes 32
  Banff National Park 46, 50-72, **51**, **65**, **71**
  Bow Falls & the Hoodoos 50, 52-3, **51**
  Bow Glacier Falls 52-3, 65-6, **65**
  Burgess Shale Geoscience Foundation 124-5
  Carthew-Alderson Trail 219, 220-1, **217**
  Cascade Amphitheatre 52-3, 57, **51**
  children, travel with 38-9
  C-Level Cirque 52-3, 56, **51**
  Consolation Lakes Trail 52-3, 60, **61**
  Cory Pass Loop 52-3, 57-8, **51**
  Crypt Lake Trail 219-20, 220-1, **217**
  Egypt Lake & Gibbon Pass 54-5, 68, 70-1, **70**
  equipment 264-6

Fenland Trail & Vermilion Lakes 50-1, 52-3, **51**
Fireweed Trail 129
Garden Path Trail & Twin Cairns Meadow 54-5, 58-9, **51**
Glacier National Park 176, 182-3
grades 31
Grassi Lakes Trail 118
Healy Pass & Simpson Pass 54-5, 59-60, **51**
Helen Lake 52-3, 67, **65**
Iceline Trail 125
International Peace Park Hike 223
Jasper National Park 134, 138-9
Johnson Lake 52-3, 54-5, **51**
Johnston Canyon & the Inkpots 52-3, 58, **51**
Lake Agnes & the Beehives 52-3, 62-3, **61**
Lake O'Hara 127
Larch Valley & Sentinel Pass 54-5, 62, **61**
Mary Schäffer Loop 140-1, 143, **144**
Mistaya Canyon 52-3, 64-5, **65**
Mt Assiniboine 54-5, 68-9, **69**
Paradise Valley & the Giant's Steps 52-3, 64, **61**
Parker Ridge 52-3, 66, **65**
Peter Lougheed Provincial Park 122
Peyto Lake & Bow Summit Lookout 52-3, 66-7, **65**
Plain of Six Glaciers 52-3, 60-2, **61**
Rowe Lakes 217, 219, 220-1, **217**
rules & permits 32
Saddleback & Fairview 52-3, 63-4, **61**
safety 105
Skoki Valley 52-3, 71-2, **71**
solo travel 33
Stanley Glacier 129
Stewart Canyon 52-3, 56-7, **51**
Sulphur Mountain 52-3, 55-6, **51**

Sundance Canyon 52-3, 54, **51**
Sunset Lookout 52-3, 67-8, **65**
trail guides 32-3
Twin Falls & the Whaleback 125
Waterton Lakes National Park 217-20, 223, **217**
Yoho Lake & Wapta Highline 125
Yoho National Park 124-7
historic hotels 15, 20, 242
  Lake McDonald Lodge 202
  Many Glacier Hotel 203
  Prince of Wales Hotel 229
historic lodges 242
historic sites 238
history 23, 236-42
  Banff National Park 90, 93, 97, 236-8
  Glacier National Park 241-2
  Jasper National Park 238-41
  land 243-4
  Native Americans 213
  Waterton Lakes National Park 229
hitchhiking 279
holidays 272
horse trails 44
horseback riding 34, 39, 44, 83-4 122, 154-5, 193, 223, **36**
Horseshoe Lake 159-60
hot springs 15, 23, 88-9, 128-29, 163, **15**
hypothermia 260-1

I
Iceberg Lake Trail 182-3, 187, **188**
ice-climbing 85, 225
Icefields Parkway 9, 96-7, 152-3, 156-7, 159-60, **153**, 9
Iceline Trail 125
ice-skating 85, 156, 162
ice walks 15
Inkpots, the 52-3, 58, **51**
insurance 270
International Peace Park Hike 223

Map Pages **000**
Photo Pages **000**

international visitors 271
internet access 270
internet resources 19
  Banff National Park 47
  Glacier National Park 177
  Jasper National Park 135
Into the Icefields 80-1, **81**
itineraries 26-9, **26-9**
Izaak Walton Inn 198, 211

J
Jackson Glacier Overlook 196
Jammer buses 20, 199
Jasper Dark Sky Festival 24-5
Jasper National Park 134-73, **134, 136-7, 158-9**
  accommodations 163-9, 173
  boating 153-4
  camping 164, 165, 166-7, 168-9
  climbing 154
  cross-country skiing 156
  cycling 135, 149-50, 152
  drinking 170
  driving 151, 152-3, **151**
  entertainment 171
  fishing 154
  float trips 152-3
  food 169-70, 173
  golf 155
  highlights 136-7
  hiking 134, 138-49
  history 238-41
  horseback riding 154-5
  information 171
  kayaking 154
  medical services 171
  nightlife 170
  planning 134-5
  shopping 171
  sights 156-7, 159-63, 172-3
  skiing 36-7, 155, 156
  snowboarding 36-7, 155
  snowshoeing 156
  stargazing 157
  tourist information 171
  tours 163
  travel to/from 171-2
  travel within 172-3
  white-water rafting 152-3
  wildlife watching 155
  winter activities 156
Jasper Planetarium 20, 157
Jasper Skytram 13, 143, 160-1, **13**

Jasper Town 160-2, **160-1**
Jasper Train Station 162
Jasper-Yellowhead Museum & Archives 162
Johnson Lake 52-3, 54-5, **51**
Johnston Canyon 52-3, 58, **51**
Junior Ranger Program 40

K
Kananaskis Country 23, 121-4
kayaking 35, 154
  Banff National Park 78, 80
  Jasper National Park 154
  Waterton Lakes National Park 225
Kicking Horse Mountain Resort 37, 133
Kicking Horse Pass 125
Kootenay National Park 128-31

L
Lac Beauvert 162
Lake Agnes 17, 63
Lake Agnes Teahouse 17, 63, **17**
Lake Agnes & the Beehives 52-3, 62-3, **61**
Lake Annette 161
Lake Edith 161
Lake Louise 9, 22, 94-5, 96, **8-9, 36, 114-15**
Lake Louise Gondola 96, **114**
Lake McDonald Lodge 197, 202
Lake McDonald Valley 197
Lake Minnewanka 22, 91
Lake O'Hara 127
lakes 22
Larch Valley & Sentinel Pass 54-5, 62, **61**
Legacy Trail 73-4, **74**
legal matters 271
lightning 263
Lodge of the Ten Peaks 96
lodges 23, 168
Logan Pass 196
lookouts 21
  Apgar 195
  Aylmer 91
  Bow Summit 67, 81
  Mary Schäffer 143
  Mt Brown 184
  Peyto Lake 66, 81
  Signal 149

Simpson Valley 59
Sundance Canyon 54
Sunset 67-8
Swiftcurrent 189
Loop, the 197

M
Maligne Canyon 162
Maligne Lake 12, 162-3, **12**
Maligne Lake Area 162-3
Maligne Lake Boathouse 154
Maligne Lake Road 151, **151**
Maligne Tour 163
Many Glacier Hotel 203, **15**
Many Glacier Valley 198
maps 271-2
Marble Canyon 129
Marias Pass 198
Marmot Basin 36, 155
marmots 250-1
Marsh Loop 89-90
Mary Schäffer Loop 140-1, 143, **144**
measures 273
medical services 259
Medicine Lake 163
Miette Hot Springs 23, 163
Mina & Riley Lakes Loop 140-1, **142**
Minnewanka Loop 76-7, **77**
Mistaya Canyon 52-3, 64-5, **65**
mobile phones 18, 272-3
money 18, 272
moose 249-50
Moose Lake Loop 140-1, 143-4, **144**
Moraine Lake 11, 95-6, **5, 11**
Moraine Lake via Tramline 75-6, **76**
mosquitoes 260
motorcycle travel 276-7, 278-9
mountain biking 12, 33-4, 39, 117, **12**
mountain goats 248
mountaineering 36
mountains 244
Mt Assiniboine 14, 54-5, 68-9, **69, 14**
Mt Assiniboine Provincial Park 127-8
Mt Brown Lookout 182-3, 184, 186, **181**
Mt Edith Cavell 160
Mt Norquay 91-2
Mt Robson 162

Mt Robson Provincial Park 172-3
museums 41, 86, 90, 117, 157, 162, 212, 241

N
Nakiska 37
national parks 46, 134, 176, 216, **45**
  opening dates 19
  policies 19
  regulations 19
Native Americans 213
  Blackfeet 213
  Kootenai 213
  Salish 213
newspapers 273
nightlife 170
North American Indian Days 24-5
North Boundary Trail 162
Northern Highline–Waterton Valley 182-3, 190-1, **191**
Northern Lights Saloon 209
North Fork Hostel & Square Peg Ranch 209
North Fork Valley 198
North of Jasper Town 163

O
Old Banff Cemetery 90-1
Old Fort Point Loop 140-1, 142, **142**
On-Line Sport & Tackle 154
opening hours 272
outdoor activities 31-7, see also individual activities, individual locations, winter activities
overlooks, see viewpoints
overnight hikes 32, see also day hikes, hiking
  Banff National Park 68-72, **69**, **70**, **71**
  Egypt Lake & Gibbon Pass 54-5, 68, 70-1, **70**
  Gunsight Pass Trail 185, **185**
  Jasper National Park 146-9
  Mt Assiniboine 54-5, 68-9, **69**
  Northern Highline–Waterton Valley 190-1, **191**
  Skoki Valley 52-3, 71-2, **71**
  Skyline Trail 146-7, 149, **147**, **10**

Tamarack Trail 220-1, 224, **224**
Tonquin Valley 148, **148**
Waterton Lakes National Park 224, **224**

P
packing 41, 266
paddleboarding 20
Paradise Valley & the Giant's Steps 52-3, 64, **61**
park entrances
  Banff National Park 47
  Glacier National Park 177
  Jasper National Park 135
Parker Ridge 52-3, 66, **65**
parkitecture 176, 177, 198, 239, 242
Path of the Glacier & Cavell Meadows Trails 138-9, 140-1, **138**
Patricia Lake 161
payphones 273
pets, travel with 42-4
Peyto, Bill 93
Peyto Lake & Bow Summit Lookout 52-3, 66-7, **65**
Piegan Pass 182-3, 184, **181**
pikas 250-1
Plain of Six Glaciers 52-3, 60-2, **61**
planning 18-19, see also individual locations
  activities 30-7
  calendar of events 24-5
  children 38-41
  itineraries 26-9
  pets 42-4
  repeat visitors 20
  tips 47, 135, 177
plants 251-3
Pocahontas 163
Polebridge 209
Polebridge Mercantile 209
postal services 272
Prince of Wales Hotel 229
public holidays 272
Pyramid Lake 161, **175**

Q
Quartz Lakes Loop 182-3, 188, **188**
quiet spots 23

R
radio 273

Radium Hot Springs 15, 23, 128-31, **15**
ranger programs 40, 155
ranger stations 205, 227
recreational vehicle rentals 277
Red Rock Parkway 220-1, **222**
rescue & evacuation 263
Rising Sun 196
road conditions 279
road rules 279
Rockaboo Adventures 154
rock climbing 82-3, 36, 128, 154, 193
route finding 265
Rowe Lakes 217, 219, 220-1, **217**

S
Saddleback 52-3, 63-4, **61**
safety 258-63
  avalanches 262
  bears 262
  crossing streams 262-3
  cycling 263
  driving 84, 279
  hiking 105, 262-3
  lightning 263
  pets 43
  rescue & evacuation 263
Saturday Night Lake Loop 150
Schäffer, Mary 239
shopping
  Banff National Park 110-11, **111**
  Jasper National Park 171
  Waterton Lakes National Park 230-1
Shovel Pass Lodge 23
shrubs 252-3
shuttles 73, 92, 127, 173, 256, 275-6, 278
Simpson Monument 129
Simpson Pass 54-5, 59-60
Skoki Valley 52-3, 71-2, **71**
skiing 21, 36-7, 155-6, 193, 195
  Banff National Park 36-7, 84-5
  children, travel with 39-40
  Glacier National Park 193, 195
  Jasper 36-7, 155-6
  Kananaskis Country 122
  Kicking Horse Mountain Resort 133

Mt Assiniboine Provincial Park 128
Tonquin Valley 156
Waterton Lakes National Park 225
Skoki Valley 52-3, 71-2, **71**
Skyline Trail 10, 140-1, 146-7, 149, **147**, **10**
Smith-Dorrien/Spray Trail Road 123
Snake Indian Pass 162
Snocoach 16, 157, **16**
snowboarding 21, 36-7, 155, **37**
  Banff 36-7
  children, travel with 39-40
  Jasper 36-7, 155
Snow Days 24
snowshoeing 37, 156, 193, 195, **115**
Snowshoe Trail 222-3
Spirit Island 163
St Mary 209-10
St Mary Lake 195-6
Stanley Glacier 129
stargazing 157
Stewart Canyon 52-3, 56-7, **51**
Sulphur Mountain 52-3, 55-6, **51**
Sulphur Skyline 140-1, 145-6, **146**
summer activities 31
Sun Point 196
Sun Point to Virginia Falls 180, 182-3, **181**
Sundance Canyon 52-3, 54, **51**
Sunrift Gorge 196
Sunset Lookout 52-3, 67-8, **65**
Sunshine Meadows 11, 23, 92, **11**
Sunwapta Falls 159
sustainability 256
Swiftcurrent Lake Nature Trail 182-3, 187, **188**
Swiftcurrent Pass Trail 182-3, 188-9, **188**

T
Takakkaw Falls 14, 124, **14**
Tamarack Trail 220-1, 224, **224**
taxes 273
telephone services 18, 259, 272-3
Thompson, David 240
ticks 260

time 273
toilets 273
Tonquin Valley 12, 140-1, 148, **148**, **12**
Tonquin Valley Adventures 155, 156
Tonquin Valley Backcountry Lodge 23
tourist information 112, 171, 205, 231, 273,
tours
  Banff National Park 78, 97
  Brewster Tours 97-8
  Canmore 118-19
  Discover Banff Tours 98
  Glacier National Park 199
  Kootenay National Park 130
  Jasper National Park 163
  Waterton Lakes National Park 227
trails, see individual trails, hiking
train travel 277
travel seasons 18, 31, 116, 207
travel to/from national parks 275-7
travel within national parks 277-9
trees 251-2
trekking, see hiking
Tunnel Mountain 91
Twin Falls & the Whaleback 125
Two Medicine Valley 16, 23, 197

U
Upper Hot Springs Pool 88-9
Upper Waterton Lake 225

V
vacations 272
Valley of the Five Lakes 150, 152
Vermilion Lakes 90
via ferratas 20, 83
viewpoints 21, see also lookouts
  Castle Cliffs 79
  Glacier Skywalk 159Jackson Glacier Overlook 196
  Kicking Horse Pass 125
  Simpson Monument 129
  Spiral Tunnels 125
  Sun Point 196
visitors 18
volunteering 274

W
walking, see hiking
Wapta Falls 125
water purification 260
waterfalls 22
  Athabasca Falls 159
  Bird Woman Falls 197
  Bow Falls 86
  Cameron Falls 225
  Hamilton Falls 124
  Snake Indian Falls 162
  Sunwapta Falls 159
  Takakkaw Falls 14, 124, **14**
  Wapta Falls 125
  Weeping Wall 196-7
Waterton Townsite 225, **226**
Waterton Lakes National Park 216-32, **216**, **217**, **218**, **228**
  accommodations 227-9
  activities 217, 219-25
  camping 227-8

canoeing 225
cycling 222-3
drinking 230
driving 216, 220-1, **221**, **222**
entertainment 230
fishing 223
food 216, 230
golf 223
hiking 217-20, 223, 224, **217**, **224**
history 229
horseback riding 223
ice-climbing 225
kayaking 225
medical services 231
road distances 216
shopping 230-1
sights 225
skiing 225
tourist offices 231
tours 227
travel to/from 231-2
travel within 232
weather 18, 269
Weeping Wall 196-7
weights 273
West Glacier 208-9
Whistlers Summit 140-1, 143, **142**
Whitefish 212-15
Whitefish Mountain Resort 37, **214**
white-water rafting 14, 21, 35, **14**, see also float trips
  Banff National Park 80, 82
  children, travel with 39
  Glacier National Park 190
  Golden 132

Jasper National Park 152-3
Kootenay National Park 130
Whyte Museum of the Canadian Rockies 86
wildflowers 253, **252**
Wild Goose Island 196
wildlife 84, 246-53
wildlife reserves
  Grizzly Bear Interpretive Centre 131
  Northern Lights Wolf Centre 132
wildlife watching 11, 21, 35-6, 131, 132, 248, 246-53, **11**
  Banff National Park 84
  Jasper National Park 155
Willmore Wilderness Park 173
winter activities 23, 31, 85, 132, 156, 225, see also skiing
  children, travel with 39-40
  cross-country skiing 37, 85, 128, 156
  dogsledding 119, **22**
  ice-climbing 85, 225
  ice skating 85, 156, 162
  ice walks 157
  Jasper National Park 156
  snowshoeing 37, 156, 193
wolves 247-8
women travelers 274

Y
Yoho Lake & Wapta Highline 125
Yoho National Park 124-7

Map Legend

Sights

- Beach
- Bird Sanctuary
- Buddhist
- Castle/Palace
- Christian
- Confucian
- Hindu
- Islamic
- Jain
- Jewish
- Monument
- Museum/Gallery/Historic Building
- Ruin
- Shinto
- Sikh
- Taoist
- Winery/Vineyard
- Zoo/Wildlife Sanctuary
- Other Sight

Activities, Courses & Tours

- Bodysurfing
- Diving
- Canoeing/Kayaking
- Course/Tour
- Sento Hot Baths/Onsen
- Skiing
- Snorkeling
- Surfing
- Swimming/Pool
- Walking
- Windsurfing
- Other Activity

Sleeping

- Sleeping
- Camping

Eating

- Eating

Drinking & Nightlife

- Drinking & Nightlife
- Cafe

Entertainment

- Entertainment

Shopping

- Shopping

Information

- Bank
- Embassy/Consulate
- Hospital/Medical
- Internet
- Police
- Post Office
- Telephone
- Toilet
- Tourist Information
- Other Information

Geographic

- Beach
- Gate
- Hut/Shelter
- Lighthouse
- Lookout
- Mountain/Volcano
- Oasis
- Park
- Pass
- Picnic Area
- Waterfall

Population

- Capital (National)
- Capital (State/Province)
- City/Large Town
- Town/Village

Transport

- Airport
- BART station
- Border crossing
- Boston T station
- Bus
- Cable car/Funicular
- Cycling
- Ferry
- Metro/Muni station
- Monorail
- Parking
- Petrol station
- Subway/SkyTrain station
- Taxi
- Train station/Railway
- Tram
- Underground station
- Other Transport

Note: Not all symbols displayed above appear on the maps in this book

Routes

- Tollway
- Freeway
- Primary
- Secondary
- Tertiary
- Lane
- Unsealed road
- Road under construction
- Plaza/Mall
- Steps
- Tunnel
- Pedestrian overpass
- Walking Tour
- Walking Tour detour
- Path/Walking Trail

Boundaries

- International
- State/Province
- Disputed
- Regional/Suburb
- Marine Park
- Cliff
- Wall

Hydrography

- River, Creek
- Intermittent River
- Canal
- Water
- Dry/Salt/Intermittent Lake
- Reef

Areas

- Airport/Runway
- Beach/Desert
- Cemetery (Christian)
- Cemetery (Other)
- Glacier
- Mudflat
- Park/Forest
- Sight (Building)
- Sportsground
- Swamp/Mangrove

OUR STORY

A beat-up old car, a few dollars in the pocket and a sense of adventure. In 1972 that's all Tony and Maureen Wheeler needed for the trip of a lifetime – across Europe and Asia overland to Australia. It took several months, and at the end – broke but inspired – they sat at their kitchen table writing and stapling together their first travel guide, *Across Asia on the Cheap*. Within a week they'd sold 1500 copies. Lonely Planet was born.

Today, Lonely Planet has offices in Franklin, London, Melbourne, Oakland, Beijing and Delhi, with more than 600 staff and writers. We share Tony's belief that 'a great guidebook should do three things: inform, educate and amuse'.

OUR WRITERS

Brendan Sainsbury

Banff National Park, Jasper National Park, Plan chapters An expat Brit from Hampshire, England, now living near Vancouver, Canada; Brendan has long relished the 'thrill' of masochistic endurance events in remote wilderness areas and thus jumped at the chance to cover Banff and Jasper for Lonely Planet. He particularly enjoyed scrambling around the Cory Pass Loop and canoeing in Vermilion Lakes with his son. When not scribbling research notes for Lonely Planet in countries such as Cuba, Mexico and Spain, Brendan likes refining his cross-country skiing technique, trying to master flamenco guitar, and following the Premier League exploits of Southampton Football Club.

Read more about Brendan at:
http://auth.lonelyplanet.com/profiles/brendansainsbury

Michael Grosberg

Glacier National Park, Waterton Lakes National Park, Understand and Survival Guide chapters Michael's first experience of Glacier National Park was something of an ad hoc one. Young and unprepared, driving back cross-country from Alaska, he set up a tube tent for the night in early winter somewhere in northwest Glacier. He recalls not sleeping because of the cold, staring up at the night sky and the sublime mountain silhouettes and listening for the paw-steps of approaching wildlife. He's since made other trips to Glacier and around Montana. This is nearly his 40th book for Lonely Planet.

Read more about Michael at:
http://auth.lonelyplanet.com/profiles/michaelgrosberg

Published by Lonely Planet Publications Pty Ltd
ABN 36 005 607 983
4th edition – Apr 2016
ISBN 978 1 74220 618 9
© Lonely Planet 2016   Photographs © as indicated 2016
10 9 8 7 6 5 4 3 2 1
Printed in China